I

N THE LOCOMOTIVE-GOD

THE
LOCOMOTIVE-GOD

BY

WILLIAM ELLERY LEONARD

PUBLISHED BY THE CENTURY CO.

NEW YORK   LONDON

Copyright, 1927, by
THE CENTURY CO.

PRINTED IN U. S. A.

FOR THE READERS OF

"TWO LIVES"

NOTE

SUCH relevant facts as have had to be omitted from the following study, however instructive in their psychology or irony, would not modify the essential problem. The date of reference throughout is the middle months of 1926. I am indebted to Miss Lucy Banks, one of my graduate students, for faithful and timely help on the proofs.

W. E. L.

MADISON, June 15, 1927.

THE LOCOMOTIVE-GOD

*Nothing at last is sacred but the
integrity of your own mind.*

EMERSON.

I

THE LOCOMOTIVE-GOD

I

I HAVE recovered to sunlight and sound, after a long strange search, the lost years of my childhood, and have traced them inexorably at work through fifty years of devious life, as the unseen companions of my loves and hates, of my books and my pen, and of all my goings and comings east and west in the world. I know more startlingly than Wordsworth or Dryden, who recorded in their rimes only the intuitions and observations of their brooding maturity, that the child is father of the man and that men are but children of a larger growth. I know it more intimately than Freud, who even in his clinics records only the stuttering revelations of the tongues of others. For I have followed, with a later cunning than any available for Socrates, the ancient counsel of the Delphic temple, and have deepened for my spirit, beyond all meanings intended by Greek ethics for the conduct of life, the meaning of "know thyself."

But this most personal of adventures has become for me an adventure in humanity. What was so poignantly my subconscious mind reveals itself, by the laws of our common organic structure and development, as the mind of mankind. My own pain, my own struggle, has been, even to myself, a spectacle, a laboratory. And my findings differ in some ominous particulars from the previous record of poets and psychoanalysts. I have been persuaded, in spite of the shrinkings of privacy and the demands of an insistent profession, to set them down: persuaded by the desire to frustrate, by a neat and unexpected turn, those Demonic

3

Forces which, as appearances go, have backed me for so many years against the wall. Beset by phobias, shell-shocked in a civilian war, hampered and harassed, I have done little enough to justify the ambitions that awakened long ago and that have not yet been willing to die. So out of very suffering and very failure I would create value: the value of a scientific document; the value of a work of art. Something, as science and art in one, to help others to human and humane living. Much of the best that man has ever done has come about this way: when time and circumstance have ultimately defeated him, see, he uses defeat; and finds in defeat the only raw stuff he can really use at all. Exile, for instance, has made many poets. And I have been persuaded too by friends, famous men of science and letters, and unacclaimed mothers of the children in neighbors' houses: they have heard my report, and have said others should hear it.

The reasons, so grim and urgent, that suggested the search, and the technique, involving some ingenuity and much patience, by which the search was conducted will be more intelligible if integrated with the later chapters of the story. For my method of telling must invert the method of finding. Day by day, night by night, not least night by night in sleep, I penetrated year after year deeper and deeper into the dusk of a tangled jungle more unknown to me than, once upon a time, the Upper Congo to explorer Mungo Park. I went back, back, back, guided and lured by sporadic bits of light, emerging, now here, now there, through the mists and shadows, till I found myself standing agape, an infant of two years, four months, and ten days, on the shining planks of a railway-platform, one bright hot afternoon in a far June, dead and not dead . . . when every month made a calendar year and every day throbbed with portents of increase. I was caverned under skies more vast and blue, with a splendor more untarnished than the human eye ever sees by the time the human tongue is deft enough to sing them. I know, indeed, by scientific evidence

4

to be faithfully recorded later, that the poetic imagination of maturity is often but the controlling reverberation of early childhood impressions: the poet doesn't sing the stale sky he actually sees; he sings unwittingly the sky he saw, fresh and new, so long ago. It is only when he explicitly tells us what his child-fancies were that he becomes so often sophisticated, self-deceived, and tenderly sentimental. So I will start from that June afternoon . . . it was five by a visible watch-dial . . . and relive in the order of time a life, now gray, which, individually considered, it is quite enough to have lived once.

But, if I have friends to follow the story, let them distinguish it, in kind (no less than in fame), from the world's literature of reminiscence, say the "Prelude" or Marcel Proust, or the earlier chapters of Augustine's and Rousseau's "Confessions." The difference is fundamental, founded in the psychological difference in the process of acquiring the data. Memories that one has consciously carried down the years sometimes interpenetrate or become fringed by alien experience, emotion, or imagination, till they have imperceptibly changed their content. Memories that are tapped by the literary process—forgotten bits that pop out on to the page from the point of the hurrying pen —are more likely to be pure and aboriginal; but they may fuse with the colors and motifs and possibly vanities of the moment of composition, even at times to an artificial reconstruction in the unconscious service of wish and theory. Goethe, wise in so much, was wise in this too: he called his reminiscences *Dichtung* no less than *Wahrheit*. All memories haphazardly salvaged and intermixed are generically different in origin, in tone, in psychological accuracy, from the memories procured by auto-psychoanalysis: I have been enabled to compare the two kinds. The latter need in fact a new name; they are not memories in the ordinary sense. The mind doesn't *remember* its childhood experience; it relives that experience in all its immediacy. The child-mind wakes up, it becomes you . . . intensely, overwhelmingly

5

you . . . a second, ten seconds, a quarter of a minute . . . while the mature mind stands by and takes note, with a partial disassociation of personality, at times painful, but always awesome and difficult to explain with this our human speech that has been created by and for the affairs of a more workaday and external world.

An illustration, in one picturesque particular, may help. Lying on my back, relaxed in the hypnoidal state (twilight sleep), I see an image of a gigantic, but friendly, woman eighteen feet tall, three times my own stature to-day. It is my young mother as I looked up to her at two and a half . . . over forty-seven years ago. During the first second of the vision the mature man's natural correlation of the size of physical objects with his own size in maturity creates this grotesque magnification. But the distorting present subsides, and the infant eye is suddenly doing the seeing . . . where mama is just naturally so much bigger than I. Astonishment too subsides into comfort and well-being, and the infant mind is doing the feeling. And then the mature eye and mind, detached from the experience, contemplates it, yet from *within* still. A hundred objects—such as houses, trees, a playmate's father, a policeman, and the locomotive that is the protagonist of this story—have come to me by this process, colossal and stupendous things, till readjusted to the bygone years . . . two and a half . . . four . . . seven . . . nine. They then take on the emotional meaning they had at the time . . . the mother and the tree friendly, the policeman and the locomotive still colossal and stupendous, but for reasons of the infantile, not the mature, mind. (So too our puzzling dreams of enormously magnified objects are but the memories of the child in our nightly slumbers.) This is to relive experience, as distinct from remembering.

This reliving then becomes ordinary memory, however, and in two ways: one remembers the recent psychological phenomenon itself, this intrusive repetition of the past; and one soon resets its content in the normal world of en-

6

larged memories. But childhood thus realistically restored fails to create in us—in me, at least—the wistful mood so characteristic of mere reminiscence. And if the mature mind adds anything, it well knows what it adds. I did not *remember* the hour-hand at five in the watch-face that a stocky man snapped open and showed me on the platform, waiting for the train. In my twilight sleep only a year ago I suddenly saw it—and so big that for many months after that visionary seeing it seemed as on a clock-tower, and so persistently associated with an old terror that I seemed to be running toward it as toward my mother. Obviously I could not "tell time" in those days; but the image lay photographed in my brain and I read the hour at last . . . forty-seven years thereafter. Then as the months of psychological probing continued, the dial shrank finally to its normal size in the stocky man's very palm, and shifted, as an infantile event, to its proper place in the series of infantile events I was reconstructing, disentangled emotionally from the moment of terror—which had been in fact not simultaneous but subsequent. I now remember both the original experience in its natural setting and the secondary experience in the twilight sleep, and I clearly differentiate from each the interpretative moment of telling time. The validity of these data is absolute, not merely relative; and the exploring and rationalistic mind that has collected them, however far it has voyaged from normal experience, has never mislaid its compass. Whatever else my story be, it is not a story of delusions and insanity. I have had my chance to go insane, and I refused to take it: I would not escape life by that door.

II

∠ I AM standing agape on the platform. But I cannot communicate either the world about me or the world within, exactly as it is to me; for my consciousness is still so largely nameless objects and nameless feelings and thoughts. I think largely in terms of things, relations, emotions. My speech must be a blend of childhood's vocabulary and manhood's craftsmanship. But the data, external and internal, are scientifically exact. I am some two hundred and fifty feet from my young mother and her friends. I have been pulling on her skirts, bothering her. She has yielded to my nagging and let me walk up to the further end; for she wants to talk undisturbed with the family doctor about the bright ways and promising future of her little boy. Nurse Tina, the pretty negress in a plaid bodice, and a stocky man, have now let go my hands. I have promised both her and my mother not to go near the tracks. This is my first journey so far from home, since a baby in arms . . . a mile from home into a world more venturous and engrossing than I can ever know twice. How big and brave I am! I had been looking round a little nervously toward my mother three or four times as our steps had increased the distance from her; but my curiosity and courage have conquered. I look back past the length of the long red station to the diminished figure of my mother with her red parasol. There too is little Mary. She is nearly four, I say to myself . . . she is so much bigger, yet not nearly as brave as I . . . she was afraid to come 'way off here with Tina and me. And, besides, her mother was afraid to let her. How wonderful I must seem to her 'way off here! And I hitch up the little black leather belt of my clean white dress (there

8

are blue anchors on the sleeves), and stalk about in the sun for her distant, admiring eyes. And Mary loves me. How proud I am that Mary loves me, more even than that mama does! Though I do not know it, I am already lover and hero . . . the aboriginal masculine of the race. ⇒

But I almost forget Mary. For forward and all around me I see so much that astounds: 'way down below right under my legs, beyond a protecting wooden rail, painted blue, lies the gulf of a cross-street that is spanned by the iron railroad bridge. A man drives along in a red-wheeled buggy and disappears marvelously under the bridge, to my right. Across the street, before one comes to the bridge, is an enormous white house, with great shingles, reached by a curving driveway—that is the Quaker Meeting-House, Tina tells me. And on my side of the cross-street, down in a little square of dirt marked by squares of white lines, a boy and girl are knocking balls with a sort of shovel back and forth across a net—how fast the balls fly, and how both the boy and the girl jump around! Still farther down the cross-street from where the man in the buggy came, stands another white house with a steeple; it's facing me, for it's really on Front Street, the street we live on—only our house is far along the other way. Behind the steeple in the open fields is the pond gleaming in the light with the ice-house on its hither border. Out on the pond is some one in a row-boat . . . "What is he doing, Tina?". . . and beyond in the immeasurable distance (of two or three miles) are the long hills of the Blue Ridge that I have never, never seen so long and so blue from our porch or dining-room window. But see, across the track to my right in another field, a big man is batting a ball and several other big men run to snatch it right out of the sky . . . again and again. Over there too is a huge house, round and gray. Tina says it is the gas-tank. We have gas in our house, blue inside the yellow. But more and more it is the track itself that fasci-nates—those lines that stretch so straight, yet getting nar-rower and narrower, so very much farther from me than

9

I am from Mary and all the folks . . . right up to the edge of the low blue air where they seem to shoot into the woods. This is to be the Path of the Train. "Papa is coming from Westfield on the train?" Tina says, "Yes, from Westfield." "When is the train coming, Tina?" The stocky man snaps open his watch and says, "It's five o'clock." I know vaguely a train carries people to far away and sometimes back from far away, and I have seen trains going by on the embankment off behind our back yard and the empty lots. But now I shall soon really see one, Tina tells me.

The size of the world, its bombardment of our curiosity, the thrill in new experience and in anticipating new experience, the intense surrender of the self to its sudden universe—these are but the pallid phrases of makeshift analysis for the incommunicable vitality of a consciousness already in richness and complexity beyond either psychologist or poet. The few who have thus relived the birthday of their intellectual passions, the first great hour of their imagination in this world of wonders, will realize with me that nothing in all their experience thereafter is so beyond our ordinary instruments of expression, whether in words, color, or music. Not love, not death. Yet always the nearer we come home to reality the harder to find the word: the politician finds a hundred for his universe, the artist finds one . . . and then hardly. And in the greatest art words are perhaps no longer words at all. Perhaps Dante could give something of the infant's stupendous reality by that sunny tract of rails and water overarched by more than God—I cannot . . . beyond the bald confession that I cannot.

From out of the woods, a far whistle, a puff of far smoke. The Train! On the Path. Beside the interminable row of poles and wires. It moves. Toward us. I beg Tina to let me go—I want to look straight down the Path and see just how IT comes. Yes, I promise not to get *too* near the rails . . . and the Stocky Man strolls over after me. He stands and lights a cigar, looking idly up the tracks. The Train. Nearer. I can see it sway. The great black, puffing head-part. The length of moving sheds behind it. The chug-a-chug-chug, louder and louder. The almost musical rattle, with humming overtones, of the rails, louder and louder. I lean over to get the view more nearly head-on. The sky is back of it, farther and farther back of it. The Thing lengthens out, swaying this way and that. And it seems to surge up and down. A Train? What *is* a train? Curiosity before the unknown now suddenly becomes apprehension . . . dread. . . . We are human from the start. We do not need to see a man die to know death. Death is born with our birth; the self that craves life shrinks by the very law of life as instinctively from the constriction and blockage of that craving. A little child . . . what should it know of death? All there is to know, O sage of Winander. The Premonition is upon me. I realize with horror what a Train is. It is a gigantic Caterpillar . . . gigantic beyond anything I have ever seen in our garden or Mary's. I am fascinated, rooted to the barren planks, while the Caterpillar roars and wriggles and arches along. The Stocky Man puffs his cigar, Tina is lolling by the blue rail, and calling idly, "Come back away from the tracks, Ellery," while curiosity overmasters even my horror at my own well realized disobedience; my mother is still talking doubtless with the family doctor, who brought me into the world, about the bright ways and promising future of her little son. But for the little son the universe is the Caterpillar . . . then the jerking angles of the driving-rod and the long boiler-belly make it for one tumultuous instant a tremendous Grasshopper . . . till it towers and lowers and grins in one awful metamorphosis, more grotesque than the most bizarre dreams of Greek mythology, as Something indescribably greater than Caterpillar or Grasshopper. As It roars over the bridge, with the engineer . . . I see again to-day his face peering out of the cabin window high above me . . . madly pulling the bell-rope, while the clanging fills

what just now remained of silence in the world . . . as it
roars with thunder and smoke over the bridge, scattering
dust and a strewn newspaper, the black circle of the boiler-
front swells to the size of the round sky out of which the
Thing now seems to have leaped upon me. It sets up conscious reverberations of a picture in Uncle Oliver's insurance office . . . up the same stairs as papa's newspaper
office . . . a locomotive on a calendar of the Ætna Company which floods my mind . . . even as a generation later
a picture on another wall is to set up subconscious reverberations of this Aboriginal Monster. My eyeballs, trans-
fixed in one stare, ache in their sockets. The head-light glass
in a square black box above the Black Circle flames with
the reflected light of the afternoon sun down there where
my mother is. But I am to postpone these realistic deductions for forty-seven years. To me at a little more than two
years, the Black Circle flashes a fiercely shaking Face of
infinite menace, more hideous and hostile than Gorgon-
shield or the squat demon in a Chinese temple, with
gaping Jaws, flanked by bulging jowls, to swallow me down,
to eat me alive—and the Thing is God. Coetaneous with the
Face and Maw, a long lank Arm shoots out low down from
around the further side of the engine, with an end half-
spoon, half-claws, to scoop me up, to ladle me *in!* (This
was a fantastic transfer from the swift vicious thrust of
the driving-rod visible on my side.) God roaring from
heaven to slay me for having disobeyed my mother and
gone so close to the track. Guilt . . . remorse . . .
Mary . . . in air above the great puffing smoke-stack, a
tumultuous image of Mary's house . . . small hands
clapped to eyes. My heart leaps to my throat . . . I think
it is coming out of my mouth. "Al-leady" (i.e., "I am all
ready. Come!") I moan inside me, summoning the resolution of an absolute despair.

The locomotive sweeps by, and my physical paralysis
ends in a sudden leap away. The steam discharges from
under the piston-box into the child's anus, with hot pain

through his kilt-skirt. "God kills me *here too,*" he thinks
with a scream out loud, and presses his hand to the pain.
I am to feel that pain a generation later . . . for ten
years, it will wake me from sleep. His little straw hat with
scarlet band whirls off in the blast and roar, as the Stocky
Man makes a futile grab. The monstrous boiler on the
monstrous wheels rolls by, topped by the clangor and swaying of the bell. If I am dead, I think, how strange that I
can still move so fast. It *is* God—God thunders out of the
sky . . . I have heard him . . . this *is* God, I think in my
panic . . . for I still think. The Face, that Face. Then the
flight. Our house, so safe, but so horribly far, floods my
mind. The parlor, with its carpet-designs in red and yellow
and its maroon plush chairs, becomes an image so intense
and vivid, with feel so protecting and close, that I am bewildered between being there and not there, with a paradoxical interpenetration of experience best comparable perhaps to our dream-states of maturity. The Face, that Face.
The distance from my mother and Mary is terrible and
hopeless: the proud moment in getting so far has supplied
the suggestion for the terror of the immeasurable far-
awayness from safety. The flight, down that long, level,
narrow highway. And I can't see my mother. The Face, the
Face, the Face. A baggage-truck down there has rolled
between . . . blockage . . . I am shrieking. The cars
keep passing me. I am so small that I see under them, past
their tangle of iron rods, to the freight-depot on the other
(the left) side of the track. The wheels pound and bump,
one after the other, where rail joins rail. The Face. A
thought more awful still: This Thing, God or whatever it
is, will kill Mary. I must get to Mary. The Face, the Jaws.
The end of the station grows nearer. I see a white frame
house just beyond the station where the platform ends.
The Stocky Man runs after, Tina runs, and a dog races
beside me. It is fun for him. I see to my right the awnings
on the stores on the street across the way from the station-
park. The last car has passed. A slight relief. I stare toward

its retreating rear end. My side aches . . . that frightens me too . . . I put my hand on the ache . . . I have lived through all thus far; I can live till I reach mama and Mary, I say to myself. My mother sees me and signals with her red parasol. Relief. But where is Mary? . . . a new despair . . . till she darts out from behind the two mothers and is running toward me. Spiritual relief . . . a little. Then I stumble and flop flat. The dog noses my neck. My anguish lies watching my mother's hurrying steps . . . This anguish will burst from the subconscious, as the university professor overhears himself saying half asleep (i.e., in twilight sleep) the apparently meaningless phrase, "Æneas rushing at me," and "Æneas" will be a Freudian pun for "her knees," and the informing point will be that he lay there unable to raise his infant head to her face, eyes fixed on her legs bending under her skirts. . . . Meantime Tina picks me up, and I sob and shriek my tale of the God-Face in my mother's comforting arms. The talk with the family doctor has been interrupted.

"Now you're all hunky-dory," says my mother, setting me down beside the baby-carriage of sister. I rush behind the baby-carriage to Mary. She caresses me. I cling with my arms about her, long . . . like a lover . . . a little shy (believe me, or not) lest the mothers see how hard I cling, how that clinging is all the world to me. I feel a sweet comfortableness in my body too. . . . And when she starts away at the joyous sight of her father descending from the train, I am jealous and grieved. I lean against my little wagon. Tina gives me an orange to suck. I am getting myself together and thinking matters over. What a fool I am, I think. A Highlander, in costume, stands with his bagpipe against the station wall, laughing. The people on the platform are staring. Rows of heads too from all the car-windows. The world is all eyes. I am the Great Fool. A generation later I will be reading books that say little children don't feel shame, until taught and mistaught; and I will know that, though one needs teaching a plenty to be ashamed of the little naked body that nature gave him, he needs no teaching to be ashamed of lapsing from himself, as Intelligence and Courage.

The train didn't bring papa after all. So we all walk through the station with Mary's folks. They drive off with a span of horses, Mary on the front seat with her bearded papa. She seems almost to pay no more attention to me, and that hurts. She too must think me the Great Fool. Then my mother leads me back to the Engine. A man is oiling the wheels. I am urged to touch them and the cow-catcher. I do . . . gingerly. My mother shows me that it is not really alive, that it has no face, that it has no long arm, that it is not God but a Locomotive. I am trying to convince myself . . . but am still nervous and a little skeptical . . . especially when it starts to move away.

I ask on the walk home, when but a few rods from the station, with my mind full of my little lover riding away behind the turning span of great horses: "Mama, do you suppose Mary thinks I'm a fool?" She cajoles and chides me: "You mustn't talk like that." I brood, deeply troubled. And again as we near our house at last: "Mama, do you suppose Mary loves me?". . . My papa arrives in time for supper, after all. Mama is telling him how scared I was, and how I thought the Locomotive was God. I am such a little boy that she thinks I don't understand her big words. But, just as I lift my glass of milk to my mouth, I see for a second the Locomotive-God plunging at me through the hall door. I shriek out. My father's face is troubled, a kindlier face than the years are ever to carve out for his childless son. . . . The Face of St. Francis. . . . He is very grave, worried about the shock and what it may do to me . . . perhaps (as I am to speculate when I am a dozen years older than my father is now) worried too that the shock may affect my love for the good God whom he loves more now, as a newspaper editor in a small city, than when before my birth he resigned his pastorate in far-off Evanston because he no longer liked the Baptist God. Yet what he and my mother had already told me of the Heavenly Father that thunders and his Power and Love of Good Little Boys was, it seems (I conjecture here), enough for my reconstruction of the Locomotive-God. Sometime the race of man will be wise enough, courageous enough, not to talk about God to little children at all. My mother is crying quietly . . . she is depressed before her husband as having failed in her care of the son—*his* son. The next day he takes me to the station and has me stand and walk about on the spot of my fright. I think how silly I was. I didn't know that it was already too late to think how silly I was. Three days later my mother makes an insert in the diary she is keeping in my name . . . she forgot the item at first. What made her forget? Here it is:

Tuesday, the 4th [June, 1878] I went to the *depot* to meet my papa for the *first* time. I never had been so near to a Locomotive, or "locomoti" as I call it. I was so frightened when it came rushing along past us that I screamed and mama had to hold me in her arms. My papa did not come home from Westfield on that train and so we had to come away without him, but I have been to the *depot* and seen a *"locomoti and the pattenger cars"* and I have been talking a great deal about it ever since.

The italics are my mother's. Forty-seven years later my mother is to remember only how lovingly she dried my tears. Mary will remember nothing, or at least will fail to answer my letter. My father and Mary's will be dead. But Mary's aged mother will write me verifying the external outlines of the episode as I have recorded it. I am to forget it—in a few months—for forty-odd years. But it is not going to forget me . . . *jamais*.

That afternoon changed my whole life. In recovering my lost years, I have uncovered a hundred dreams dreamed in the years not lost: that afternoon was involved in their pattern. I have uncovered conduct and motives for conduct: that afternoon was in their pattern. Emotions, opin-

16

ions, scholarly interests, materials in my poems: that afternoon was there too. Long years of unexplained, intermittent nervousness, followed by fifteen years (to date) of a
chronic neurosis, with all its accompanying limitations and
handicaps: that afternoon was in their pattern. Can ten
minutes' time control fifty years? It can. Children's diseases
—measles, scarlet fever, infantile paralysis—how parents
dread them, for, even if the little lives are saved, they
may be maimed, in eyes, ears, or legs, for life. And nurse-
maids must not drop or bump them—for a scar is a lifelong misfortune. We must guard their morals and manners
too—training them not to tell lies or to spit or to do nasty
things in the clothes-closet. But a scare, with a few shrieks
and tears, is soon a neighborhood joke. Yet what was this
scare of mine? Sex, self-respect, self-confidence, friendliness to the world, the will to roam and the will to know,
basic forces for normal manhood, here unfolding with
wholesome promise, were abruptly disintegrated in the explosion of complete collapse before the attack of alien and
incomprehensible power, to be replaced by terror, guilt,
shame, and the cringing need of shelter. In a nervous system, a little more than two years out of the womb. I was
born again that day.

Had I been, I query, from my first birth destined by
temperament or inheritance to suffer shock, where many
infant minds are hardy or immune, even as my body has
always been hardy before wind and cold and heat, and all
but immune from disease? I can only conjecture what my
temperament was before that day. The diary records affection, mischief, babble, runnings-off, sidlings-up, shyings-
away; nothing but a small nuisance that mama and papa,
and Clare, and then Tina, mistake for the Remarkable
Child; nothing to suggest deranged susceptibilities. This
commonplace evidence is all the more significant in the
light of so many later entries: "he is a very nervous little
fellow." My inheritance, I know, is from very old colonial
New England stock, ironmongers, small manufacturers,

farmers, and mothers of huge families with the familiar
infant mortality of the good old times. Anglo-Saxons, with
but one exception—the French army officer who was the
father of my mother's father's mother. Earnest Baptists,
Quakers, Congregationalists, Episcopalians. On my father's
side I am directly descended from a younger son, among
those boat-loads, compelled by the law of primogeniture to
forgo estates and titles, that landed here in the generation
after the founding of the New England Canaan, and did
perhaps as much as the Puritans to create Anglo-Saxon
America. My mother's grandfather was one of the Boys
of '76, but several of the Leonards (I grieve to say) were
for a time in Halifax. On both sides for generation after
generation they would refuse to die before their eighties
or nineties. My father died at eighty-three, with never a
day in bed. My mother at seventy-six writes me letters in a
hand indistinguishable from that of the diary. There is
nowhere, as far as the family record goes, any insanity . . .
though a paternal maiden aunt, who once would scurry
about in a faded red shawl to collect the rent of her numerous shanties, was sour, suspicious, and peculiar; and though
my maternal grandfather, a designer of iron grilles, gate-
ways, and garden-pieces, cultivated an artistic taste, to
judge from the filigree nightmares in his buff-covered catalogue, horrendously different from Ruskin's or mine. My
sister, unmarried, physically robust, has been kindergartner,
actress, social worker, feature-writer, Christian Scientist,
Spiritualist. We are strangers. My father and mother were
the first in the two lines, I believe, to go to higher schools,
though the copy of Sale's Koran and a Latin dictionary in
my library reminded me that grandfather Whitcomb had
intellectual interests creditably higher than his esthetic.
My parents, as transmitters of stock, had integrity of body,
head, and heart. Both had self-reliance and opinions of their
own, my mother with the more rigidity. My father's lips
never shut so tight, though he opened them less. My father
was gentle and kindly by native instinct, indignant only at

injustice; my mother more by a sense of duty and by a troubling aspiration of perfection. My father's eyes were blue, my mother's black. Both felt deeply, swiftly—yet both quietly, my father by instinct, my mother by self-control. My father read the New Theology and Science of the sixties and seventies, and "In Memoriam"; my mother Emerson's Essays and the German verse of Freiligrath. My father wrote free-trade and single-tax editorials; my mother much poetry, with spells at the piano. Both were playful of spirit, but without rollicking mirth, trenchant wit, or much humor, though each had a little bag of good jokes, with a faint scent of musk. It was my Uncle Oliver who was the perennial funny man of the family circle. I saw him last at grizzled eighty: his wife and eldest son were long dead, and his younger son at forty a problem; surviving sons of several of his best friends were derelicts from drink and women; he was poor, broken, and lonely, and his only job was his sixty-year-long clerkship of the Baptist Church, where he and my father had accepted Christ in the home town where we were all born. But he still shot off one quip after another with the same pop and flash. Still the funny man . . . only a little weary. Both my parents dwelt more with ideas than with imagination or with facts: my father came to believe in the Baconian ciphers, my mother in New Thought; though ultimately both believed everything together. My mother in widowhood still wears, as her only jewelry beside her wedding-ring, my father's fraternity-pin. He was an Alpha Delt. They were increasingly melancholy during my boyhood: my orphaned mother had grown up in affluence at an uncle's in a college city when my undergraduate father-to-be played with her as a meditative little girl; but Uncle Briggs had gone bankrupt, shortly after his niece's promised dowry had gone into fur coats and earrings for his flashy second wife. His gold watch is all that came down: it is in my pocket. My father had inherited homestead and houses and lands: a third of an estate that had been blocked out of the Leonard farm

. . . the Leonard farm . . . now a millionaire suburb
of New York. He never talked about his business
affairs with me. But I know he bought up that local
newspaper just after he had come back with his bride.
I used to overhear worried talk about a Mr. Niles, then
about Mr. Niles's cousin. The homestead went to Mr.
Niles's cousin when I was thirteen. I inherited from the
Leonard estate another gold watch; it is a stem-winder.
My father was, as editor, the Horace Greeley of the pro-
vince. As manager, he was without a school. He already
refused patent-medicine advertisements back in the seventies. He always gave subscribers and other debtors a feeling that they needn't bother. They didn't bother. His
stanchest supporter with the populace was the town's leading saloon-keeper. Rafferty had long ago been to the office to
arrange for a liquor ad. My father had explained his quiet
"No." The Irishman understood. He could admire an ethical principle applied to business. So he subscribed for the
"Central Times." For years on my route I left him his copy
under the swinging screen door. Rafferty always paid for
his subscription. My father was not a business man. By
the time I was ten my mother was often silent over the
dish-pan; and my father was sitting, like the setting sun,
in abstracted silence on the back porch. When we had company, especially some old college friend of my father's
from out of town, we had canned salmon and ice-cream.
Each on its platter, fresh from its mold. In later years
when everything was gone, they arose up marvelously.
Cheerfulness became a cult. Their strength and their hope
was more and more in the Father of Mercies. But God is
the verbal surrogate for many things; and their strength
was, in fact, their own indomitable spirits reclaiming themselves, and their hope . . . the divine providence that they
felt would provide for their own old age . . . was in fact
their final delegation of the practical battle, with unconscious shift of attitude and unconscious relief, to the son.
They could not foresee that the son would have on his

hands more than one battle of his own. There was nobility
and pathos, and just a breath of unsuspected Meredithian
comedy, in this fine, faithful marriage, to them always such
an unprecedented event. Thus my immediate forebears,
though somewhat specialized personalities, were sound
enough to transmit the essential soundness of the stock.
From my mother I get my looks and eyes; from my father
my walk, gestures, and even handwriting. From both much
besides, but surely from neither any diseased predisposition to trauma or neurosis. Crisis and influence, as far as
created for my life by their lives, have been created, not by
any hereditary taint, but by the human fact that I, as I,
have lived my life with them, as them, in the immutable
relation of sonship . . . for many, many years. Great
good indeed have they done me; but like all parents who
ever lived—like myself if I had had a child—momentous
harm, the more tragic because they loved so well.

Had anything gone wrong with me in the womb?
Stepping on snakes as the explanation of birth-marks is
folklore of course, with no more biological meaning than
my mother's explanation of my facility in German as due
to my prenatal absorption of her Freiligrath. But the fetus
is a nervous system and organized for living long before
the conventional date of its birth—the three months before
the destined nine are up can be lived in sunlight as well as
in dark. Some of the sensations that can happen to its
plastic make-up in those months when, prematurely, it lies
in the incubator or pillow can happen as well when it lies in
its mother's belly. Did some physical lurch startle me out
of my omnipotence, as I lay huddled and curled and yet
adjusted as never again in life to my environment? Did
some thunderclap penetrate the walls of her engirdling
flesh? Or did anything go wrong with me in that labor of
thirty-six hours, ending with the moon risen a second night
on the undrugged anguish of a young girl? Being born is the
greatest adventure in human life. A sudden first use for
lungs and bowels and eyes, now first really *ours*. And all

sounds now suddenly so much nearer and louder. The compulsion to fight on one's own . . . for one's own. Does this experience not *register?* Life is one long adjustment to social limitation and egoistic frustration, after an initial experience of omnipotence. Something may depend, after all, on how it begins. And did my ears surge at my mother's groans? My doctor-friend has a record of three thousand babies; and he smiles at my fancies . . . he used to smile, too, at my phobias.

Had, perhaps, life itself, in those forgotten first two years, been undoing my ancestral hardihood? I had no sickness: the glory and the mockery of physical energy was mine even then. But I turn over the leaves of the diary.

Sunday Feb. 8th [1880, æt. four years, two weeks]. While I was washing him to-day, he wanted to know the names of different parts of his body and if boys had *"dinners"* as he calls the breasts, and asked the name of "that little ball," pointing to the navel. I told him. The darling little pure boy. . . . He asked me about the way babies nurse and then I told him that God gave the mothers this milk food . . . because they could not feed themselves and that it was the best kind of food for little babies. Then he wished to know why it was God did not give *all* mothers such food for their babies and why it was some babies took their milk from a *bottle.* Then I gave him a satisfactory answer.

I speculate dubiously on this early lesson in metabolism and theology. A satisfactory answer? . . . I craved a universe of facts, and facts in rational coherence. I wanted them without sentiment—like other small fry when they ask questions. But our good mothers begin the buncombe of life for us: their love creates the first frauds. . . . The next sentence goes on thus:

He does not seem to remember when he used to nurse, but likes to hear me tell about his lying in my arms so much and sleeping and nursing as I [an ominous mistake for *he*] did so many hours at a

22

time. I really think the darling little boy is drawn nearer to me by
these little talks about himself and his babyhood. I wonder if in some
distant day, when perhaps he is a man, he will look over these pages
and realize how mother loved him. . . .

The man has looked them over. They were written, not by
my mother, but by the Eternal Madonna, who needs the
Child in her arms for the fulfilment of her own being—
and the richer the being the more poignant the need. But
the Eternal Child lies there with his own fate before him,
needing iron, more even than milk. *He* is not there for the
emotional satisfaction of another; not primarily for his
own either. The mother's need is real; the child's is real.
Each has its rights under the law of nature: but the child is
helpless. I copy these words with reverence, far beyond
the reverence of one son for one mother.

The entry is a year and a half later than the flight from
the Locomotive-God; but its items (with many others)
reveal that there were at work upon me and within me,
even long before the flight, precipitates of thought and
tensions of emotion of a sort to impair eventual resilience
to that aboriginal racial fear of Uproar and Onset shared
even by the stolid cattle. Mother-love is the greatest blessing . . . and the greatest peril . . . in life. Some readers
will understand.

III

I CANNOT say just how long it was before the onset and uproar of the Locomotive-God, "glowering on mortals with his hideous face," disappeared from the region skies of conscious memory into the subconscious. In trailing the course of later shocks, I have observed that the conscious memory has always preserved in sunlight for years the bald fact, the general circumstances in place and time, and fragmentary details of secondary or no emotional importance, while losing entirely, even in a few weeks, days, or minutes, the vibrant picturesque core of the experience, as drama. Something like this seems to have been the case here. Even when standing on the spot the next day, I seem not to have remembered the God-motif. But I was still occasionally thinking about that queer chimney-pot of a smoke-stack for a year, perhaps two; and later on in the same year, when the autumnal rains had swollen Green Brook to a flood in the lowlands, I was explaining sheepishly to Mary that I hadn't really been so scared as she thought. We were munching crackers in the back seat of her father's phaëton, before a dark red house with its fence half under water (as I recalled at forty-eight through a dream-picture in twilight sleep). And the conscious manifestations of this infantile trauma were immediately detached from the original objects of both fact and fancy: I developed no specialized fear of locomotives or of God. On the contrary, trains became a childish passion and God a more than ordinary childish speculation. To several other objects that were thrust with all their living light down so deep into my

impressionable intelligence on that afternoon, I owe odd avocations that I took up with strange zest in maturity after my breakdown

nel mezzo del' camin :

in my smash-up at thirty-five, that primal Afternoon finally vindicated its long power both by the phobias it generated and by the interests and occupations it suggested. To those objects, too, I owe, in part at least, sundry lines, even themes, in my poems. That Afternoon created ill, and created good for me . . . like my mother, my father, my friends. That is the law, however, of all human afternoons, in one degree or another.

But I developed very soon secondary nervous phenomena sun-clear in their origin to any specialist to-day. Indeed, if our affable Family Doctor, with the carbolic smell in his beard and the red-headed coachman out in the buggy, had known what was even then beginning to be known in the psychopathic clinics of Paris and Vienna, he might have left his paregoric and his quinine for once in his black leather case. At least he might not have added to my troubles . . . except perhaps by renewed unction and still longer words. Nervous phenomena sun-clear to any enlightened parent to-day. And even in those days, why not sun-clear, as a simple untechnical fact, to my mother—whose good wits and intuitions were so dominantly occupied with the child? She showed fine sense in dealing with my fears. I noted how she had me touch the locomotive. She later got me a little drum, that by beating it myself I should overcome my new terror of the tom-tom and rap-a-tap-tap down Front Street, where the parades went by under the elm. Both she and my father always recognized my panics with gentleness and intelligence for what they were in suffering: why never for what they were in origin? There is a significant gap in the diary of seven months immediately after the brief entry about the "locomoti and the pattenger

25

cars." The very first that follows begins the new theme. Its date is February 7, 1879; but it refers back to the preceding Christmas:

. . . His papa put a wooden train on the tree for him and as soon as he set his eyes on that there was nothing else that he could see, so great was his delight. But he is a nervous little fellow and the excitement almost made him sick.

I have succeeded only in reclaiming the vague outlines of this experience; but by inference from other experiences fully reclaimed, even to factors subconscious at the time, I see in this abnormal excitement the reverberations of each of the initial emotions—the interest and the distress recorded above. The diary proceeds:

He shows quite a timid nature. He has been [as something new] very much afraid of all noise . . . cars . . . church bells . . . everything of the kind.

Later entries list hand-organs and bands:

He will run a great ways to avoid them.

She fails to note that I always ran *home* . . . even into the rear closet under the back stairs. How could she have made all these entries and never have guessed the truth, so clear as cause, however mysterious in psychological process? Why did my father never guess . . . when he held my trembling hand as I walked one Sunday morning under the sudden outbreak of the horrible pandemonium from the Baptist Church tower, or when he saw me pull myself together for the desperate plunge under the railroad bridge, impossible to take at all when the cars were roaring across on the tracks above? . . . impossible till my eleventh year. They had spoken anxiously at the time of possible aftereffects. But unconsciously, I think, instinctively, both suppressed the suggestion of the true cause: my father for my mother's sake, my mother for her own sake. So the explanation became "nervousness." . . . In later years, my mother explained these panics as a phase of my peculiarly keen intelligence: I used only to be frightened, she would tell me with satisfaction, before what I didn't comprehend. That explanation was an escape too. My father never referred to them. But both were to feel the pain of them a generation thereafter . . . grievously . . . in a far-distant city . . . in their crippled old age . . . in a second cycle of years.

I carried with me into manhood the vague memory of two or three specific frights (misdating them several years too late), and how in general I used to be afraid of loud noises. I explained the phenomenon physiologically, as if I had been cursed with over-sensitive ears—that magnified, like the electric receivers of the deaf, the racket of a civilization already noisy enough. Having now relived these same frights, with many others besides those recorded in the diary, I speak with scientific precision when I affirm that the core of each new fright-experience was uproar and attack, and that in no case was the sound loud beyond what it must have been to other children in the neighborhood, and that the attacking object, even when transformed, was never transformed into anything that deceived the sight. The deception was essentially in the reaction-feel, in the undefined transformation of the Significance. When I was alone in the house, aged six, with my sister one morning, a whimsical cow stuck its head into the window of the downstairs back bedroom and lowed at me. She might, of course, have startled any child *qua* cow. I knew cows; I had seen this very cow tethered in the field between our house and the next. She did not startle me *qua* cow. But the feel of uproar and menace was overwhelming. The cow-idea disappeared in the idea of imminent death. I was too paralyzed to scamper away. I pulled my sister—as much bewildered by my antics as by those of the cow—to her knees beside me. I prayed God. I made her pray. The cow looked on

27

and lowed again. I fled with her to the attic, to a closet in the attic. I prayed again. I heard footsteps rumbling and creaking on the floor below. The Cow coming up the stairs! Then my mother called for me. The adventure took its place in the family anecdotes. . . . Another illustration, from about the same period. I had gone on an errand a little way down Front Street toward the stores. Suddenly, spread across the street, man beside man, with drum-major before, came marching the Zouaves, to drums and brasses. I knew they were men and the noise men's noise. And they underwent no transformation to either physical sense; but the feel and significance was totally alien and un-motivated—that of monstrous power inexorably sweeping toward me to destroy. I was called an imaginative child. I was. But these were not, genetically considered, tricks of the imagination, conceived either as insight into reality or as reshaping reality. They were the reverberations of buried experience, set going by specific objects, and these reverberations, not the sympathetic or creative imaginations, gave in turn to those objects their horrific meanings. The distinction is of wide application. I ran shrieking home. Into a closet under the back stairs—till I was sure the band had passed. I knew then, as well as now—as well as I know too now in regard to my present phobias—that there was "nothing to be afraid of." So my chat, a few minutes later, with my father and the Episcopal minister (who was al-ways dropping in) served only to pain me. "Why, most boys don't run away from the bands; they run after them, and with their mouths open," said the now seated rector, laughing encouragingly behind his cigar in all his fat. I knew they did. I wished I could. The rector was the Stocky Man who had grabbed for me beside the Locomotive-God.

I recall from these early years only two frights that did not conform to this type. But they were also reverberations from the same afternoon. The first. Ten or a dozen little boys and girls, with their wraps half on, were spitting and crying and gagging in our upstairs hall. A great hubbub and my mother indignant and bustling about. What an end to that happy kindergarten morning, when they had been making the balls in different colored worsted swing back and forth in their wooden frames, and folding squares of glazed paper, pink and yellow and red, into original geometric patterns so demurely before little tables all lined off like chessboards, or caroling in a circle, "Thumbkin says I'll dance and sing," or marching around the parlor school-room with bean-bags on their heads. What an end! But I have forgotten the name of that youngster who passed around the April-fool candy. Mary had swallowed the most—the blue-eyed, golden-haired little girl. Her spasms grew worse. She was nearly in convulsions on the third step of the stairs to the attic. Or did she only seem worse to me? My mother told me to fetch a pitcher of water and a glass and gave me the accursed box to dump in the kitchen. I was in horror. If Mary should die. I trotted speedily back with the pitcher, and slunk off into an adjacent bedroom, both ashamed of my dread and half realizing that it was groundless. But, as we have seen, it wasn't altogether groundless. This episode came up from the subconscious after I had been startled by a distant dream-cough heard in twilight sleep.

I could fill a book with my adoration and solicitude for years. Over at our house . . . up at hers—a long walk up Front Street far beyond the stores—in a vast mansion with verandas and a tower, with gravel walks, huge flower-beds, a summer-house, a rustic bridge over the brook, and, inside, those wonderful new things, a telephone on the wall of the landing and a bath-room upstairs. What an event for me to do number one in that bath-room. One morning I flung my shoe across my bedroom, angry at my mother. Mary was downstairs waiting to take me to her house—supposing she knew, oh, the shame of it! My best jokes were for Mary, inspired by Mary. We were singing in a standing circle, she opposite,

. . . love, the best of human ties . . .

29

I gave my little neck-bow a meaningful yank as we came to the last word, and she nodded an approval so kindly and intelligent that I mulled over my triumph for days, determining sometime to do something still funnier. But there was only one episode that could be called indelicate: I would just as soon tell it, though the motherly Mrs. —— that was Mary might not just as soon have me. But it was trivial and casual and not implicated in the frights of childhood or in that neurosis of maturity where she, in other connections, came to play so distinguished a rôle. Yet, lest the reader, too steeped in Freud, be getting suspicious and nervous, let me assure him, besides, that my story will involve no sex-perversions, though from first to last the fact of sex. Male and female created she them. Had it been otherwise, my neurosis would have been otherwise—or rather, never have been at all; yet it cannot be called, in the accepted sense of modern psychopathology, a sex-neurosis. When the whole case has been outlined, this contradiction will be automatically resolved.

I have wondered what my life would have been, if this child-love had unfolded through adolescence into a mating of the man and the woman. Byron loved at eight, Dante at nine. The world has marveled or doubted. I was loving at two and a half, and continued with a faithfulness as great as the young Dante's, and certainly considerably more than Byron's. This is not the sentimentalizing of reminiscence, grotesquely transmuting an infantile and sexless affection through the retroaction of later-born emotions. I have relived those years, with their own convincing emotional tone and texture. I had my little girl friends; but Mary was my *Bien aimée*. It was not imitation of my elders. Most, indeed, in children that we call imitation is the life-urge to get into the game of life. The emotion was of the same sort as what we call being in love . . . less engrossing, less turbulent, less possessive in aim, and, of course, entirely without the passion which we miscall physical, but still an incipient form of that adoration and solicitude and

spiritual comfortableness in the companionship of the beloved, which creates the bliss and the miseries for ourselves and the jokes for our friends, between the years when
we put on long pants and those when we send out our wedding announcements. There is nothing for astonishment,
except as all life is an astonishment to the few that know
anything about it. How should it be otherwise? The first
fact proclaimed over each new-born is the fact of sex: "It
is a boy". . . "It is a girl." Parents cheerfully, proudly,
note the masculine traits and the feminine in their waxing
offspring—the prowling instincts of the one with the broomstick gun, the tent-pitching instinct of the other with her
rag dolls. But that the darling little boy should fall in
love is too ridiculous. Yet we become what we are; and we
are what we become.

There are some special reasons why the development of
this little love-affair into maturity might have protected me
from the long latent power of the Locomotive-God. My
neurosis is not due to suppression of infantile sexuality;
without those special reasons in play this love-affair would
have been for me, as for the millions of love-affairs of the
little ones all over this magnificent earth, a sound training
in personality for the future mating with one or another
yet to come forth. But this love-affair had involved my implicit manhood in disintegrating emotions, notably shame
and terror. If Mary had been a boy, the Locomotive-God
would have still scared the wits out of me, but would not
have created an experience involved with sex, even as the
neurosis of the past fifteen years, with its abnormal clinging
to house and wife, is involved with sex. But Mary was not
a boy; she was Praise and Need. So I wonder: would love-
fruition have eventually assimilated and destroyed the
shame-complex and the fear-complex?—which, detached
from their object in consciousness, went on to thrive so
disastrously for the host, underneath by themselves.

As a matter of fact, very favoring psychological circumstances would have been necessary to develop the ex-

pressive lover, after that initial collapse. Though Mary never made fun of my fright, the fright tended to undo the feeling of masculine superiority with which I had strutted so wholesomely before her on the platform: she became more the superior, and has remained so in life, in curious ways that I realized long before I became a "case." But all other factors contributed to undo it: the advantage of a difference, so enormous in childhood, of one year and a half in age; her precocious intelligence (she graduated from high school at sixteen . . . in simple white . . . with a valedictory in the theater, beginning "We are told that our Aryan forefathers". . . and I remember my father correcting the proofs for his paper . . . in which Mary's father was now a chief stockholder); the quiet, though never prim, reserve of her graceful figure; and the local fame of her gold hair, fair skin, and budding beauty. And above all, estranging was the difference in money; her father was the richest man in town, mine more and more nearly the poorest. This difference has now been leveled out between the families. Mary's father, a boy in town with mine, stood, as the only spectator, beside the sexton and undertaker, when my father was laid away in the ancient burial ground. Mary's father, as the symbolic deputy of our scattered household . . . of mother, son, daughter, who were all unable to follow the casket southward, was himself laid in a near-by plot six months after. Now the two widows exchange letters, her mother from the great empty mansion, mine from a small back room in the house of a friend in a New England village . . . my mother has nothing in riches; and to hers riches are nothing. But I couldn't foresee all this: the money in Mary's family, though always unpretentiously in the service of simple worth and dignity, began, as soon as my social consciousness had awakened (and that was long before puberty), to accentuate my inferiority complex. In a renewal of our contacts in young manhood, after some years in different quarters of the world, this was, in fact, the only inferiority I was aware of;

32

till, when I would try, rather awkwardly, to counter on it by shining for her intellectually, her kindly but convincing amusement would house in me a second inferiority devil worse than the first. "They say the Germans are so much freer with profanity than we are," I remarked to her on her veranda (a few years after her graduation at twenty from Wellesley with an A. B. thesis on Kant) ; "but the words don't have the same function in German : *'um Gottes Willen'* isn't really the same as 'for God's sake,' for instance. So any German lady can say without gaucherie or vulgarity, 'Um Gottes Willen, reichen Sie mir das Butter.' " "But, Ellery," still at her sewing, "no German lady *would* say that; *no* German lady." "Why . . . I'm . . . I've . . . *what* would she say?" "She'd say *'die* Butter.' ". . . I never dreamed of courtship . . . not consciously, and, as far as I have probed, not even subconsciously. But it was she to whom I took in chief the miseries of my first upset in manhood's love. . . .

If she could know the history of her subconsciousness, as I have come to know mine, I wonder what she would find as precipitates and influences from those years of our childhood play. Probably very little. Just as the station-fright blocked my masculine emotions, it also undoubtedly fixated them about her—made her, far more dominantly and permanently than might otherwise have developed, a center of masculine energies. It is practically certain that she was spared any such distortion of childhood's normal grace and good. When she thinks of kindergarten days, she thinks not of me but of my mother : "I owe her much for life ; she is a remarkable woman," she wrote me a year or two ago. And, if as the busy wife and mother, coöperating in his work, with a famous man of science, her Austrian husband, she should chance upon these pages, she might well be hugely surprised . . . but counting on her humane intelligence, I don't think she would be vexed. My mind, in spite of all the tricks it has played on itself, has salvaged, in this relation as in many others, its quantum of whole-

someness. I think my "case" is instructive, with regard to
Mary and to all other phenomena, of how a normal personality may undergo devastating abnormalities from turmoil in the subconscious and still carry on, hampered, but
not exactly defeated, in normal activities and work; and
hampered and deflected, but not defeated, in the evolution
of normal values of the inner world of thought and emotion. One Mary was a subconscious complex; but the other
is an old friend.

The abnormal terror lest Mary should die, reverberating from the onset of the Locomotive-God, was to awaken,
along with terrors of my own destruction, long after in
association with women whose names were not Mary.
But only long after. The one other spell of terror that did
not conform to the uproar-attack type was as follows. My
father and mother, with sister and me, had walked out
into the middle of Brooklyn Bridge . . . that I now remember to have seen not long before in the building . . .
the great white cables swung in space between the two stone
towers, high up as our Washington Rock in the mountains.
They were tired. My petition to be allowed to proceed as
far as the Brooklyn tower was granted with the usual cau-
tions. I proceeded, exploring. I went through the tower-
gate, arching so high above my head, disobeying. I stood
gazing off at eerie Brooklyn, which then looked, however,
more like New York than it does now, though nothing
stuck up so high as Trinity Church spire. When I decided
to turn back, a man, blue and definitive as a railway conductor, blocked me at the gate. I think he asked a five-
cent toll. I hadn't a cent. Whatever the cause—and for this
experience I have made no continued probe—I found myself suddenly blocked from my center of safety. I began
to sob. The man set me free, and I was forthwith at the
old business of fleeing "home." I shrieked then; I never
shriek now . . . but I flee faster than then and much
oftener. This came back to consciousness rather pictur-
esquely. During several evenings I had seen in my crystal-

34

gazing the spot of light take shape as two oblongs on end, meaningless as objects but powerfully associated each time with the idea of *Brooklyn Bridge and long ago*. Then I waked up one morning with a brief dream—scarcely more than a picture, but as real as life: the majestic sag of a great white cable, and two men swinging high up in the meshes with paint-brushes at work. This was the entire dream; it was not a wish-fulfilment (as some are) except as repeating the original wish to get to safety, nor a sex-complex (as some are), but an unmixed instant of the Past (as many are . . . we shall see). The rest came back at once after waking.

It is clear that this and several other scares had normal elements: any five-year-old might be frightened, too far away, by a hostile man; any child might run, as I once did, from a mother hen suddenly bouncing up from her chicks and flapping madly on to his head. But several were utterly unmotivated in the normal fear-psychology of a child; and those not motivated by the Locomotive-God afternoon were accentuated by it. There had been set up a fear-reaction, as well as a fear-pattern. But all the fear-reactions connected up with the fear-pattern, directly or indirectly. For this I have the positive evidence of the tangled ramifications of subconscious associations, as well as the negative evidence of absence of fear, in consciousness or subconsciousness, in certain fearsome situations when this pattern did not enter. I can almost say that I have never been really afraid of anything in life, except the Locomotive-God.

These childhood terrors plagued childhood, but the student of the case must see them in their setting. They were intermittent and brief. They were my plague; but other childhoods have suffered others far worse: sickness, cold, foul air, starvation, beatings, parental ructions, orphanage, spiritual dark. The reader must already have caught glimpses of our old gambrel-roofed homestead through the street elms, with its pillared front stoop, be-

35

side the field (owned by my Aunt Cornelia of the Shawl) with the shadowy pine-cluster toward the front and the big apple-tree in the back. There was lots going on for me. Always. I had my box of blocks, in smooth hard maple— squares and triangles and plain oblongs twice as long as squares, and oblongs with a half-moon cut out of them, and the half-moon block there too, all in geometric correlations both felt and analyzed . . . the raw stuff of the bridges, houses, and above all railway stations, to be built on the floor. I had my paper money for playing store, and shared with the still smaller sister the big doll-house my mother made us (a stove and coal-scuttle in one chamber, a bedstead and a dresser in another, yet five rooms in all, though our real house had thirteen besides the enormous attic). I romped with sister over the rookery and under the orange trumpet-vine by the side door, or rolled her about the big yard in the discarded baby-carriage (whereupon my mother wrote another poem), or pulled up the periwinkle or upset the milk-pan where the cream was setting for my father's coffee. I must have learned to skate in my sixth year . . . down on Green Brook where the dam made it into Randolph's Pond, across the street at the foot of the slope of the back yard of Uncle Oliver's tenant, down where the long wooden shed still stood that had been Grandfather Leonard's hat factory fifty years before. I had already coasted down that slope, and my father on his skates had already pulled me around on the ice on my sled. I have skated ever since; and will skate as long as I can walk. So will my wife. I would not, I think, accept a call, however distinguished, even if freed from my neurosis and able to take train or ship, to a university where there was no skating. Nor to one where I couldn't see the sun coming or going over open water. We ultimately choose our values. My father and mother had once often skated and ridden horseback together. So they told me. I never saw them. . . . In Rochester . . . on the Genesee River . . . along on the bank of the Genesee River. I must have learned to skate in my sixth year . . . did my mother once or twice skate with me? The trail of my search into the subconscious has not led close to Randolph's Pond. The name itself I remember only as the by-product of a study for other data of psychologic recall, when I was looking up old maps of our home town (in the Atlas of Union County, New Jersey) here in Madison's State Historical Library. The dam was washed away in a flood, and the pond had disappeared from my front window early. Later I sailed boats on the brook that was left over . . . with my sister. So as a physical child, I lived the normal, happy, first years of millions of us born in the seventies . . . or after or before . . . years so useless except in their own right to happiness and in their meaning for the future. Companioned by other children from similar homes.

Similar . . . except that my mother was apparently the only parent in the group, perhaps in the town or the State, who had a vision of the scientific education of early childhood. She was read in the great subversive and reconstructive educators, Rousseau, Pestalozzi, Fröbel. The Montessori System—*she* was Montessori. She went two summers to Martha's Vineyard, where there was a new school for the new science; and brought back ideas, self-dedication, and little clay jars, parti-colored in fantastic streaks. Colonel Parker, whose name is on the big stone lintels of American city schoolhouses to-day, looked me over. "That child is all intellect," he said. This worried her and pleased her both . . . unduly.

She had started to teach me to read at four. I remember, but let her tell it.

Feb. 5th [1880] . . . A word more about his study of the alphabet. He has been greatly interested in it, and often, taking the alphabet-cards, would point out letters of his own accord and tell wherein they resembled other letters and how they differed. O was the first letter he learned, and he observed that it had no beginning or end, but was just a curved line. He would then with delight find Q

37

and say that it was just like O but had a *tail* attached to it. He is quite fond of using big words and uses them frequently and *always* correctly.

Let us, with all charity to a mother's pride, delete the underlined "always"; but there remains nevertheless the embryo of both philologist and poet—the scientific interest in language beside the creative—that have seemed so puzzlingly incompatible to my friends; we are what we become.

But the same entry announces that she is skeptical about teaching a child his letters so young. He must first be trained in objects, mastering directions, relations, colors— both the world of sensation and the world of analysis. So she turned to kindergarten methods —first for my sister and me—soon for twenty-odd other tots. It was one of the first successfully organized American kindergartens. Most townsfolk smiled: to-day there is a kindergarten in every public school in the land. Some remonstrated, Mary's father among them, first that I was not taught to read till I was eight, and then not by spelling but by "sounding the syllables." My first book— a History of the United States in Words of One Syllable, with pictures of Eric the Red, of Columbus, Pequod Indians, Puritans in Shovel Hats, etc.—I knew by heart before I read it. The reading *process* was a trick learned in a week, or less, when the time came. All my reading since has been merely perfecting the trick and applying it to more complicated problems. My mother and I don't always agree in our views, in these latter years; but I still believe in her, as the scientific educator of two children at least—of the small son and of Mary.

My mother kept up her kindergarten, with my father teaching Mary and me writing and arithmetic in the graduate school, till I was nine. The income helped stave off Niles and Niles's cousin. She also scissored and pasted together a school reader, a manuscript that finally came back from the publishers for the last time. For several years

38

she and my father called it the ship, for it was to bring in silver and gold.

The child's ambition of perfection, the normal urge, the will to live humanly, was stimulated in many ways, designed and undesigned. I watched the mark, made by my father with ruler and pencil on the white dining-room door-post, ascend inch by inch, year by year. One year I grew half a foot, and I considered it my most successful year in all essential respects. But as on each birthday I straightened up to be measured, with the book laid flat on my head, I never tried, by taking thought (and lifting my heels unperceived), to add one cubit unto my stature. The meaning of the high mark was for me in its truth alone.

March [no date, 1880]. He thinks he will become a very strong man if he keeps on eating oatmeal and such things. [Such things were still plentiful in the pantry, then.] He thinks he "will be strong enough to pull the house down" or do some other wonderful things. Indeed he says he "thinks he will be stronger than Samson."

The family ideals were being drawn already from the Bible, though not from the family Bible of tradition. So much for physical perfection. Now for moral. From the same entry. I am not quite so ambitious.

He says: "I cannot be as good as Jesus but I can be as good as Dr. Channing."

Dr. Channing (William Ellery). They had named me after the sturdy Unitarian divine. The names we all bear tell more about our parents than about us, yet the names help make us. This early realistic good sense, as to my ethical limits, which I have just copied with some satisfaction, has unfolded into still greater perspicacity. I now know I can't be as good even as Dr. Channing (I dropped the surname long since), however highly I admire the fearless author of the devasting appraisal of the Military Intellect in that

39

essay on Napoleon. Channing was in this wiser than the wisest of our countrymen; for his spiritual pupil Emerson missed the true insight—compare the two studies. Not as good as Dr. Channing, but better than if I had been named Adoniram Judson. Nor was it to no purpose that, long after, in college days, I used to stand before his statue by the Public Gardens of Boston.

So too my father and mother coöperated with the unfolding urges of curiosity and meditation about the world and my place in it. They were not like the Plumber . . . out in the pump-room, beside the coal-bin and shelf with the shoe-blacking. He had opened the boards and was half-way down the well, beside the big pipe where the water wouldn't suck up. I stood over, as near as I dared. "What's this for?" . . . "Why do you do that?"—"Get out of here—you ask too many questions," as he banged his wrench on the pipe.

My mother had given me a physiology book. "He has been delighted in looking at all illustrations of various parts of the body." I was four. I remember the illustrations: man erect with arms parted like the zodiac-man of the almanacs; but man repeated—in skin, next with the garment of skin stripped off to show the banded muscles, then a nervous system, then a naked skeleton, still erect and indisputable. The traditional pictures that have come down the centuries: I recognized them a few years ago in their historic source—as plates in the anatomy of the Renaissance master, Vesalius. Yet I did not turn over the amazing leaves of that first edition in Professor Miller's library —famed as the best collection on the history of medicine in the Middle West—with as profound a thrill as I had the leaves of the debased copy. The first experience was knowledge of eternal nature herself, the second a brief item in bibliography and the history of knowledge. The pictures made me doubly curious, not morbid.

One day he sat upon the floor very quietly (under a window in

40

a corner of the dining-room). He was so thoughtful that his papa said, "Ellery, what are you thinking about?" His reply was simply, "My bones."

A little later my father took me to the office of the Family Doctor. He unlocked a great ebony case, like a grandfather's clock, that stood in a corner of an inner room. There, erect and indisputable, were all the bones, and all in order. I couldn't reach up as far as the bulging rows of white ribs; but I could stroke the legs and wiggle the toes. This record contains no fancies. Where I don't remember, I don't invent and know that I don't. But I think I compared notes, feeling bone for bone my own skeleton. Certain it is that I gazed with a pop-eyed trepidation exactly the same in intellectual origin and quality as that of any of the bigger men of science—the bigger men to whom nature is still more than the subject-matter of a monograph which will start talk and bring academic preferment. The bones! Those bones, my bones! It is never reality that makes us morbid. Later, a student of Germanic philology in Bonn, I traversed the dissecting-rooms.

He likes to look over his body and once said, "Why did God make my toes so that I would have to examine them?"

No one could tell me. Who can? . . .

Our house was full of windows:

One day while in a meditative mood he wanted to know if birds did not have souls. I explained to him about birds having what is called instinct and this is what tells them how to build their nests and how to care for their baby birds, etc., etc., etc. He then said, "That isn't a spirit. *Ours* is a spirit." . . . "Why isn't everything straight," he said, as he still stood by the window observing birds, trees, etc. . . . "What does God make the thunder roll with? Does God push it?" "Who put the stars in the sky?" When told that God does, he said, "God is standing on his toes."

41

And a reminder of our central story:

I like thunder better than hand-organs.

Our house was full of windows. And there came a strange new Light one summer into the skies. Out from far beyond the solar system, the Great Comet of 1882. My father waked me, and led me half asleep up into the attic, with a candle in hand, under the shadowy beams, oak, ax-hewn, a foot thick. We trailed past the boxes and trunks. Over to the far end. I waked up, I did. There it hung, with a head more radiant than a Jupiter, and big almost as the moon. With the vast shining sweep of motionless silent tail, killing all starlight. For two weeks or three it hung by night in the sky, over our house. Even in daylight I could see it. It did not frighten me. That which had frightened so many millions of mankind through all history, the men in tents, the men in cities, did not frighten me. But I was already destined to see in mid-manhood another, a far different, great light in the heavens, and to shriek in collapse, "No! No!" All alone.

Nor did the reality of death frighten me. Death did not enter our house. Nor Cousin Elston's, till later; then it came every year, to Cousin Elston's, for one aunt or uncle or little cousin of his after another, for it was a very big house, or rather two houses on the same big lawn. But it didn't frighten me. Not even when I looked straight down at its handiwork. My father took me one July day of 1885 to New York. In the City Hall we filed in the long line, each taking his look, past the dead body in a blue coat. The lips that had given the commands before Vicksburg were thin and tight and very silent. The hand that had written, "no terms but unconditional surrender," lay crossed over the other. I felt all this. I never forgot in normal reminiscence the scene—for I was already nine—though not till my psychological investigation did I relive it to discover just how I felt. This visit to the dead body gave deeper

42

intensity to my reading of Grant's Memoirs in my middle
teens. Grant still interests me more as man than as military
man. Grant refused to visit the tomb of Napoleon. Grant
didn't strike a pose for the Nations: "Lafayette, we are
here." Grant fought his greatest fight from an arm-chair
up the Hudson. I was to listen in Madison some day to
flamboyant laudations of the commander by one of his
staff, who had subsequently been postmaster-general, senator, and Orator of the Great Lakes. I knew the old warrior
better than he.

But we are not yet in Madison. May 22, 1880, was the
date the kilt-skirts came off and the little pants were fitted
around my little buttocks, buttoned and safety-pinned by
my mother on her knees, in the upstairs sewing-room. I
have since taken three academic degrees . . . minor affairs.
Out I bounded to stand on the gravel walk by the flowering
almond. I still know all about it. Hands in what were called
pockets, head up, chest out. Jack Horner is a pallid myth.
The last entry of the diary is the next day. No object in
writing about the baby any more: my mother respected my
manhood. She simply chronicled two sentences:

May, Sun. 23. "I love God. Is God happy because I have pants
on?"

I have restored realistically to consciousness nearly
everything in the diary from the date of the Locomotive-God, with numerous supplementary details of scene
and action, and above all of my own states of mind. And
many episodes not there at all. I even recall her writing in
the diary. "What are you doing, mama?" "Writing about
you. Sometime you'll read it." She sent it to me to read for
the first time after my father's death, with a new title,
"The First Four Years of the Professor's Life," penciled
and pasted in white on the flexible cover of each of the two
volumes. I had already begun my search for those years
and could verify objectively at once the reliability of all my

43

initial findings. The reading of the diary itself stimulated my subconsciousness to further recall; but there is no question, as will be more manifest later, of illusion and artifact. And where infant episodes were told me in boyhood, I have recalled the moments of telling, as well as the moments told about—each as a distinct item. My power of realistic imagination is one thing; of realistic memory another. The difference is absolute when the process has been completed.

I have sketched something of myself and my world up to my enrolment in the public schools. I see that youngster in myself to-day. But a good piece of him in the youngsters around me to-day. It is not an hour ago that I was down in the yard, back of our third-story apartment, burying a mother squirrel whose young were frisking in the tree. A little girl, a stranger, stood watching me, who had seen the two dogs kill it. "Dogs certainly are mean to squirrels," she pondered. "How old are you, kiddie?" "Four and a half." My childhood stood there in that little girl. Before I had relived that childhood, I was well read in "child psychology." A friend of specialists in childhood. I knew nothing. What we get from mere reminiscence is flimsy; what we get as observers is flimsy; what we get as behaviorists misses the matter altogether. But I can communicate to my fellows little, ultimately, of what I now know. The literal experience of being a child over again, while we maintain the mature powers of adjudging and realizing in thought the experience, needs words that pass over into colors, light, bodily sensations, attitudes, longings. Where are the words? But when the little girl said an hour ago, "Dogs certainly are mean to squirrels," she spoke to one in her own world, who knew what she meant, in intimacy of discourse incommunicable from one world to another. Parental love furnishes the only other clue . . . but even that bungles.

My search has added six or seven years to my life . . . at the other end. It would seem that those attacks of phobic terror, especially one to be analyzed in the next chapter,

44

were gradually suppressed, as disagreeable experiences so often are, and in sinking into the subconscious dragged down with them much that would normally have remained as childhood memories. At forty-five I had only a few isolated pictures and vague general memories of the old homestead and its life before my tenth year—the date when the Locomotive-God whistled and thundered in my brain again, with all of his primal fierceness, and with vastly more than the subconscious fierceness of the intervening years . . . though I was to live to face Him more terrible still, after twenty-six more years, for all my manhood's mastery of philosophies and foreign tongues and all the strength I had won at last from Alps and ocean. Of early pictures in this isolation, the earliest was of my mother daubing her nipples with black liquid from a pan on the stove, as I sat on the floor, a curious observer. She weaned my sister when I was two and a half. The next was of my father stumbling, shaking and pale, into the house to be led by my hurrying mother to the lounge. He lay speechless a few moments. The shadow of Niles, with the mortgage, thought my mother . . . and she asked about "the property". . . but it wasn't that—yet. He had received a telegram from Washington: "Garfield assassinated." My father took his country's politics seriously. All summer I was looking at the illustrations, I now recall, in "Harper's Weekly"— the special railway built out over the sands to the house at Long Branch, the patient white face pillowed up in bed for a look at the salt sea, with the nurse and the wife beside him. "You've one chance in a hundred," said the surgeon. "All right, we'll take that chance, doctor." And he set to work. Garfield was not a great man, but he put up a great fight. He died September 19. I was disappointed that he lost out. Both these normal memories have been verified and amplified, as the reader will note, by the psychoanalytic process.

I need tell little more about those years. The realistic training on the part of the parents of the young mind, with

its own normally realistic bent, incidentally spared me all
bugaboos—Jack the Giant-Killer, Little Red Riding-hood,
and the rest, I heard about, primarily from old Margaret.
But I played at them, as I played a little later at Robin
Hood: they were thus both truly objects of *make-believe,*
opportunities for the creative imagination, not obsessions
of shuddering credulity. Margaret, just over from County
Cork, with her brogue and proverbs and ballads . . .

London Bridge is falling down . . .

was fundamentally herself a realist. My mother had sent
her up into the country for a vacation. She was back with
us in two days: "there's more coompany in payple than in
shtoomps." The nearest to bugaboos were Indians. Rumors
of Western troubles still floated to the Atlantic seaboard.
Dodge's "Our Wild Indians," with its colored plates and
woodcuts of the aborigines crawling under the moon in the
prairie-grass with their tomahawks toward the caravan of
Oregon Trailers, was just out, and in our library and
often in my hands. My father took me to the Picnic Ground
near where Grove Street crossed the Brook to hear an
Indian open-air revivalist. I wanted to see a live Indian,
curiosity having got the better of fear. My awe disappeared
with my curiosity when I saw the same pious Prince Albert coat and gestures and heard the same pious Prince
Albert phrases as Dr. Yerkes's, Uncle Oliver's pastor's.
But that didn't cure me of Indians. I felt I had been
hoaxed. "That preacher on the platform, for all his dark
skin, isn't a real Indian." I was right. Gipsy-camps were a
little mysterious; but the circus was only a show. The
Christmas stockings for sister and me were filled by mama
and papa, not by Santa Claus . . . and the excitement was
to hear them down there fixing things up, in whispers, after
we'd gone to bed. That was fun enough . . . and real
employment for the imagination. What would we find in
the morning? Santa Claus, too, along with Jack the Giant

Killer, was a creature of the play-spirit. Once he burst, with all his beard and padded coat and bag and cotton snow and rollicking laughter, from the suddenly opened doors of the back parlor. Into the gas-light. A dozen tots screamed as much with scare as joy. I clapped my hands in a blaze of triumphant recognition: "Uncle Oliver!" I got my fun out of the thing as *joke and drama* . . . also out of my superior insight. I would only question "is that a true story" when the story was itself built on the laws of reality. Conventionally, one would say I had no training in the imagination. Yet the only training that counts is that which both correlates the imagination with life as *made* and stimulates the make-believe, the *play*-spirit. I had that training. I could be absorbed in the world I saw; and absorbed in the world I made, quite as to-day, except for subject-matter and intellectual overtones of feeling. And, quite as to-day, I knew the difference. A comet, a bird, a tree, a skeleton, are the best training for the realistic imagination; a rag doll, a broomstick, and Jack the Giant Killer accepted in the category of rag doll and broomstick, the best for the creative. The child who believes in fairies is not necessarily imaginative; the poor helpless little silly has probably simply been buncoed. My training in beauty was an undesigned realistic by-product of training in sense-perception, in getting things put together right, and in learning about life and nature.

It is clear I never had to get over Orthodoxy. That struggle, so tragic and devastating a crisis for so many of my contemporaries, was fought out in our family a generation before. My father's intelligence and honesty beat down, when the time came, as I know, the to him so terrible spiritual assaults of grieved kindred and teachers, of ambition, of obligation to those who had invested in him as the boy with the authentic call, even of parishioners who said, "Stay, believe as you will, we want you." But I think the shock did something to him for life. His theological library was all burned up in the Chicago Fire. I dedicated a little book to him about the "Poet of Galilee." My mother was a Boston Unitarian from girlhood.

But my parents' intelligent realism broke down in several particulars. It wasn't that I never got punished; I even got spanked, as that realism was finally faced with choice between theories of moral suasion and a still fractious child again in the peach-basket or cake-box. But they inculcated an unrealistic social attitude: it was nobler never to punch back. I myself felt it was merely sometimes safer, and came to use nobility as a subterfuge for cowardice. That subterfuge was thoroughly bad; worse even than the flight from a good row. And their philosophy got noised about among the urchins. On the other hand, Cousin Elston's Cousin Willie, whose father had been an old Yale baseball captain, being taught always to punch back, once punched a rangy stranger before a bar out in Nevada and woke up in a barn alone with a broken jaw. The stranger was a professional pugilist of fame. They inculcated exaggerations about my parental opportunities: my father would assure me of a most unusual mother; my mother of a more than most unusual father. Now a normal child takes this sufficiently for granted in any respectably conducted household. Anything more is to delay unduly the inevitable self-weaning of the free spirit. Moreover, it tends to devastate during adolescence its own purpose. The time comes when we see through the good home-folks, however good; they have to come down. We've no use for the sentimental bunk. By thirty-five we may have the facts. Exaggeration of my own personality was fostered less by any over-praise and indulgence; more by the indirect effects, later in school-days, of my mother's intimacies, on principle, with each successive teacher: the two dames were always talking me over; and I knew it with satisfaction, but didn't want my schoolmates to know it.

If God is to come into the child's life at all, their God was the best. I said my prayers. I was christened from a marble font by the Stocky Man, a Low-churchman, before

all the people in the shadowy pews. At five . . . somewhat
timid and puzzled (a recall verified by the parish records).
Sunday-school for several years, before service. The rector himself as superintendent:

On-ward, Chris-chan so-o-ul-jers . . .

My father was superintendent . . . a short time . . . bits
of chewed hymn-books . . . little tin spit-ball shooters.
My father was also a lay reader for a cool little brick
chapel, ivy-walled, 'way off on the sandy flat outskirts of
town. He usually chose Phillips Brooks' sermons. . . . My
father was sitting before me on a rock in a field on one of
our Sunday afternoon walks. "But who made *God,* papa?"
"My son" (when deeply moved, he always called me "my
son"), "my son, the Great First Cause is the Great First
Mystery." I was seven . . . but we were two children together.

It was in sex-training, however, where their realism
went all to pieces. Of this, later.

IV

At eight I had my biggest thrill at seeing a close-up of the heroic . . . long before movie days . . . a stand-off against odds. The family was for two weeks summer boarders at a salt-air farm-house near Atlantic Highlands. I had got up alone at five o'clock in the sunny silence, up from sleep in the attic with its smell of new-sawn pine boarding and its white mosquito-netting, to explore some more of the Hull, a derelict schooner that lay in the sands between the tides and the goldenrod hills. I was just crossing over on a sunken dirt-road when a switch-engine on a siding came chugging round the curve and the thickets, and maimed the front legs of a half-grown cat. It bounded with a wail, this small affair in white and gray, hobbling and sagging, and a dog pounced for it. Backed against the inner embankment of the hollow, it turned and fought for its life—fought with what was left. Its two stumps quite peeled to the bone, with bits of sand on the white gristle and the dangling fur. "Kill him, pussy! Kill him, pussy!" And I ran up to do what I could. The cur slunk off. The engineer got down, hunted up a dead bough, and put it out of pain. I knew he did right, but I cringed as it lifted its stumps for the last time, backed in the flying sand. The picture stayed by me all the years; but, more than that, the emotion plaited itself into my subconsciousness. An influence on our morale is primarily not in the example as remembered *qua* example, but in the integration in our emotional life of the example as something lived with, whether we remember it or not. Wordsworth is the poet who knew this best. But the cat got tangled up in the unseen web of my thought with the instrument of its

50

death—the locomotive. A generation later it came back in strange ways. Meantime I started school and soon was in a fight of my own against odds.

A month before I entered the public schools, I made my first boat. I chipped a hole in a loose brick from the back doorstep, set a stick in it from the woodhouse, and secured it upright with rigging of twine from the kitchen-drawer. *Pinta* and *Niña* and *Santa María*. The *Constitution*. Eric the Red. I launched it in the tub under the spout in the pump-room. It sank. Instantly. All my soul with it. I fished it out. Fished out my soul. I hunted in the woodhouse. I found a suitable block. I tried it out in the tub. It floated. Good. I fitted mast and rigging. Tacked on a bowsprit. Pinned rags on the string. Nailed a rail about the ends and sides. Laid a tack-claw with sawed-off handle in the stern— the anchor. I launched my second boat. San Salvador. Greenland. Cannonade on the blue sea. When is mama coming home from Aunt Lizzie's? I tucked my dripping boat under my arm and darted out the front gate down the street to bump into her right by the pine-cluster of Aunt Cornelia's field. By the next day, remodeled into a two-master, with rope-ladders, and sails well sewed to boom and rigging, she was bobbing about in Green Brook. Shortly after, they took me to have my picture taken again.

The one notable item above is the brick. Nine years old . . . with a realistic education . . . and not know a brick will sink. I need not speculate; I can read off my mind of that excited morning. I did know bricks would sink; but, engrossed in a tremendous creative idea, I never stopped to think anything about the law of the raw material. The idea was more than the brick—but the brick didn't care about that. I had a good lesson; and before tinkering further, I made doubly sure of the practical conditions by preliminary experiment. Let all mankind do the same.

I was to enter the third grade of the Washington School, over there in the yard next to the new Catholic cathedral with its brick and marble. The old homestead was on the edge of the tough ward. All the mickies lived over there on Liberty Street and the cross-streets beyond the railway bridge. The quarter, with its saloons and gangsters, was known as the Boulevard; and I have never yet succeeded in restoring its lexical meaning to "Boulevard," though there were two or three blocks of decent folk at the school-end of the street, toward the outlying countryside. I was to take my chances in democracy. I was not to be pampered; and, besides, I could manage the only real phobic terror that hadn't died out in the last year or two— I need not pass under the railway bridge when a train was passing over. I always knew the train wouldn't fall through; but to be under the roar still made me wild. I always waited and then made a dash. "Fraid Cat."

The morning arrived. New blue suit, red bow-tie, straw hat. A long block down Front Street away from the stores, a turn up Liberty toward Fifth. With my mother . . . past so many picket-fences, yellow and white and brown . . . I talking. Under elms . . . elms. Then rows of saplings— now after forty years elms too. I had often been over that way before to the cemetery where Grandfather Leonard had been buried when I was a baby. No, really never before. Only one block more: I see the flag on the great white staff in the playground beyond the high pickets. Boys. A half-block: the balustraded porch on the side. Boys. Then the whole massive square pile . . . its gray-painted brick doubly transfigured—by the light from the September sun and the light from the child. Past the Fifth Street gate of the boys' yard right up to the big front steps. We are before the balustraded platform all across the front, with lofty portico in the middle. The windows, guarding mysteries behind their opaque shimmer, are four times the size of ours, and ours are big. But these are all in one row; ours go up to three at the gable-ends. We mount to the huge double doors. "Mama." Inside, the kind lady principal by her desk. Miss Humiston. She and mama have it all arranged: "Shake hands with your new teacher." Miss Bond leans over, and her necklace of black beads dangles away from her white shirt-waist . . . a neat wiry little lady with freckles, of twenty-three or four. I learned her age later.

But what an amazing inside! One vast high chamber, its ceiling and its windowed walls all a-dazzle, as if that chamber had captured half the bright day. With intersecting rows of pillars shiny in fresh brown varnish, and hundreds of little desk-tops in assorted sizes all about, with five other big desks on platforms, like the one near where I am standing with mama and the two nice ladies. From pillar to pillar up in air, glass-frames hang rigid and perpendicular, crisscrossing under the ceiling and bordered by blackboards along their lower sashes, these also high in air above our heads. Here and there two pillars are connected down to the floor by a doorway, the doors being now all open. St. Peter's will not seem so amazing, nor Cologne Cathedral, nor the Mosque of Cordova.

The interior had, for a fact, been constructed on a plan unique in the architecture, ecclesiastical or secular, of the globe. The president of the Board of Education— Dr. Stillman, let me give him to fame—convinced that climbing stairs was bad for children's spines, had requisitioned—rather, himself designed—a compact, well lighted, one-story structure. As I first contemplated that chamber, with the youngsters beginning to file in, it was the assembly-room. . . . And there I was, bewildered in my seat with my beaming mother by Miss Bond's, as childish treble raised in meek chorus its first morning song and the Principal stood tuning them along with a stick, beyond the shiny pillars and behind a stack of little flags on her desk. Assembly over, the teachers lowered the blackboards to the floor, inclosing their charges, demure or rebellious (from grades one to six), for the ritual of the day . . . under light from the high frames at the top of the inner wall and from the tall windows, shades up, on the outer. White plaster. George Washington.

I have been at some pains to make this interior clear;

53

for its bizarre contraptions added in two weeks an item to the disaster I am about to relate, and much embarrassment, nearly forty years after, to the process, already intricate enough, of psychological recall. It had totally disappeared from consciousness along with all, even to the name and location of the school; and when it first began to come back in disconnected fragments—greenhouse frames, pillars, door-knobs, blackboards overlapping in and out of place, one desk, six desks, big room, little room, eerie flashes of light—I was for a time almost persuaded that the creative imagination, with its stimulus perhaps from the new art of the "Dial," was insisting on supplying me, by a *tour de force,* with a substitute for what I could not get by memory—and a substitute as crazy as a dream. But right there was the clue and the hope. A dream isn't crazy. What was coming back was yet a dream—wait and the meaning of the dream will be clear. To-day the whole is as organized and intelligible in consciousness as the commonplace class-room I lectured in this morning. With every detail objectively verified by photographs and correspondence except just how the blackboards were operated in their movable sashes—I think that when up they partially covered the glass-frames, and were merely shoved up and pulled down by hand. The teacher's arms could reach so much higher than ours.

My mother sat beaming by the teacher's desk till recess. Then she took me out to the little girls' yard, and the small white coop behind the lattice. To make sure that I was all hunky-dory. I had been taken to the Family Doctor more than once, for a common childish affliction in my sleep; and when awake I had often enough to stop my play a moment under the laws of nature. She kissed me good-by at my seat —four or five seats back down the line from Miss Bond's desk and the clock over the door behind her. She waved from an outer doorway at the further side of the class-room, and disappeared into the girls' yard. I dreaded to have her go. But excitement, challenge, curiosity carried

54

me through that first morning, as it was doubtless carrying a million other small Americans in a similar plight that same morning. But they hadn't all come from such a home to such a school. Nor all with their mothers.

I found I could do it. I found I could go to school. I ask the reader to know—and without sentiment—that they were very happy days, those two weeks. And I was all set to make good. How like a little soldier I took my place in the yard from that very first afternoon, at the clang of the bell over the boys' door—toward the tail of the line among the diminished heads—and how I pounded out my steps, as we filed through the first-grade room between its wall and seats into ours. How neatly I made my little figures on my slate for Miss Bond down the aisle to look over and correct. How straight I stood beside my desk, thumb and little finger distending the page of the Reader, and how carefully I pronounced the words—this time "always correctly," for a fact, since they were baby-words to me! How carefully I arranged my ruler and pencil-box and books in the desk drawer. Miss Bond (who to be sure was taking me rather dryly) would realize in time just how bright and just how good I was. I would keep at it.

Four times back and forth every day, through the hole in the rear pickets of our fence that bordered the path in the field and by short cut down a back street over to Liberty. Alone or with fifth-grade Florence or stray urchins that I was getting to know better in a common cause. And only one rainy day. Rubbers in the cloak-room. Out in the school yard at recess I threw pebbles bang against the back-boarding that divided us from the Catholic Cathedral, or stared through the pickets that divided us from the romping girls, or got ordered away from the flagstaff tackle by the janitor, or played tag as one already used to playmates, though not many so red-headed and freckled. But the boys didn't tease me beyond laughing at my mother. I had done nothing in particular to be noticed in such a busy swarm, and was not squeamish about dirt. My parents were

delighted with the way things were going; but I heard my
father say something would have to be done at once about
the filthy condition of the boys' toilet behind the school-
house. I didn't mind that as much as the dash under the
bridge. But I would keep at it.

So the great era began and rolled on. Till the end of
the second week. That Friday morning at half-past nine,
I raised my hand. I had been forgetful about tending to
myself just before out in the yard behind the lattice. And
Miss Bond was impatient if we asked too often. I wished
mightily I hadn't forgotten.

I shall have to ask the reader to go through the rest of
that morning with me, if he is interested in the scientific
and humanistic purpose of these pages; both of us to save
our laughter for another day . . . for everything that
is serious is funny—that's perhaps the main reason it's
funny. I have a fifty-page manuscript that records the bare
outlines of my consciousness from 9:30 to 12:30 of that
morning in September, 1885. If I recorded all the details—
every object living or dead with its shadow, every motion,
every thought, every feeling of mine item by item in that
three-hour segment of the stream of time and the stream
of consciousness—all that I now remember after my two
years' search during 1922–24 for the reality of that morning, I should need not fifty, but a thousand pages. There
are no other three hours of my life that I know so well,
minute by minute—beside which Joyce's "Ulysses" would
be but a sketch. I speak with precision. What is time? . . .
The thousand pages will never be written; nor will the
fifty be printed. I shall simply pick out the psychological
moments that most clearly echoed the boy's younger days in
the years and the fears already lived and that most clearly
reverberated down all the years and the fears to be; and
shall leave their setting of bodily and mental torture to be
reconstructed, in its ineluctable crescendo, without help
from me, by any reader humane enough to understand and
scientific enough not to wince.

We have been in our seats only a half-hour. I am ashamed to bother her so soon. She shakes her head and goes on talking about plus and minus. That is all the meaning I have to her. I drop my hand. Perhaps I can wait till recess . . . only an hour. But in five minutes the signal is lifted again. To remain lifted. Over the heads of all. The snickering children see . . . if Miss Bond won't. Plus and minus.

She will dislike me. And my world is in her praise. But discomfort becomes pain. And pain is great. It can destroy fame and good report. My right shoulder aches. I lift my left arm. I begin to watch the clock. The longer hand jerks forward, minute by minute, up, up toward the quarter. My left aches . . . left . . . right . . . I cross my legs, this way and that way. The shooting pains frighten me. "Oh, Miss Bond, if you only knew." My eyes stare at her without tears. My lips are tighter and tighter. The hand is past the quarter. The reading-lesson begins: Little Slider-downhill.

I look at the door beside and behind her desk, into the first-grade room, the highway to the boys' yard. I look at the outer door into the girls'. I am in the very middle of the room. Surrounded. It is terrible to be surrounded. The social law, incarnated in that harsh and remorseless face, and vast humanity, incarnated in my classmates, become something alien and menacing. Helpless isolation. Dread. The two doors? Oh, if I only dared! The minute-hand jerks to ten.

I look at the glass-frames up in air, at George Washington, at the white plaster in the corner. I even risk turning my head toward the rear window. Perhaps by the next time I look at the clock it will be a quarter past ten . . . I look: it is 10:05.

A new plan. Miss Bond can't see, if I'm careful, nor the children. My underdrawers and pants will hold the water that my body can't hold any longer . . . a little of it, if I'm careful. But a pool grows on my seat beside me.

57

Quickly I cover it with my slate. Did Kathleen across the aisle see it? No. She's looking at her book and then up at Miss Bond. She may have to stand and read next. Supposing Miss Bond calls on me. No. Miss Bond probably won't call on me. Miss Bond's eyes look this way and that but always past my lifted arm. Miss Bond's lips say, "Mamie, you," "Dennis, you" . . . Little Slider-downhill. The pool grows, the pain grows, the ache, the isolation, the terror. "Mama, papa." Our house so far . . . so far, and papa's office two times as far. A mile. I am dying. You will never know . . . My eyes are raised to the clock, as to a God who will not save me even when my teacher has given me up.

I hear a low cough and then a hiss from small Kathleen. My head turns. She points a stubby finger of disgust to a pool under my seat. Horror and shame. She makes a grimace with her tongue out. That face will startle me with shudders from sleep in a distant city long after Kathleen is dead. The laws of organic nature create us, and we bear witness by a willing or unwilling obedience or we perish. They unite us as one race. They unite us with a thousand races, around us in fur, feather, hide, and shell. With the races before . . . back to the Silurian and before. They are older laws than the laws of man's etiquette. They may be ugly, but they work. Even the more recent have worked for fifteen million years—since the Jurassic mammals and the beginning of thirst. They can vindicate their prerogative even against the laws of the school-house.

A whistle blows. The sound of a south-bound coal-train. I have heard, I have seen the empty cars trailing back to be refilled in the Appalachian mines, year after year along the embankment over yonder through the orchards and cottages behind our yard. But then I was always on the *other side,* where our house was. An instantaneous surge of panic engulfs even pain, shame, despair. So strange and new that the very surprise of the visitation challenges the boy's reason. What is it? What is it? Surely death. Papa, mama,

58

home, suddenly so infinitely far away in *feel,* though I know
they are no farther away in fact than the far-away of before. The imprisonment suddenly in *feel* horrible beyond its
previous horror. I count desperately, 1, 2, 3, 4, 5, on up the
decades. I lower my hand. I grasp my slate and pencil. I
make frantic marks. To get myself together. The panic
was both its own alien self and a secondary panic created by
the intellect in its bewildered dismay and premonition: the
primary state itself rumbled death; the reason, contemplating the state from its own corner, drew its own devastating conclusions from the symptoms. But I subdued the
attack. Rather it passed . . . with the passing of the Locomotive-God on toward Pennsylvania.

I have made no sound, no motion. The turmoil has
been all inside. But the puddle has meantime been whispered
up the aisle and down. The boy to my right has seen. The
news is all over the room. One youngster on the front seat
of Kathleen's aisle leans 'way around and peers low with
leering grin. Miss Bond suddenly notices something is very
wrong. She steps down beside her platform. Her face
flushes. She nods. It is nearly 10:25.

That nod meant life. Quickly and quietly I get up and
walk down the aisle, amid the buzz and rumor, and out
down the side of the first-grade room with a turn between
teacher and forty little faces, not too little to see my plight.
I apologize as I pass: "Excuse me, Miss Anderson." She
wears a black dress. She smiles gently. That helps. I take
hold of the knob of the outer door of the class-room . . .
I will later take hold of it many times in twilight sleep
before understanding to what door in what house and city
it belongs. There is a little hall by the cloak-room. A big
boy there. He sees. "Hello.". . . "Hello." I get the
school-yard door open, fly down the steps, off down the
boardwalk to the lattice. Swift as my flight is, the eye
photographs for my subconsciousness two nuns over on
the grounds of the Parochial School walking peacefully
about in black and white. They will later walk in my dreams

59

under Wisconsin oaks with the Dominican Sisters of the Convent of the Sacred Heart in Madison, near the bungalow home I am some day to build on Lake Wingra.

The physical anguish relieved, I know my difficulties are not over yet. In the ordinary reminiscence of maturity we lose an appreciation of the relative maturity of the child. We graft on a genuinely childish situation childish reactions of thought quite specious in their childishness. My awe before the constituted authorities was that of a child—at least of a well bred American child of forty years ago. As a man, I'd simply walk out of the room when I got ready and out of the neighborhood, with the decisive comment, "You may all go to hell." To be sure, I would *not*, if I found myself under Authority as awesome to me now as Miss Bond was then . . . but where is there any such Authority? The man knows no experience of Authority equal to the child's. That, rather than the pain and the shame, was the childish situation. That, too, rather than my terrors at nine years . . . for they were largely conditioned by abnormal subconscious forces that have generated phobic terror-phenomena of exactly the same emotional texture in my maturity. The childish situation in a broader sense was of course my social relation to my childish group. But I cannot differentiate my practical, intellectual reactions, at this point where relative freedom of action begins (as opposed to helpless subordination), from my normal intellectual reactions to-day. The situation, the objects, were of the child's world; the effort to handle them was already out of that same world of intellect from which has sprung all my effort, successful or not, ever since. I wrung out my blue-flannel knickerbockers and adjusted my clothes in the fetid acrid closet behind the lattice with all haste, well realizing the recess-bell would soon set loose the pack. I decided not to run home, but, in case of jeers, to get back into the school-house. Miss Bond would know it was not my fault, and the lady-in-black was my friend. The scandal, I thought, would be the sooner forgotten so.

60

This, with all its nuances, had scarcely passed through my mind when the bell clanged. That intellectual energy of self-preservation which we call foxiness decided forthwith for a run out from behind the school into the center of the yard, as strategically a better position—for the clangor of the bell was not alone this bell, and it initiated the premonitions of the flight-motif. I was well out there when the doors burst open and the pack, big and little, yelled and bounded at me *en masse* down the steps. "Hi, fellers, there he is." Instantly their uproar and onset became the Locomotive. That is, without fully losing their external appearance in sunlight as faces, clothes, hands, and legs, they generated so fiercely the *feel* of a locomotive that the reality of sight had actually less meaning in that instant than the objectified subconscious state. I may say that the pack in its uproar and onset was, as it were, veiled in a wraith of a monstrous locomotive. The nearest analogy in everyday experience would be an accelerated fade-in and fade-out of the cinema. I have distinguished in my phobic attacks three states of such subconscious projection: (1) simply the feel, (2) the feel with the wraith, (3) the feel with the completed objectification of optical hallucination. In no case have I ever lost rational consciousness or the power (no matter what the degree of terror) to size up objective reality for reality. Even in the third state, experienced but once and at thirty-five, I knew in my collapse, the skyey Horror in all its visibility for a Hoax, though I could not then know the meaning and origin of the Hoax. It was only in the original trauma on the station-platform that I believed with my whole being what I saw and felt. And let it not be forgotten that at the time of which I write absolutely all recollection of that episode had disappeared from consciousness for at least five years . . . and the core of it for seven. The reader, following this tale, will know, for many chapters still, much more about what was really happening than ever I did at the time.

The Locomotive rushing down from the steps staggers

61

me, and almost simultaneously I am obsessed with a feel, strong almost to the point of emerging as hallucination, of the red-brick railway-station off in air opposite beyond the school-yard picket-fence. But the reality, the mob of hooting boys, compels a swift calculation of chances, though the fear itself is at least half phobic reverberation: I am really *running away* from the Locomotive-God. I see they can head me off before I can make the only exit—the Fifth Street Gate—toward home, too. I strike off diagonally toward the picket-fence on Liberty. My shoes beat the pebbles past the flagstaff. My eyes eat up that brown sunny floor of grit and dust. The abnormal sense of immeasurable distance from safety—the dominant motif in my present neurosis—floods me. But above all, even in my flight, Mary's personality, in all her pink and gold of ten years, is a poignant presence in an emotional matrix of terror, yearning, and shame . . . It is to return so poignantly and persistently in my psychoanalysis that I will be writing her about it in the year 1923, before I have got back to the Mary of 1878, and she will answer:

No. I do not remember ever being in the neighborhood of Liberty and Fifth Streets, as a child, for either play or any of the small businesses of life—dentist, doctor, dressmaker.

But what is the meaning of *to be?* She *was* there for me, though indeed for none of the small businesses of life . . . By the time it takes to read these lines on Mary I have reached the pickets. A hundred, perhaps two hundred hooligans yelling nearer and nearer. No. It is now not alone the Locomotive-God that makes my shoes beat the pebbles and my mouth gasp for air. "Get him." The Mob, the Mob. The fence is higher than my head. I mount the lower scantling. "Get him." I grasp the picket-tops. I get my left knee on the upper scantling. "Get him." I lift myself, exhausted, unnerved, breathless. And half jump, half topple over. One of those sharp pickets digs a wound into my right thigh. I light full on the back of a passing dog, who scurries off. With my hands in the gravel of the side-walk. I get up. Dash across the street. A lady going out of a front yard and a man with a cane on the opposite side of the street stop some distance off to observe the show.

On the tree-lawn, I pick up a stick. I turn and face them. I shake the stick. I shake my fist. "Come on, you devils." Winded, broken, yet for an instant full of fight. A hundred. Two hundred. Dozens and dozens of them clambering on to the fence, heads in rows, like buzzards. One great jeering and cursing red-head towers over the pickets, bigger and redder than all the rest. He alone could wring my neck with one hand. And the swarm behind still running up. And the pandemonium of yells. "Get him." They start to throw stones, the hundred, the two hundred. I hurl a rock. Let them kill me. I'll stand my ground. I was the maimed cat. A generation later I will be the maimed cat again and I will have to face another pack more cowardly still.

But the red-headed giant seems as if about to climb the fence. And I see a dozen making south for the Fifth Street gate. The Mob, the Mob. To head me off on Liberty Street from home. The flight-motif. The chase, the fox-hunt, begins again. I see through the pickets one little runt tearing along, waving his arms in an ecstasy of delight over this unexpected fun. He gets his courage, like all the little runts, from the tribe. I think, even though I have much else to think about, "You'd be running the other way, if we were alone." I am at the corner of Fifth and Liberty. A dozen are already through the Gate out on to Fifth Street, fifty yards away. Shall I dash into the corner house before me? No. The screen door may be locked. So I spurt, gasping. The stones fly. Street-stones bigger than the playground pebbles. I have scarcely crossed the street, when from the enfilade a rusty corn-beef can of heavy tin hits me fiercely on my left temple, and bangs along on the sidewalk before me. I think, as I see its jagged half-opened lid, "A narrow escape for my left eye." A milk-wagon

passes. I think, "That protects me for a minute." I pass
a lady with a baby-carriage . . . the reader will recall that
at the station there was a baby-carriage . . . "They can't
throw with her there," I think. And, for a fact, they don't
follow. I am safe, I think to myself, but think I'd still better
keep running to the end of the block. Fifth and Fourth.

Then a whistle blows again. This time up from Pennsylvania. The alien spell that had seized me in the class-
room seizes me again. I recognize it for the same. I think,
"That passed, this will." But it does not pass. It surges
with an indescribable intensity of Horror. Home again
becomes immeasurable distance, only more immeasurable.
And the distance of three blocks to the railway-bridge
girders is, in feel, an infinity of street in the sun. I totter.
I fly. I open my shirt to get air on my bare chest. There is
a white hitching-post by the gutter near the end of the
block. My imagination creates that as its goal, as its refuge.
If I can get to the hitching-post, I am saved. I get to the
hitching-post. There is a pile of bricks on the tree-lawn and
mortar in a mixing box. I stumble on a pail. I fall down on
the gravelly sidewalk. All my strength is gone, but with it
something of the seizure of panic is gone. I crawl and wrig-
gle a few feet to get that much farther from the school, and
I look back, from where I lie. Farther than one can throw
a baseball, I say to myself, with one more reverberation
of 1878. They are gone. They have had their fun. I look
up at the wooden tower of the old Catholic Chapel, facing
me over a garden from Fourth Street. Not the new Cathedral. I have a strange dread lest its bell should begin to
ring. But I can no longer move . . . not one inch.

My temple and thigh pain. My tongue is dry. My wind-
pipe aches. My side. I need water. All the water has gone
out of my body. By all highways: the water from the blad-
der, the water from under the skin. Sweat is socially the
more respectable water; but the body knows no difference.
I can still use my eyes. Across the street is a house and a
barn beside it with a dilapidated wooden arch over the

driveway entrance. An old buggy with top up clatters toward me. I can't call. I don't think of calling. I roll nearer the pile of bricks to be out of sight. In the back part of the buggy are two hen-coops. The hens have their heads out between the slats. They see me. Through the lower interstices of the palings I can see the grape-vines in the garden, and yonder a man on a scaffold repairing the chimney-top. But, mostly, I look down the street toward the girders that I am unable to reach, or up toward the chapel belfry with the bell I am dreading may ring. Exhaustion . . . all except eyes and brain.

A gray cat strolls across the street a little in front and crawls under the fence. A lady in black comes up from a grocery store. Toward me. With a basket on her arm. She leans over. I cannot answer. She sets her basket down beside me near the fence-gate. She runs up the side-path to the ell of the house, which itself faces on Fourth opposite the old Catholic Chapel with the square little belfry. A slip sticks out of the packages in her basket: "six pounds of sugar". . . etc. I can still use my eyes. She runs back, with another woman. They beckon, frantically, to a man yonder, burning in the gutter the yellow autumn leaves of young elms. He runs toward me, his rake still in hand. He becomes terrorizing onset, attack, though with my reason I know he is a man. I shut my eyes, too weak to clap my hands to my face, as I had done before the Aboriginal Locomotive-God. I feel Death. "Mama, papa, oh, my boat, my boat." If not a swoon, very near. The man lifts me. I still was alive. I have felt Death many times since . . . and I am no less alive still. When it comes at last and for the last time, it will be a kinder thing. The man carries me in, past the patch of corn-stalks and stray pumpkins, and they lay me on the bare floor. The man sits in the doorway with his straw hat on his knees. An old crone in a rocker on a rag mat is peeling potatoes for dinner. I find speech, and can tell my friendly deliverers my father's name. The strange lady who had found me searches up the address in a directory

65

hanging in a corner. But that was before telephones in suburban houses. They look me over. They see the rent in my knickerbockers. They open my clothes, though I try to roll over, in my shame, to prevent them. They bathe the bleeding bruise. They see my breeches are all so damp. I gasp, without tears, the nature of the catastrophe. They had heard the yells. Neither the old crone at her potatoes, nor the man with the hat, nor the old crone's daughter with freckled fat arms, nor the visitor-lady, thinks it funny in the least, nor the shame of it my shame. The visitor-lady lifts my head. She makes me swallow a spoonful of liquid. From its taste relived, I now know it was brandy. On the inner wall of the low room just below the ceiling hangs a long gaudy frame, inclosing an image in pallid wax. It is Christ on the Cross.

I can get up. They set me at the table. I drink a glass of milk. "No, I can get home alone, thank you all." But they let me go upstairs first to reconnoiter. From the upper windows of first one bedroom, then another, I survey the school yard. It is empty and silent. I have only bodily pains now, and I can manage them. "Thank you, for being so nice to me," I say from the hall-stairs doorway, not as one taught but as one grateful, and decide to go down from the ell through a front hall, evidently inhabited by a "wealthier" family, out by the Fourth Street exit . . . farther from the school. I open the front door and see the janitor turning up the corner—this way. I return, apologizing for making more trouble. The visitor-lady accompanies me down the hall and explains to the janitor at the gate. He goes away. The lady shuts the door . . . and doubtless in a few minutes is on up Liberty Street from the ell path gate with her grocery basket.

I stand an instant on the front porch, with its pillars and wisteria-vines. Another whistle, the third, from the Pennsylvania way—for the Central New Jersey was even then a two-track and a main-traveled road. It does not raise a panic—but yet a pressing problem. From the sound

66

it is about at Evona—a mile and a half. The express!—I know the time-table. Only too well. Can I get under the bridge before it passes? I pound down on air by each hip with each clenched fist, in resolution to try with all my strength. Another whistle. As I leap down the steps and unlatch the near gate, the façade of the Catholic chapel becomes the onrushing wraith of the Locomotive, its belfry the stack, the roof the engineer's cabin. To the eye a monstrous wraith, but to the feel (that created the wraith), again, aboriginal reality of attack, swelling at me to the compass of the horizon. The phenomenon comes and goes almost instantaneously. I cross the grass-grown street, stumbling into a hole out of which I will be building a nightmare in 1902 in Dresden. Past the chapel, round the corner, with a straightaway now to the girders. I must beat the train. In retrospect I note hundreds of details—elm saplings with yellow leaves, scarlet woodbine, a stranger-child smiling down at me from her swing as it mounts to the highest point of its giddy pendulous curve, my shame that she sees me running so fast, a rickety corner saloon, a yard full of old iron (wheel-rims and pipe-joints)—a hundred details—a hayrick with oxen up Liberty, for instance, the hotness of the September sun in old Jersey, for instance —before I reach the bridge.

I have been racing against the incoming roar of the train. Evona, Grant Avenue, Plainfield Avenue. Can I make it? To wait till it passes is impossible; for another flight-motif is the abnormal poignancy of the instinct for home. I must beat the train, for I must not be blocked in getting home. Two men across the way are sitting on the unroofed stoop of a slate-factory office, under a big lettered umbrella, such as used to be stuck by the driver's seat on delivery-trucks. One yells, "Johnnie, get your gun." The train is still three hundred yards away. I can make it. Then I bump into the Dog—the dog I had tumbled on over the school fence. I stop, as he runs at me. Nervous. Pat his back, high as a pony's would be now. The delay is fatal. The Path of the Train. The Locomotive. I dash forward. There is a siding by the slate-factory sheds, descending from the embankment. Just as I get opposite the end of that siding, the locomotive reaches the spot where the siding switches off. The *feel* is instantly as if the Train were about to dash over on to the siding and run me down. Again—need I use adjectives any longer?—that feel of onrush and attack. I say to myself, "What's the matter with you, you young jackass?" That is—and note closely—I am perfectly realistic in eyesight and reason, knowing both that the train will not run me down and that the idea of its running me down is nonsense. But I don't know, you see, that the Train I really fear is neither in eyesight nor in reason. I don't know that it is the Locomotive-God . . . and I won't know for many a year.

The terror at being so far from home, still with so many trees and houses between, mounts above the terror of the roar overhead. The locomotive, wheels and boiler, has already crossed, and a cinder blows down into my eye, and a smell of anthracite into my nose. I live through the seconds of Uproar. The cavernous coolness and the shadows help. I am on the other side. I look back at the retreating rear platform, in two or three minutes to draw up at the station. The Station becomes a moment's obsession. Mysterious shame sweeps through me. All the people in the train must see and know my disgrace of this morning . . .

Jump over the years, my friend. In 1923 I will be seeing half asleep a dream-picture of the side of a passenger-car, with people facing all one way in the windows, at a time where my search has already recovered most of the external action, but as yet little of the internal (the psychological states) of this school-day episode. This dream-picture will awaken to memory some items in the action of the last few paragraphs. The car will be recognized as this car. But one point will puzzle me: it will be facing the *wrong way*. The real car of 1885 headed away from Pennsylvania. The dream-car headed toward Pennsylvania. But, as the psychological detective, I will know that this wrong way must mean something. What? Can you solve this? It will mean that car from Westfield as it stands in the station before the two years' child. It was this associational fusion of the car of 1885 toward Westfield with the car of 1878 from Westfield that represented one of the first shadowy, elusive manifestations in my recall-states of the 1878 experience; another was recalling that the boys on the steps (already recalled as boys) had reminded me of a locomotive. Their psychological significance was not resolved for a year, however, after their recall as psychological data.

The train has passed. I feel weak and nauseated, and all but resolve to ask help in the first house. But no. I *must* get *home*. So I scurry round the first corner into the back street, the familiar short cut . . . and bump square into Pat Lynch. He may mean nothing to the reader, though it is hard for me to put myself in the place of any human being who from earliest boyhood has not known Pat Lynch. The six-foot, two-hundred-pound terror in blue coat and blue helmet, with the brown billy on a thong at his wrist. Terror of every school yard, every vacant-lot ball-team, every swimming-hole in Green Brook, every sidewalk game of marbles, every empty house with broken panes, every blouse bulging with apples. "Cheese it, fellers—Pat Lynch." He turned up everywhere and at any hour. I could never figure out his beat—now down by the railway-station where he had an apartment on the ground floor of the jail, now pacing, with hands judicially clasped behind him, in majestic stride past our house, now suddenly standing with undemonstrative dignity and heavy upturned visage underneath some isolated cherry-tree on the borders of town, sagging with succulent fruit and small boys. There must have been other policemen in town. But Pat Lynch was our policeman.

And now he turns up here in my alley. He questions me. He is a truant officer. I admit running home, and explain why in my trepidation. An old man and woman inside the moldy fence say, "Let him go, Pat." A tinner, patching the roof, calls, "Let him go, Pat." I try to flatter or scare him with the power of the press: "I am the son of Mr. Leonard, editor of the 'Central New Jersey Times,' Mr. Lynch." But he is obdurate, or suspicious. I stare up, high up, though I have a good nine years' growth, at the badge on his immense chest, with its big number. If my story of the stoning is not true, I must go back and be punished for lying and playing hooky; if it is true, I will be needed in the investigation for the punishment of others. He is not Cruelty; he is Justice, the Law. He takes me firmly by the collar and starts me *back*.

So near home—so near at last—and then this. I think of mama, who could almost hear me from the house if I called very loud. I think of facing the Mob, the Mob, again—but at least he won't let them stone me. I think of going under the bridge again—but at least there won't be another train for a while. So I stumble, abject and hopeless, along beside him . . . a hundred feet . . . two hundred feet. Then by one of those instinctive resolves that become action quite literally, before we know it, I duck my head and scoot. I am many rods away before I fairly realize my freedom. By a roadside apple-tree, I look around. He is pacing and swaying along just under the bridge with hands, as normally, behind his broad back. I make straight down Liberty into Front, without turning round again. But later in the day—to conclude with Pat—I was much worried. I had resisted an officer. I had defied the law. I wrote Pat Lynch a respectful letter, explaining my case and urging him to regard me as by intention and general social habits a law-abiding citizen; and gave it to my father for personal delivery. "Be sure to see Pat Lynch," was my final admonition, as my father, already delayed by my affairs, made a belated return to his sanctum. At suppertime, I was at the door: "Did you see Pat Lynch?" My father smiles: "Yes. I saw him. It's all right. He believes you told the truth.". . . Three years ago, when I had got this memory all back, I wrote to the present chief of police in the old home town for the number on Pat's badge. The answer verified my recall, and gave me the one definitive assurance that the big fellow would never trouble my normal life again.

August 9, 1923

The number of Pat Lynch of the Plainfield Police Force in Sept. 1885 was No. 2. He died about 11 yrs. ago.

P. H. KELLY.

The way around the corner up Front is the last lap. I am running simply to get home. Now under the big elms of old colonial plantings. Past the house where I returned the umbrella, yes, past the house where Florence Runyan lives —sixth-grade Florence. I make a detour into the gutter to dodge the cow tethered in the front of the field between her house and ours. Just at the nearer Front Gate—for Grandfather's old rambling manse was big enough to possess two—I am seized with horror lest mama be at Aunt Lizzie's—a mile away—and nobody at home—and how far beyond my running-power now is the long distance to papa's office. Up along the side of the house, and round the ell, between rain-barrel and woodhouse . . . "Mama," "Mama," "Mama." With one surge of premonition, "What if Mama isn't home?" Abyss . . . isolation . . . alien sky. I come to a stand before the opened pump-room door of the lean-to. There she is already in the doorway, with anxious and astonished eyes. I rush into her, burying my head in her skirt, with arms clasped about her thighs. I sob long. The first tears and outcry of the morning.

The seventy-odd-year widow writes the psychoanalyst, upon inquiry, January 28, 1923:

Yes. You ran in and I met you. You were dreadfully pale. . .

71

Not flushed from the furious run and the heat of a cloudless sun, but "dreadfully pale": terror is the supreme emotion of life, and it borrows its color from its Master, Death. The letter continues:

and I saw how badly you were feeling, and, along with my surprise at seeing you at that early hour, my sympathies were deeply stirred and I made every effort to comfort you. I drew you close to me. We stood right there for a little while, till you told me what had happened, before we went into the kitchen and up the back stairs to your room.

I have often noted, in getting help for my recalls or verifications of recalls, that my mother's letters themselves reveal, like those of some other of my correspondents in the same study, interesting phenomena of recall. In all that relates to my boyhood troubles for instance, she remembers with most certainty and detail and satisfaction her own motherly emotions and mothering acts. She is not less a man's mother for that.

Yes. Up the back stairs to my room, a low-ceilinged room with low little square windows in front, and a high-set window at the side, overlooking the roof of the ell-front, and next to a projecting chimney-flue. I clamber up to this window to see about the cow. I am phobic with unguessed reverberations of old unhappy far-off things and battles long ago, as well as with the exhaustion of the battle of the morning. I get myself "sponged off" at my wash-bowl. I rub vaseline on my thigh—from the pudgy bottle on the little shelf over my wash-stand. I get my clothes changed with her help. She has me lie down on the bed beside her. She is playful. She raises her thumbs with her arms at sides:

Thumbkin says I'll dance and sing.

Then I go down with her, and, making sure from a lower

window that the cow has not got into the yard, hang my clothes on the line between woodhouse and elm. We are sitting, shelling peas on the step of the low back porch off the kitchen, when we hear papa's feet in the hall. There is much indignant talk at dinner—chiefly about Miss Bond. My little sister sits eating, detached. I sit long in my father's lap after dinner. I need his lap and his arm and his voice, but I feel silly, being so big. I don't know that I have been shattered back into my infancy again. After he is gone, my mother, with a purposive, businesslike speed, gets out her portable desk, lays it on the dining-room table, and writes Miss Bond the vigorous letter of an outraged young mother. I beg her never to tell Mary. In the middle of the afternoon, Florence Runyan, as little errand-girl, comes in by the side door where the trumpet-vine is and lays my hat and books and slate and pencil-box on the same table. I tiptoe away out of the next room.

I stayed in and about the house for several days. The episode became for the School Board and for the city superintendent, Julia Bulkley, crony of my mother's, a black-eyed gifted woman full of energy and methods, a crisis in American education. For me it meant (then) transfer to the Franklin School in a more civilized ward; and to Miss Bond sharp rebukes, official and unofficial, and almost dismissal from her post and ruin. I don't know what her defense was. She was then, like so many, an inexperienced, much bossed, youngster-pestered girl, and, moreover, presumably she did not wish to annoy Miss Anderson in the next room by letting her charges pass through. Dr. Stillman, in his concern for children's spines, forgot their little bladders.

Early in 1923, still utterly confused in my distorted recalls of the Washington School, though having already recalled some main items of the catastrophe, I made inquiries by sundry letters, and discovered, with strange sensations, that Miss Bond was still living. In a Jersey village, pensioned and retired. I wrote her at length, saying how well I remembered her because, though we were both now gray, she had been my first teacher, touching on the catastrophe (but in a way to minimize her responsibilities), and explaining something of my manhood's neurosis as being in part due to that childhood's stoning, and how I was trying to get over the neurosis through getting back the experience. I knew at the time of writing her nothing about the Locomotive-God. Her reply began:

You can guess my reaction to your letter, no doubt, and what memories it recalled; but the incident to which you refer is not one of them. I do remember you as a rather pale, slender little boy with dark eyes and seemingly rather diffident . . .

She inclosed a neatly drawn and precisely notated plan of the school; and was thereafter most understanding and helpful in answering many little questionnaires (apparently so trivial) and in verifying my little maps of the neighborhood streets and houses. She had taught, I found, in the Washington School many, many years and had walked up and down Liberty Street many, many years . . . conscientiously absorbed in her quiet duties, as one of the thousand aging women, single and lonely, to whom the school becomes more and more all that life has to give in interests and affections. She had taken up photography as a hobby, "specializing," she told me, "in children." She sent me several snap-shots of the same school yard, with youngsters in all sorts of sportive and happy postures. The one that pleased me most showed a tousled boy with legs set and bat raised for a good crack, and an eager, laughing face that must have been looking toward her. He was about nine years old.

I have sent her some of my books—which she has read on her porch; and I have won from her the coveted praise for good work at last. But why should she have still seen in memory my face from behind the more than a thousand small faces of the thirty-eight intervening years? She had

74

never seen me since that morning, and, before, but for two weeks. Why? Clearly, for the same reason that she had forgotten the real reason for remembering that face. A distressing experience, so perilous to her peace and reputation and career at the time, set at work the psychological mechanism of suppression, from the same hour that it began reinforcing the image of the child that was identified with it. I am truly glad she has forgotten. In all my letters I laid all the stress on the trouble in the yard and street. I would not have her read these pages. I shall not send her this book. Her real name is not Bond.

Besides, it was not wholly her fault or even that of the urchins . . . or even of my physical idiosyncrasy or my temperament. Without the Locomotive-God, I would have suffered the same bodily pain. I would have suffered shame and fear both of teacher and urchins . . . but not of the same kind or intensity. The episode had its moment of primordial courage and, throughout, a certain alertness of intellect, even in several matters a definite sense of the insufficient motivation, objectively, of my state of feeling. But the Locomotive-God made the difference. It always has. It has always made grievously harder the hard places of all my life: that is what a phobia is for. The dynamic terror-factors of 1878 operating in 1885 must be pretty obvious to any interested reader—the locomotive-factor itself (in five distinct moments), Mary (twice), the need of mother and shelter, the feel of infinite distance from shelter, the clock, the sensation of Death. The God-factor seems not to have been manifest on any level of consciousness or co-consciousness I have been able to examine; though it was still alive down below, as this true history will demonstrate later on. But there was a number of manifest peripheral factors, associations that doubtless assisted in creating for 1885 a likeness with 1878, as the dog and the baby-carriage, and (perhaps not altogether peripheral) the hot day, the hot, panting body, the running itself, and the falling down. In some of these factors the relationships

75

are very subtle: for instance, the fact that I had fallen down in 1878 gave in the complex of factors, already before falling full of 1878, a set of mind for a fall, beside the physical facts of the pail and the exhaustion; whereupon the actual fall became a new link in actual experience with 1878. There was even the negro-motif in a familiar Negro Baptist Church on Liberty (among many items not mentioned above), on which I had my eye set when nearing the railroad bridge. Contributory also were the phobic panics of the years between 1878 and 1885—the bridge, the bell, the cow (themselves of the same brood). A cat was there too, though from a different emotional complex. But 1885 modifies the old pattern of 1878, by resetting the emphasis in subconsciousness: the dominating content of the 1885 terror was *distance* from home, *blockage* from home by an intervening object (the bridge-inhibition). Blockage too from mere freedom (the confining school-room walls). Many a troubled dream in my maturity about being helplessly confined and bewildered in some bizarre house or hotel with glass partitions and interminable doors has come back to me—to be recognized by my common sense and to be revealed by experimental tests of association and emotional reactions, as a subconscious memory of 1885. Distance and blockage: we will need to remember these items when we get to 1911 and after.

The memory of the on-sweeping locomotive-wraiths (hovering in front of boys and chapel) seems to have vanished even before I reached home—before in fact I reached Pat Lynch. They formed no part of my more than worried state of mind as he started to trot me back. We will meet an analogous but far more strikingly swift lapse of memory, in 1911, where I have curious and indubitably objective proof. A sketch-memory (growing ever fainter) of the generalized external facts—the disaster in the classroom and the stoning and the running home—lingered on for years, present or latent, in consciousness. I even entertained my fraternity brothers with the yarn in college days.

76

The three details that lasted all down the years were shame in my seat, wringing out my blue knickerbockers, and the boys on the steps; but even these had for mere normal reminiscence scarcely one tenth the distinctness and none of the immediacy of reality that they acquired by psychoanalysis. Other details, very few at best, were inventions, distortions, fusions. I can compare: reminiscence is not recall. The commonplaces of dinner-party chatter on the unreliable nature of childhood memories concern the phenomenon of reminiscence, not psychological recall.

The manifest effect of the episode on my mental life in the immediate years was far less than the reader might expect. It produced no new phobias, it revived no old. That night in bed (in the guest-chamber, to be nearer father and mother) I lay thinking with infinite relief, "Well, it's over with anyway." I suffered some anxiety for a few days lest I might have injured my urinary organs; but my chief negative emotion was grief—grief at terrible failure. All my energies and longings had centered about making good in school. This emotion soon disappeared . . . into the subconscious to burrow and mate with the emotion of disgrace and failure at the station in 1878. The common resilience of healthy childhood, and a certain incorrigible drive that I cannot but observe as a characteristic of mine more pronounced than in any other of my kindred, near or remote, except perhaps my mother, urged me on. I was soon absorbed in another, more strenuous effort to make good. My new teacher, also, was very considerate. On the first morning she came down to my seat and whispered, "If you want any time to go out, don't ask—just go." Considerate . . . and perhaps not taking any chances. In a few weeks I was advanced to the fourth grade. By spring I was in the sixth.

Yet it still had certain social effects. Two years later I was ashamed and uncomfortable because now in the same class-room with Agnes Morrison. I had meantime come to know that the lady with the grocery basket was her aunt. And for four or five years, though I scarcely ever went

near the Boulevard quarter again, I was as likely as not any
day to be assailed with jeers or stones by some hoodlum
that had strayed out of his bailiwick . . . on my way to
school with Mabel or Walter, on my paper-route, on an
errand to "the stores," off skating, off swimming, off playing marbles or ball. Time and again, I vanished into a
butcher-shop or tinsmith's or livery-stable to avoid an encounter, though as much from loathing as from shame and
fear. I was a tradition in the Boulevard; I am probably
a tradition still. I even had my name among the clan.
Names are a venerable habit in the Isles. A fellow in the
Icelandic saga of Salmon-River-Dale (I now teach the
language of Eric the Red), for having dreamed that an old
hag had cut out his bowels and stuffed his insides full of
little sticks, was ever thereafter known as Twig-belly. Another Viking—in the Grettir saga—whose shoulders one
day spurted white blood, with a miraculous explosion under the stroke of an irritated companion's battle-ax that
yet didn't seem to hurt at all, became Bottle-back: the astonished gang had found in uproar of mirth that he had
packed as private provisions under his sark a sizable skin
bottle filled with whey. Possibly these degenerate young
Celts from the Boulevard were the heritors of a naming-
tradition from the days when the Vikings, crossing the Irish
Sea, chased their monastic ancestors over the coastwise hills
or held barbaric court in conquered Dublin. But their name
for me was not as imaginative or nice as "Twig-belly" or
"Bottle-back," though it had its own appropriate anatom-
ical connotations.

Liberty Street . . . the Washington School. I have a
full set of photographs of each as each now is. Mr. Maxon,
who succeeded Miss Bulkley as superintendent before I
left the High School, I discovered was still superintendent
when four years ago I began retracing my boyhood steps;
and it was he, or rather his son-in-law, who so kindly photographed in 1922 block for block the route of my flight in
1885. The neighborhood is still depressingly ramshackle

and sordid, though many old buildings have tumbled down and many new ones in frame or brick have been set up. Yet the old wooden chapel, around the corner on Fourth, still stands; and I have identified the trunks of many great elms as the great elms . . . or the saplings . . . of long ago . . . and the railway bridge. I have blue-prints, copied for me to scale from contemporary maps in the office of the city clerk. One of the colleagues with whom I began this study stopped over at Plainfield thrice on Eastern trips, and got in touch with old inhabitants—indeed, with the aged contractor (himself remembered by me) who had built several of the original houses. My colleague's data, like other data, served both to stimulate and to verify recalls . . . old gardens, barns, fields, alleys . . . now gone. As a special test of the objective validity of recall, I gave him for his second stop-over twelve items about the exterior of the house into which I had been taken in collapse, its color then, its porch, its vines, its two gates, etc.; and he found that I was correct in all twelve.

In this entire investigation wherever an objectively verifiable recall has finally taken on a vivid tone of reality in integration with other reality, objective inquiry has proved it correct; hence I have come to trust that tone for recalls not objectively verifiable, even for recalls of states of mind. It was some time, however, before I was expert in distinguishing accurately that tone of reality from the tone present in simulations by the imagination or in fusions of two or more different memories. Sometimes, when the data have been very evanescent and vague (as so often when a new memory is just starting), my mind has feigned a complete structure which has at first seemed like memory, memory far and tenuous; but, if it is in fact merely a structure of the imagination, it continues in that pallid tone and leaves me emotionally undisturbed. Very seldom, however, has the imagination really feigned anything without some cause sooner or later being revealed as a specific subconscious stimulus: the so-called feigning itself means something

79

achieved, even as its refusal to take on this vivid tone of reality means something not yet achieved.

Four or five times in the first two years of my search I was grievously disappointed, and on the point of doubting the objective validity of even vivid recall. Further search and experience not only dispelled skepticism but established more firmly my reliance. In each case I had not yet learned to recognize in truly vivid recall just what its own tone of vivid relived reality is and just what emotional reactions it produces within me to-day when relived; in each case I ultimately disentangled details of real memories out of pseudo-memory. An example. I thought I remembered men playing ball in a field by the railway bridge over Liberty Street. I had seen dream-images of men batting and of balls flying. I had heard dream-sounds of balls batted. I had the strongest *feel* of baseball as associated with the railroad and my fright of 1885, even a vague memory of playing ball there myself a few years later. But I didn't recognize then that, however vividly the *feel* of baseball was identified with the 1885 fright, the *place* of the game had not integrated itself vividly, realistically, at all with the already vividly recalled physical surroundings that were well organized in my conscious memory. Further recall gradually filled the block realistically with the veritable houses which my colleague's report and the maps had so disappointingly convinced me must have been there, and I went on to find the ball-field where it really was. It was, of course, the 1878 ball-field by the 1878 track. I ultimately discovered, as already hinted, many intrusive elements from 1878 present, and long unexplained, in the recalls of 1885. The ball-field where I played later was another field and also alongside the *track*. The earlier stages of recall merely merged baseball, track, and terror in a recall-experience at once blurred and unintegrated as *vision* and realistic as *feel*.

A dozen or so snap-shots of the old Washington School, inside and out, from one specific position and another (as requested), were prepared for me by the gracious priest of the Cathedral. It is now one of the parochial school buildings. The fence is now of wire. Climbing would be easier now. The city's Washington School of to-day . . . over that way still . . . is a new building of which I have not seen a photograph. But I have heard about it. Only a few days ago I was talking with a young girl in pink and blue, the office-stenographer of our English Department. She had interested me for her quiet efficiency in this world of flapperdom. "Where was your home?" "Plainfield, New Jersey." "I declare—my old town." "Yes, I knew about that." "Did you go to school there?" "Yes, to the Washington School." "What!" . . . She didn't know about *that*. . . . And in further talk I learned that her favorite teacher in high school had been the lady of whom I speak in a later chapter as my classmate and rival; and that she had had her sewing class in my old Franklin School. "Leonard will do anything for you you want now," a colleague told her, amused at my discovery and at my new interest in her welfare. This is one of a thousand examples in my career of coincidences impossible in fiction. . . . only because an unobservant world continues to think them impossible in life. So it was that the anonymous critic in the "London Times" pronounced some phases of the story of "Two Lives" artistically impossible. I knew sooner or later some one would say just that. Art is now so superficially, so factitiously, impeccable in its motivations that when the artist makes no compromise with reality he seems to be distorting reality.

V

THE Franklin School was in the middle eighties a new three-story structure of brick, in everything, except patent ventilators, bubble-fountains, and indoor toilets, presumably identical with the Big Red School-house all over the land to-day. It provided instruction through the seventh grade; the eighth and ninth in that ward were housed in the lower floor of the High School, an older brick structure in gray paint, at the further end of the same block. The two had the same playground inside the same high boardings—and the same wall-eyed Mr. Clarkson, policeman-janitor, with the same grouch for the young probationers in each, who, taking their mid-morning recess in successive periods of fifteen minutes, were to him all one plague of harum-scarums in pants long or short—to be shooed away from the pump or ordered down from the fence.

Our public schools at this time were beginning to share with those of Quincy, Massachusetts, a certain outstanding reputation. Neither subjects nor methods were revolutionary, it seems to me, but there was an emphasis on learning by doing, and we acquired craftsmanship with knowledge. I still have a set of my own maps, in unfaded watercolors, with scalloped mountain-chains and lettered cities by the winding rivers. An emphasis too on learning *by study*. There was an awesome tradition of thoroughness. I remember a visit of Miss Bulkley to our seventh grade, after the quarterly test in arithmetic. She held, poised in her hand at a meditative angle, a foolscap folio covered with childish numerals and scratches in black ink, at the top of which were two large digits in red of my teacher's devising. That rubric was the occasion of the visit. She summoned me into the hall, and my mother's friendship did not save me: "Ellery, this must never happen again." I had fallen five points below the passing. Any youngster who didn't have an efficiency of 80 per cent was in disgrace —and he usually felt it as a disgrace, not as a joke. It never happened again. Except for the principal of the High School and the science teacher, all the instructors were women, chiefly young women of the new order, though two were faithful servitors from long years before . . . one of them, prim, thin, sallow Miss Niles, was mysteriously related to the Mortgage-men. She was especially kind to me. We had no dances, no organized athletics, no school paper, no band, no ribbons, no yell—in short, no school spirit. We simply liked our teachers, our schoolmates, and for the most part our work. Grade by grade, as the little laggards or rough-necks dropped out, we became more and more homogeneous. I entered High with the brightest and best-bred boys and girls in the city, most of us already good acquaintances. The lubberly poor were by now driving grocery-wagons; the lubberly rich had been from the beginning in the city's flourishing private schools where the pace was more leisurely. The solution of the high-school situation to-day is quite simple: get such young folks; get such parents. The teachers will do.

Competition was a class-room affair. In the grammar-school, it was for a "reward-of-merit card," that gave the successful aspirant a free Friday afternoon; or, perhaps, for some humble prize offered by the teacher—I got "Little Men" for writing the best compositions in the same grade where I got the dreadful 75 in arithmetic. There was a substantial prize, awarded at commencement for the best final in United States history, open to all the children of the city of ninth-grade standing, a six-hour written examination. I received second; but, when the papers were returned in the fall, the committee, a civic group, had some embarrassment in explaining to my father how my paper hap-

83

pened to be marked 98 and that of Jennie Carter, the winner, 95. I myself was quite old enough to scent the injustice of favoritism: there were people in the town who didn't like the editor of the "Central Times." In the High School, the chief commencement prize was for an essay on an assigned subject, open to all four grades. As a freshman, I came in second, my subject "The Isles of Greece." This brought Miss Bulkley again to my class-room . . . also with my foolscap paper in her hand. She summoned me to her office. "What do you expect to be?" "A college professor." "You aim high." I thought of my earlier ambitions— house carpenter, bridge-builder, locomotive-engineer. I smiled firmly. And now I smile again, but not so firmly, I guess. The next year I took first, with a screed on the "Weakness of Force," ominous of my opinions in '98 and 1914-18.

But the prize was the standing offer of a wealthy High-tariff man and Seventh-day Baptist, often publicly vocal against my father's politics and religion; and when we opened the set of Shakspere late that evening on the dining-room table, I thought I understood my father's quiet mortification as he turned over the cheap paper, blurred print, and pinchbeck binding—so unlike the magnificent set with its morocco, gilt, and engravings that had gone to Alderman Archibald's son the year before. The insult destroyed the glory for all of us. Cowardly fellow, I have forgotten your name—"Uncle George," a ragamuffin young nephew of your wife (your third wife, formerly housekeeper), used to call you. But I have not forgotten your voice. A couple of weary farm-hands were pleading with you to let them finish unloading the hay they had brought in from the country-side for your thoroughbreds. It was a Saturday afternoon. You made the yokels unhitch, and ordered them to come back and finish the job next morning, their day off. You explained the Seventh day. You said, "Remember the Sabbath day to keep it holy." A few days later there was a barrel of lime on your tree-lawn.

Smithie and I dumped it on your broad front veranda the next Friday evening . . . after your manorial lights were out . . . to test your orthodoxy. And to Dickie, that rapscallion fourteen-year-old nephew, you with your silver cane and stove-pipe hat, you with your aristocratic gait and gray mustache, introduced a new puzzle into the already puzzling universe of sex-emotions and sex-morality; "But *do* you suppose such high-toned folks as Uncle George ever——?" . . . And the ugly monosyllable, as the only available term in his plebeian vocabulary, was uttered with a gasp of such preternatural solemnity that I almost hope the reader will guess what it was.

In the grades, geography, especially South America, and the history of the United States absorbed me most. Both were affiliated with my stamp-collecting; and this was something more real, too, than purchase of packages from Scott and Co. and swapping with schoolmates. I had access to old attics—especially to a hair-trunk, with its bundles of grandfather's letters . . . O, pompadour of President Jackson. But hair-trunk, crinolines, and great-grandmother's lace-shawl and grandmother's flowered dress disappeared when we left the old homestead. The great mahogany secretary, with its drawers within drawers and with its glass portals on high behind which were Grant's "Memoirs" and "Our Wild Indians" and so many other books, went with us on our journeyings for years . . . to disappear too, at last. The mahogany dining-room table was the only heirloom that came through till my father's death. This was sold to pay for ten years' storage. We left the old homestead the year I finished the grades. I remember how I used to lie in my bed beside the low front windows thinking how humdrum our family life was . . . when *would* something exciting happen . . . always in and out the same gate, always the same old peach-tree by the same old side fence . . . and the same old trumpet-vine and lilac-bush. Only one thing had ever really happened

. . . that was when the disused corn-crib had been taken down, and the house and blinds repainted—years ago too.

We moved into a small cottage on Arlington Street owned by Uncle Oliver. Organized study, as scholarship, method, progress in power and knowledge, began only with beginning Latin, in the first year of high school. The stimulus was perhaps threefold: (1) the philological bias of my mind, (2) the rivalry with thirty or forty industrious classmates, (3) my father. My father was always indulging in reminiscence about his college days, especially about his Horace and his professor of Greek, Dr. Kendrick. Real study for me already meant the Classics. Though dead, Dr. Kendrick's spirit still worked vigorously in his pupil's son. I always studied out the Cæsar lesson by myself; and always read it, on my own initiative, to my father before the class met—always. A *pensum* of two or three hours every day. We finished, with a thorough review, the four books in March. If I have not forgotten my Latin, the reasons are very simple. My father also went over the rough draft of my "monthly compositions," pointing out unclearness and magniloquence. He would quote with pride what his professor of rhetoric had said to him: "Mr. Leonard, you will never have any difficulty in being understood." This reminder, with five other comments picked up as the years of scribbling went on, was all the instruction in writing that ever started anything in me. As a matter of fact I reduced my composition courses in college to two quarters. With me writing has been mainly a function of growing up. The five other comments are:

(1) My professor of Latin's: "Of course you can justify the phrase, but it's no good if it doesn't justify itself";

(2) My professor William James's: "Mr. L., you have an amazing knack at putting things concretely";

(3) Emerson's: "Poetry . . . in proportion to the inspiration checks loquacity";

(4) The Frenchman's: "The secret of boring is to tell everything";

86

(5) The Stoic's: "To speak well is to speak truth."
My father also gave me useful pointers on how not to do it, when I went into training for my assembly recitation.

> When the British Warrior-queen
> Bleeding from the Roman rods . . .

and the next year . . .

> The Isles of Greece, the Isles of Greece,
> Where burning Sappho loved and sung . . .

when Dr. Kendrick underwent a particularly startling rebirth.

Our only outside activities were the two literary societies, the boys' and the girls'. The themes were the big ones we laugh at now, but they were the initial challenge to many I have been thinking about ever since. "Resolved that Greece has contributed more to civilization than Rome " was the subject of the public debate of our sophomore year. I was principal for the affirmative. That six months' reading and note-taking in Guizot, ancient Mediterranean culture, the Roman Church, and modern European institutions, with attention eagerly concentrated on understanding and controlling a definite problem, in continual conferences also with my associate, would be worth to-day about four credits for two semesters toward an A.B. degree in Wisconsin. I have my "extempore" opening speech still in MS. to prove it.

But it was my last extempore speech for many years. I had not been "extemporizing" four minutes, when I got tangled up in the text as finally revised a day or so before, and lost my syntax, my argument, and my nerve. But not losing altogether my cheek, I fished the unsuspected MS. out of my desk and brazenly read the rest; excusing myself from the hall at the end, as if too ill to remain. I did feel sick for a fact. I walked the streets for hours in abject mortification, unable to invent any explanation that could possibly rehabilitate my hitherto growing reputation as an orator, "who didn't need even notes." Sheepish and unconsoled for weeks, in spite of congratulations on the decision in our favor. Possibly social reverberations of shame and panic of 1878 and 1885 were evoked by that the biggest audience I had ever faced and by the locally distinguished Judges. No associational data of my probings establish the connection; but the experience was clearly stage-fright, like that of 1896 to be analyzed later, with the audience suddenly transformed into a horribly alien world, not so different from that I had faced twice before. Possibly stage-fright has always such hidden roots. However, if the Locomotive-God was responsible for this disaster, it was the only one during adolescence.

Though heckled and mauled now and then by rowdies in the grades, and though joshed by friends in high school, and though often restless in my seat during the two long sessions, with the usual misdemeanors and the usual disciplinings, I certainly did not find school Shelley's world of woes, nor walk forth upon the glittering grass to weep. Quite the contrary. And I was as little isolated from my schoolmates by lonely grandeur as by lonely sorrows—we were all bright and merry together, weren't we, Henry, Phœbe, Champlain? And though I was a little more highstrung than some, wasn't it John or Oscar, or F——, the son of the lexicographer, rather than I whom you would have picked out for the prospective phobiac—or Stennie with his St. Vitus dance in his face? For I didn't have even the stigmata of the poet—at least not alarmingly. I remember speculating, as a wakeful twelve-year-old, one night in bed, on my eventual career, and discarding, among others, that of the poet . . . because all the subject-matter (roses, sunsets, brooks, girls, April showers, etc.) was already nearly used up and would surely be entirely so before I was old enough to start, say, at twenty. But four or five of us boys wrote verses by the time we were fourteen—

usually in sportive amatory vein, ironic toward both love
and the lyric art, to Bessie and Mamie and Maud. This
to Bessie:

> And when I am married and sober—
> For marriage will sober me through—
> And am burdened with burdens parental—
> My eldest I'll name after you.

This was considered particularly funny and daring. But at
fifteen I wrote the "Battle of Marathon," perhaps the outstanding achievement of our *Dichterbund*. Before that, it
had been the "Ballad of Hairy Bill," by Walter Sampson:

> There was a man in our town whose name was Hairy Bill;
> Of adventures and old stories he always had his fill—
> And this is what he told me . . .

Out of school, these same years had the same normality of interests and tone. I read the books boys used to
read: Scott, a little Dickens, Robinson Crusoe, Jules Verne
("The Mysterious Island" six times), "Ishmael or In
the Depths" (five times), and even the trash of E. P. Roe,
half knowing it was trash. I followed Stanley into Africa
and Kane and Franklin and Greeley into the Arctic; and a
new book called "Sunny Spain," with towers of Seville and
Alhambra's heights and ladies in black mantillas peeping
from behind fans on upper balconies and gay-skirted girls
with castanets dancing in market-places, became for my
early teens what the gaudy Child's History of my country
had been a few years before. Sunny Spain . . . Sunny
Spain. . . . One Saturday morning in my eleventh year I
came running from my seat by the dining-room window,
with an opened book I had just found behind the glass
doors of the secretary shelves. I had to tell my mother in
the kitchen about that wonderful old man of long ago . . .
who was always asking questions . . . just like me . . .

and they put him in prison . . . and gave him a cup of hemlock juice to kill him. I called him Soak Rats. My mother was interested but I wondered why she smiled. For many months the hemlock-tree in Aunt Cornelia's pine-cluster made me feel queer . . . We are what we become: a generation later I told a thousand others in a little book of my own called "Socrates, Master of Life" . . . we become what we are.

My first vital literary experience was at fifteen, in Virgil, "Eclogues" and "Æneid." But even this I supplemented by the sequel to "Ishmael"—"Self-raised or From the Depths." With one educative result at least for my later years—the indubitable clue to so-called popular taste. The fiction-reading millions to-day are simply the fifteen-year-old minds at thirty and forty and sixty that I was at fifteen, congenitally incompetent to learn the difference (a difference in life, more than literary technique) between writing and Harold Bell Wright-ing. I never read, as boy or man, but here and there in the Arabian Nights—though I've read as man the Koran over and over (even a little in Arabic) and possess a dusty MS. of a life of Mohammed. And I didn't read "Pilgrim's Progress." School, with its chants in concert . . .

Who is the happy warrior, who is he? . . .

and its individual drone or lilt in dipodic treble . . .

The sun that brief December day

arrested the development of all interest in English Poetry, till I happened to overhear a substitute teacher for the upper class (when I was having my own study-period for algebra) reading and explaining Keats's "Ode on a Grecian Urn": she said too that young Keats's death was a terrible thing . . . that he might have become even greater than Milton. So I kept listening . . . for days . . . till the

regular teacher came back. Then I preferred even my algebra. Incoherent literary taste merged in characteristic
fashion with untrained scientific curiosity. The first book I
drew from the public library, when at fourteen its privi-
leges became mine by city ordinance, was "The Origin of
Species"; but I was equally convinced by Donnelley's "Lost
Atlantis."

The founding of the Unitarian Church, precipitating
local acrimonies in theology, started me on biblical exe-
gesis and homiletics. It was the era too of the sentimental
Revivalist—with the soft voice and death-bed scenes of
sixteen-year-old girls who had sassed their mothers and
danced and got tuberculosis. They were always repentant,
always about to accept Christ, but always perished before
they could gasp the right word. . . . "Too late, my
friends, too late"; and the evangelist would pensively close
his Testament and lay it on the stand, and take another
swallow from his glass of water. At fourteen I could be
buncoed by "Ishmael," but not by this. One of my cronies
fainted away, and, when he came to, he stumbled to the
altar as fast as possible. He had done things with Annie
Green; yet I told him afterward it was not the judgment
of God, but the hot air of the floor-register by the pillar
over which he had been standing for an hour.

I differed from the others only by a little more intellectual independence and ambition. I studied Greek and
Roman history by myself one summer and absolved the
subjects by examination, in order to get free hours for phys-
ics, not part of the classical course. Beginning to translate
the last books of Cæsar by myself, under the August trees,
I made a discovery that revolutionized my humanistic universe. It flashed into my mind that no old Roman had ever
translated these words into English—why should I? The
Roman took in their sense through the Latin (as I take in
the sense of Grant's "Memoirs" through the English)—
why shouldn't I? My idea worked—and I felt an enormous accession of power. My parents never directed my

reading; but by fifteen I often went to books I heard them talking about, as "Childe Harold," "The Lady of the Lake," and the Sermons of Minot J. Savage, then busy in the treeing of Joseph Cooke and his kind.

I took tickets at the door for a lecture on Egypt, and the author presented me with his last book. John Fiske, florid and monotonous, used to lecture too, with hands folded motionless over his big paunch, on Virginia, Columbus, and the Critical Period. The town was in fact almost the Madison of the eighties and nineties. The Monday Club had verily the same intellectual ladies as Madison's imposing Woman's Club, with the famous addresses by Oscar Fay Adams on "The Brutal Sex" and "The Mannerless Sex," so shocking to his mother, a citizen of my home town. . . . "What *has* got into Oscar?" And the paper read by my father at the Unitarian Literary Society, on a New Book by Thomas Carlyle (the posthumously published lectures on Literature), was verily not inferior to some I have been privileged to hear (as a guest) at the Madison Literary Club. If we had no university, we were the headquarters of the Chautauqua Literary and Scientific Circle—for which my father's plant did much of the job-printing—a fairly serious institution of national enlightenment, before the development of university extension robbed it of its respectable functions and drove it ingloriously to midsummer vaudeville and William Jennings Bryan. We too had our Distinguished Citizens—judges and presidents of railroads, executors of millionaire estates on Fifth Avenue, and our own millionaire-commuters, with mansions almost prophetic of Madison's Lakewood and University Heights. And Julian Hawthorne lived up at Scotch Plains; and Mrs. Bret Harte, sweet quiet lady in black with her two dashing daughters, was our neighbor and friend.

But I was not growing up a young prig or pedant. All the games children and boys play I played: prisoner's base, Robin Hood, Indians, snap-the-whip, hockey (land and ice), hop-skip-and-jump; leap-frog, marbles (but never for keeps), boxing (with gloves), fencing (with regular foils and masks), wrestling, football, bob-sledding (on a mile slope); and some of them I played rather well, though my friends owned the gloves and foils. We rigged up by our own carpentry a gymnasium in Smithie's barn, with parallel bars, horizontal bar, ladder, and rings, and practised regularly, achieving the kip and the muscle-grinder and chinning the bar (twenty-five times). At fourteen and fifteen I still hoped to be as strong as Samson. Charlie Boone and I all alone learned swimming day by day down in Green Brook where the shallows deepened under the willow-roots. It took us three weeks to save the thirteen cents each for tights; but even then we risked parents, landowner, and police. At thirteen I swam a mile; and my parents forgave me in their pride. Later we thought nothing of a three-mile walk to South Plainfield for an afternoon's splashing and diving at Elbow Bend in the swamp by the trestle-bridge of the Lehigh Valley Railroad. Once he told me about a terribly funny and exciting book he was reading called "Don Quixote." Once we dove in on Thanksgiving day. Charlie Boone is now a Paulist Father. I had learned to ride a bicycle on big Cousin Jamie's old high-wheeled wooden affair and then had occasionally the use of his nickel-plate Columbia; but it was on Smithie's safety with its cushion-tires that I made my longest trips, even up to Westfield on the macadam of the first good county roads in America, the highways of the Century Runs and the L.A.W . . . those days when the Sunday air was full of little bells. I had from my eleventh year a carpenter-shop upstairs in the woodhouse of the homestead, and afterward in the basement of Uncle Oliver's cottage; with bench, tool-box, rip-saw, cross-cut, scroll-saw, auger, bits, draw-shave, square, level, gouges, chisels, miter-box, vise, planes, etc., all in their places. I watched the workmen at the long frame-building going up in what had been Aunt Cornelia's field, a new private school to take care of some more of the wealthy town-dummies, we said. There I got pointers on how to handle all my tools, and practised assiduously. I always wanted to get things right; and combined independent experiment with a wholesome deference to all master-craftsmen. I made, first and last, bows and arrows, bow-guns, toy boats sleds, a toboggan, bookcases, screen-frames, little tables, etc. I still hear the planes curling off the shavings of the pine. I still hear the saw crossing the grain and the thud on the floor. I still smell the sawdust. I still see the cobweb in the corner of the sun-bright window. I still hear the oriole in the elm. I saved my father the price of the tools by doing the repairs on the place—patching a sill or a rotted step, setting in a new picket, or lattice-slat for the trumpet-vine. For several years the great spring event was building the new canoe in the back yard, according to the winter's plans at the secretary-desk—a simple and inexpensive kayak, straight at bow and stern, with barrel-hoop cockpit, with barrel-hoop ribs, reinforced laterally by heavy twine, covered with stretched canvas at twenty cents a yard and made water-tight with linseed oil and white lead, and painted to taste. The voyages down under the Lehigh Valley bridge into the South Plainfield Pond, with Charlie or Smithie. One was sixteen feet long, crimson-red, with an oblong cockpit large enough for three, and two small leg-of-mutton sails. One was three feet by six, a dun-brown tub designed for the exploration of rushy swamps and muddy coves.

I occasionally snared suckers under the rocks in Green Brook, but was really never fisherman, much less hunter. I wasn't interested in firearms or killing creatures. I once took aim with my bow at a spring robin on a low branch. I never dreamed of hitting the saucy little chirp; but to my remorse down he fell and fluttered into death in the street at my feet. That is the only higher animal I ever killed; though nobody ever taught me not to. Except one rat. I can understand the primitive hunter, the starveling; I can understand the boy in whom the primitive hunter still lives, though he lived in me without blood-stains; but I cannot understand hunting as the sport of manhood—the college professor on his holiday pumping shot into wild deer and water-fowl. Somehow I feel nearer to these flying and roaming dumb things than most men do: the facts of evolution, the kinships, are for me somehow intertwined in my imagination—with my feeling for earth as the home of multitudinous life. And an animal's pain is Pain. I can understand killing for food against hunger, for fur against cold; but not for fun against boredom. We boys were all hunters, though not killers. Primitive man himself, as hunter, was not always hunting to kill. He hunted for berries and roots, and nuts and wild honey, for shelter-sites, for trails, for observation-cliffs, for flint and staves and withes, and somewhat later, for clay, for copper, for magic stones, pearls and nuggets. We hunted for the same things on all-day wanderings in the mountains, up in the Notch by the cascade for strange wild flowers, back of the stone-crusher for crystals, and other minerals (to be tested in school with the blowpipe), off over the second ridge for hickory and chestnut and persimmons, up on Washington Rock for a view of the two airy white filaments between the two towers that were Brooklyn Bridge twenty-six miles away in the afternoon sun. Along the three brooks, Green, Stony, and Cedar, we hunted for mussels and sassafras in the woods. We hunted for springs and caves. We hunted for short cuts.

And, when with the frost the spirit of the chase called, we played hare and hounds. I was usually one of the two hares, as being fleet and foxy. With our bags slung from the right shoulder, we would chalk our trail on the sidewalks from the high school gate, in a five-minute start for the golden country. We were soon off to the mountains, scattering the bits of paper now, adding many a false scent on the cross-roads, in the brisk clear air of an October Saturday morning. Never crossing an open field, always hug-

ging the ledges. . . . Two hours and then half-way up a
too sparsely covered slope—the pack, the pack, down in
the valley. Twenty or thirty throats yell with the lust of
the man-hunt. They had seen us first. But I know a trail,
if we can only reach the top with our shaking legs. So we
escape. In the middle of the afternoon we sit, weary
enough but uncaught, on the curb by the high school gate
as they come straggling back. They charge us with skimp-
ing outrageously on the paper-scent.

And now in these last fifteen years, since my neurosis
has made impossible all free wandering, I find that my
dreams have gone back in both wish-fulfilment and memory, not to the great spaces of the Alps and the Campagna
of my student-travels, but precisely to these neighborly
meadows and groves and foot-hills of my boyhood's first
home. I have recognized in my psychoanalysis a hundred
shadowy landscapes of friendly sleep; but I am always
wandering through them bewildered, a man as I am to-
day, with a most troubling dread lest I lose my way or find
myself suddenly too far from wife and house in town.

I knew all about baseball, the batting averages of the
Big Leaguers, Buck Ewing's stunts in "catching-off" without a mask, Captain Anson at Chicago's first base. As
twelve-year-old sporting editor, I had passes to the Saturday games of the local semi-professionals where Sammy
McCutcheon, old Yale captain and then Wall Street
broker, played short, and John Lee, the ironmonger, center, and both in those hardy days without gloves. A little
later I wore the uniform of the Arlingtons, the champion
boys' team of our new ward. I was catcher. I learned to
throw left-handed, when a left-handed batter was up. "The
feature of the game was the base-throwing of Ellery
Leonard," said the "Daily Press," though edited by a
Democrat, no friend of the "Weekly Central Times." I
knew all about Kilrain's bare-knuckle fight with John L.
down in Texas—was it in '89? I saw with boyish thrill
James J. Corbett himself dash by me into the surf at Ocean

Grove, when training for John L. A few weeks later Gentleman Jim had delivered the punch; and John was sobbing on an upturned pail beyond the ropes: "Booze done it; booze done it." This amused my father, and became one of his favorite quotations. Meantime, I had myself learned to punch; and was no longer standing any nonsense. Thus far my adolescence, in spite of young years socially over-sensitive to the genteel poverty of the home, was normally hardy in body and mind. If I differed at all from other boys, the differences were chiefly in my favor. Those childish shocks of themselves would never have made me a phobiac. They needed help—long strain and sapping of normal energies, and then some fierce blow where a blow would strike deepest—and in the course of the years they got that help . . . with all power. And the Locomotive-God bore down on me again.

VI

MEANTIME there was another force within me, far more primitive and no longer latent. It was not, like the Locomotive-God, a creation of civilization; though civilization in its attempt to control it has given it an alien and sinister strength. The sex-instinct, as old as hunger and thirst, and far more integrated (and perilously integrated) than either of these more crassly physiological urges with man's higher life as founder of home and family and as creator of hopes and arts and religions, is a chapter in the history of every human being, indeed more than a chapter. But autobiographer, no less than biographer, so ingrained are the fictions imposed by the stupidity of civilization, either omit all reference beyond a sentimental kiss and a marriage-date, or fill their pages with a luscious chronicle of illicit amours. But I wonder if the garrulity of Casanova was not quite as fatuous as the reticence of Wordsworth, who never breathed of the crisis with Annette and his little French daughter when he told *all* about "the growth of a poet's mind" in the "Prelude." To the integrity of realistic thought, sex-experience is, like religious experience, like social, like economic, like intellectual experience, as little a matter for garrulity as for reticence. It is simply a matter to be taken up or omitted, according to its relevancy at the moment for the ulterior meanings of life. Specifically, in its typical conflicts with civilization the sex-force has been proclaimed by some men of science as the primary cause of all the neuroses of modern times; and by all men in the least enlightened it is recognized as the only too potent cause of some and a contributing cause in others. For these pages of mine,

98

as a study in a long-continued and unusually complicated neurosis, the question of the sex-force has its moments of peculiar relevancy. Have my sex-training and sex-experience had anything to do with that neurosis? The return of little Mary I defer till the return of the Locomotive-God.

Before little Mary at the station, there had been those prolonged hours of nursing, and afterward, still before my fifth year, that mother-urge to make the child share the intimacies of motherhood emotions; my critical attitude here is conjectural. There was too a strong urge in my mother to develop love to my little sister, and I caressed and fondled her much in early childhood; my attitude here is conjectural too. The subconscious has revealed nothing that bears on my sex-life: I know only what the Freudians have said. But there is nothing conjectural for me in sex being sex from birth: "It's a boy". . . "it's a girl." Not alone because of the presence or absence of the little telltale tassel. The structure is psychic as well as physiologic: broomstick gun of the boy, rag doll of the girl, though the make-believes may interchange more readily than later. That at a little over two and on during the years that the Freudians call the latent period I had a gracious male to female reaction to Mary I have already tried to make clear. At about twelve I had a few months' devotion to a boy friend, analogous to a sorority house crush. I wanted to serve him; I was peculiarly hurt and jealous at inattention. It was not like my other boy-friendships. But the pre-puberty sex-life of boyhood is quite normally more unstable and plastic than of maturity; plenty of boys have had such crushes, though they are certainly not to be encouraged. Nor are the gross physical contacts of some boys in their early teens to be interpreted as prophetic of peculiarly homosexual tendencies. They are in fact less homosexual than juvenile crushes, though certainly less respectable; and in my case the abysmal privacies of personality made such rendezvous revolting even to my moments of grosser sexual tumult. However, educators might as well realize that boys

99

in sex-moments are dominantly animals, lusting and shameless. The young sodomites usually grow up into decent and useful citizens. Yet I stray from my argument. Sex is sex from birth, but the bearing of sex on my own emotional life and neurotic history becomes clear to me, if clear at all, first in connection with my training in sex-education.

I have no detailed prescription for sex-education. If, as I often think, civilization is man's effort to organize his instincts in social control, civilization has failed as completely in the concentrated sex-instinct as in the more diffused possessive instincts: our marriage is too often a makeshift, even as our wars to end war are a delusion. And Nature makes a male in our zone biologically active in sex by fourteen; and she herself still defers his intellectual qualifications for even crude parenthood by at least three years; but it is civilization that defers his economic qualifications from five to fifteen years more. Meantime, sex-passion, the redintegrations of the breeding organism, aboriginal, authentic nature, is during these earlier years incapable of complete assimilation with the higher and finer feelings in an idealistic growing boy of my sort, and incapable of acquiring for his imagination that sublimation generally achieved in maturity even by relatively commonplace humanity through romantic love and family-life. He is now two individualities: the unfledged idealist, the sex-animal. Even his mooning about girls belongs to the idealist in him; for his sex-speculations and secret gloatings he chooses feverishly some young wench of the plebs, like Annie Green, whom he really despises. In his emotionalized muddle of half-information half comprehended, he wonders if he dare ever really marry Bessie, so fair and blue-eyed and demure, because he fears that when they come to go to bed together undressed he may disgrace himself and shock her purity by a seizure of sexual excitement. And if physical sex and Annie Green's image and the adventure in the empty house that Bill told about suddenly get him hard in a fit of auto-eroticism, he feels indeed such a sweet

girl as Bessie should never be the mate of such a vile creature as he.

I have no detailed prescription for sex-education; but I
know that any sex-education that widens and deepens
this split in personality for any boy is wrong; worse
in fact than learning from "the other boys." It is from the
other boys indeed, "the nasty boys" whom good mothers
dread, that he generally gets what little realism and common sense there finally lodges in his pate. I suggest that
mothers keep off the premises entirely. I suggest that
fathers, unless themselves more trained in reality than
would seem probable from most of their social and political
activities in this generation, keep off too; except for ar-
ranging some three or four appointments, over successive
years from ten to fifteen or so, with a competent doctor.
Nor is that so easy: a doctor at once sympathetic and
matter-of-fact in manner, realistically acquainted with both
the psychology and physiology of adolescent sex. Bah, hum-
bug everywhere in the world—even at the doctor's, the
helpless boy is likely to be told that auto-eroticism leads
to the insane asylum. The doctor will probably know
jolly well it never did with him; but he'll think it good policy
to throw a scare. I've heard doctors say just this. Yet more
than any time ever again in life that boy now needs and
is now entitled to truth.

My good parents were progressive realists. The question had been settled long ago: little Ellery was to be told
no myths about Storks and Baby Buntings under Rose-
bushes. He was to learn, in well timed lessons, step by step,
the divine facts of his divine origins and to live and move
and have his being in the contemplation of his own divine
potentialities as progenitor . . . until the divine day on
which, a white soul (hitherto sexless), he should lead to
the altar a soul as white (and hitherto as sexless) as he.
And it was from his mother that he was to learn them.
Well. . . . Such facts as I got were distorted into a new
mythology; and the facts that I didn't get at all were the

facts that chiefly mattered for the moment. My father never inquired about my sex-life but once (to discover whether puberty had really set in). I can separate loving intention from results; but it is alone the results that concern us. In our family sex was too holy . . . when it wasn't too embarrassing or too recondite.

Just when or how it was that I first learned that babies came out of their mothers' insides has thus far eluded my search into the yesteryears. I can recall no juvenile thinking that, however askew in other genetic particulars, did not presuppose this fact. "Playing family" on our back porch, I "played being born" by crawling out from under eight-year Effie's petticoat. But obstetrics is the least part of the sex-problem for the child—or for any one. What did puzzle me was why I knew only one lady named "Miss" who had a daughter named "Miss" and why neither of them ever visited anywhere but at my mother's, never even went to church. And why Mr. Thorpe, tall and cadaverous and sad, and Mrs. Thorpe, florid and short and plump and sad too, had no children at all in the neat little white corner-cottage with the rose-vine entry. The two would stand after supper looking up at their ivied chimney, like a corn-stalk beside a pumpkin, and sometimes they gave me grapes from their arbor. I recall that I finally solved the Thorpe mystery with the reflection that people didn't have to have children and perhaps they didn't want any. I learned in time that the two Miss Marvins never went to church because Mama Miss Marvin had been expelled sixteen years ago; but even then I couldn't understand why they expelled her.

Though in many things, especially the whys and wherefores of moving machinery and natural objects, I was so pestiferous with questions, I seem early, like many children, to have preferred to solve the meanings of life for myself. I might still ask, like Helen's baby, what makes the wheels go round; but I was not so ready to ask, by my eighth year, why some people die and some don't. So with sex-matters, particularly of personal concern. Those instincts of privacy, integrated with the sex-instinct itself (for even two savages prefer to woo unseen), prevented me from telling things youngsters are supposed to tell their mothers. When I came home from my one ride with the wheedling milk-man, I would never take another; but I would not tell my mother the reason—I hated him now because, though ever so jolly, he had tried to tamper with my groin. What I told later of nasty boys' talk in school, was detached from personal privacies and an opportunity to play up to her desire for my confidences and to curry favor as a nice little boy. Of course I was merely a nice little cad; and knew it too when tearful Arthur Salter, packing up all his school-books for the very last time, came over to my desk and hissed, "You dirty little sneak, you've got me into a peck of trouble." Let mothers accept the fact that some things are none of their business; and that in others a boy has some prior duties to his clan.

I don't like myself much better in some other eight or nine or ten year postures. I was sitting on the floor as my young mother stitched. She had been telling me of her desperate birth-pangs, in bringing me into the world. I knew her point: in proportion to the trouble and sacrifice, so should be my gratitude for the blessing of life and my love for her. Thus I answered: "Mama, oh, how thankful we should be that all went as well as it did." I recall my mood perfectly: I knew with responsive thrill that I was saying it to please her, without accepting the implicit logic at all. I see no reason why a child should take part more than once in its own parturition. When no longer a child he can respect his mother's birth-pangs with the universal cry, "O Mary, pity women"; without in the least being grateful to them. My good mother struck this falsetto note more than once; till I finally ceased piping my shifty falsetto answers. By fourteen, already fractious and morose toward her grieving heart, I would tell her: "Well, I never asked to be born, did I?" And then I'd be sorry, seeing her so silent, and patient and hurt . . . and then I'd be more resentful than ever . . . for why should I be sorry, I thought—isn't it the truth? Poor mother, poor kid. I like better a remark of hers of only twelve years ago when we were discussing sex again . . . on my birthday: "No child was ever wanted more than you." Stark reality at last.

But her sex-education regarding my own body was diabolical in its unwitting cunning. By the time I was twelve, she would be sitting in the dark by my bed whispering deep things. In the dark . . . whispering. Long before the new psychology, she grasped the potency of twilight sleep suggestions for the child in assorted monotones. But she failed to bring into the room the right suggestions; she failed to realize that it was perilous for her, the mother, to bring into a small son's room any suggestions about sex whatsoever. No knowledge is almost better than half-knowledge. And there is little to choose between the technic of threatening the member with the chopping-block and threatening its possessor with spiritual corruption and mental collapse. I owe to these "suggestions" many intervals of abject horror and despair in adolescence. But baseball, Latin, my own clan, kept me going till I got the facts straight for myself, in spite of the criminal assistance which the patent-medicine almanacs gave to her cause. Nothing I could find to read did me anything but harm, except a plain-spoken, though inadequate, chapter in "Our Family Physician" by Dr. Beard: but why was it hidden in the parental bedroom dresser?

Moreover, these very suggestions precipitated the curiosities and experiments they were designed to prevent. The reiterated tale was the peculiar sanctity of my *membrum virile*. I could see no reason for contemplating that physiological incident as anything more sacred than ears; and, like ears, I had considered it simply as useful. But I kept my doubts to myself. More insistently I could see no reason why touching it with my hands, whether urged to by wicked boys or not, should do me any more damage than

touching my ears. Besides hadn't I touched it often enough
in tending to natural needs? And anyway why should boys
urge me, and why would they be wicked if they did? But I
kept my doubts to myself. Well, by at least a year and a
half earlier than either wicked boys or wicked nature might
have suggested anything at all, her suggestions suggested
to my utterly skeptical intelligence, out of mere curiosity
with no sex-urge whatsoever, empirical tests that stimulated
sex. In adolescence, still obsessed by the reverberant suggestions of doom and degradation, I hated her for having
herself been the cause of temptation. Adolescence has a
hard enough time in any case in loving the mother; adolescence thus spiritually hampered is embittered through and
through. The warnings that came later against "impurity"
with girls were not so harmful, even though, in common
with all the boys, I could not figure out why it should be so
"impure" for us to do the things that our parents did. I
solved this by assuming that "pure" parents did such things
only to beget children; and that of course begetting children would be practically out of the question for me a long
time yet. The social habits of our set of young people were
so directed toward fun, study, and friendships, or harmless
flirtatious banter, so fundamentally deflected from the
dance and the petting-party, that no specific warnings were
necessary. The fact is that for the animalistic sex-urges
that constitute sex in the adolescent male there is no emol-
lient and solvent equal to a friendly young schoolmate, even
if her laughing bosom is rounded out like a woman's.

Meantime after awakening animalistic sex, nature, who
takes her time with *Homo sapiens,* begins her prodigal creation of the life-giving sap. The father-story comes into the
mother-story. Possibly there is a useful clue in pollen-dust
and fertilized birds' eggs; but if so, only as scientifically
explained, and in the broad light of day. A boy may be
interested to hear that natural processes are universal, that
man shares the laws with all the kinds of life. But senti-
mentalized pollen-dust and sweet little birds' eggs touched

by divine ichor, as proclaimed in the handbooks of progressive mothers' clubs, are balderdash as alien to the
youngsters' matter-of-fact curiosity as the very storks
hatched from the eggs of the earlier mythology. Again and
again: the sacredness of sex and generation cannot be an-
ticipated; it can only be experienced; and it can only be
experienced when sexually animalistic adolescence has
ripened into the potentialities of sex-love. And even then
its sacredness is sentimental moonshine, unless correlated in
thought with the sacred rest of reality. For the adolescent
male, the generative fluids are another problem altogether.
The remorseless prodigality of nature, in nothing more
prodigal than in man as progenitor of mankind, overstocks
and fevers the lad, and in spite of all the "Y.M.C.A. Sunday Talks for Men Only" and all the Sanctities, she will
have her way—she will have her way. She will send him
dreams, and he will awake with a start which is not a nightmare, but a begetter of nightmares. The dream itself is
wicked, and its accompaniment presages a brain sapped to
imbecility, and a broken physical frame: so say the patent-
medicine almanacs and the advertisements in the barber-
shop periodical literature; and the other fellows, a little
secretive, aren't sure they are not right. The one fact of
ripening sex that it is most imperative a lad should know
by the time he is fourteen was never mentioned in my sex-
education. It was as if the sex-education of a daughter
lacked the item of menstruation. I refused to be humbugged
by almanac and advertisement in the end; worried and
harassed, I read what I could find in medical books, and
added a quantum of analytic intelligence of my own. But I
never asked my father—much less my mother. My sex-
education made sex for me an impossible topic in the home.
And the Family Doctor was only for colds and cuts and
bellyaches.

I recall one particularly burlesque and distressing episode. I had scarcely passed puberty when in my broodings
over sinful handlings and in my zest for physiological in-

formation (no longer merely about my skeleton-bones) I came across a hidden tome on Hydrotherapy (no one could ever hide a book from me very long). I was soon at Chapter X on "Venereal Diseases." Its Dantesque opening was like the inscription over the Gates of Hell:

We now come to those most loathsome and hideous of all the diseases that afflict erring and degraded mortals.

Here must be something meant for me, of course; and in fifteen fierce minutes I had complete enlightenment as to just what my mother's awesome warnings must have referred to. Here was all the dope. I made a speedy corporeal examination. Of course I discovered the symptoms of the primary stage, dozens of them, little white nodules, telltale chancres. I passed a night of horror. The next day I confided in Bill. He too made an examination. He too had the same symptoms. Two nights of horror. But at any rate I had company. Another conference. We'd have to tell our parents. Besides, nothing mattered any more. We were going to die anyway. But first we consulted Ned. Ned had them. Somehow this didn't frighten us so much, though at first it frightened Ned. Jack was consulted next. Jack had them. But Jack was a little older, and the white nodules proved to be everyday gooseflesh, follicles of incipient hair-processes, and on the scrotum, at that. The years go by . . . we tell the joke. We beget sons. We see to it that they go through the same—joke.

I made other scientific researches. I had read about "sexual drain" and "lost manhood," especially the insidious and unseen seepage in one's water. Unlike Falstaff, I tested my own water. There could be no doubt. The bottle, sequestered behind a box in the basement corner, revealed, as furtively uplifted day by day against the unflinching sunlight of the cobwebbed window, day by day more and more sedimentation, more and more sinuous and suspended films, beautifully variegated and iridescent for the artistic eye but increasingly horrific for the scientific—with the increasing chemical disintegration of the organic structure of the fateful solution. There could be no doubt: the result of my laboratory researches spelt doom—until I decided, after two weeks or so, that there was more hopeful evidence in the fact that my base-throwing was still the feature of the game. The gradually discovered fact that discharges and auto-eroticism were common among our clan assisted balance more than anything else; but it was many years before I realized that the latter was as physiological and universal a phenomenon as the former. Both, as physical functions, are subject to control; but the only control is through the boy's non-sexual interests in his games, his jobs, his books, his enlightenment. The miseries they normally entail are not physical, but mental; and mental only because he moves about in an unreal world created either by the silence, the misinformation, the stupidity, the cowardly fictions or commercial lies of the grown-ups. Morale? The effect on his morale is serious, I admit: to live during the years of all unfolding energies under a cloud (or with a cloud in the offing) of impurity and degradation, however hard he struggle, is not good for his morale. I should say not. Not always permanently serious, perhaps; yet those years themselves have their own right to all the sun there is in the sky. But this cloud is a monstrous phantasm conjured up by foolish older folks who have apparently learned nothing from their own adolescent sex-experience. In this, as in so much else in human life, slow-learning mankind itself creates, by its institutions and beliefs, the system that creates the sufferings of mankind.

In only one particular was my sex-education a good training. It was a damnably good training in thinking. The boy had only one guide, his young wits, wherewith to see him through not only the mysterious fires of enkindled nature, but the fogs and bogs of sentimentalism and the stench of the harpies who traffic on boyhood's ignorance and fears. And in this hard and difficult thinking, so much of it

108

alone and lonely, I first learned not only the vast sweep of human follies and fictions, but first something of the primacy of *fact* in all successful living, and something of independence and courage before folly and fiction on the one hand, and fact on the other. It was a good training in thinking—and useful on more than one occasion in the remoter future, in other connections.

I developed no complexes, however, Œdipus or otherwise. The undoubted strains of my adolescent sex due to the system of thought around me are related to my neurosis only as generalized preparation. Along with the experiences of another order in the next chapter they did their part toward untightening and softening the fibers of nervous strength and mental resilience; did their part too in establishing emotional attitudes of ashamed timidity toward sex-love and toward social life. The only complexes, save one, which are associated with sex, whether boy-girl or son-mother, are phases of the original complex of the Locomotive-God. This one was a deeply suppressed, suddenly released and recognized, and readily resolved and assimilated memory of exhibitionism and contacts sometime before puberty, and, in the opinion of experts probing with me at the time of its recovery, in no way involved in my neurosis. But the phenomenon of emotional readjustment after recall was instructive. I *felt* degraded, even lustful, and *knew* that the feelings were ridiculous; there were a few hours where pubescent feeling relived (from long ago) stimulated the maturer physical sex-feelings (of the present), both sets of feelings in a brief conflict with mature intellect—an illustration from another terrain of the intertwining of my infantile emotional with my mature emotional and intellectual life which we will be tracing in my neurosis where, on the contrary, the mature intellect has been powerless to achieve the resolution.

The matter of sex-experience in maturity, before marriage in 1909 at thirty-three, is relatively unimportant for our problem. I had no concubines noi pick-ups. Reverberations of boyhood bedside suggestions doubtless still worked. Even when I was jollied as a freshman for being innocently in love with a specified blonde, I did not blush for my secret: I turned white as death. When, a few years later, a liaison would have been feasible with a certain respectable girl old enough to take care of herself (and me), I shied away, my burning curiosity and desire conquered by an unmasculine timidity, which I masked in those callow days as "morality." In general, girls of my sort were out of the question, and for girls of the street I had human pity combined with sexual revulsion and quite sensible fear of venereal disease. I visited houses of prostitution in Germany, as a social study, quite in the way I had visited the poorhouse on Governor's Island in Boston Harbor. I never visited them in the States lest I might encounter an acquaintance and each of us have something to explain. I make no doubt whatever that I would have been better off in tone, self-confidence, stability of moods, if I had lived during my twenties in expressive and satisfied sex-life, with one woman or more than one woman, preferably companionable in all ways, but even if companionable only as woman; assuming a social order where I was not degraded from without —that is, where what was in itself normal and decent for me would not have been muddied by a social opinion retroactive on my opinion of myself; and where I would not have any wrong to another on my conscience—that is, where through me the woman would not have been wounded or wrecked. I make no doubt of it: I would have been the gainer, even in higher values, and in no wise rendered coarse and heartless, and unfit for the home life deferred through no fault of mine. However, civilization is a sorry compromise; and on the whole, discomforts and distresses (diffused, rather than acute, as with most men) of my celibacy probably were a cheap price to pay—especially here in America, hypocritical in sex beyond all other lands—for an escape from serious messes of diverse sorts easily to be conjectured.

This celibacy, preoccupied too with study, travel, scribbling, and pressing personal problems, and seldom tittilated very grossly by the social flutter of skirts and bosoms, and little assisted by the street-woman in scarlet or pink, and not practised in gallantries, assuredly occasioned no sex-suppressions or sex-strain of moment to my breakdown. During those years I suffered far more from homeless loneliness and bewildering insecurity of place and career, than from unsatisfied sex-desire. To conclude our clinic: we may omit the subsequent sex-life. My neurosis is not a symbol of a suppressed sex-fear, whether of impotence, of perversion, of incest, of neighbor's wife, or whatever else may be on the list. I know that now; I did not know it five years ago. Analysis on the one hand has failed to reveal even shadowily any dragon of that breed; on the other it has succeeded in revealing with a burst of light another dragon puissant enough for ten.

VII

WITH the beginning of the high school course which I was never to complete, my father had surrendered, along with the homestead, his editorship and what may have remained of his stock in the paper and press-room. I never knew, I don't know now, the story of his vanishing properties. He never spoke. His troubled blue eyes by the lamp over his account-books were all I knew . . . and after a time there were no more account-books. It remains the Mystery still.

He had talents, as an editorial writer, in an age when good editorial writing was in demand. He had had some apprenticeship after leaving the Baptist ministry, as editor of the "Chicago Illustrated Journal" and as editor of the "Denver Tribune" in the frontier days before Eugene Field. During my first two years in high school, he wrote the leaders in the summer months for the "Daily Journal" of Elizabeth. His newspaper employers, like his parishioners, early and later, would write him out of grateful hearts their farewell letters. He kept these letters, and after his death they came into my hands: always the same unsolicited praise for good work. He kept also many of his editorials, in bundled clippings. After his death they came into my hands: realistic, clear, and courageous thinking in the plain style on political, social, economic, religious issues of the day, local or State or federal—on Garfield, Blaine, Harrison, our new mayor, on temperance-reform, on single-tax, on the Beecher Trial, on the liberal movement in the churches. At a time when Labor was trod underfoot by the Republican Elephant and kicked by the Democratic Jackass, he could, while deprecating "a despotic spirit and the

112

pride of its clan," applaud with economic insight and a sense of humanity

Every intelligent effort that is made by labor to protect itself against a tyrannical infringement upon its rights by the employer.

This in summarizing a series of concrete editorial studies on the Homestead Strike. But for organized labor to demand the right of continuous employment might be dangerous to labor itself: Capital might turn about and

compel continuous service, which would be only another name for slavery.

Sparkle and epigram are seldom to be encountered in his editorials, but independence, justice, honest study always, even where our study would register different opinions. A provincial Horace Greeley, a provincial William Cullen Bryant; but other papers in Northern New Jersey, even in New York City, would copy his words. He was editorial writer, however, not newspaper man, not journalist. No James Gordon Bennett, no Pulitzer, no Hearst, no Munsey. The "Times" was a hang-over from the days of the country weekly, and totally without features, at first even without "boiler-plate." And his attitude to truth was the hang-over of his scholarship; he would spend half an afternoon running down an item too haphazardly noted by the reporter. The composing-room was a hang-over too with its archaic machinery—up on the third floor of an old brick block with a slow and creaking freight-elevator in the rear shaft that handed up the print-paper. Old marble-top tables with forms half pied or locked, rows of slanting cases by the dirty windows with their high stools and compositors idling with "sticks" in hand and flinging jests back and forth. Mr. Runyon, silent and bearded, working the foot-press with an ancient leg, and feeding in the cards with a white old hand—now for a Sunday-school program, now for a business announcement of Mr. Peck, Ladies' Hosiery

and Laces. Wednesday afternoons Mr. Jackson, and sometimes me, on the platform feeding from the big-press top
each large white sheet, nipped and yanked down so tight
around the huge roller to be first pressed on the forms that
rode back and forth on their tracks, timed to the feeding
of Mr. Jackson or me and to the inking by the little
rollers—and then to be flapped by the up-and-down wooden
frame, with hinges on the lower lateral, on to the increasing pile of the receiving-table. And faithful Old Black Joe,
whose big knuckles were on the walnut handle of the fly-
wheel and whose sweating bare arms and bent spine, bony
through his clinging undershirt, made the whole thing go.
One Wednesday it was already 3:30 and Old Black Joe
had not come. There was no telephone. There was no con-
venient tramp in the street. So Mr. Runyon, and the loafing
compositors, and even my twelve-year self took spells at
the wheel. Old Black Joe never came back. The next motor
was an Irishman, jolly and profane. The big water-pitcher
. . . to one side of the corner sink . . . the famous printer's towel on the wall, stiff as starched linen but not so
white, the ink-smudged soap . . . the sultry smell on a
July afternoon of paper-pulp, printer's ink, glue, and human sweat. A memory too . . . but I prefer the odorous
shavings and sawdust of my carpenter-shop up the woodhouse stairs. The rumble of the presses of the "Central
Times" was answered by the eternal humming of the flour-
mill behind us down the side-street slope . . . but its wheel
was bigger and in a cooler and darker place down between
the mossy planks over the mill-race of Green Brook. And
another memory still . . . of an eight-year-old on the flat
roof gazing over the front parapet and over the intervening business roofs to the railway-station, where suddenly
a switch-engine with terrific clangor and whistling and hiss-
ing bumps into a freight-car . . . and the child rushes in
screaming panic to the opened trap-door and down the
ladder to huddle in the remotest corner of that composing-
room.

On the floor below, by Uncle Oliver's Insurance Office
(. . . The Phœnix . . . The Ætna . . .), were the editorial rooms, equally archaic, atmospheric, inefficient,
reached from Front Street by a narrow dark staircase which
was musty and dusty with powdered dirt, powdered shoe-
leather, and the powdered fibers of the worn, hollowed
steps. Here was the big base-burner glowing in January
. . . to take a winter scene; with the Stocky Man, the
swarthy Anglican cleric, and his cigar on one side—he, a
Democrat—and white-haired Daddy Dietrich, a younger
contemporary of Grandfather Leonard, with his Republican cigar on the other; and my father writing editorials or
correcting proofs at his yellow roll-top desk by the corner
window. It was a comfortable room for a lively chat and
smoke between chaps who were good-natured political enemies and too respectable to drop in at Rafferty's Saloon.
And tobacco-smoke tended to give my father headaches.
But he never knew how to go about putting a stop to it.
"Say, Will—drop your scribbling a minute—Daddy here
says . . . well, what do you say?" And the most he dared
protest was: "Excuse me, Tom, I've got to get this copy
upstairs in a half-hour.". . . without looking up . . . My
father was not a business man . . . either for projecting,
for organizing, for making, or . . . for keeping. He was
always only a scholar and a preacher . . . in or out of the
pulpit.

As a child I had accepted food and shelter, like the sun
and the sky, as a part of the natural order into which I was
born, as indeed a phase of my very self. I knew we were
poor, from the doled butter, the corn-meal mush, the cocoa-
shell drink, the patched breeches, and from my mother's
angry tears when I brought home the basket of rotted
apples a charitable neighbor had invited me to gather from
under his tree—for at Willie McCutcheon's and even at
Cousin Elston's things were so much better. But this too
was part of the natural order. I seldom envied my playmates their expensive toys, their ponies and bicycles and

long summer holidays to Mount 'Desert and the Adirondacks. These phenomena of life were for me a part of *another* natural order. And from my paper-route, and especially from the annual tips of the carriers' New Year's call (with the presentation of my mother's rimed address on a leaflet just off the press), I bettered my wardrobe and had a few pennies for school-books and bats. My balls I usually got from the City Team after the Saturday games—a perquisite along with my pass. I once saw a lady drop a coin from her pocketbook as she came out of the bakery. It was twilight. I looked about. I picked it up. It was not a gold sovereign, like Francis Thompson's, nor did I think it an angelic miracle. But like the other eleven-year-old in the story, did I run after her, my honesty triumphant over bollivers and marbles? I did not. It was now my ten cents. But I would never tell as long as I lived. And once or twice I helped myself (with grim humor) from the collection-plate at Holy Cross service, at the same time embezzling for my own uses the nickel I was supposed to deposit there. I felt mean—so does the chap who steals a loaf of bread, doubtless. I even expected to repay—so does the bank-cashier. I had perhaps as much *moral* sense as I have now. But I have now more fortitude . . . more experience in privation . . . yet if I were starving, I would steal—but not from the starving. Also now more resourcefulness in getting and conserving the minimum of cash needed for my affairs. As a child, I had no instincts for trade whatever: lemonade-stands in the front yard were not for me. No instincts also for a trade, a craft, as a commercial asset, no instincts for job-hunting, for money-making. Young Edward Bok, just over from Holland, was a far more promising American.

In high school I was still accepting food and shelter as a matter of course, preoccupied with preparatory studies and the ambition of a college education. By the time of the second declension in Collar and Daniell's Beginner's Latin, I had determined on my future, but the college professor-

ship in the classics was naïvely envisaged as a career . . .
not as a job. A habit of thought early and inveterate,
destined several times to be sadly jolted but never cured.
And now with but one book of my "Anabasis" completed,
my father has accepted the pastorate of the Unitarian
parish of a far-away New England village and the family
is to move in April. Food and shelter may be still a matter
of course; but, in my helplessness, now so is all else. As
a matter of course, I will not finish the "Anabasis" with my
schoolmates, nor my Vergil, will not read with them either
Cicero or Homer. As a matter of course, I will not give the
Valedictory, for which as a matter of course my classmates
have in goodly fellowship already so vainly nominated me
in their hopes. My world was upset.

Less than a twelvemonth before this we had first opened
our Vergils, in the spring of our second year, thirty of us.
It meant adventure for all of us . . . and still harder work
too, that first eclogue right after the *his rebus cognitis,* and
the *pervenit Labienus* of the "Commentaries"; but for me
it was dawn of the spirit of poetry as the interpreter of life,
a delayed but magnificent dawn. I remember getting my
first lesson. I have told about it before:

Fresh from a starry sleep, on a school-boy morning of April
　(Over the meadows a mist, oriole out in the elm),
Fresh from my dreams of the Marvelous Book I had opened at
　bedtime
　(Pictures of altar and urn, Sibyl, Silenus, and lyre),
There in the homestead at Hilton I sat by the window with Vergil:
　Under the morning star, words like woods to explore.
Tityre, tu patulæ. . . . O eerie quest in the silence!
Magic of dawn on the earth, magic of dawn in the boy!

The rest of the story is in the volume, "Tutankhamen and
After." But the "Æneid" in our junior year was the radiant
light and music that transformed all the days . . . *Arma
virumque . . . tempus erat . . . O lux Dardaniæ . . .
Provehimur pelago . . . Anna, vides? . . . et debellari*

superbos . . . sunt geminæ Somni portæ. . . . Our
teacher, Mr. Hunt, a recent graduate of Amherst who intended to go into law, was adequate in conventional equipment and routine instruction; he heard our translations,
quizzed us in forms and constructions, and taught us a
little scansion. He was a good head, very handsome, a fine
presence. But he was rather remote, deliberate, and impersonal. Yet day by day, we sat on the edges of our seats
ready to be called on in turn to take up our ten lines of
the story with words of our own eager shaping. Instinctively we were trying to create in the afternoon sun of a
New Jersey class-room, through our juvenile alien phrases,
the masterpiece of the Mantuan and the *tanta moles Ro-
manam condere gentem.* And we did not lounge as we stood
by our desks. Vergil was so much greater than Mr. Hunt.
And some of us caught not only the imaginative lure and
the majestic ethos, but something too of the *lacrimæ rerum.*
I am not wistfully reminiscent. I am scientific: the evidence
is in the precisely remembered tones of my classmates'
voices in recitation, as well as in the precisely remembered
emotions of my own breast; for I can analyze the implications of each. If school-room rivalries played a part in
our zeal, Vergil himself would accept the tribute. Educators ask, "What can boys and girls get out of Vergil?" It
depends who the boys and girls are. Beware of shutting
the gates against those who can enter.

But all is to end in a week or two. I will not be with
Phœbe and Albert and Fred when they reread those first
six books in the swift, firm voyaging of the spring review,
reward for whatever toil there had been with grammar
and glossary. I will not be with them to finish the "Anabasis" and to read Homer. "What will you be doing next
year?" asks Mr. Hunt at the farewell party to our family
in the recently built Unitarian Chapel (for he has to ask
something). "I expect to study by myself." "That doesn't
generally work," says Mr. Hunt, as remote as ever. And
no matter how hard I study I will not be valedictorian.

Memories of Mary on the platform at last commencement come back . . . "We are told that our Aryan forefathers." . . . Mary is now at Wellesley . . . This proved to be the greatest disappointment of my intellectual life. A generation later, the neurotic handicap that prevents all travel compelled me to decline an invitation from Harvard to come back and deliver the Phi Beta Kappa poem . . . in the tradition of Lowell and Holmes. What a burst of rehabilitated joy and power after so many years of discouragement and imprisonment to have seen again old Kitt, with his Jovian beard, to have stood with bardic triumph, a good gray poet, in Saunders Theater where so long ago I had received my M. A. from President Eliot, to have mingled as the guest of honor with cap and gown on the gravel paths where so long ago I had been a nameless nonentity. The prestige of it too among scholars and literary folk—and the importance of prestige! But I wrote that it could not be; and spent a quiet evening at work on my monograph about the metrics of "The Cid." It was a disappointment; but immeasurably greater was the disappointment that I was never to be Valedictorian in the High School of Plainfield, New Jersey, of the Class of '94. For then I was not used to life.

I call on Miss Niles. For good-by. Quietly. On her front porch. She urges me to go on studying, writing. She says I remind her of the young Macaulay. She is sad. Thinking about me? Thinking about her kinsmen, the mortgage men? . . . The mahogany table and secretary and all the beds go into the chartered freight-car for Hudson, Massachusetts, to be unloaded two weeks later from the vans behind the weary horses in front of a big frame-parsonage in the hills four miles from any railroad. We are off by express for New England . . . in a way going home. For most of our ancestors are buried there and—at least I shall see Boston Common and Bunker Hill.

I was helpless; for the very preoccupation with studies made impossible the practical enterprise whereby I might have saved my school-days by getting a job in town. My father was doubtless as helpless as I—or would he have been quite as helpless had he known the perilous abyss of my despair? But there was a big attic with an unused room at Uncle Oliver's—and I could have made my board. There was my Aunt Cornelia, and the rent from one of her shanties—or less—would have kept me in school. The Old Maid. There were all my father's well-to-do friends, and the kinsmen of Aunt Lizzie, his brother's wife, called Uncle This and Uncle That. They all wished me well. They all knew my ambition. They all knew I had respectable gifts and tolerable promise. But such are our conventional conceptions of social responsibility, that I have no reason to suppose it ever entered the head of any one of them. It entered mine, though, and ate down into my sullen heart. . . .

My last day of school had been our last lines of the "Æneid" . . . *sunt geminæ Somni portæ*. "Finished April 21, 1893" stands chronicled underneath, like an event of some import. And on the blank page, overleaf, I had translated for that last day:

> There are two gates of Sleep. The one, they say,
> Is horn, whence glide the visions true away.
> The other white with shining ivory gleams,
> Whence send the Manës man deceiving dreams . . .

an awkward school-boy's attempt to make his own in form an art already verily somewhat his in its thought and emotion. And I had added, applying Vergil to my own life, as every one sooner or later (if he reads well) applies every poet to his own life:

> In dreams I conned of future, fate, and fame.
> I woke, I sighed—I knew not whence they came.
> Yet it is well. Man must the future wait,
> Nor know the hornèd nor the ivory gate. . . .

the awkward school-boy still . . . not because he had nothing to say . . . but because he was then quite as helpless to master words—as he was to master life. Of course he never knew: the words—even these vapid and jejune words—helped him in his grief and awe. By saying them he had completed an authentic poetic experience . . . for himself. Was he ever to complete a poetic experience . . . for others? That would depend on how far he ultimately might master both words and life.

VIII

THE Concord Coach drove up the valley. . . . I
thought of the Buffalo Bill Show on Staten Island . . . of
the woodcuts in "Our Wild Indians". . . it has left the
low meadows and the witch-grass I have been mistaking
for fields of young wheat . . . it has rattled over the loose
planks when the brooks crossed the winding dirt-road . . .
a house with a barn clapped on behind it . . . apple-
orchards with pink buds . . . though down in Jersey the
blossoms had fallen and the fruit was already greening to
the size of rose-hips. A farm-house . . . woods . . .
woods . . . stone walls . . . stone walls . . . not a rail-
fence anywhere . . . between openings in the low hills
either side, a pond here, a pond there. "Little Pond,"
"West Pond," says the elderly thin-lipped lady opposite in
the black shawl . . . whom the tired little girl calls Aantie
and thanks for the other haaf of the orange. . . . I can go
swimming at least, I say to myself, interested in the little
girl's dialect. A bend in the road . . . a cluster of white
farm-houses, each with a white barn clapped on behind it
. . . no outhouses at all . . . cord-wood piled on the
roadside . . . the cluster is called the Pan, the lady tells
me . . . only a mile more to the Center, adds my father,
for he has already been here "candidating.". . . My
mother and sister don't talk at all. . . . A cemetery, behind a low stone wall and a row of maples. I see it. "Signs
of civilization at last," I say aloud, and laugh bitterly with
folded arms. . . . The coach stops, and Aantie and the
scrawny little girl stoop and clutter out, she with a box
of new shoes, the little girl with a roll of calico. Up from
shopping in Hudson . . . the metropolis. Aantie snaps de-

fiantly from the roadside, "Yes, and we've two other cemeteries in Bolton."

The first Sunday, while we are still at venerable Dr.
Stone's cottage across from the parsonage awaiting the
Jersey freight-car and the Hudson vans, the peal of the
great bell in the steeple on the neighboring slope beyond the
elms and the Town Hall invites me skyward. I think of
how such aërial uproar used to frighten me. . . . I am indeed somehow suddenly full of memories of my past, now
first poignantly aware that I have a past at all. I will try an
experiment. So I mount up the rickety steeple-stairs, beside
the cobwebbed scaffolding which incloses the suspended
clock-weights and the yanked bell-rope. Into the belfry. I
open the trap. The Big Ben tosses to and fro over my head,
black and cavernous, shutting out all but the edges of the
clouds, its clapper pounding as furiously as if once more
liberty were being proclaimed to all the land and all the
inhabitants thereof. I don't blanch. I stand between the
swaying brazen flange and the belfry-rail while the caldron
of din flings its reverberations over the tree-tops to the four
corners of the parish and beyond. Thank God, I seem to
be cured for good of the terrors of sound, I say. The bell
slows down . . . the farmer in the lobby down below has
stopped yanking. The din dies off in eerie overtones, octave
above octave. I catch from far away, from invisible green
places beyond our uplands, now and then the faint bells of
surrounding parishes . . . from Lancaster, from Harvard
Village . . . from Stow . . . from Berlin, and even up
the valley-road from Hudson where we took the coach. I
can see the spires of Hudson . . . and to the left, eight or
nine miles, is Leominster, shining on the long ridge, which,
like Carcassonne, for the rest of my years I was always going to visit. Hills all about us, and yet Bolton itself is in
the hills, hundreds of feet above Hudson and the Boston
and Maine Railroad. Great hummocky Wattaquottoc yonder where the sun sets, with the upward brown road along
its side and the long brown farm-house on its top; the

great ledge immediately behind me with the little brick
powder-house in decay from the War of 1812, they say;
the stretches of sunlit meadow-lands, woods, plowed fields,
farmsteads before me down and off below to the verge of
every hill-foot. Bolton Center hidden under trees at my
feet with its forty houses, its little new Baptist chapel, its
blacksmith shop, and its general store at the cross-roads; its
wooden high school so-called . . . for I have already been
the rounds. Between me and the red brick of the side wall
of the Town Hall is an immense and ancient live-oak on
the sloping common, older than the oak ribs of the *Santa
María*. Across the road, down there, the distance of a revolutionary musket-ball, is the parsonage. I think to myself it
looks like the picture of Emerson's house in Concord, only
nineteen miles away. I go down.

When the second pealing begins an hour later, I take
my seat in the pew with mother and sister. My father
rises beside the pulpit desk in a pulpit high enough for a
cardinal. Fifty or sixty people, tired old farmers, tired old
ladies, tired young farmers, and tired young wives . . . all
so tired and yet kindly in their stolid silence . . . are scattered about in this house of God that had been built a hundred years before to shelter four hundred communicants.
How wearily they sing! My father is venerable even at
fifty-six . . . his first sermon is simple and earnest, un-
clerical somehow. . . . I do not recall his text, and I will
not invent . . . from Jesus doubtless . . . as much a message of his presence there as his words there. So all his
sermons. The villagers will come to respect him, to love
him . . . whether they go to meeting or not . . . though
he will not be able to talk crops with Andrew Nourse after
church nor to jolly the giggling girls by the sheepish boys
in the portico, nor to say "Damn it" in the General Store to
prove to the Cracker-Barrel Club that he doesn't put on
ministerial airs. My father's portrait will hang on the
wall of the old Bolton Church in the years I will be writing
about him. And my mother will be spending her quiet sum-

mers beside the steeple. His talk and his walk were goodly among the hills. . . .

Though, for generations, so many of its more restive sons and daughters had migrated from those wood-lots of second-growth timber and those pastures and fields, strewn with glacier-boulders or streaked with the gneiss outcrop of the Archæan age, to the cities or to the Dakotas, the folk that carried on among the hills was perhaps the sturdiest of their Yankee stock. They had the tenacity to stay by, where there was still work to do. And they had their pride—a more autochthonous emotion than the smug booster-pride of Main Street or Zenith. And every one a citizen, a real citizen in town-meeting, with real civic problems: the repair of this road or that, the election of constable, school com- mittee, or the three selectmen—the triumvirs of an agrarian republic six miles square, a Massachusetts township. If the Center, with post-office and hitching-post for the Concord Coach, and Town Hall and Spire, was Rome, the outlying settlements, the Pan, the Green, Quakerville, with their cemeteries, acknowledged no overlord. They were not municipalities; they sent in no delegates. They came to town-meeting themselves, one and all, behind the old mare, with all their politics in their heads. Now in 1926 the women-folk too . . . but in Fords. The only kind of an America where government of, by, and for the people has not perished from the earth. So different too in the primi- tive simplicity of its social structure: the Sunday-school superintendent peddles through the Center his strawberry crop; the Selectman's daughter works out for Mrs. Whit- comb; the girl that washes the Postmaster's shirts dances of a Saturday night with the Postmaster; the son of the school committeeman makes hay in the fields with the town clerk. So it has been from the year 1728, when the town was set off from Lancaster; so from long before 1728 when the neighborhood was still a part of Lancaster. The names of the voters are the names in the three cemeteries. And all

their thought and emotion comes from where their potatoes and Indian corn and hay and apples and elms come
from—from the glacier-drift and the rains and the snows
and the sunshine. And when they read books—and sometimes they do read—some of the farmers and farmers'
wives know what those books mean. To-day the library is
no longer in the Town Hall; but in a charming little stone
building, not the gift of Andrew Carnegie, up the street
beyond a neat meadowy grass-plot and gravel drive. I'm
told the librarian is Catherine Edes, with whom I used to
play "terrible Turk" in a tent. I spent my college vacations
in Bolton in extra curricular studies; I always came back
there when I could, long after my father's resignation,
back from New York or Philadelphia, back from Göttingen
and Rome and Geneva. I wrote "The Poet of Galilee" in
Bolton, though a book and a writing of more importance to
my father than to the public. It was from Bolton that I
took train for Madison. With the years, those uplands and
that upland people became mine; and, in the social mis-
understandings and personal stresses of late-middle and
aging life, I have turned many times in imagination, without sentimentality, indeed with a very realistic sense of
spiritual commonalty in fundamentals of toil, pain, dignity,
reserve, worth, humor, friendliness, to those farmsteads
and roadsides and hills that, with realistic grasp of my
neurosis, I have rather good reasons to believe I may never
see again. I became, like Robert Frost, a New Englander,
and projected long ago essentially the same artistic interpretation that he, with a far subtler sympathy and an inerrant
craftsmanship not mine at all, was destined so triumphantly to achieve. I once told him so; and he believed me.

But these comments record things learned long after
my first ride up the valley in the Concord Coach, long after
my first survey of a then alien terrain from the belfry in the
steeple. And there is this other, earlier phase, with its
own significance for the same man's life . . . and with far
more significance for that motif of his life of which this

book is the analytic record. The uprooting, the estrangement, the isolation, the struggles, the despairs of those two next years toward the end of adolescence: I find I have been trying unconsciously to postpone the chronicling. For we ever look back with the zest of thought upon all adventure, all action however interwoven with pain; but not readily will we look back upon the self where, marooned and stranded in wretchedness, it was once ingloriously, morbidly, eating itself away. Furthermore, contemplating myself in those two years quite objectively, as if another personality, I shudder no less and turn to other years: for I can't bear to contemplate boyhood so distorted—not, you see, my boyhood but boyhood itself. Such a moldy corruption of the normal meaning of boyhood is far more repellent to my feeling for life than any story of young highwayman or libertine. . . .

The initial situation scarcely needs analysis. Transfer to another city, and another school even, in a world like what I had known, would have spelt homesickness. Transfer to this village-world, so different to me, and so different then mainly as seemingly so barren, was to homesickness what acute melancholy is to "the blues." And my morose and aloof attitude at the church after services, at the post-office, on the street, my citified dress, and the wildfire tale of my remark in the coach had disgruntled the villagers. Bill Robinson, Grand Army veteran, burning brush in the meadow just back of the parsonage fence, denounced me one May morning for having cluttered his field and ruined his scythe with stones in clearing out my new back yard, and went on with other charges, not forgetting the cemeteries and civilization. I was in white ducks —cheap enough, but cleaner than his blue overalls. He cursed New Jersey roundly as a copperhead State, and me as an upstart dude, and concluded: "The *last* minister we had here was a damn fool." I was so unstrung that, once inside the house, I sobbed, seventeen though I was, with bitterness and fury . . . till the comic premises of his

127

Yankee reasoning in the final comment set me into half-
hysterical laughter. The "last minister," Ernest Montesquieu Haldane, was an ex-curate, an Englishman who on
horseback had always turned out to the left, and always
mistaken the turf sidewalk of the Center for a bridle-path.
To be sure, in a month or so I had done a deed that made
me Bill's boy and Bolton's boy forever. There was a stocky
little French Canadian wood-chopper with a pair of boxing-
gloves who was regularly knocking down the young or
middle-aged Sawyers and Jacksons and Martins every evening at dusk in the street before the post-office. Sauntering
up there—where else was there to saunter to see my fellow-
men?—I offered to meet the outlander; and, in the scrap
that ensued, my long practice in Smithie's barn-gymnasium
speedily saved the pride of the village. Rather, not so
much my practice, as my ugly state of mind: but in taking
out my desperation on the alien Canuck I acquired a reputation. Bill's boy and Bolton's forever. The fight became a
tradition, like the big black pill of Dr. Endicott, village
physician before the War of 1812. Bill Robinson, acquaintance of twenty years, is dead; but, if you go up to
Bolton, you will find others who can tell you, either as
eye-witnesses or as themselves told by Bill.

Meantime I had visited the one big upstairs room that
was the high school, and the young Dartmouth graduate
who was principal and faculty. The twenty-five young
folks, from all corners of the parish, were chiefly strangers
to me, except for distant nods after service; and, as I had
been led to expect by my father before leaving Plainfield,
the course of study offered nothing for me. Such little villages to-day wisely make provisions for their more intellectually ambitious young folks in the fully equipped high
schools of the near-by towns. I myself was soon walking
the four miles to Hudson to interview the principal; but
the twenty-dollar term-fee and the prospective eight-mile
daily tramp, especially in the heavy snows of New England—for I could not have afforded the coach—at once put

the Hudson school as far away as Plainfield's. So I settled down to fulfil my original intention. I would keep up with my class. I would prepare myself for college without help. My parents, indeed, conceded me this; and finally left me entirely to my own plans, though Aunt Lizzie had written my mother that, however good an education was for a boy, a boy should go to work if the family needed his assistance; and there had been talk of a job in the shoe-factory in Hudson. But there was sacrifice, even in this grant of freedom: my parents gave what they could. The parish was able to pay but little; there were obligations back in Plainfield. We had not been in Bolton two months when "the farm" was almost sold for unpaid taxes. "The farm," all that remained to my father of grandfather's vast acreage, was a suburban tract between the country roads, containing a chestnut-grove, rented fields of Indian corn, and a worked sand-pit. Once long before, there had been a morning of huge excitement at the pit. The workmen had found yellow grains sparkling on their shovels in the sun. The old cry, heard from South Africa, California, and the Klondike, went up on the Jersey air—"Gold, gold!" The news came to town . . . to my father. He knew it for iron pyrites. "Gold, gold"—Look in Webster:

Iron pyrites. A brass-yellow mineral with a brilliant metallic lustre; fool's gold.

Several years later, when without all income, he managed to dispose of it . . . now it is one of the fashionable residential additions, I understand; even as his Denver properties of the early seventies were worth (so we found on inquiring) hundreds of millions of dollars, before the death in 1920 of the venerable single-taxer, whose curiosity was as detached as that of his half-socialist son. . . .

So I settled down. The great secretary was installed by the end wall of my bedroom, beside the upstairs back window that looked out on Bill Robinson's meadow over to the

marsh and the birch-wood and the low oak-hills . . .
meadow-rue, goldenrod, palisades of white bark, blue ridges
and clouds as I looked up from my Vergil in summer; the
bleakness of snow and gray skies as I looked up from my
Cicero in winter. For night-work I had the light of a bedroom lamp, the sort where you see the white wick curled in
the oil beside the glass handle. I had my school-books. I had
about twenty-five bound volumes of my father's and uncle's
Teubner texts of Greek and Latin authors—Uncle Oliver
had had "Leonard's Horace" stamped on his copy of the
"Satires" and "Epistles" in his merry college days. I had collected, too, before leaving Plainfield, from Aunt Lizzie's
brother, "Uncle" Frank, a Princeton graduate, his disused
set of Anthons with their copious notes and his own mirthful marginalia. Those were all behind the glass doors of the
secretary. In time I borrowed some secondary school-texts
in French and Latin from the storeroom of the high school,
and books of rarer sorts, like Emerson's "Dial," from Dr.
Stone's across the way. The church library had some theological books, besides the "Little Women" and "Rollos."
The town library had about three thousand volumes in my
native tongue, of poets, essayists, novelists, philosophers,
historians, men of science: the minister and schoolmaster
had always served on the library committee—though Dea-
con Powers of the Baptist Chapel still kept out all the
books on Evolution he could. A year later, I had the privi-
leges of the still better equipped libraries at Lancaster and
Harvard Village, and carried home on my four-mile walks
(every place was four miles from Bolton Center) such
books as Taine's "History of English Literature" and Ben
Jonson's plays. If Boston's Public Library, the Athenæum,
and Harvard's were destroyed, Massachusetts would still
conserve in a hundred colonial villages the best of the long
record of man's imagination and thought. A little reading
circle of the ladies subscribed for the "Century," "Atlantic," "Harper's," and "Scribner's," which I could borrow
when the last lady had finished the latest chapter in the

130

distinguished serials by Mrs. Humphry Ward and others then running. There was plenty of good print about. I did not have to educate myself exclusively on the family Bible, and the "Farmer's Almanac."

I drew spiritual support from the ideal presence of my former schoolmates. I was in lively correspondence, exercising my literary ambitions in prose and rime—chiefly, satiric of "this God-forsaken hole and these country bumpkins," or lyric and elegiac on the sunsets in the hills and on the pine-trees in the cemeteries. They kept me informed of all their doings, of the class-room, the teachers, the debating society; and insisted on my competing for the prize in the poetry contest of the debating society, and awarded me that prize by mail. I drew spiritual support from the ambition to outstrip them; and indeed, first and last, I read twelve orations of Cicero to their six, seven books of the "Anabasis" to their four, the rest of the "Æneid," with some Ovid, Juvenal, and Horace—read and reviewed. I did not get very far into Homer; none of my books made the dialect very clear to me; and I was not a wizard in scholarship. Geometry I came to neglect too—of my mathematical history, perhaps a word later. I drew spiritual support from the great masters themselves: I was not reading Cicero's moral indignation against the monstrous maladministration of Verres in Sicily and Cicero's pæan to the life of letters in the Archias oration merely as stunts—

hæc studia adulescentiam alunt.

Not following the Ten Thousand through Armenia to the Black Sea, as a stunt—

Thalassa! Thalassa!

I drew spiritual support from the great languages themselves. I was already dimly aware that the greatest creation of a race is not its mythology, its religion, its social and political institutions, its folklore, its architecture, its

131

literature and its art, not its science, not its inventions, but what is the far more organic product of its experience and its temperament and its thinking—that speech which it has wrought out through the long generations, in the unconscious urges of human life. Already dimly aware; and the morphology and syntax of Latin and Greek had their own fascination, their own challenge to the mind of man that would master the mind of man. The Latin subjunctive and the μι-verb of the Greek were not easy, with the imperfect start I had had; but they were marvels, and not to understand them was the discomfort of thwarted power and curiosity. I was already dimly aware that, while the mastery of a language first makes possible mastery of a literature, linguistics is a study of still greater depth and wider scope than even literature. So I learned too something of French, from a copy of the school grammar in use down the street, a use too slow for me, and from Guizot's "Life of William the Conqueror" . . . with a pronunciation that some years later I spent four months in Geneva trying to get over.

I got moral support from my weekly schedules. Here is the card on my door:

BEGINNING JULY 5, 1893

5:30–7:30	Geometry
8–10	Greek (Anabasis)
10–12	Latin (Cicero)
12:30–12:45	Physiology
1–6	Work (Manual)
7–8	Latin Prose Composition
8–9	Greek Prose Composition
9–9:30	Physics
9:30	Retire

You cannot miss a day.

This I happen to find transcribed in a diary; and underneath in a parenthesis of some months later:

(But you have.)

Manual work meant weeding our greenhorn's kitchen-garden—I then knew a blade of young Indian corn from a plantain-leaf, a string-bean pod from a catalpa, and little more—or it meant, particularly, sprucing up our yard. During the bachelor pastorate of the Rev. Henry Montesquieu Haldane the proprietary responsibilities of the parsonage had become ambiguous: the lady in charge thought he was her boarder, the ex-curate thought she was his housekeeper; and the practical results of the misunderstanding became acute whenever the two happened to invite out-of-town friends to visit at the same time. . . . Especially when the lady's visitor was a Boston Blue-stocking writing a Philosophy of Nirvana, and the clergyman's an overseas Anglican who liked his cigar in the parlor. Meantime the place had become more and more unkempt since the young pastor had scorched the front pickets in burning the autumn leaves. I nailed up and repainted the pickets, straightened the hitching-post, trimmed the grass into the beginning of a lawn, sawed a dead limb or two from an elm, and cut the intrusive sod from the driveway into a neat semicircle. Indeed, the Village Improvement Society perhaps owed its revival to the landscape artistry of the young stranger in search of manual exercise. The tidy beauty of the Center in later years was due, I used to boast, to the example of my adolescent industry and esthetic judgment. Manual work meant also sawing cord-wood, tough old quartered oak, and splitting the billets, out in the rear ell behind the kitchen. One afternoon during manual exercise (1–6) I happened to be asking God to send a particularly knotty billet to a region where it would burn in far hotter flames than any in our kitchen-stove. There stood my good father: "My son, my son, you are first in all the line of the Leonards to use language like that." . . . I think to-day: "My father, I'm sorry for your amazement and grief. . . . I may have been the first . . . but I am the last too."

133

"You cannot miss a day" . . . "but you have." Those schedules, though applauded by my father, made a dubious moral support after all. I set myself specific tasks, so many chapters, so many pages, which I seldom was able to complete in the allotted time. I was also often too miserable, too restless to study, and the unfulfilled schedules on my door rebuked and tortured me. I did not know then that a schedule should exist to lighten, not to load, the burdens of life, as project, not as command. So I cut into my afternoons; and tried to make up for self-set tasks incompleted in the mornings and evenings by industry in general reading betweenwhiles. First and last in those eighteen months I did study much thoroughly, and did read much in widely different fields, in all fields, science as well as letters. And I retain to this day what I studied and read then; I have asked as a university professor many a question in the oral examination for higher degrees in English —on Goldsmith's "Traveller," on Dr. Johnson's "Critique of Pope's Epitaphs," on Latimer's "Sermons on the Card," on Mackenzie's "Man of Feeling," on Macaulay's "Milton," or what not in the old byways—that depended on reading done then and never done again. Memory is primarily a matter of initial self-identification; memory is excitation of the imagination, thoughts, emotions. A poor memory means initial indifference or revulsion. The schoolboy with "no memory for dates" remembers the batting-averages of fifty major leaguers. There is no such thing as a retentive memory, aside from vitality of initial experience, at least for me. And I remember—to put it otherwise—because I never worry, never even think about remembering. I am assuming of course some continuation or potentiality of the initial interest. If that lapses completely memory may lapse too: I still remember the dates; I have forgotten the batting-average even of Buck Ewing. I am not speaking here of abnormal suppressions; whether by the slow workings of the mind ill at ease with itself, or by its sudden convulsive combat with the Horrors it cannot face. Not here. But I have spoken a word before; and toward the end I will have to speak again, and more than a word. Actually, I did acquire quantities of intellectual goods; actually, I did vindicate a lad's powers of self-help. But inordinate ambition and morbid introspection killed all comfort. I was the self-tormentor. Now I insist that my intellectual affairs shall contribute to my happiness. For one thing, I am amused, not tormented, by my blunders or ignorance.

I tormented myself, too, in my very search for spiritual companionship, by the lives of those who had achieved, especially in scholarship and letters—Theodore Parker, Dr. Johnson, Milton, John Stuart Mill, Margaret Fuller, Macaulay, Wordsworth, and so on—I was always measuring what they knew and did at seventeen and eighteen with what I knew and did at seventeen and eighteen. Macaulay had read so much more Latin; Mill was an Aristotle at three; Shelley's "Queen Mab" and its recondite notes was only less great than the "Divine Comedy" (in Longfellow's translation), and Pope's heroics in the "Pastorals" were of a far more graceful and musical art at sixteen than I could achieve with an advantage of fourteen months. I did get some encouragement from Byron's "Hours of Idleness," and thought my own exercise in "Childish Recollections" in spots perhaps as good as Byron's. I was probably right. Or, with the unbalanced moods and judgments of this abnormal adolescent isolation, I would go to the other extreme. My rimed tale of the Persian Wars with its recurrent, "Master, remember the Athenians" (inserted in the original Greek . . . Athenaion . . . to rime with Aion, Bion, die on, lion, sigh on, etc.), I vowed was as good as "The Siege of Corinth"; my satire on Alexander the Great as good as the lines on Napoleon in "The Age of Bronze"—even as later in college my "Ode to Evening" was better, far better than Collins, far more like Keats and Shelley (for a fact, it was far more like Keats and Shelley). But did these realizing moments of conscious supremacy in

135

precocious power bring me peace? They did not. They brought me further torment. They accentuated my rebellion and despair: here in this God-forsaken hole genius is doomed to rot away. Smile. I smile now too. It was Hell then. I was a fool? I was a fool. But I'm not talking about folly; I am talking about spiritual anguish.

I often, and more and more with the months, read not for spiritual support but for escape, to forget, to forget— yet always finding some unhappy image of myself on every other page. In mature years, I acquired indeed the resources of escape in books. Lucretius, Goethe, Dante, Cervantes, Abelard, Shakspere, Chaucer, Homer—how I thank you! For salvation again and again. For companionship too. Humbly content merely to walk by the sides of you. Finding exaltation enough in the elemental fact that I am man enough to understand the voices of you. I would have been dead long ago but for books. Yet back there in Bolton, if I could only have pitched hay, as I learned to do later in college vacations, and have sweated out on the sun-beat slopes the poisons my system then distilled even from books good and great!

Above all from Byron. I had already known Byron through "The Isles of Greece." Now "Childe Harold" became the companion of my lonely classical studies, "Childe Harold," "The Giaour," "The Curse of Minerva": Byron spoke out my emotions, Byron reinforced my imaginings, on Greece and Rome. We were together. Soon, however, the peculiarly Byronic in the classical mood became mine:

> O Rome, my country, city of the soul,
> The orphans of the heart must turn to thee.

Byron . . . Rome . . . the Bolton exile. Then the Byronic mood itself, which had made increment of Greece (sad relic of departed worth) and of Rome (childless and crownless in her voiceless woe), became mine; or rather (without attempting a too subtle analysis) interpreted and reinforced my own moods, of self-conscious adolescence, of isolation from my kind, of world-pain, of the tragic grandeur of my fate. The Corsair had leaned beside a pillar in the hall, darkly scowling at the dancers. I visited a country dance under the oil-lamps in the upstairs of the Town-Hall and leaned and scowled too and withdrew into the night. I dramatized myself as Byron. This is the Byronic bane for adolescence, especially for an adolescence conditioned, as mine was, to meet the Byronic more than half-way on its own miserable ground. There was no bane for me in his so-called immoralities, either sentimental as in "Parisina" or farcical as in "Don Juan"; and I doubt if there is for anybody. I caught something of the veritable spirit of nature, of the heroic, of the sagacious in Byron; but the chief blessing, beside the bane, was the thorough-fares he opened to English literature around and before him. I followed one lead after another in his text or in the notes, and in the Byron biographies, to Shelley, Coleridge, Keats, Wordsworth, Crabbe, Gifford, and to Milton, Pope, Collins, Gray, Dryden, Johnson. And in their works, in turn (some of them of course already familiar to me in parts), I got other leads. I had no "Century Outlines" or "Century Readings"; no manuals. My mind did its own sorting out; and it got the chronology straighter than most students I have ever assisted in examining for their master's degrees. And, incidentally, I found that the simplest way to know *about* when a thing happened was to know *just* when it happened. And I knew just when it happened because the date meant to me a moment of Reality . . . 1688 . . . 1700 . . . 1744 . . . 1788 . . . 1809 . . . 1812 . . . 1815 . . . 1824 . . . 1850 . . . *1876.* I knew every line of Byron—this is not a figure of speech. I knew "Childe Harold" practically by heart—this is not a figure of speech. And reverence and pity and love for Byron, need for Byron, was the nearest I ever came to that worship which the Christian heart and imagination experiences toward the divine Son of its creed. A slighting

137

comment on Byron by a professor in my freshman year made me flush and tremble and all but sob in my seat . . . (Byron, I'd like to talk this over with you sometime in the Elysian Fields.) Later Byron marked out for me much of my own pilgrimage through Europe—by the exulting and abounding river, by the castled crag where I became a university student, by Lake Leman mirroring the stars and mountains, in the pass where Jura answers from her misty shroud back to the joyous Alps who call to her aloud (where my own amazed ears heard the same thunder), even down to Italia. . . .

> Italia! too Italia! looking on Thee
> Full flashes on the soul the light of ages,
> Since the fierce Carthaginian almost won thee,
> To the last halo of the chiefs and sages . . .
> Throne and grave of Empires. . . .
> The fount at which the panting mind assuages
> Her thirst of knowledge . . .
> . . . Rome's imperial hill.

And only not to Greece because too poor of purse. As I think of the great companion that led me through Europe, no longer a boy but still young, still free to follow light of mountain or sea or poet, of what his great voice did for my eyes, for my spirit, must I not forgive his part in the tragic buncombe of Bolton days? Byron too gave me my doctor's degree at Columbia. Byron made me an official examiner of Samuel Chew's Johns Hopkins dissertation a little later . . . which was so good that, in sad prescience, I realized my brief career as "perhaps the leading Byron authority of America" had about run its course. Yet when Drinkwater told me in Madison a few months ago of his new book on Byron, I said, "They'll ask Chew to review it, but they'll ask me too." And they did. "They" meant of course such people as Canby, Sherman, and Van Doren on Manhattan Isle.

My verses were obviously more and more Byronic;

Byronic in mood, Byronic in theme, and manner. Worthless of course. Interesting, not for any outstanding poetic promise, but, possibly, for their part in fixating my morbidity, and for some suggestions on the psychology of composition. To re-create by self-identification as reader is a vital process, but not so vital as to re-create by self-identification as writer. And, worse, with me the re-creation found much stuff available inside myself. The Byronic imitation was not mere pose. I had, too, something more than Juvenal's *cacoethes scribendi,* scribbler's itch. I had the authentic need, the double urge behind all art—the urge to shape, to objectify, to get it off my chest; the urge to communicate, to propagandize for my state, to tell the world—the double urge that converts brute experience into human experience—to get it straight for yourself and to make it plain to your friend, whatever it be that has come home to you. I had too the external form of verse. I never learned meter and rime. Verse was for me only a specialized application of organized sound through speech, implicit in my original learning to talk. I had the stuff, not only an aching and a yearning heart, and a sense of human life, but a love of nature, first awakened in these hills, and wrought into my emotions of self and of life, a sense too of something far more deeply interfused. . . . Never again was I to vibrate so entirely as poet. But I failed to function as poet because I could not objectify and could not communicate. I lacked the stabilizations that come from the intellect and the self-reliance of an unmastered personality, using its own tongue on its own feet. I was undifferentiated splurge. There is no prophesying from youth. What the two urges become depends on the unforetellable nature of his future experience and what his intellect and his character can do with it. For every ten thousand at seventeen who scribble so-called promising verses, only one will be saying anything at thirty-seven. They really never transcend seventeen. And if they learn to *be,* they never learn to *speak.* Growing-up means getting the use of one's tongue as well as of one's experience.

When not alone with my books and my verses, I was alone with the woods, the birches, the pines, the oak-groves, alone with the Wattaquattoc sunsets, immense over the valley and intervales of the Nashua, with golden and crimson clouds flung from darkening Mount Wachusett, eastward to Blue Hill by Boston—such sunsets as only the Gods on Olympus ever saw before—alone with the cattle down by the meadows and willows of either pond for a swim in primeval nakedness, alone on the slopes of the blueberry patch, alone with the brown thrasher and orchard-oriole and cardinal, alone by a roadside stone wall after supper with the whippoorwill, the whippoorwill that will sound New England twilight in my ears forever. Alone on another hill up the main road from Hudson to Lancaster from where I could see Emerson's Mount Monadnock cut into the New Hampshire blue. Alone on Powder-House Rock back of the Steeple, looking at Leominster on the long ridge. Alone when not with a book or note-book. These were goodly things to be with; but to be alone with at seventeen not altogether goodly. If my sketch seems too lively, let the word "alone" give it sobriety. As a sketch it suggests too much of what I felt later when not alone. Before those earlier vistas and landscapes the exaltations were too chafed, the resignations too bitter.

I was alone not only because the young people were widely scattered in the outlying farms, but because they were busy with work or with recreations outside of my interests or experience, and as withdrawn from me as I from them. I had no friends of my own age, whether boys or girls. In the two summers, I seized on the transient companionship of two college book agents, and of two lads from preparatory schools who spent some holiday weeks within walking distance. But all four depressed while they cheered —they were in school. My sister too went her way, which was not mine. Except, indeed, for early childhood and for two years or so in my early twenties, when she was successfully at work as a kindergartner, we have never been close.

Before that time I was indifferent or gruff; since that time worried by the difficulties that kept her from sharing more effectively the economic responsibilities in an all but penniless household. Inasmuch as the emotional reactions inside the family circle are so often active causes of the neuroses, it seems necessary for clarity in presenting this case, to state that the failure of correlation between these two beings of the same blood and roof-tree, however sad a failure in living, is not specifically implicated in my trouble, as cause—or even as contributing cause, except as any failure contributes its general emotional strain. And not symptomatic of neurotic predisposition, either: that our paths have led so far apart is due to the same normal reasons that tend to so many human separations—fundamental differences of taste, opinions, activities, that are more powerful than biologic origins or the social pressure of conventional sentiment. The relation between us repeats—families so often repeat—the relation between my father and his sister. I am glad of that two years' experience in a brother-sister situation; but even if it had continued I cannot see how that would have protected me from the neurosis that came when it came. I sought also little companionship from my parents. Contrary to the village opinion, my father neither directed nor assisted my studies. I sometimes talked over at table what I was reading, even sometimes read some of my verses. But not often. I was instinctively withdrawing, resentful on being snatched from my schoolmates, superior in my increase of intelligence, rebellious at having, as the minister's son, to attend church every Sunday morning. Church-bells had ceased to be a phobia; they were now often a depressing nuisance. Yet I had moments in the pew when my father's kind eyes and earnest voice, so human and unprofessional, touched me to a feeling for transcendental things and thrilled with the desire to be a good man. God was the name objectified from these states, and from my broodings on Wattaquattoc Hill; but neither there nor ever after has the religious consciousness been more definite than this. And, less than some men, have I been deluded by the clarity of the majestic monosyllable into thinking there was any clarity to the mysteries for which we make it such an easy symbol and surrogate. The God that has been my fate was the Locomotive-God.

About the Center, my human contacts were chiefly with the very young or the very old. I played Indian at seventeen in the groves and pasture with two small brothers of ten and twelve from across the street, built them a canoe, swam with them, had apple-fights in peltings back and forth from ammunition of August sweetings, the windfalls under our respective trees. I sat in a tent with seven-year Catherine and nine-year Ella, as their lord and master, playing Oriental Despot or narrating them my adventures among the Aztecs with Cortes. The next year's high-school teacher was friendly, but off for Boston every week-end; and I was a little diffident in my few visits to his study. He could have done something more for me, had he known . . . or had I let him. I had help from him only in making out some sentences in his Spanish books . . . Spain will come into my story again. There was a very clever and buxom twenty-three years' girl teaching in the district school-house in the Center (situated beside the fire-department shed, with *semper paratus* above the double doors); but it was only in college years that I bicycled about the country with her. Adolescence needs adolescence, and six years, especially between the sexes, is an age at seventeen. . . . To satisfy the craving for life in its surge and mass, I sat on the post-office steps waiting for the evening mail-coach, with seven or eight; or on an upturned nail-keg in the blacksmith shop.

The Blacksmith Shop was the rendezvous of the parish, even more than the Cracker-Barrel and the Stamp-Window. Meet Andy Simpson, émigré from Nova Scotia, with a dialect quite priceless to a philologist, quoting snatches from Burns's "Death and Dr. Hornbook," as his left arm pauses at the bellows and his right readjusts with the tongs the horseshoe in the live coals—

Horn sent her aff to her lang hame,
To hide it there.

Or, with buttress under his armpit and upturned hoof between his knees—

Ah, Tam! ah, Tam, thou'll get thy fairin'!

Meet Dr. Reuben Holbrooke, retired dentist, with dapper beard at sixty, always in a boiled shirt, the village atheist. He doesn't believe in novels, for they are lies. He is a man of decision and unwavering convictions. Twenty-five years ago he quarreled with his wife over the price of a bonnet and has never spoken to her since. Each morning she gets him his breakfast and spends each day next door sewing or cooking with her sister, Bill Robinson's wife. The other meals he gets himself. Nobody has ever been in the house, but the village says there is a chalk-line in the kitchen, renewed once a week. Bill Robinson has just remodeled his barn into a G.A.R. post and hall for village suppers and musicales. Reuben refers to it darkly as the Mormon Temple. . . .

Meet florid Uncle Joel with his goatee and cane. He is eighty-six and a little cracked. Mr. and Mrs. Newberry keep the old house for him. It fronts the main street between parsonage and post-office. He will stand inside the gate and hail strangers passing in their buggies. One will get out a little puzzled, and follow Uncle Joel into the house. "My wife," he says, pointing to the gilt frame and the work of an itinerant artist in crayons. "My wife; we were married sixty-two years." He had been a watchmaker in his prime and once long ago the big clock in the ancient steeple had been his to keep in order. That big clock was still always on his mind. Along with the crayon portrait. Whenever the great hands on its four faces failed to keep up with the sun, or whenever the bell crazily struck twelve as the haycock shadows lay longest or as the harvest moon

rose over the barns, the villagers, looking up from culti-
vator or milk-pail or woodpile all over the parish, would
say, "Uncle Joel has got into the steeple again." They kept
the portico door locked. But he would filch the key, or steal
in during service or repairs, and toil up the steeple stairs
and tinker with his crippled fingers on the old familiar
springs and wheels. Buzz, whizz, zip! And then he would
descend triumphantly happy. They kept the door locked.
They did not particularly object to the clock's being wrong;
but they didn't want Uncle Joel to break his neck. Robert
Frost, meet Uncle Joel. . . . After Uncle Joel's death the
clock stopped going too. (Hawthorne would have made a
tale of this.) I get a letter from my mother, writing in
Bolton on June 14, 1926:

> The clock in the old church is doing duty after a silence of many
> years. The town is now in charge. It struck 200 when first started.

Making up for lost time. . . .

Meet Miles Boughton, who will fling up the biggest
forkfuls on to the load at eighty-two, wiry, olive little
man, who brags of his lawsuits won. He lives with his son,
former widower, who has just brought back a widow and
her eight-year-old Mamie from South Boston. Her Irish
temperament does not like Bolton, and her Irish temper
revolts at the wiry, olive little man, especially after a drink
of whisky. I am passing with a pound of butter and Mamie
rushes out. "Oh, Ellery, ma's killin' granpah." I jump in,
Mamie weeping after. Ma has him pinned against the
kitchen wall, with left hand on his Adam's apple, and in
her right, poised high over his wisps of gray hair, an empty
white chamber-pot of conventional pattern, viciously
gripped by the handle. . . .

Meet Mike O'Malley, three feet and an inch or so
tall, once clown-dwarf with Barnum's, marooned for drink,
now adopted as Bolton's town pet. He paints red or yellow stripes on buggy-wheels and tail-boards for a living,

but gives the blacksmith shop many a whimsical hour betweenwhiles, with circus anecdotes and Celtic philosophy.
Once in two months, after a visit to Hudson, he shoots up
the village, yelling comic defiance at man, woman, and
child, and pointing with mock bravado his clay pipe like a
Derringer. He knows he is drunk, and is having a ripping
frolic with his misfortune—until his lanky, mysterious wife
sticks her head out of the shanty door and shrieks: "Mike,
you damn fool, come here right away.". . .

Meet James Mansfield, called the Town Bull. He has
a farm on the Lancaster Road, and he, too, a wife, Prudence Mansfield, sour, childless, and past child-bearing. It
is Prudence who stands one afternoon looking into a baby-
carriage before the store as John Marshall comes along.
"Whose brat do you say that is, John?" "Why, Sally Jen-
kins's!" "Oh, yes, we all know that much—but I mean who
do you say its father is." "That's what's got us all guessin',
Prue." "Well, I'm not guessin', I guess. Who is its father?
—my better half.". . .

Meet "Old Graves." But if you really want to talk
with him, drop in at his peddler's junk-shop, opposite the
general store, after supper. It was he you saw riding home
with his fat paunch profiled between the nag in front and
the load of brooms, pans, and wash-tubs on the wagon
behind him and his taciturn dame. Nobody knows where he
came from three years ago, or why he chose Bolton as
headquarters. But he'll recite you the "Essay on Man"
from end to end, and long stretches of Pollock's "Course
of Time." There are some second-hand books on the shelf
with the empty fruit-jars. I bought from him my Kames's
"Elements of Criticism."

There are others to meet in the blacksmith shop or in
hay-field, in the cow-barn, working out the taxes on the
road, at bean-suppers and corn-huskings, on door-steps, lay-
ing stone walls, beating eggs, sewing, feeding chickens—
and a story, many stories, in each . . . as of the little old
deaf lady who lived all alone in Dr. Stone's woodshed, and

the quiet young bride, daughter of the blacksmith, who dropped dead on the kitchen floor in her last hemorrhage. But this would be the chronicle of Bolton, not of the Locomotive-God. And, during these years that concern this chapter, though I often sat on the upturned nail-keg, I had not then realized at all the inexhaustible treasures of humanity about me. Tragedy, Comedy, and eloquent Commonplace. Here was God's plenty, as Dryden said of the Canterbury Pilgrims. The realest people, all in all, I have ever known were the Bolton villagers . . . or is it simply that a village four miles from the railroad is the only spot now left in the Western World where we can get near enough to people, and long enough, to know how real they are. That in part, but in part, too, such a village gives human nature its best chance to become individualized and real, in a world more and more *en masse* and standardized.

There was one old man who never went to the blacksmith shop. He never went anywhere. He sat all a summer's day in the cottage porch behind the woodbine, all a winter's in a little study bedroom, on the ground floor before his wood-stove . . . reading the Psalms in Hebrew and Plato in Greek . . . or the "Odyssey" . . . or Sophocles. With his widowed daughter who had married late, and Ella the golden child. He had been the village pastor a generation before, during the Civil War, after he had been dismissed, as an Abolitionist, from the Unitarian pulpit of witch-hanging Salem. He had come into this world three years before Emerson, and graduated from Bowdoin College a year before Hawthorne and Longfellow had matriculated. At ninety-three and four he was certainly one of the most extraordinary creations of spirit and flesh since the human race began. Old Age was never more awesome, more beautiful. A quiet little man, but unbent, with ruddy cheeks, and narrowed eyes still bright and cheery behind their moistness, under the lids that were closing but had not yet closed; with a thin crinkly beard and long iron-gray tresses unshorn over his shoulders. Scholar, Saint, Prophet.

Dr. Thomas Treadwell Stone was the last of the Tran-
scendentalists. His name will be found in old books about
the movement, as O. B. Frothingham's History; his initials
in his own small scholar's hand will be found under some
articles in his copies of Emerson's "Dial" along with the
initials of the other contributors, unknown even to scholars
to-day. An old volume of his sermons, "The Rod and the
Staff," may still be picked up in the dark back shelves of
Boston's second-hand book-stores. But he was one who
worked chiefly through others. You will find, if you know
what I know, Dr. Stone in Emerson's Essays, in Hawthorne's Stories, in Whittier's Poems, in all the prosemen
and poets of the Great New England Period. And I would
like to think that my friends will find something of him in
my own books. He was the one intimate friend that the
seventeen-year-old boy had in Bolton. His one bodily in-
firmity, except for a slow and cautious step and the drowsiness that sent him to bed at eight o'clock (with "Good
night, my children," to all the folks in the parlor, though
aged sixty and seventy years), was his extreme deafness,
which he mitigated by no adequate apparatus. But so long
as I could frame tolerably astute questions, distinctly and
loudly enough for him to hear, his deafness did not matter.
It was for him to talk, not for me. One question was often
enough to start a whole afternoon. If I had had the enterprise of Boswell or young Edward Bok, I could have written out and marketed his talks. Talks about Washington,
just as he had in his own boyhood questioned the veterans
of the Continentals; about the *Constitution* and the *Guer-
rière,* Waterloo, Monroe Doctrine, Missouri Compromise,
Monterey, John Brown—like authentic interviews with the
dead beyond the unforded River. Vivid in concrete detail,
and in the settings of a philosophy of history. Advice on
study: "The secret of learning a language is perpetual review." Talks about Shelley, talks about his talks with Dana
the elder, on Byron before Byron himself had died. Critical
comparisons between the "Æneid" and "Paradise Lost."

Arguments for the unity of the "Iliad." The eternal message of Plato. The significance of Coleridge's prose for the New England Transcendental Movement. Talks about walks with Emerson to visit Thoreau at Walden . . . about a two hours' ride in a closed carriage with the shy and cloaked Hawthorne where there was no talk at all. Talks about Emerson's talks with him about Thomas Carlyle . . . regret over his one disagreement with "the good man Emerson"—on the matter of translations versus the originals: "Yes, I would tell Emerson there is no knowing Greeks without knowing Greek." With Whittier he always used the Quaker speech, but was careful, he said, to improve the Quaker grammar,—"thee," but not "thee" when it should be "thou." He was fond of reminiscent anecdotes about eccentric obscure folk whose bodies were sixty years under the sod . . . old college teachers, old-time parishioners, or fellow-pastors. Fond of anecdotes about himself —how, for instance, on his parish rounds in the bibulous and social thirties, he had to resort to ruses to avoid too many sips of the cup which cheers because it inebriates. He would begin with a ventriloquist chuckle, as if the far echo of the mirthful noise of the original comedy; then his body would begin to shake, as if the old ribs would spring loose from the spine, and the tears would stream down his cheeks; and then at last the outburst of good laughter, yes, with some resonance, not an old man's cackle. I subsequently rimed one of these anecdotes, and it made my first poem in legitimate print, "Parson Moody's Prayer," in the "Century's" "Lighter Vein," sometime in 1899. He never repeated himself, never lost the threads of narrative or reasoning. Nothing could perturb him . . . he was at one with the Universe of Plato and Emerson, one with Pervading Spirit. I saw him in autumnal dusk lying on his back on the boardwalk between cottage porch and street gate. I ran in, thinking him dead. He said apologetically: "I came out to look at the moon, and I lost my balance." And he was still looking at the moon . . . cane fallen beside him

. . . time enough for somebody to pick him up . . . sitting or standing or lying, what difference did it make between him and the Oversoul? He left the gate just once. The Worcester Conference of Unitarian Parishes was meeting at Bolton. My father guided his steps up the adjacent hill, through the portico, into the lofty pulpit. He gave his last public message . . . standing . . . without notes . . . with Isaiah's seraphic coal touching his lips. Perhaps three hundred heard him, country parsons and delegates and Boltonites, as compared with the thirty or fifty millions who have listened in to Coolidge or Bryan— the Rotarians, Fundamentalists, Republicans, and Democrats. What has greatness to do with fame in a world incapable of knowing and using greatness? Noise is for the noisy . . . and the noisy are the world. A year before our coming to Bolton, he had made his last voyage out into the contemporary earth. It was to Bowdoin's commencement, as the oldest alumnus, as the sole survivor of the class of 1820. . . . As he told me about it, I thought that Longfellow's "Morituri Salutamus" somehow lost something of its venerable pathos and dignity. When back home during my freshman year in college, I shouted to him as best I could something of my *vita nuova,* for he wanted to know all about it. Then one day he said to my father, "I feel as if some one were taking the light away from me." My foreboding father came home, himself whiter-haired than Dr. Stone, with troubled eyes. So Goethe had said, *"Mehr licht* —the light, the light!" He lay in bed only three days. He wanted to see me. I came. An eighteen-year-old college freshman. He had a solemn message for me, on his back, half-rising from the pillows. For me, not for my father, or for Emerson. Clear-headed, clear-spoken, resolute, majestic, but deluded by a cruel echo in his brain. People, he thought, were defaming him; for the first time in ninety-four years mankind was questioning his integrity. He would not, he could not, bring himself to say what. But: "When I am dead, Ellery, go to Bowdoin, go to President Hyde—

149

I am leaving Bowdoin my library—go and tell him it is all a lie, a lie, a lie. Tell him that, for all these seventy-four years, I have never done or said anything to shame my alma mater." I tell Bowdoin, I tell all the colleges and universities of the land. Has Bowdoin such loyal lovers to-day . . . has Harvard, has Wisconsin? . . . To live ninety-four years in spiritual peace . . . only to die in spiritual torment. Man can be greater than any god I have heard tell of. . . . After his death, I picked up his Teubner text of "Iliad" and "Odyssey" bound together, a gift of his son on his seventieth birthday. It contained the entries of his re-reading of Homer in the past twenty-four years when for most men the fires are dying in the grate, or already dead. There were twenty-five entries. I own his pocket Vergil.

Such a friend, alone, it would seem should have borne me up. Not if the reader thinks twice. Much spiritual and intellectual good was stored away for the future years; but under those conditions, in spite of his extraordinary vitality, the nonagenarian was not the companion for a lad. Adolescence, more than any years earlier or later, needs its own kind. He was to my subconsciousness one more reminder of the grave; and I was more and more expecting to die young and soon. I had been to the village doctor early in the winter for a new thing—a bad heart. He called it nervous palpitation, and I believed him. I tried to get more exercise—chopping wood for our primitive stoves, skating with the little girls or taking them sledding, going up the street for the mail with my lantern on moonless nights, exercising (per schedule) with dumb-bells, chinning myself (per schedule) on a cross-bar in my doorway. I took my measurements. Six years ago I happened to find the memorandum. I measured myself again. After more than a quarter of a century, absolutely the only differences were in my right biceps and forearm—I had lost one fourth of an inch in the one, and a half in the other. But by that time I had ceased worrying about my physique. However, one can worry over nervous palpitation, and I did. I knew well enough that chronic nervous palpitation is itself a diseased condition. I knew that my low tonality was abnormal, though I did not realize that my extraordinary intellectual drive indicated a deep-seated vitality. I worried most over sex-conditions. A worse setting for the development of adolescent sex could hardly be invented by the devil himself. All the normal sublimations of wholesome objectivity in sport and companionships with both sexes of my own years were impossible; and much was in the situation to over-stimulate. It is a fool's mistake to suppose that brain-work *per se* destroys sex. It is a fool's mistake to suppose that youth can walk off its sex. Study and walking may feed sex, lonely study with its aftermath of fantasies, lonely walks with their company of fantasies. I was abnormally sex-conscious. It was not love-mooning; it was just raw sex. But I was not a peril to the rural virgins. Nature, dis-torted nature, avenged herself upon me in sleep. Even though no longer completely at the mercy of the patent-medicine almanac, I felt with profound gloom that I was not right. I am not dependent on casual reminiscence or even on the recalls of auto-psychoanalysis. An old diary is before me—in all its miserable morbidity—where, along with my reading and exercising, I chronicle from day to day my sex, my palpitations, my depressions, my broken sleep, my attempts at cure:

Sat. Aug. 11, '94. Am trying Horseford's Acid Phosphate for a change.

What were my parents thinking about all this time? Is there not irony in this lame conclusion to the careful train-ing in childhood, to the old solicitude for my education and character? I don't know their thought. But there was no money; my mother had to undergo a serious operation in a Boston hospital; they were more and more now trusting God's providence; they had problems more defined in con-nection with my sister; they felt I was shifting for myself —as oblivious, apparently, of the nature of adolescence, as they had been in general actively and practically awake to the nature of childhood. And I never told them anything to the purpose. But they did what they could. They gave me a trip to my schoolmates in Plainfield the second spring. I was eighteen. Circumstances had never permitted a long journey alone before. Had the abnormal conditions of the past year (which, while emphasizing my intellectual self-reliance, had undermined my self-reliance toward people and the world) shaken loose any of the buried phobias? I recall without psychoanalysis a few significant items. Two or three times in remote and silent twilight, when several miles from the house, cross-country afoot or down a strange road, on a borrowed bicycle, I had experienced momentary moods of the terrors of *isolation;* of immeasurable distance from home; and remarked them at the time as alien, calling them symptoms of "my nervous condition" (see Diary, *passim*). These states, I now know, were associated with the initial isolation-motif at the railroad-station; indeed one at least was set off by a train-whistle; but in their form they were casual prophecies of the form it was to take many years later, rather than repetitions of the old form in the first fright, which indeed had already been given a modification in this direction by the school fright of 1885. I was, however, still a long way from chronic phobias. The trip by rail to Boston and Fall River and by boat down the Sound, to-day (and for fifteen years) exactly as unthinkable as a walk along a steel girder thirty-five stories in air on lower Broadway, or an airplane ride to the Pole, was made with exultant expectation and almost hysterical expansiveness in the burst of freedom and power. I walked the upper deck of the *Puritan* in the salt winds of an April night, with stars twinkling above and shore-lights twinkling either side far away over dark waters. At Point Judith the great Atlantic, known from all-day Jersey picnics to Ocean Grove, rocked us from the east, and I chanted my "Childe Harold." And when I went to bed in a bunk with the rest who could not afford state-rooms, it was to sleep with a fresh security in life. I would give much that a man of fifty prizes most dearly to be able to make that trip when April next comes by.

The two weeks' visit at Henry's with Mary (not the original Mary), back from Smith on vacation, and with all that fine family, was of course a new lease of life. I forgot that I was about to perish from nervous palpitation and sapped manhood. I showed off my year's progress in learned lore. I was full of the old pranks. Fred and I happened to read together "The Rape of the Lock." This put an idea into several heads. We incited an amorous swain to try to rape a lock from Effie's chestnut hair—or was it raven? This was the beginning of a series of mysterious "poems by several hands," the two chief authors acting as the two chief detectives in affecting to ferret out the authors. There were so many others who could scribble smooth Popian heroics that I was not *a priori* suspect. Yet it involved finally humiliating a good boyhood friend; and the final lesson for me was ethical, not poetic: to use another's personality for your sport is only less unworthy than to use it for your preferment. I learned it a little earlier than some. Otherwise, I took back only joy from those two weeks . . . except for the Homer class. They had taken me to the Homer class. I had a book . . . I could follow, but, oh, so haltingly. Fred, whom I had always outshone, if only a little, in Xenophon, was translating those Ionic datives in εσσιν, those un-Attic infinitives in μεναι, as easily as if they were those Attic imperfect singular middles that went last year with all the parasangs of the first book of the "Anabasis." I must indeed have been a queer Dick—you will say, perhaps—to sit in a class-room in Greek with a breaking heart because my fate robbed me of a chance to sit there the week after. . . .

The week after. On a leaf of the Diary I find this:

Once more among the hills and yet once more.
Once more removed from busy haunts of men—

My solitude is happier than before.
For I have mingled with my kind again . . .

and so on to the end of the stanza. Any one who can't give
the rime-scheme of the rest is no competent reader of this
chapter. In the next stanza I feel

> The freshening wind
> That drives the cloud and bends the apple-bough.

I was sitting in Andy Simpson's orchard under an astra-
khan-tree. A real seat, a real day, a real situation, a real
mood, but only three words that sound real. . . . Which
three? There is no proof of unreality in imitation; but the
only proof of reality is straight talk of one's own make.

My solitude is happier than before.

But not for long. The poignancy of separation and frustration is more acute than ever. Phœbe is appointed valedictorian. I write her a merry letter of congratulations . . .
my disappointment was not jealousy. She understands.
Nearly all the boys and girls are going to college in the
fall . . . Philip to Harvard, Fred to Amherst, Esther to
Vassar . . . or into business in New York. All are to be
going on, full of power and confidence. During the summer
my father writes some letters of inquiry to old college
friends . . . expenses, opportunities. He shakes his head.
I write for catalogues, and study both entrance requirements and expense-tables—even in those days $350 with-
out the tuition was the lowest figure. Impossible. I get a
set of Harvard entrance examinations. I arrange hours to
simulate the busy Cambridge sessions of the boys up from
Phillips Exeter or Roxbury High. I take the examinations.
I correct them. I know that I pass, all except geometry and
Homer. The hardest examinations in the country at that

time. I pass. But what of it? I study the catalogues—Amherst, Brown, Dartmouth, Williams—for their enticing accounts of opportunities for self-help . . . tutoring, table-serving, furnace-tending, gardening, part-time clerking, lawn-tending, dish-washing: all the college-towns are on the jump to get such services; college students alone solve the labor-shortage; and they are always preferred, being always so bright, willing, and honest. . . . Some of these things I could have done; but how to get them to do? How to dare to ask, to dare to do? And how to do them, when study itself was the thing to be done? If I was practically no go-getter when I left Plainfield, I was now as socially timid, as economically ineffectual, as a child of eight years. The long months in Bolton had undermined whatever energies of self-support there might have been latent in my character. I could pass the Harvard entrance examinations; but the very thought of asking for a job frightened me. It was, I believe, a mild form of phobia, and allied to the phobic timidities of these later years; a neurotic condition in any case, and indubitably allied to the abnormal existence of the preceding years. For the first time in life I really want to die . . . or the conscious part of me thinks I do.

A business man, a friend from the Plainfield Unitarian Society, who has just moved to Boston, visits us in the village during the first week in September. Perhaps he had heard of my miseries. Perhaps my father has sent for him. In all my conjectures, there is always the possibility that my father did more than I knew. For he was a silent man, a tragically unpretending man . . . just like his own father, Uncle Oliver used to tell me. Mr. Nichols takes me back with him to spend two weeks at his home in Roxbury. The change, he says, will do me good; and he wants to try me out in a new business venture of his. He has backed a new patent window-ventilator. With a sample under my arm, I am to canvass from house to house about Roxbury, demonstrating by opening the sash (assuming the housewife opens the door), inserting the sample, taking the measurements, and taking—the order. All very easy. And easy money. What good to say "no"? What good to say "yes"? So I get out of Bolton. . . .

IX

THE Nicholses are kind people. There is something to the change. There is something in the fact that I can ring a door-bell and explain my errand. Not quite as hard as asking for a job. I even sell a ventilator or two—though presumably more by the eloquence of shabby clothes and plaintive timidity than of expert salesmanship. After a week's canvassing, I take a day off to see Boston. I check in the guide-book the places of interest that are free to the public. One is "Massachusetts Genealogical Society, 12 Somerset St." I'm led thither from Faneuil Hall and the Old State House and King's Chapel and the Old North Church, out of curiosity to verify the family descent made out for me by Uncle Oliver. Uncle Oliver had what he called a hobby. Aside from fire insurance and Baptist Church clerkship, he copied the inscriptions in the ancient cemeteries and he pored over old deeds and old maps and old family letters of Northern New Jersey's colonial settlers. He had one large room the four walls of which were full of filing-cases, alphabetized in contents. He called it a hobby; but he had in both knowledge and method the equipment of an historical scholar. He wrote for technical periodicals now and then; but he studied more than he wrote . . . inverting the activities of some contemporary professors of history—and other subjects. I get to 12 Somerset, off to the side of the New State House, up from Tremont and Park Street. About eleven o'clock in the morning.

I have cursed compositors for their misprints; but there is one unknown compositor whom I would bless. He made the biggest difference anything ever made in my life

. . . except the Locomotive-God. 12 Somerset was not the
headquarters of the Genealogists (the number should have
been 18), but of the College of Liberal Arts of Boston
University—a façade of red brick, with registrar's office
to the left off the corridor of the ground floor. I saw my
mistake; but I got a melancholy thrill out of entering and
asking for a catalogue. A friendly man behind the grille
leaned forward to question me. "Coming to B. U.?" "No,
just looking around." I had sold a ventilator to a man last
week who had questioned me in the same way and recom-
mended his alma mater B.U. as a poor man's college. "Why
not try us?" as he shoves out the catalogue. "I haven't any
money." "Lots of boys here in the same boat . . . I want
you to run upstairs and talk to the dean." Let the reader
make up the gestures and interplay of features. I'm not
making up this dialogue. My memory is as certain as a
phonographic plate. Not a word about my credits, my
credentials. "Why not try us?" Mr. Rand smiled. All
registrars smile . . . but Mr. Rand with a difference. All
registrars smile; it is their business . . . so do dentists.
Mr. Hiestand, nearly a generation our registrar at Wisconsin, smiled . . . for years in the outer office, then for
years in the inner. One unflinching smile from 9 to 5, especially during the last week in September, as the bewildered
boys and girls, just up from Baraboo, Oshkosh, Eau Claire,
Sauk, Fond du Lac, Jug Prairie, or Vilas County filed by.
"Sorry, you lack two entrance credits in math" . . . "Sorry,
your school has been dropped from the accredited list". . .
"Sorry, you'll have to take special entrance examinations in
history and French to-morrow.". . . But the same unflinching smile along in May, when the other boys and girls,
hard-boiled seniors, hoping to graduate in June, file by.
"Sorry, but your class-adviser should have seen to it that
you absolved those two credits in modern languages". . .
"Sorry, but I can't count these credits in German—you have
three above the maximum". . . "Sorry, but you have not
made up that condition in Mr. Leonard's Anglo-Saxon; and

you'll have to stay to summer-school." Good, loyal, well posted, long-suffering, and ever smiling Mr. Hiestand has smiled his last smile here. I wonder if as he got to the Heavenly Gates (for he must have been headed that way), St. Peter smiled and said: "Sorry, but you're short two credits in Flexibility and two more in Interpretation-of-the-Rules-of-the-game-of-Life." Or will he let him in for that remorseless sense of duty to an academic ritual after all not of his devising and for that—remorseless smile.

I went upstairs. The dean was out; but his associate got enough from me to insist I come back the next day. I came. The dean, Dr. Huntington, afterward president, heard my story. "I want to talk with your father." My father comes up from Bolton. We three sit together. He verifies my story, adding details. He knew more about my doings than I had thought. Dr. Huntington says: "We want you. We offer you a scholarship; you can enter on your two-year credits from Plainfield, and pass off the other requirements at the fall or spring specials." Apparently my story had hit him hard. Twenty-five years after, he referred to it in a letter. So I came to college. Four years later I was instructing in Latin at B.U., six years later their traveling fellow in Germany. The rigid gate-keepers of Wisconsin would never have risked such peril to the machinery. I could not have enrolled in Madison. But Wisconsin is vindicated nevertheless—Dr. Huntington was a graduate of Wisconsin.

My parents called it Divine Guidance. . . . Others good luck, or chance. Words. Realistic analysis readily discovers that the determining factor was the set of mind . . . from years before. So it is in all that we call Guidance or Chance. The enormous welter of life, the infinite, interlacing series of events with infinitely varying meanings, in infinitely multiplied details, is round us all as we walk along and wind our way hither and thither on the teeming, surging earth. If I had been walking Boston that morning, dreaming of becoming a bridge-builder, I would presumably have "chanced" on something to the purpose about

159

bridges. We select our means as well as our ends. A thousand other chances were round about me, waiting their man, for a thousand other dreams . . . but I passed them by. Very possibly there were other misprints that might have led others to other doors, but not me; certainly of the other thousands that had read that misprinted numeral 12 in the guide-book, not more than two or three had been led to seek out the Genealogical Society; and certainly no one of the two or three had, on getting to the wrong door, stopped there because, with sudden change of interest, they realized it was the right door for them. This is the deep truth of knock and it shall be opened unto you; of seek and ye shall find. But does it always work? I fear not always. One may be moving in the midst of series of events too alien or disrupting; the specific chance may not be there. It may be Hiestand, and not Rand, behind the grille. There is to all realistic analysis of human destiny the element of hit or miss. But the central idea, the invigorating thought for creative living in a world where we are too prone to surrender our acts to the Will of God or the Sport of Fate or the Cruelty of Society is that chance means simply *your* chance. You take a chance; you also partly make a chance; and you end, if you are a man, by making something out of the chance. Perhaps it all comes to that: here is an individual center of creative energy of specific direction. There yonder are the interlacing series. Pick out your item, your chance. I said an individual of specific direction; but every individual has actually more than one direction, and potentially many more. If he doesn't find one chance, he finds another. Creatively he will find another . . . or he dies. And he makes of that other something that becomes his. In my own career, apparently so peculiarly hampered in commanding its own destiny, early and late, I seem to have traced a peculiarly striking example of external and accidental situations, that is, of myself embarrassed in the midst of relatively alien or hostile series of events, which altered my whole subsequent history . . . but altered it in ways ulti-

mately created by me, that is, by the turn my creative
energy gave to the situations. Creative freedom means having a purposive spirit, but complex and plastic enough for
several purposes, and making the most (a wise phrase) of
what you can pick out most adapted to one or another of
your natural purposes from a world not constructed in itself
either for your benefit or your bane. In this sense, realistic
and without rhetoric, a man may be master of his fate. So
far as I see, in this sense only . . . unless I am to believe
the success-mongers of the full-page advertisements.
Chance, as *the* chance, as *my* chance; chance as source-ma-
terial and point of departure for creative freedom, is one
of the secondary motifs that run through this story of the
Locomotive-God. It runs through many life-stories whether
the protagonists know it or not.

My father gave me ten dollars, hoping soon to give
more. I installed myself in a cellar-room at a dollar a week.
Off the basement-kitchen of a lodging-house kept by a poor
widow of old American stock . . . in fact my mother's
elder sister, who, in the smash-up of the family due to
the Civil War, had not had my mother's opportunity to live
with the rich husband of her father's sister. I did not believe for an instant that I could remain in college long. But
if only long enough to see what college was like . . . if
only till Christmas. That was the beatific vision . . . till
Christmas . . . one whole term. The first days were indeed a strange dream. The college had no campus, no ath-
letics. No morning sun over elmy walks, no twilights behind gray ivied towers, no Venetian nights over any lake
with lanterns and rockets, no bonfires after home-coming
victories. But I had never envisaged college in such wise.
Another Light, another Fire. College was professors,
books, lectures, recitations (now even to be my recitations),
examinations, students. College was study. College was the
great vista into the past, into the future . . . of man, of
nature. The interminable corridors, upstairs and down,
went by doorways of chambers dedicated to Homer, to

Horace, to Shelley, to Washington and Lincoln, to Goethe and Heine, to Egypt, to astronomy. Wandering about before my first classes with now one, now another, of the forty or so new boys who (with about eighty girls) made up the entering class, mostly from the small towns of Cape Cod and the Massachusetts littoral, I saw this Prophet and that Prophet ascending or descending the stairs, each with his green bag and exalted countenance, the forefront of mysteries within. An affable upper-classman, on the lookout for rushees, but himself to me (naïvely oblivious) only a little less majestic than the Prophets, approaches, as Vergil approached Dante on the threshold of another world, and points out the mighty spirits. "That's old Buck —he used to be head master of the Roxbury Latin School —teaches Greek, great on Socrates, ornery old chap. But easy to get under his skin. . . ." (He died at ninety-odd in Germany during the World War beside his German Frau.) "That's Bowne . . . Harvard and Yale wanted him . . . the greatest philosopher since Aristotle." (Dead.) "That's young Billy Warren, with the mustache, son of President Warren—teaches math—look out for him, he's stiff.". . . (Warren is now dean of the C.L.A.) "That's Lindsay, the Latin prof, awfully genial . . . dresses well . . . wise guy though. Belongs to the Century Club. Only prof at B.U. who smokes." (Dead.) "That's Perrin, German . . . he's American but talks it in his sleep . . . likes beer, they say . . . new methods . . . won't work you too hard." (Still there.) That darkish bustling little chap?—"Geddes. Has all the Romance languages in his pate—no wonder he looks scared. . . . Gets medals from Europe." (There still, and still getting them.) This was college. Probably only once before in my life had life seemed so marvelous and strange, so thrilling an intellectual, a human experience . . . only once before . . . when I stood on the station-platform looking about me ere the Locomotive-God came forth. Perhaps only once before in the life of Western Civilization was the love of learning a more absorbing passion than mine . . . when from beyond Alp and North Sea came the thousand ragged lads to Abelard and built the Paraclet. Father . . . Uncle Oliver . . . Dr. Kendrick . . . college . . . collegian. I'm simply telling an honest story; not propagandizing for outworn sentiments, as *laudator temporis acti*. And so I'll match it with another honest story. A few years ago, I overtook on Breese Terrace an eighteen-year-old who was gazing college-ward with perhaps as much inward vibration and longing as ever I. Off yonder down in Camp Randall the football squad was at practice under the golden October afternoon. I have an absent-minded habit of addressing any one who looks interesting; but besides, as an old Wisconsin professor, all the boys are mine to talk to. "This your first year, I suppose?" "Yes, sir." "Never mind; it's no sin to be a frosh. . . . Know the game—going in for football?" "Gee, I hope I can. Gee, that field over there's just what you read about. Gee, *that's* college."

In a cellar-room at a dollar a week. Breakfast, oatmeal, badly cooked by myself; suppers, bananas (ten cents a dozen from the street vender) ; dinners, beans in Pie Alley (ten cents). By two weeks half sick of course. My father came down. Oliver Wendell Holmes had died the night before, and my father and I left cards on the Beacon Street door-step. I did not ring and ask for an autograph. The Beta Theta Pi boys had wanted me, in spite of my worn-out suit, and at my father's request let me room with one of the pledged boys, at $1.25 a week, in expectation of my pledging later. My father gave me twenty-five dollars. The Vermont boy and I arranged to have eating utensils and oil-stove sent us from home, and cooked passably nutritious breakfasts and suppers, from milk-bottles and canned goods, with a box now and then from up-country. Our dinners, by meal-ticket, cost seventeen cents. The Vermont boy was drowned the first year out of college in trying to rescue a girl. His name was Ernest Perry. I lived during the college year on $156. The scholarship covered only tuition.

Henry's father in North Plainfield, as president of the Board, bought ventilators for a school-house, by mail-order. Other Plainfield residents suddenly desired fresh air without dust and drafts in their private homes. One or two B.U. professors too. My ventilator commissions amounted to $50. I sold a "feature article" to a New York paper, how an American merchant, a resident of old Bolton, had negotiated for Napoleon's escape as his valet to America after Waterloo. I acquired four gold pieces, in literary prizes offered by the "Beacon," the college paper, which I was to edit in my senior year. And I wrote to my thrifty Aunt Cornelia, telling her about my college studies and my economies —leaving it entirely for her to draw the hoped-for conclusions. Uncle Oliver wrote my father with amusement that something would surely come of Aunt Cornelia's troubled state of mind. Something did—an appreciative letter and six pocket-handkerchiefs. I was amused too . . . but when, in my senior year, she was laid away and her shawls and shanties distributed according to the will, I inherited $500 "with which to finish college." Uncle Oliver's amusement over my supposedly astute letter brought me twenty-five dollars from him . . . he was always the funny man.

Meantime the news had been taken, by friendly Boltonians, to rich Mr. Thayer of Lancaster Village, whose hobby was helping (by gift, not loan) ten boys a year through college. He put me on his list for $200 a year the next fall. I earned a little—by haying in Bolton, by literary hack-work in Boston, etc.—but it was Mr. Thayer, a stranger, who put me through college. My expenses even in the more opulent living of an upper-classman were far below the minimum in the catalogues. Except for perhaps five fraternity banquets, twenty-five cents was the most I ever paid for a meal —then only on an occasional Sunday. For raiment, I watched the fire-sales. But youth, supported by surrounding youth, and by the work and hope of its heart, can stand much roughing it, without knowing. For long I felt some humiliation in this help. I might have exchanged humiliation for self-help. My phobic dread of asking for a job had disappeared; and jobs, I suppose, could have been had for the asking. Some of my classmates had jobs. But the craving to own my time for the intellectual quest overrode humiliation. I am glad it did. In my shame I was the victim of our conventional ethics: in such a case the only humiliation would be to misuse the help. I did not misuse it. I can say that. I returned Mr. Thayer his principal and his interest in the specie of his own spiritual kingdom. And if Mr. Thayer helped me, I helped Mr. Thayer. If one is going to college with all his soul, he cannot earn his way. To have to, is only a blessing in so far as man, from his very youth on, instinctively insists on wringing some good out of limitation and misfortune. But it is at best a blessing for character; I have never known a self-supporting, earnest student in college who was not thereby robbed of something which the college was there primarily to give him, and which he was there primarily to receive. The fact that this opinion runs so contrary to current American opinion is readily explained: aside from the concealed implication that making money (even a little) is the first duty of man, to current American opinion college-work has lost the depth and the scope of its ideal meaning. So long as laying the foundations of a business acquaintance, acquiring a smattering of knowledge and technique for a degree and a job, trivially broadening one's social experience, and training one's executive or political talent by managing class vaudeville or jockeying class elections, are considered the essential purpose of a college education, a boy can, to be sure, earn his way through. He'll have plenty of time too for pool and poker and necking. I have been in and about the American college for thirty-odd years. I know . . . better than the Old Grad.

Incidentally, if half of our several hundred colleges closed down and fifty per cent of the undergraduates in the other half were sent home to useful employments about town, the higher education in America might make a solid beginning in experimental democracy: that is, by whole-heartedly concentrating great opportunity where it realis-tically, greatly, counts toward an informed, a dedicated band, trained under only truly informed and dedicated scholars, for authentic leadership and service in letters, arts, science, technic, government, or business too if you will. To-day the college, by and large, even quite aside from ath-letics, seems to me one of the most wasteful illusions of the generous-spirited, self-complacent, American public. I know . . . better than the Old Grad.

Behind the brick façade, on Beacon Hill up from Boston Common and the "Atlantic Monthly" offices, this College of Liberal Arts was in its own small way such an experi-ment. Its enrolment was scarcely four hundred; few of its young men and women were brilliant minds; but fully ninety per cent were dedicated to mind and a career of mind and zealous to master by hard study and hard thinking the world into which they were born and which they hoped to serve. From the band of young men, there in my years, has arisen no major prophet; but a strikingly large percentage became leaders of the good life of humane intelligence in diverse smaller centers of American civilization: leaders in the secondary schools, librarians, modernist clergymen, newspaper editors, college professors. Indeed, of the forty or so men that I knew best, at least fifteen became pro-fessors, and three of them leaders in leading universities. The teachers to a man lived in scholarship, and inspired respect for mind, and a respect for their minds in all of us —and in me indeed so profoundly that to this day, as a scholar myself, I feel the reverberations of our undergradu-ate deference—most uncomfortably, for instance, as I specu-late on the Jupiterial head-shaking with which Bowne would greet my ultimate defection from his metaphysics. Lindsay, though no discoverer in Latin lore, was as good a Latinist, for intimate familiarity with Latin speech and Latin litera-ture, as any I have met on this side of the Atlantic; and his *obiter dicta* on life and letters were the best evidence of the transcendent humanistic function of the classics as taught by a humanist. It was an intimate intramural world, with much talk between the hours, with much loitering after class beside the professors—but the talk itself reached before and after and round about beyond the walls. As in high school, our social interests and activities were offshoots of our class-room. Our athletics consisted of pulling weights and tossing the medicine-ball at the City Y.M.C.A., and of interfraternity baseball on Franklin Field or Boston Common, where my base-throwing was still, however, the feature of the game. "The distinguished speakers" that did not come to B.U. came to Boston or lived in Boston, and we heard them all, from Dwight Moody and General Booth, to Henry Cabot Lodge, Edward Everett Hale, Grover Cleveland, and the boy orator of the Platte, already in 1896 full of Jehovah. Those were the days too of the Boston Symphony Orchestra and noontide oratorios, the delight even of ears as untrained as mine. There were the theaters: their rush seats to Nigger Heaven, my pass all one winter to the first balcony of the Castle Square, my personal contacts as fellow-actor with Irving and Terry— as the one supernumerary intelligent enough in appearance to be assigned a vocal part (three groans as First Knight of the Round Table, with glance averted from the kneeling Guinevere). There was Boston's Art Gallery. Boston University was to me Boston in a far more cultural intimacy than later Columbia was New York to me. I caught the spirit of the City, of the crowd with its mysterious individual fates, of the organization of society *en masse* into institutions, with their external symbolizations in colonnades, domes, hotels, spires, counting-houses, railway stations, wharves, ships, markets, and monuments of National Effort, the obelisk of Bunker Hill across the river, the statue of Channing by the Public Gardens, the Shaw Memorial. I caught the spirit of the city, as I had caught, or was now catching, in my Bolton summers of lonely study

167

and lonely walks in an aloneness no longer lonely, more and more of the spirit of the Country.

And just as I projected Robert Frost for rural New England, I projected Sandburg for Boston, and before I had read Whitman. My scholar's ambition to know and to interpret, was then, as long before and still longer after, companioned by the poet's ambition to show and to interpret: and, unawares, this poet's ambition was stirring in three realms: the city with its State House on the hill, the village with its orchard and oaks on the hill, the individual with his passions and struggles trying to climb another hill than Boston's or Bolton's. Frost for our period did the village, though not Bolton; Sandburg did the city, though not Boston; and it may be that, when all the estimates are in, America will discover that in my own no less authentic speech I have done for our period the individual, though not the Roosevelt or Bryan or Wilson, though not the Ford or Gary. Or am I still in effect the twenty-year-old that used to dream complacently on a bench in Boston Common; who would say to himself as the unregarding populace passed by (bootblacks, newsies, shop-girls, blue-stockings, lawyers, policemen, clerks, and financiers, each to subway or an easement-station) : "O thoughtless generation, little do you realize that he who broods on this bench, with thumb and forefinger under his chin, and elbow on his left crossed knee, and eye on yonder pebble, is none other than one of the three or four, probably the greatest of the three or four, American Poets of the Next Age." Robert Frost and Carl Sandburg, we are all three in the early fifties together; and so we must have been in the early twenties together—what were you two thinking about in those pregnant days? You have both since then learned a more racy, a more valid American idiom than mine; I talk still, even as bard, too much, they say, like a professor. I admit my idiom is nearer the tradition from the isles overseas, even from the isles of Greece, and not so readily perceived to be mine. Yet mine it is (say I, still dreaming on

the park bench) ; but, as the idiom of the Individual with
its passions and struggles up that other hill, it has been
learned not so much from America as from the race, especially from those who have attempted that hill through the
centuries . . . as Sophocles, Dante, Milton, Wordsworth,
Byron. Yet, "reviewers and anthologists," admit you must
that there are a few turns and monosyllables at least in my
"Lynching Bee" that would have shocked all the Old Masters, sufficient reason for my disappointed hope that it
might please you. It would seem there is no escaping the
odium scholasticum. But worse than that: while the littéra-
teurs want to discredit my poesies because a professor's,
some professors want to discredit my scholarship because
a poet's. Man has not yet learned that a man is to be
appraised as a man. . . .

My school-boy project to become a college teacher of
the Greco-Roman civilization was less and less a dream,
more and more organically integrated with my actions and
environment, and with a tenable future. I passed off most
of my probation-subjects (Cicero, "Anabasis," etc.) at the
"October Matinée." These special examinations in the
fall were from two o'clock to six, open to all comers. The
student went to the proctor's desk for his special papers
and set to work. I did four papers that afternoon, in my
flurry not realizing that each student had two hours to a
paper. This made an unexpected hit. So I was permitted to
defer the examinations in the "Iliad" and entrance French
till after I had taken courses in the "Odyssey" and in Advanced French. The school, you see, had no sort of discipline. I was four years under Lindsay, with Sanskrit in my
senior year. All the Greek at B.U. after the sophomore year
was under the Socratic Buck, and, though I remained his
young friend, I did not remain his pupil, but I am not about
to prepare an alibi for *lacunæ* in my Greek scholarship. Its
lacunæ are due to preoccupations, not to good old Buck's
grouches. No teacher has sufficient sinister power to block
intellectual desire if there is any vitality and independence

169

in the desirer: I went on with Greek by myself and have read Greek off and on all my life ever since. Our recalcitrant spoon-fed undergraduates, however, continue to identify the possibility of knowledge with courses in the curriculum: "I never studied 'The Tempest' because I never *had* Shakspere." And actual knowledge in the courses they have had is to them knowledge for the course, not for intelligence. They talk about an absolved course as if it were a children's disease: "they've *had* it." Yes, and like a children's disease, they've got safely over it.

The Greco-Roman civilization was my main theme; but I wanted to know it in its setting of all civilization. And, besides, other themes had their own independent challenge —economics, philosophy, history, modern languages. I seldom elected courses in English literature, and then usually to get the professor's point of view and a résumé of materials already familiar, as indeed was sometimes the case with other subjects, even Latin—I had read Juvenal before I "had" Juvenal. Our science courses, except astronomy and mathematics, were at that time given at the Massachusetts Institute of Technology, at a distance and a time usually for me very inconvenient, but the course in geology started me on a lifelong hobby, and scientific reading and affiliation with eminent men of science among my colleagues at Wisconsin or visiting at Wisconsin has probably been the equivalent of several "introductory courses" in this or that, biology and anthropology, for instance. I think I am by nature artist more than scholar, if there is any significance to the data I have captured from my own instinctive emotional reactions; for instance, a misprint that distorts the beauty of my sonnet uniformly causes a far deeper distress than one that distorts the facts or ideas in my learned monograph. But I am not so sure that I am by nature humanist (scholar) more than scientist. In my special field, linguistics and metrics, the two are merged. In psychology likewise. I know that my interest in the sciences never flags, and that it is not merely the common lay interest in the gen-

eral results; it begins with search and method. But, aside
from the four years' investigation that lies back of this
book, my experiments have been vicarious; as on visits to
Guyer and Loevenhart; and the chief regret of my intellectual experience is that I have never had any laboratory-
work . . . and no field-work beyond measuring Indian
mounds and grubbing up skeletons, arrow-heads, celts, and
other artifacts on the borders of the lakes of Southern Wisconsin, with Charles Brown, curator of the State Historical Society Museum, in those years when I was free to roam
the goodly earth. The scientific interest certainly antedates
with me the humanistic: I was feeling of "my bones" very
early, and it was a scientific curiosity about a supposed
phenomenon of nature that got me into trouble for life.
And geography appealed to me far more than Jean Inge-
low. I think my preoccupation with humanistic scholarship
rather than with natural science is another illustration of
how we make our chances into our selfhoods. All through
the years, at home, in the grades, in high school, Bolton,
and college, the initial chances for my intellect were dominantly humanistic rather than scientific. Yet the division,
so far as concerns attitude and operation of mind, is superficial: humanism implies the inquiring act of science; science
implies the imaginative act of humanism: both culminate in
man—that is, even Astronomy and Geology are muses, and
it is ultimately for the difference that they make to man that
man listens. And the Germans have one word for both:
humanism and science, both are *Wissenschaft*. And the
artist may absorb either—or both, like Lucretius and Mere-
dith and Shelley and Goethe. We become only in part what
we might; for the rest, what we get the main chance for;
thus when each one of us dies, a hundred unfulfilled selves
die with us . . . and we never know what.

In college mathematics was the only subject to which I
felt repugnance. Miscellaneous reading, however, in bio-
graphy—in Macaulay, Goldsmith, Emerson—flattered my
vanity: the poet couldn't be a mathematician. My imbecile

recitations became eloquent (though sometimes painful) witnesses to a bardic destiny. Yet I was not quite satisfied with my logic here. Moreover, the professor of mathematics had told us that Plato had said over the school of philosophy should be inscribed, "Let no ungeometrical man enter here"; and I did not know then (what the professor apparently did not know either) that Plato was not thinking of propositions to be demonstrated and corollaries to be recited (for in his day was no Euclid) but of spatial figures to be mystically intuited, as symbols of the Platonic entities of spirit, the "ideas." But I did want to be a philosopher. So I worried. I recalled with depression that ominous mark of seventy-five on my arithmetic examination in the grades. I began to speculate on an eventual "psychological defect," and to read books on education. I had many theories. For years afterward, in Schopenhauer and others, I examined the problem of the non-mathematical mind. It could not be identical with the non-philosophic; for the very chap that got an "Excellent" to my "Conditioned," in trigonometry, got in metaphysics a "Conditioned" to my "Excellent" (or was it a Good $+$?)—the very metaphysics which by faculty vote I had been allowed to substitute for a second "Conditioned" in trigonometry. Even long after I was a university professor myself, I felt uneasy about this chapter of my undergraduate life. It was my one intellectual collapse. So, one winter, I tutored in trigonometry a girl here at Wisconsin who had also been conditioned—page by page, doing the exercises and problems a day ahead, using ordinary wits where I had forgotten algebra. I conferred often enough with the professor, who was also the author of the text-book, to know that I was on the right track. Well, though I had once received a second conditioned, my pupil did not. Then at last I lit on the correct explanation: mathematics had not interested me because to me then it was mere sterile manipulation, just tricks (often enough pedantic *reasoning* where the eye already could *see*), with nothing to satisfy my desire to *experience* life and nature, and, not being interested, I scarcely ever *opened* the book. It is not so surprising that I got "conditioned" in trigonometry as that I succeeded in not getting conditioned in solid geometry and college algebra. As soon as mathematics became to me a study of the processes of thought and of the framework of nature, the "psychological defect" disappeared. I was really more of a Platonist than my teacher.

In my senior year, when the streets began shouting "War," I had to make a profound readjustment in my practical universe. War had been something for the detached imagination, something far in the past or far overseas. Now it meant bombardment insurance for Boston, and my own classmates volunteering for a murderous march on their fellow-men. The heroic note was engulfed in the monstrous horror of it all. But to horror succeeded an intellectual interest, tuned to grief and indignation. I soon realized: that economic interests urged and the newspapers fanned the issue; that "something doing" to break the monotony of life's routine was the motif of the patriotic bustle of the populace; that "Remember the *Maine*" was the tribal cry of blood-lust; that the Spain on whom we declared war, whatever the stupidities of her colonial administration, was not the Spain of the nineteenth century (or really of any century), but the Spain of the *negra leyenda* of the Inquisition, the Conquistadores, and the Armada, a Protestant tradition inherited from our Elizabethan ancestors. And such were my comments in the men's study and at the fraternity house, scenes of so many agreeable discussions in the past three years. The answers were: "Lamp-posts for traitors." It was a good propædeutic for 1914–18; and the beginning of a little closer realistic scrutiny of politics and economics. The attack on Charles Eliot Norton made me say this:

America, my country, is there hope?
Thy doric treasuries are piled with gold,

Thy navies ride the oceans; manifold
Thy flags wave o'er white city and green slope.
But in thine ancient senate halls there cope
With thy vast destinies the dull, the bold,
The base; for strength forsakes the tried and old
And party seals the lips that truth would ope.
And up and down the land applause is theirs,
And when one man, the last of all his race,
With eye still fixed upon the eternal, dares
Uplift his voice and point to thy disgrace,
Thy people, heedless of his good gray hairs,
Proclaim the patriot, "traitor" to his face.

The verses were published (I hardly understand how it happened) in the "Boston Transcript" and brought a grateful word from the grieved and stricken old man eloquent. He must have forgiven their bombastic crudity as speech for the sincerity which that crudity, perhaps, did not quite obliterate.

In the sketch of these undergraduate years I have left all the people behind the mists, and pictured only a foreground of library and lecture-halls, and myself as there. People, young and old, with the young of both sexes in jest and earnest there were; but the difference they made to me, as characters in distinction from intellect, was less than that made by the Bolton folk, and, excepting three or four, the mists are thickening between them and me, and the grave has closed over others. And I have never been able to return to the reunions. I have desired simply to emphasize my intellectual zest and the normality of my interests and general tone. I suffered at times from low spirits; I was poor, but that was not it—I made a jest of my rags. My parents were poor; but that was not it—they had house and home and economic security, however humble. I had, I think, acquired a set toward depression from the abnormal adolescence of the earlier Bolton isolation, and was certainly half hungry much of the time. But even so, no one, fellow-student or teacher, would have marked me for some future chronic neurosis, except, presumably, a certain young Polonius, pompous and chary of jest, whom I used to heckle and gird at, under a mask of feigned stupidity. And in my reading in abnormal psychology, I used to say to myself even then: "Thank Heaven, I'm not afflicted with any such crazy wheels in *my* head." I was a somewhat specialized individual, devising my own pranks, following my own leads, ambitious, loquacious, idealistic, enthusiastic, somewhat at loose ends in temper but not asocial or fractious, on the whole getting along with my kind and liking my kind —intellectually and physically (rather than socially) aggressive and self-confident. But, however annoying or absurd in self-conceit, I was certainly not pathological; and the subconscious forces, if compensatory and not merely aboriginal personality, generated no delusions or crotchets, no grisly chronic fits and starts in passion or conduct—nothing that I can check up by the lists in the books—and conceit had much of the time a wholesome companion in its own ironic humor. I never tasted alcohol till years after, and then only as I taste chocolates or olives. Drink, as a vice, is doubtless far oftener the result of disease than the cause: Poe's tragedy was not drink, but a psychic condition that needed, yet could not support, drink. Drink occupies no place in this chronicle. But what of the Locomotive-God, what of old onset and uproar, flight to shelter, and shame before a thousand eyes? Did the bell still ring . . . the locomotive-bell, the recess-bell . . . sunken bells under the sea? Were there any reverberations from the traumas of childhood? I think there were.

During those years in human worlds, in Boston or Bolton, both so friendly, so very friendly, I had still two rows. I am not interested in the picturesque or the picaresque or the ethical moment; and interested in the psychology only for one moment: the overwhelming resentment before attack, even to physical constrictions in throat and chest, out of all proportion either to the occasions, to the respective gentry, or to my normal emotions and conduct.

I noted the phenomena as extraordinary, on reflection
shortly after; and my fraternity brothers thought my
antics all the funnier because so "unlike Leonard." Taken
in connection with similar phenomena later where there can
be no doubt of the specific subconscious memories seeking
expression, these reactions were reactions less to my visible
opponents than to the onset of the Invisible Locomotive-
God and of the Recess-Mob. In twilight sleep I have started
at the vague face on the boiler-front merging into the
vague eye and nose of some one of the Mob of 1911 . . .
Locomotive-God, Locomotive-Jack . . . and have caught
myself dreamwise seeming to shake my fist at the Double
Thing. So it goes with most folks, at one time or another:
they are furious at something they hate from of old and
taking it out on an accidental scamp of the present . . .
not that he may not be a scamp too in his own right,
however.

Psychiatrists speak of the over-reactions in the emotional life of the neurotic, as if characteristic of his whole
emotional life and of all his situations. To judge from
what I know intimately of myself and not entirely superficially of a few neurotic acquaintances, over-reactions are
emotionally specific and to specific situations with precisely
such specific subconscious causes. I over-react to the attack-
situation, but not to many others; and I over-react for the
same reason that used to cause over-reaction to the uproar-
situation. Psychiatrists may well err too in what they judge
to be over-reaction. The apparently same situation may
actually not be the same as between one who reacts normally
and one who over-reacts. The facts themselves may be
different to the *senses;* the neurotic with no ear for pitch
will react to a piano out of tune far more "normally" than
a perfectly robust nervous organization with a fine ear;
they are reacting differently because reacting to different
situations, which are incommensurable. Again, the facts
themselves may be different to *thought.* I will illustrate
from my own experience. A psychopathologist among my

friends insisted that I over-reacted as a typical neurotic, when once in the midst of a public reading I stopped and commented, though with admitted restraint, on the now exceedingly "normal" habit (acquired perhaps from the movies) of people passing in and out during the performance. I reacted simply to a different conception of social art and of social courtesy, prompted by, but thinking not only of, my own annoyance. And there was still another moment, the fact that I was not intimidated like a "normal" person, in speaking my thought. One of the many necessary afflictions of the neurotic is that his neurosis becomes for his fellows the glib explanation of all his acts—even his acts of intelligence and courage.

So too the psychopathologists make egotism the chief of the nerotic's stigmata; whereas the neurotic may be preoccupied with himself, in the same way as a man with cancer in the stomach—each has himself forced upon himself in pain. Or in the same way, for that matter, as the man whose golf is going to pieces—each has an absorbing problem of immediate personal concern. Egotism is often enough a genuine neurotic symptom, but it is quite as often only the inevitable preoccupation with pain and with the problem of getting rid of it. I permit myself this divagation, convinced that the psychoanalysts in discussing neuroses sometimes forget very elementary data of everyday human nature. One or another of them, if he reads this paragraph, will surely discover a "defensory-complex," unable to realize that perhaps the problem of the neurotic, however much it concerns me as a neurotic myself, may concern me likewise as a speculative mind along with other problems of science . . . and unaware that perhaps my first-hand experience of fifteen years may itself be as significant for truth as his own ready-made terminology and stereotyped thinking.

Egotism, anyway, in psychological analysis, is a variable, and may mean several phenomena. Preoccupation with one's self may phrase itself in one or another attitude to the self, to society, to the world; and the diversity in the phrasing is what reveals the character of the ego under examination. If my training and disposition has given me any power to objectify and analyze my own personality at all, it is clear that egotism quite antedates neurosis; and functions in relation to the neurosis precisely in the same way that it had functioned in relation to other factors in my life. Egotism here is not a symptom, a result. But will it be found to be a contributing factor, indeed both in originating and in perpetuating the neurosis? My discussion will have to deal, as best it can, with this ticklish question on a later page.

But reverberations of shame before a thousand eyes and of flight-to-shelter are to be noted too. All through college I never spoke in public, though we had a vigorous debating society that staged once celebrated interstate contests in Faneuil Hall. I managed to deliver the class poem, that was all—with manuscript in hand. I laid my dread to the stage-fright in the high school debate; but it now seems fairly clear that both the social timidity of the earlier Bolton years and the original traumas of childhood reinforced this set toward panic before a crowd. The connection with the original traumas is practically established in the following episode, where the flight-to-shelter motif is present also.

The chief event of my sophomore year, the first experience of my life in a single large coöperative undertaking successfully completed, was the Latin play, of itself worth an honest note. Harvard had given the "Phormio" of Terence, with Terentian elegance; B. U. now announced under Lindsay "The Captives" of Plautus with Plautine abandon and jollity. We worked on our lines, our action, our ensemble for six months, and gave three public performances in the old Bijou Theater, at first before classical audiences from various colleges and schools of New England, and the last chiefly before Boston's own theater-goers lured there for a good evening's laughter, Latin or

178

no Latin, by the reports that went out through the press
and patrons. But nobody had more fun out of it than the
actors, and none of the actors more than I. . . . Of those
roaring boys, with the leading parts, Bell was professor of
history at Olivet (till his death), Churchill was on the
staff of the Library of Congress and is now a professor of
history, Evans is head of the German Department at Ohio
State; Sanborne is ranking professor of philosophy at Van-
derbilt, Bugbee (I understand) pastor of a large church
in Minneapolis, and I professor of English at Wisconsin.
I was *Ergasilus,* the parasite, the cheeky wit, querulously
in search of a dinner about the town whose young dandies
and gourmets are now off in the war; and in the end pran-
dially rewarded by an old man for the information that
relieves the old man's paternal heart and disentangles the
plot. The part had several soliloquies and offered excellent
opportunities for comic make-up and character acting. I
lived it for months . . . in a deeper sense than I knew. I
myself was in effect hungry and ragged, and in effect supported by others in return for my wits. My zestful imaginative management of the part was comic irony toward
my own situation in life. "How does that fellow act off
the stage?" asked a spectator in a box. "At bottom, not
so very different," answered the other who knew me. My
part was the most thankful in itself, and my dramatic relation to my part surely the most organic (in the way just
noted); and so in the performances where all did well Ergasilus made the most noise. School-girls wanted his picture; and a theatrical magazine began its notice: "The
question is not have you seen Salvini in Othello [then
playing in Boston], but *have* you seen Leonard in The
Captives." This josh so set me up that (for a week or
two) I reconsidered my decision to be a college professor,
as originally announced to Miss Bulkley, in deference to
the loss which this decision might occasion to the American stage. But the realistic satisfaction of one bit of acting
well done was enough for me. No small part of the enrich-

ment of life is in doing one's best, for once, what others do, as their best, for a career.

But the devil alone knows how near this success came to failure, with my very first steps before the footlights. I had been getting more and more nervous as the time drew on, and had tried to protect myself against eventual panic by learning my lines (several hundred) so thoroughly that my lips would keep on saying them even if my head were cut off. Wise prevision. I am in the wings. Mike Carroll, the Prologue (now Boston lawyer), with golden wig and pink cheeks, is nearing the

Abeo, valete judices justissimi—

abeo, "good-by"—my cue. Out there is vastness, isolation, and no help except from within one's iron soul. Out *there,* the thousand eyes, out there is for *me,* with the opening soliloquy. In terror lest I run away, I dive tumbling into the abyss of the footlights before Carroll is off-stage, so that to this day neither of us knows whether the uproarious applause was for his parting smile and bow and retreating curls or for my black scraggly beard, shuffling gait, and ashen lugubriosity. It was fortunate indeed that the stage-directions called for shaking knees, distracted eye, drooping mouth, broken voice, and when at a standstill, for an initial posture bordering on collapse—for suppose the part had been Richard the Third. . . . My mind is in a terrific turmoil of horror . . . beyond the front-border of glare are those thousand, those million hostile eyes in the shadowy gulf . . .

Juventus nomen indidit . . .

I forget totally all about my lines. But I am thinking, thinking in that turmoil of horror . . .

Scio apsurde dictum . . .

180

here all, all depends on me . . . six months' work . . .
twenty people's work at stake . . . Professor Lindsay . . .

Estne invocatum an non est . . .

father and mother out there . . . up from Bolton . . .

Est planissume . . .

Now all, all wrecked . . . at the very start . . . I *must*
not drop . . . I *must* not run . . . I'll die rather . . .
then at least is no blame   . .

Quasi mures . . .

I am dying. . . . I am dying. . . .
Oh, oh, oh, to be home, to be in Bolton . . .

nostris dentibus . . .

Oh, never, never to have come to college . . .

quos ligurriant . . .

And then the spell broke. I came out of the trance; I was
suddenly gloriously in the game. There must have been
an almost complete disassociation of personality. I afterward questioned many who had been in the audience, and
not one had noticed that anything was wrong. Those who
saw all three performances could notice no difference. I
had said the first fifteen lines while all the brains I had
seemed to be otherwise fully occupied. That this stage-
fright was in the phobic series which this book is tracing
seems clear on the following grounds:

(1) On the first night of the formal investigation
four years ago (an account of which will occupy us later),
in the first use of the crystal, the first object to appear was

a stage as seen from a wing with a figure (Mike, the Prologue) in a toga. I had of course never forgotten the Latin
play, nor the general fact of that stage-fright. But the crystal brought it back in vivid details; and the objects that
soon followed in associated series were of memories of
other phobic moments derived from the complex of 1885
(the school-run, already noted as indubitably associated
with 1878). (2) An analysis of the ideas in the stage-
fright (as isolation, the crowd, flight-to-shelter, blockage
of flight) reveals only too clearly the miserable fixations
that make up the central ideations of my phobias now.
(3) A reliving of the fright in twilight sleep reveals an
emotional tone identical with that of every phobic attack
since I became a neurotic. There is indeed a fourth link,
one directly connecting the stage-fright (1896) with the
school-fright (1885). In rehearsals, Professor Lindsay,
more sensitive than I to the niceties of civilization, had
counseled me to modify my initial posture away from its
slight suggestion of a scared child in urinary distress—itself probably a reverberation. And his counsels were in
my subconsciousness. I have discovered the urinary moment of the 1885 trauma in many dream-states and hypnoidal relaxations of my auto-psychoanalysis: particularly in the acrid stench of the Washington School privy,
blown down the years across all the intervening perfumes
of apple-blossom times, hay-fields, and scents of cinnamon
and lavender in rustling silks. Yet there is one ghostly odor
that the winds, the doubly invisible winds, have blown still
more persistently and pungently from out of the past . . .
the odor of the cigar in the hand of the Stocky Man at the
station in 1878 merged with another cigar in another hand
on the lake-shores of Madison in 1911. But of the Cigar,
later.

By checking the progress of the stage-fright attack
and achieving indeed self-mastery and social glory, I
doubtless inhibited any phobic after-effects, though the attack itself left its precipitate in my subconsciousness, along

with earlier traumas. Had I been able so to check the attack of 1911, I might have been spared my neurosis. But the attack was immeasurably more violent and my resistance immeasurably weaker, and I was as unable to check it as a man, falling from an exploded aëroplane, is unable to check his plunge down the abyss by seizing on the wispy end of a cloud.

I went to Harvard after graduation. The money left me by Aunt Cornelia was not all gone; and I had room and board at Cambridge with an old man and his wife, summer residents of Bolton, in return for informal companionship. Dr. Dunning, long blind, his hands distorted by disease into stumps and his feet swathed in prepared shoes that he might hobble to Samuel Crothers's Church or the concerts in Saunders Theater and achieve too the exercise his still powerful physique of seventy-seven still demanded, was to me another of those outstanding beings that I have set in my own Hall of Fame, indifferent to the Votes of the Committees. He had been a dentist in other days, and Emerson and his kind had sat in his chair. He would quote to his Concord patient from a favorite poem, "Brahma" or "The Sphinx." "Mr. Emerson," he would ask, sorting out of the tray the right picker or scraper, and looking down the very throat from which had welled up the transcendental music, "Does it mean so-and-so?" "Yes," Emerson would reply as soon as he had the use of his jaws, "it might mean so-and-so." After his blindness he had lived with the poets. He knew "Saul" by heart, through joyous effort. He did not excuse himself, like my graduate students more than fifty years his junior, on the grounds of atrophied memory and mature preference for meditation and analytic. And several other poems quite as long. He would sit saying them over to himself a long evening; he would recite them to friends at the house with a simple eloquence that came from unseen places very near where the poems themselves came from. He knew by heart all the sonnets of Shakspere and had just finished dic-

tating to his eager and faithful wife a book which he felt
solved the mystery of their spiritual meaning (published
as "The Genesis of Shakespeare's Art," by Lee and Shep-
ard). . . . He was amused by a postal card from the
forthright other old man, Furnivall, across the water. He
used to recite its text with chuckles:

Mr. Furnivall begs to acknowledge the receipt of Mr. Dunning's
book and to state that he considers its theory utterly worthless. Mr.
Dunning seems to mistake Shakespeare for a nineteenth century
American sentimentalist.

Always the *odium Americanum* from the Old Home. Over
there they don't like it if one American pokes into the
dusty rolls of the Public Record Office for facts about
Shakspere's London residence on Silver Street, or if another finds the queen's pardon that at last explains the
murder of Kit Marlowe. Yet Shakspere and Marlowe,
and the English language are ours as well as theirs; and
we have an equal right to our discoveries . . . an equal
right to our blunders. . . . Dr. Dunning was happy in
the opportunity he gave me. Overhearing my regret that
I couldn't own the Mermaid Series for my Elizabethan
drama with George Baker, he purchased a set, saying he
wanted me to read him some of Ben Jonson. I was meeting good-will on all my way. Let the reader understand
how much good-will, how much on all the way . . . all
the way to Madison. The greater the shock when at last,
a man of thirty-five, I found Hatred and Slander, like the
Mob in the school-house yard, like the Locomotive-God
on the Path of the Train, bearing down upon me to an-
nihilate . . . with weapons sharper than stones, with a
breath hotter than fire and steam.

My record at B.U., with Lindsay's personal word, enabled me to enter the Graduate School, contrary to the
rules then in vogue demanding a Harvard B.A. before
admission to the Harvard M.A. But I was required to

take five instead of the normal four courses—"required"
when my only regret was that I couldn't find time to take
six. Latin (Vergil, antecedents and influence) with Mor-
gan and Marsh, Shakspere with Kittredge, Elizabethan
drama with Baker, Anglo-Saxon with (I declare I've forgotten), metaphysics with James. Stiff year-courses, several with long papers. I had been there but a few months
when B.U. asked me to instruct, as a substitute, nine hours
a week in Latin (Aulus Gellius and freshman composition). An opportunity, they said, though involving the surrender of some graduate work and the degree. I accepted
the teaching-offer. But in the meantime, through a good
word from James, the Harvard administration allowed
me to remain a candidate for the M.A. with a half-course
less. I was deceiving B.U., my alma mater. But after I
had made sure that they were satisfied with my teaching, I
confessed I had taken the degree too. They forgave me.

But the double task was indeed a grind. I studied practically all the time I was awake, except at breakfasts and
suppers with the Dunnings or on an occasional stroll with
the old man. I studied on the way down the elm-walks to
Massachusetts Hall, on the way to and from Boston on
foot (for the only exercise) over the Charles River
Bridge, amid the clatter and clutter of plates and coffee-
cups in Pie Alley at lunch, late into the night in my room
(where Mrs. Dunning would not let me smoke . . . the
only cruelty in all those years)—eighteen hours out of
every twenty-four, counting classes and teaching. What
supported me? Not now, I fear, the intellectual quest itself; for there was not time to follow through anything
for its own sake, not time for the imagination to create
the absorbing lure so that it makes midnight strike when
we think the hour scarcely nine. Intellectual pride and ambition supported me; the sense of power itself supported
me; youth and health and Mrs. Dunning's cooking supported me. I did a stunt. But I had started in at one hundred and sixty pounds stripped, by the Harvard Gym-

nasium scales, and at the end of the stunt I had lost ten, with scarce three pounds deviation to this day. I could still wear the clothes I wore at twenty-two (or at eighteen); as indeed some friends probably think I still do. Except for the vanished ten pounds (which anyway belonged more to Mrs. Dunning's oatmeal and steaks than to me), I suffered absolutely no constitutional ill-effects either in body or mind. Certainly, if a born neurotic, if a constitutionally weak nervous organization, I could not have stood such a strain.

The loss was of a different order. I lost Harvard. I had no time to linger under the elms to watch Royce and James strolling after class back and forth between Pluralism and the Absolute on the gravel before Seaver Hall, no time but for one chat with Münsterberg as host of the Philosophy Club, for but one visit with Norton, though at Christmas eve when he read us under the candles from Luke, for but one cigar in his study with Kittredge. No time but for one visit to Mount Auburn's Dead. No time to know really any of the graduate students, gathered, not as Boston's, from all the colleges of the land. In one chat under a willow in a field, some nameless classmate read me the new poem, "The Man with the Hoe," and described a wonderful teacher in his college down in Sewanee, Tennessee, a certain young Professor Trent. The name of the man that sat taking notes in the seat ahead in Elizabethan drama I learned only later in Shakspere's house in Stratford-on-Avon, where he signed the visitors' book just before me: G—— was his name, now an authority as he was almost even then. I remember one other by name, for his methodistic long hair and Western accent and irritating disputatiousness that the too kindly William James never shut off soon enough. He teaches philosophy in a denominational college of the Middle West. No time to know Harvard, as well as no time really to know my own subjects of study. No time to know Harvard? And yet Harvard is for me almost identical with the Idea and the Ideal

of the American University. How so? How, if not because
I drank in more than I knew of what was so dear to my
temperament, assimilating it too to the Harvard of all
my reading in the lives of all the great New England dead
in Mount Auburn on the Charles and in Sleepy Hollow
at Concord. . . . Emerson once gave there the Phi Beta
Kappa address on "The American Scholar." Lowell once
read the "Commemoration Ode" there; but when Harvard asked me to come back with a song she was willing
to trust, as not shameful to these dead, there could be no
coming back any more; and I lost Harvard a second time.

Aside from Dr. Dunning, I really had only one friend
in Cambridge. But that friend was William James. In
1898 James was just beginning to think out the pragma-
tism, already implicit in his psychology, by which he is now
known to all the world. Our class was a discussion-group,
working with special texts, and my copy of "Appearance
and Reality" is enriched by marginalia prophetic in idea
and phrase of passages of his then unwritten books. Alas,
not as enriched as it should have been; for James, with
his famous toleration for another's point of view, surrendered much precious time to four or five conceited dispu-
tants who taught me nothing, and certainly taught James
nothing. He was not a great lecturer, except by a more formal preparation than could be demanded in class-work;
nor did he sufficiently guide and control the class babble to
be called a good pedagogue. But his high business should
have been to do the talking, informally, all of it, except
for an honest question now and then. Whenever he allowed himself to shut up the prophets from the hinterland,
that room was a wonderful place: the place where the
first original American contribution to philosophy was
taking shape. In the class-room I always wanted to hear
what my professors knew and thought; I could hear all
I needed from fellow-students out of class. I now assume
my students want to hear me, rather than their classmates.
And art is long and time is fleeting. And so, assuming a

man has a right to teach at all, I defend the lecture system, or the talk system, as against the discussion system. The latter is wasteful and disorderly, except in small specialized groups, even with a skilled master; and the students who thus pass such "interesting and lively" hours have mistaken the pleasures of self-expression and cerebral excitement for learning, for thinking. The "lecture system"—the system of Aristotle, of Abelard, of Kant, of all the great masters in all the universities of Europe. The "lecture system"—the trouble with our lecture system is in some of the lecturers (who fail to lecture) and in some of the listeners (who fail to listen), not in the principle.

But I had a better chance to hear James talk. That winter his family was away much of the time, and he would invite me now and then to supper all alone in his home. But I have no table-talk to edit, nothing even from the library-talk. He told me how he wrote his psychology, why he took up with psychical research, what philosophical puzzles he was just then most bothered with; and he answered the questions that the class babblers had given no opportunity to ask. Good talk, but not as good as in his books. James was, I think, the only philosopher who ever really talked in a book. Yet not even the technical student who follows the great talk in his books can experience the rich humanity of that nature, at once so simple, sincere, deep, and broad, in those days communicated even to me, a casual, but lucky, outsider. He had an uncanny power of getting into another person's mind, of remembering everybody as a concrete person; and a naïveté, genius itself, in overlooking external differences in reputation and position. Let a man be an authentic personality with authentic experience, and James wanted to use him: James might spend an hour listening to Royce in the college walks in the morning; and in the afternoon another with the house-painter. And he'd quote in class the opinion of either with equal candor and respect. In the friendly solicitude of voice and features, in the stocky set-up, in the gait that seemed always to be on some errand, though unhurried and unabstracted, in whimsical humor, even in the beard and the quiet neatness of his clothes, he seemed one's ideal of the Physician rather than of the Philosopher—an Hippocrates rather than a Plato.

I had come direct from his exact opposite in method, ideas, personality. Bowne, genial but remote, philosophic idealist, rationalist, had acclaimed supreme trust in the technic of the abstract intellectual process (above all, as wielded by his own intellect), positing a world-ground on the pattern of what we humans mean by intelligence, and girding with trenchant jests from his *cathedra* at all opponents of his doctrine from Empedocles to Spencer. His lectures were undeviating masterpieces in analytic subtlety and eloquence, granting the ultimate, and unexpressed, premises of his type of thinking; with peculiar power to lift one into the realms of Intellectual Beauty. . . .

> Hinter ihm in wesenlosem Scheine
> Lag was uns alle baendigt—das Gemeine.

James and Bowne were friends, and Bowne's "Theism" was one of the three books in our discussion-group. "Bowne is a fine fellow," he said at supper; "I wanted him to take my work one year; but he wouldn't budge from B. U. He has one trouble, though—everybody who doesn't think as he does is an *ass*." A few days later, I could have presented the pragmatist with an empirical demonstration of his insight. James had written an indignant letter to the "Boston Transcript" on behalf of the Filipinos, beginning with a strident cadence like the beginning of Cicero's first Cataline:

Shall Governor Roosevelt be allowed to crow all over the national barnyard and no equally shrill voice be raised in reply?

As Bowne's young colleague pro tem. in Latin, I asked Bowne if he'd seen the letter. "Yes; and I see James has been making an *ass* of himself again." . . . "Professor James, did you ever get Royce to take nitrous oxide gas?" I inquired after reading James's experimental proofs of the Hegelian philosophy it induces. "I tried to, but he said he didn't need it." . . . "Mr. Leonard, damn the Ph. D. degree." . . . "Good-by, Professor James" (overtaking him in the Yard after commencement). . . .

Many years later, some paragraphs from an essay of mine on Paul Carus, another philosopher-friend then dead too, reappeared, translated from the "Dial," in a magazine of Reykjavik. There I read, in the very language of my beloved Icelandic sagas, that Professor Leonard was "the distinguished successor of William James, in the chair of philosophy at Harvard." Perhaps a wish-fulfilment, dreamed by proxy.

X

My father, in the meantime, had resigned his pastorate. At sixty-two, without other earnings in sight, he gave up the quiet security of food and shelter and service that might have been his to extreme old age—like that of his colleague Dr. Bartol, for sixty years pastor of the Lancaster parish. He said he felt that his usefulness in Bolton was at an end. The villagers said "stay"—for spiritual reasons. They loved him. My Baptist Uncle Oliver with great urgency wrote "stay"—for reasons practical as well as spiritual. He loved him too. Young, impractical, and detached from my father's actions though I was, I foresaw with anxiety the long result . . . for him, for all of us. But I said nothing. I knew my advice would mean nothing, and in the persistence of the juvenile father-son relationship I shrank from advice anyway. Somehow he must know best, I thought. I loved him too.

I shall never be sure that I have understood my father's attitude to life from this time forth. He then had, I think, a little money from the sale of "the farm"—perhaps it *felt* like a permanent security to him. He had a humble, but sincere, belief in his powers as needed in the world—perhaps this *felt* like security to him. He knew I was now a man, a college graduate—this doubtless *felt* like security to him. He had a mystic's trust in the Divine as light and leading, as the maker of a place for him. This of course felt like security to him. I shall never be sure that I understand, but it would seem that, as the years went on, his vision, especially prevision as respecting himself and kin, became, by some deep-rooted developments within, more and more deflected from terrestrial fact and the laws of terrestrial cause and effect. I cannot presume to disentangle this phenomenon from the accompanying spiritual deepening; the spiritual deepening may have quickened a practical change already implicit; it may have been quickened by the deprivations due to the change; it certainly assisted him in supporting those deprivations. Yet there was nothing in the least fanatical or eccentric in his religious experience or conduct, beyond this instinctive dismissal of concrete fact. He secured a little parish in Bath, New Hampshire, at a still lower salary in cash and with no parsonage. He was there two years, alone or with my mother, as a boarder in the village, with skim-milk for his coffee, while the other boarders (summer boarders) got cream. After two years he resigned once more, but the practical hardships for my mother were a contributing cause. Thereafter, for a number of years, he earned now and then a Sunday's fee as a temporary supply in towns near Boston; but that was all. I had begun to advise and to plead, especially that my sister, who had long given up her brief kindergarten career, should be more steadily and practically employed. I had begun to prophesy, sometimes with unlovely desperation. There was always one answer from all: "Everything will turn out all right." Throughout four years in Boston when I had begun to be an economic assistant, my father edited, for a New Thought Crank, a little magazine called "Practical Ideals." Month by month his employer promised him a salary . . . month by month my father wrote, without salary, his spiritual counsels for the few subscribers and pasted on the "dummy" the lucubrations clipped from other New Thought magazines on how Thought Controls Being, how Thought Controls Success. Finally it ceased: the printer would advance no more credit . . . "Practical Ideals." . . .

Their living conditions became narrower and narrower. The mahogany secretary had long ago disappeared. My own anxieties acuter. My education practically cost the family nothing, except shelter in school-days and during college vacations. It was not till I returned from Europe that the actual conditions had become pressing; though, even while overseas, I felt a twinge over many a ten pfennigs spent in the cafés for beer, thinking of their narrow circumstances. Should I have given up, after Boston University, or at least after Cambridge, all thought of the farther quest? Should I have gone out to earn them a house? Paradoxical as it may sound, I could have done nothing that would have grieved the aging man more. It would have crushed him completely. He did not know it, and I did not know it, but to him I was the Fulfilment, the deferred Self, of Scholarship, Leadership, Humanity. As well as the Son—the Son too. I was to go on, on, on. I was to know and to teach more largely, more wisely than he. If I ever mean anything to my country, let my country thank my father, not me. The Madison Mob that later tried to murder the son was trying to murder a good old man . . . as good as ever lived . . . and then very old . . .

After Cambridge, I planned to teach, to save, to become B.U.'s Traveling Fellow. My eyes were on Göttingen, famous for me because of the famous Americans, Motley, Everett, etc., and of the memories brought back by Professor Perrin. Germany had from childhood been the great Other Country. My mother had grown up with Forty-eighters in Rochester. She talked German. She had learned the kindergarten from Germany. Miss Bulkley had been in Germany to study the school system. Older Folk and schoolmates in Plainfield had been German-Americans.

And Fräulein Lena Fliege, who became long before so unexpected a visitor in the homestead, had come from Germany. Let me tell you how she came and how she went. The station-master had found one afternoon an elderly lady in black pacing distractedly back and forth on the railway platform (which has come into this story before). Pat Lynch (already equally well known to the at-

tentive reader) took her in charge, and over to his home
in the jail. Mysterious cringing terror in the corner . . .
mysterious alien babble. My father fetches a German-
American friend. She tells a wild story of escape from an
insane asylum in St. Louis. But will tell nothing more,
cringing and shaking in the corner. My father gets the
town to transfer her, pending investigation, to the home
of the German-Americans across the street from our homestead. I sit in the window watching with excited ten-year-
old eyes. A crazy woman from Germany . . . almost as
interesting as a wild Indian. Everything she does is crazy.
She sits in a chair in the yard, with unread book in her lap,
gaping at the sky—just like a crazy person. She twists her
hands together—just like a crazy person. She walks into
the house when people stop and stare at her over the pickets—just like a crazy person. One day she escapes out
the gate, down the street, and looks at the funeral procession
starting from the Baptist Church—just like a crazy person. Her German-American guardians report that she won't
talk, but mumbles about her brother in her sleep—just like
a crazy person. However, my mother had been watching
too. "That woman is not crazy; she is in desperate trouble." My mother sends me over in the morning with Freiligrath and Goethe and an invitation to call, written in her
best German. That afternoon, summoning trust at last, she
tells my mother the story that the police and outraged citizens afterward verified. She had come from Germany two
years ago as governess of her widowed brother's little children in St. Louis. He had treated her cruelly. She had in-
advertently learned something of his embezzlements and
adulteries. He feared her. By collusion with another scoun-
drel, he got her committed. After six months, apparently in
new fear, he took her out and put her on an east-bound
train, with a plausible story. At Jersey City, a conductor
shipped her back to Plainfield. Her Lutheran Pietism saw
the hand of God in that conductor's action. I didn't. The
town raised a fund—sufficient to send her home and to sup-

port her simply for the rest of her life. Incidentally, there was a clean-up in the St. Louis asylum. Incidentally, her brother contributed roundly to that fund—under threats of immediate prosecution otherwise. Meantime she came to lodge with us. Dear lady, aside from the memory of this cruel experience, she brooded till her death twenty years thereafter over another sorrow and mystery. To her my mother was second only to her Saviour. She all but prayed to her over yonder in far-away Königsberg and Tilsit, as to a Guardian Angel incarnate. Yet it was plain from her letters that my mother caused her confusion and distress: her Saviour-friend was not an orthodox Christian; her Guardian Angel was doomed to Hell-Fire. How could her God have appointed one of the damned to save her, to guard her? How could she be one of the damned? Her theology was at war with her heart, and not even the shade of the sage of Königsberg could help her out. She needed a simpler "Critique of the Practical Reason" than Kant's. Probably Fräulein Lena Fliege did more than any other experience to set my eyes toward that Other Country.

Meantime I planned to teach. The sick professor had returned to B.U. Lindsay's personal efforts for a college instructorship elsewhere had apparently fallen through. James wanted me to tutor a friend's boys in the Adirondacks, but I had to be near Boston till the next year's job turned up. Harvard had only my impersonal grades at the employment bureau, and I had small claims for help. I joined a teachers' agency, and hung around the deserted fraternity house of B.U. with another friend in similar plight. We amused ourselves on hot evenings writing sardonic recommendations for each other. My intellectual quest had been purposeful preparation for a career; but I had envisaged the career as implicit in the quest. I had prepared for a career, without preparing for a job. It was many years before I realized that in my profession, as doubtless in others, no small part of planning a career is active planning to get the proper job for the career. There was no little of my father in me: I thought in ideal terms of my equipment, of quest, of service, without prefiguring where in the actual world I was best to give them meaning, and get, incidentally, the truly equivalent wage. So the first call that came I accepted. It was the principalship of a small high school, with two other teachers. At $750. A few days later I had a college opening . . . too late.

That year in Plainville (Wrentham), Massachusetts, has fallen out of my life. Every life has a year (or more) that has fallen out. I taught Vergil to eight or nine bright young girls, who may remember me. I read Cicero with one boy after hours. I taught other boys and girls some American history, English, physical geography. And elementary astronomy, wandering about on the knolls to pick out constellations. I taught French. I kept order. I got my fun out of the game of "teacher." Back of my desk were glass bookcases that made, from a certain angle, an excellent mirror. I would turn absently as if to look for a book; and then reseat myself at the desk. After a moment: "By the way, John, you might bring me the rest of that apple Jennie just gave you.". . . "Nellie, don't pass Sammie any more notes." . . . I discovered who cut the electric wiring by watching closely what happened to facial expressions when I asked in assembly (so naïvely as they thought), "Who did it?" . . . We played the game together, and I, being older and in a strategic position, usually beat—and they liked to be beaten, and liked me for beating them. That's all there was to my "excellent discipline." I wasn't so excellent at Jobbs Ferry or Lynn later on. I had got sick of the game. I knew subjects and game; but I knew nothing of secondary education . . . nor of the problems of adolescence . . . and cared nothing. I was an M.A. There is one little face, compound of bright eyes and stupid mouth, the only face I remember vividly . . . a freshman boy. I studied. I lived on five dollars a week. I got company by week-ends in Boston. I learned how to kiss a young schoolma'am. I did not like the superintendent. He conducted a teachers' class in pedagogy. He had a big mustache, and pulled on it. His name was A. B. Call, and I dubbed him A.B.C. . . . later Aristo Feigns for his mispronunciation of Aristophanes. The teachers, in high school and grades, liked me better than he did. I wrote verses . . . about the mountains, the White Mountains. I was in correspondence with Maude. I was looking forward to Europe. But I was at least sufficiently interested in the school to procure it a better principal than I was, who remained there for several years. I hope I earned my $750.

I had measured the success of my first year as a worker in the world, not in social terms at all, but for books read, poems written, and money saved. The job had nothing to do with my career. Several later jobs, likewise nothing. And the long maladjustment, instructive in itself, is not without bearing on the central problem. In my case, such preoccupation with the intellectual quest, without practical forethought of my own, and without all training or example in the family, would have involved me, economically handicapped as I was, sooner or later in frustration and embarrassment anyway. But lurking neurotic forces augmented the complex of these embarrassments as the secondary cause of some and the primary result of others. My quest, both as scholar and poet, was to be against greater and greater odds, in summary: (1) against the maladjustments due to exclusive dedication to the quest itself, (2) against financial family-responsibilities, (3) against the Locomotive-God. By the time the first two had been mastered, the Locomotive-God had mastered me. Against other odds, too, perhaps: against the dominating ideas and practical conditions of American life.

But there is to be first a gracious holiday. Parts of the two summers, before and after my school-teaching, I spent at a mountain farmhouse overlooking the Wild Ammonoosuc that dashed down the valley of my father's new pastorate . . . overlooking from the west long Moosilauke with the Presidential Range to the northward. Maude and

Annie and I, all three from the same Jersey town, all three again weaving together a moment of life out of old familiar threads. Yes, I too have been in Arcadia . . . with the nymphs. Such a ménage as we had, with our own breakfast room, our own hammocks, our own corner in the orchard, even our own piano on rainy nights and our own dancing-party of three, chaperoned all the while only by the gnarled but amused old couple who pattered about asking no questions and suspecting no ill. The two sisters were as unlike as could be; Maude, the musician, a flashing, black-eyed, black-haired brunette with her dialect stories and gales of laughter; Annie, the younger, blue-eyed and fair, as golden as all her namesakes in song, with her sketch-book and her sly chuckling queries so much more devastating to the master of arts than her sister's forthright girding. Such reading of Keats and gathering of columbine. Such quiet looking at the moon, with me in the middle. Was I in love with Maude or with Annie? . . . was one or the other in love with me? They were sisters. Was I their brother? That wasn't quite it. But if sex would only stay at that stage of its subtle career what an idyl life might be—

> *Dem* Augenblicke dürft' ich sagen:
> Verweile doch, du bist so schön . . .

But there would be no begetting of children. And we had our old rig and old Dobbin who would trot off with us up the Wild Ammonoosuc, through the forests and upland meadows, over to Echo Lake and the Great Stone Face. Mountains . . . mountains. The great earth is greater in the mountains; silence and shadow and thunder are greater. Mountains . . . mountains. They remake the blue sky, even as they remake the green earth, its pastures and its pines. They remake sun and sunset and moon and stars. They remake Time. They remake the mind of man. I had never lived in the Mountains before: I had never seen the

Mountains before except from far away. And no one had
ever told me about the Mountains, not Vergil, no, not even
Wordsworth and Byron. And whom have I, poor babbler,
ever told—in those boyish sonnets written in those days and
printed in "The Vaunt of Man"? . . . The whistle of the
White Mountain Express. . . . To be for the first time in
the mountains is, in simple psychologic truth, to be startled
by the discovery of an unknown and unimagined dwelling-
place for our human kind. But to be there for the first time,
in a visionary mood already exalted by the presence of ideal-
ized girlhood, companioned too by veritable girlhood in
skirt and blouse, sharing the cosmic, the spiritual mystery
. . . well, it would seem this was the nearest I ever came to
immortality. And when we would halloo from the skyey
lookout over Echo Lake out toward the vast side of
Lafayette, from that mountain wall the eerie reverberations seemed as if we had wakened the wailings of the dead
from the beginning of time. And the Great Stone Face
looked on across Crawford Notch, with closed eternal lips,
as if he could tell more but would not. The Mountains . . .
and Maude and Annie. Every life has its one loveliest un-
shadowed memory. This was once mine. And I destroyed
it. Wait . . . till I return from overseas.

I destroyed it, but not yet. The day after to-morrow I
leave. "Maude and Annie," I say with mock-heroics on the
road in the Notch, "I am going to say farewell to America.
I am going to the top of Lafayette." And I strike into the
forest. Lafayette, only a few hundred feet lower than
Mount Washington, is far abrupter in its slopes, and without roadway, and, so far as I know, without clearly defined path. At least the only path after the first thousand
feet I could then follow seemed as much the steep dry
channel of a forest-cascade as a trail. I reach the timber-
line and for the seven or eight hundred upward feet still
ahead I see my bleak course marked by a line of loose
rocks and boulders, set there I don't know when. I reach the
top—a little plateau scarcely twenty-five feet square, ram-

parted by unplastered stones of unknown, but human, builders. I stand, transfigured, on the Mountain. All there is to see of the world—and there is so much, from gathering thunder-head to the vast wooded gulfs below—is mine, is mine. The storm-wind begins to bend the scrub-oaks of the timber-line and tears at my wet hair. Thunder to the south. I laugh with primeval joy. Mountain and I . . . and I on the Mountain. But I come to myself . . . I descend in fifty minutes. . . . The old crone who sells picture-cards in the road-house won't believe that I made it. There hadn't been time enough. I describe the top. She says I have been there before. Maude brushes my coat; Annie mops my cheek. Dobbin trots us back through twenty miles of rain and darkness. . . . The whistle of the White Mountain Express. . . . The day after to-morrow I had exchanged the Mountains for the Sea.

XI

Out of Boston Harbor into the Unknown, with only a dress-suit case and a fellowship and savings (compactly reduced to traveler's checks), and all my freedom. And so this was Ocean. The Sea was not so new as the Mountains. I can now trace my experiences with the sea into my fourth year . . . to long before Atlantic Highlands and the derelict in the sand. But I had seen it and smelt it only to the east, rolling in upon America, with all America at my back. Now it is everywhere with its blue swell and its blue skies, and all its salt winds. On the mountain-top I had been at the center of the world for half an hour; here I was at the center for a week and a day. A whale spouted to starboard; the dolphins raced beside us on the port, like seahorses on a steeplechase; but I remained in the center. A three-master with all sails set see-sawed westward against the horizon. I watched it from my center. Whether the stars came out, till they had filled in, one by one, the bright angles and squares and clusters of all the ancient patterns of the sky, or whether the sun rose, with a wing-spread of long, low crimson clouds, like an apocalypse, there was always this radius between myself and the encircling rim of the universe, as if I looked out over the primeval waters, before even the Laurentian ridge had emerged as the chine of the first continent. One breathes more freely too, from the very feeling of escape. A week and a day with no news . . . till wireless destroyed the last refuge. There is a strange abandon toward one's fellows. We are indeed all in the same boat, thrown so much closer together than in the land-world; and never to meet again after we make port. The life together on the ship tempts to confidences; just as the thought of that port with the quick dispersion into a thousand different highways makes each yield so readily to the temptation. Besides one must pass the time. So secrets cease to be secrets. The love-stories, the divorces, the business-failures, the diseases, I know. And the now gray-haired ladies that then heard all about Maude and Annie. The hectic young servant-girl that was crying all day as we steamed up the Irish Sea past County Cork. I knew her secret. But it would make no difference who knew in six months.

I crossed over to Chester the first evening. I sat by the bridge of the River Dee. I saw my first cathedral, my first Roman wall. I knew I was in Europe. I exulted to be so totally alone, without any shelter beyond what my own desires suggested, hither or thither, for I was *my own center* of power and of safety. This mood, so emphasized on the mountain-top and on the high seas, remained with me throughout my two years in Europe and remained indeed, though later subdued by practical duties, till my breakdown. The outstanding phenomenon of my neurosis is the diabolical cunning with which the neurosis has wrought in me the precise opposite of that mood. My chief delight in those days was the feel of freedom and inward security, even to seeking and creating vivid situations for the more poignant thrill; my long dismay and torture is to live now so haunted always by insecurity that even the minimum freedom of normal, cautious daily living of an eighty-year-old lady in going and coming about town, is impossible, a walk to Capitol Square down State Street impossible, to be in my own house alone is impossible. The same absence of external center that was my main joy, as expanding my selfhood, is now my main terror, as the very collapse of selfhood. The greater for me the misfortune and pain. But the two states of mind may be correlated in something beside such ironic antithesis of meaning and effects. The very excess of the former, for it was more than mere Wanderlust, may have been the subconscious over-compensation for the latent timidities of the childhood traumas: in other words, the Locomotive-God may be the cause of each. Aside from the general correspondence of such a mechanism with the findings of modern psychology, I have discovered in my own analysis no evidence, beyond one, but one important, observation. This: from the very beginning of the phobia (i. e., my insecurity-mood), I noted its peculiarly antithetical character, and felt powerfully that the two were profoundly related. I say "felt" advisedly, for there was less of analysis or reflection than I at first supposed. Where did this *feeling of their relationship* come from? It was, I believe, the authentic testimony of psychological fact welling up from the subconscious. Let no reader pooh-pooh this as obscurantism. Later pages will give ample demonstration of how I have accepted one or another explanation of specific phobic phenomena, as supposedly given by a process of reasoning, only to realize afterward by psychoanalysis that this rational explanation was the direct bubbling up into consciousness, through some little crevice, of matters, so to say, known in the immediacy of fact by the subconscious —the subconscious telling me something by generating a suggestion, sometimes as idea, sometimes (as in the present case) as a feeling. I seem, then, to have felt in consciousness this synthesis of antitheses because to the subconscious they were synthesized, as of one and the same origin, in childhood traumas, the one mood resulting in a restive and blatant over-compensation of timidity, the other in a huddling exaggeration of timidity. Just as I have found much that I had supposed was due to my imagination, due in fact to subconscious memory.

A main motif of this chapter will be this glorified abandon—the manifestations of this fearless and defiant ego at home anywhere on earth, at home with people anywhere, because so certain, so secure, in itself. I took train, as I supposed, for Stratford, and found myself by mistake on the way to Coventry. "Sent to Coventry," I thought. What of it? A good joke. The old town was crowded from all the country-side, for one of the ancient fairs. I had to double up with a long-bearded loquacious patent-medicine faker, who prayed well on his knees before he put out the candle and climbed into the high bed beside me in that fifteenth-century upper chamber. I had met him in our third-class coupé, and he had already told me about his marvelous mandrake pills. His circulars showed a male duck with a bearded human face. He gave me the address of the cheap boarding-house where I stayed in London. I walked from Coventry to Stratford, sending suitcase ahead to the Oxford station. By cottages and hedges and meadows in sunshine, through the heart of England. To Kenilworth village. An old man sitting by a brook. I ask him. He says he will take me to the famous ruin. He says he has retired from forty-five years in a London counting-house; but he has evidently strayed out of Wordsworth's poems. We sit high up in the castle overlooking the meadow, and talk about Walter Scott, the festival of 1575, and the American Revolution. By gray Warwick Castle, seen through a sultry luxurious brake, deep in from the main traveled road. I get to the borders of Stratford at sundown, shoes in my hand, foot-sore, walking on the grass. An affable and lively representative of the little burg runs up to meet me. "Show ye Shakspere's House for a penny, sir," says the eight-year-old fellow-townsman of that dramatist formerly referred to by American travelers as the Swan of Avon. "I'm not interested in any Shaksperes." "Stand on my head for a penny, sir.". . . I lodge in the Red Lion—I think it was the Red Lion—anyway such a tavern as I'd read about. I see a quiet River meandering through meadows, and a church, and a house, and a school. A grave and an epitaph. I stroll over to Shottery and see an enormous live-oak behind a long cottage. I am in England with the father of Henry Leonard, before the twenty-year-old boy took ship for Boston in 1640 . . . the first to return. I study at Oxford—three days—taking my exercise in Addison's Walk. Towers of Magdalen, Bodleian, High Street, Shelley's Cenotaph. . . .

> He has outsoared the shadow of our night. . . .

A week in London, with the family friends of the bearded Man Drake. I hear my first cockney from a grocery-clerk boarder and his fiancée of the milliner's shop, and my first Scotch of Scotland from the ancient landlady— "Maaster, here is your bonnet." I ride the buses on top. The Tower and the Ravens, Westminster and the Great Hall of William Rufus, Parliament and Bankside. The Thames. London Bridge. . . .

> This city now doth like a garment wear
> The beauty of the morning . . .

I am quoting verses, wherever I come to a stand, or remembering the silenced hum of mighty happenings wherever I walk or ride. The Monument. Whitehall. All over London. Hyde Park. The British Museum . . . five hundredth anniversary of Chaucer's death . . . Ellesmere Manuscript under glass. The Poet's Corner . . . O rare Ben Jonson. Bank of England. Strand. Underground. Trafalgar Square . . . Piccadilly . . . Byron. Paul's . . . *si monumentum requiris* . . . Sir Christopher. I have several letters of introduction; but the literary folk and scholars are out of town in late August. Except William Archer: he gives me an autographed copy of his new book, "America To-day," and I feel distinguished myself.

I visit the Tate Gallery once, the National three times. I must learn about painters and painting. My state of mind was the same as when I used to go again and again to the New York or the Boston Galleries. I loved to look at pictures, mainly for colors and for reveries. But I knew little and had no critical training; and my quest through the galleries of Europe was impelled more by ambition to improve myself than by delight to live with the masters. Probably the Preraphaelites and the Turners of London, the Böcklins of Berlin, the Murillos of Dresden, the Rembrandts in Amsterdam and in the Hanoverian town of Cassel, and Michelangelo's frescos in the Vatican and his sculptures at the tomb of the Medici, and the Venus de Milo in the Louvre came home to me with the most power and the least mediation. At least, I was not admiring simply because of double stars in the guide-books. My keen interest in the Italian painters, except Michelangelo and Titian, was intellectual, rather than esthetic. In the Dresden room of the Sistine Madonna I was more amused by the self-conscious whispers and gasps of the American female visitors and clergymen than overwhelmed by the image they were gasping at. Yet my memory has retained a thousand pictures and statues from those days of free vision; and what study I have since given to the fine arts has had only these memories to work with, and a few prints. I have a keener insight now—mainly, however, the transfer of my art-intelligence in poetry to the plastic arts—but now I have no more opportunities. I thank the gods for the old, free days of the quests and for the rich stores they have permitted me to retain: I have scarcely seen a picture since. I mourn most for Velásquez. . . .

I sail away from England, in a freighter for Rotterdam, down the Thames from Blackwall Street, London, through low-lying Kent, the terrain of the isle where Julius Cæsar first landed his legions. I had purchased a through ticket up the Rhine to Mannheim for seventeen shillings, without state-room and food supplies. It turned out a tough passage. But before we cross the North Sea in the moonlight:

> Welcome, welcome, ye dark blue waves
> And when you fail my sight,
> Welcome, ye deserts and ye caves!
> My native Land—Good Night!

Few situations in those days were complete without a verse,

oftenest a Byron verse. I had perhaps been remiss in not quoting this when sailing out of Boston Harbor; yet England had still seemed my native land. Here was my speech; here had lived my poets and the scholars and the statesmen and the artists of my speech. And in my brief sojourn of a little over two weeks I had seen so much, of past and present, that was typical of the England of my imagination—provincial towns, landscapes, rivers, university, feudal battlements, ruins, historic monuments, graves, the folk, the City. I had even been approached by a recruiting-officer of the Boer War. I had felt less the transition from New England to Old England than that a few years ago from Plainfield to Bolton. Indeed, the older we grow the more we take in the human race and the earth itself as one. To-day, if I could travel at all, I would find nothing particularly alien even in Tibet or Etah.

There was no sleep on the North Sea for me. The peopled hold reeked with cheese and dried sweat, and the bedding in my bunk was moldy. Herr Stein, the Göttingen student, one of my pick-ups, didn't mind. The other did—Arthur Stone, the Oxonian . . . of all things an Oxonian on this Dutch freight-barge. So he came to think too. The Oxonian and the Harvardian pass the night against the smoke-stack on deck, watching the maritime moon that had once belonged to Hengist and Horsa and Olaf Tryggvason. We are off the coast of Holland in early dawn. By the first light, I see, over the wharves of Rotterdam, a huge figure, pictured with a broad-brimmed hat, looking westward. Underneath was the legend "Quaker Oats"—the Americanization of Edward Bok's countrymen had already begun too. I walk the twelve miles to Delft and back that Sunday, in a world well swept and scoured, and see canals and windmills. . . . Hans Brinker, Diedrick Knickerbocker . . . the Oxonian and the Göttingener are with me. We talk about Ricardo, the economist. Dutch soldiers at Delft scowl at us, hearing the English language. We had put our packs aboard the Rhine freighter at the docks of the Maas,

and return there to pass the night. Silence and darkness of
the waterfront at the warehouses—like a stage-setting for
a murder. Low fires in the deserted boat. In the hold, not
even bunks—only a long low room in the forecastle with a
wooden bench around the walls and a couple of deal-board
tables. And cold down there. Herr Stein sleeps. Oxonian
and I pass a second sleepless night against a smoke-stack.
Morning. The slow all-day trip against the broad swift
muddy Rhine, between the interminable flats with those
monotonous windmills, was a subtle soporific that we did
not need. Our fare was coffee from the crew's cook and
crackers and cheese from our own supplies. To get water
for our unshorn dirty faces, we lowered a cracker-tin over
the gunwale. The swish of waters nearly jerks it off the
cord. There are no passengers, but many boxes. We tie up
at the German border from six to midnight. Here at a
riverside tavern in the little town of Münden, Oxonian and
I eat our first raw ham. He didn't know it was raw till too
late. "Bah, civilized nations cook their meat." The tavern
fills with peasants and lower bourgeoisie. An excited young
Dutchman shows a paper signed by the queen; he is on a
search up the Rhine for his kidnapped little daughter.
After the long racket and rattle and clank of the lading,
we are off again. We descend the stairs into the hold. Here
lies in the shadows, on benches, tables, and floor, an indistinguishable mass of skirts and trousers and hair and arms
and shoes, all the peasantry of the Germany of the lower
Rhine unstirring in their sleep. Herr Stein lies down in a
corner of the pile. "Foul, beastly hole," says the Oxonian,
as we turn away. For us there is no smoke-stack now. The
deck is crowded with crates of fruit. There is only a narrow alley between. Round and round we walk. I steal apples
and plums from the crates. The Oxonian won't steal, but
he will eat. At four o'clock we pry into an empty cabin on
the rear deck, for so-called "first-class passengers." We arrange eight camp-stools in a double row. We doze . . . to
be kicked out in a half-hour. Three nights without sleep. It

is hard work, this getting into Germany. The German student, feeling fine, gets off with us at Cologne. The Oxonian's destination is Bonn. Mine much farther up-stream; but my ticket is good for any one of the boats of the line; and I must stop for sleep. I see the cathedral in a dream . . . not of vivid exaltation but of bewildered unreality. There is a strangeness to all the world, as seen in sleep; but that is nothing to the strangeness of the world when seen without sleep. Later, during the first year and a half of my neurosis, I lived my life and did my work most of the time in a similar penumbra of unreality, projected by something within me more profoundly wrong than the ephemeral daze of drowsiness, and accompanied by the abnormal fears that this drowsiness had been totally free from. Herr Stein buys our tickets for Bonn, and leaves for Göttingen by an earlier train, with instructions for travel. At the gateway of the Bonn Station, the guard wants to arrest us for coming in a third-class train with a fourth-class ticket. At least, I manage to gather that is what's the matter. The Oxonian can't speak a word of German; and mine, poor as it is, has gone to sleep. The guard thinks us drunk. I stammer: "Schlaf, Schlaf; wir suchen Schlaf." We find the rooms of my old college-friend, Evans of the Latin play, my predecessor in B.U.'s fellowship. But sleep is more pressing than friendship. For years, thereafter, I was to be turning up fortuitously in the cities where Evans was living . . . more and more to him, I think, like a strange man in a daze.

The following midnight, I embark on the next boat, a duplicate of the first, except that there is not a passenger visible in "the foul, beastly hole." I am now again absolutely alone, but without all fear. Without all fear, too, when after a few miles the boat anchors mysteriously till dawn in the heavy fogs of the narrowing river-valley. Fortunate for me was this unexpected delay. At daybreak from over the top of the fog I saw we were directly under the castled crag of Drachenfels, where the mountain ruins and

the terraced vineyards and the shining villages in the green
hollows begin, that go on and on for so many winding
leagues of peace and loveliness. To have passed, unwittingly, all this in the dark—what a calamity I had escaped
. . . Bingen, too, and Ehrenbreitstein. There emerges on
deck an unsuspected companion, a startled young chap with
beard and a beer-bottle and crackers. We communicated
all day in a hodgepodge of Latin, English, and German.
He was a ragged journeyman-printer, with the typical German capacity for sleep, beer, and friendliness. He pointed
out all the landmarks on either side of the river: "Das sind
die berühmten Loreleifelsen". . . but I'm not writing a
Rollo book. We disembark in the lights at Mainz, instead
of at Mannheim. He has been drinking beer all day, far
beyond my capacity to accept his hospitality. He has friends
in Mainz. He will show me the city. He will get me a con-
cubine. He is desperately hurt that I don't want a concu-
bine. I see he is drunk. In an alley-way, I deliberately lose
him. He was my first friend in a land of friends . . . and
he guided me first through the region of Germany that was
later my dearest home . . .

An den Rhein, an den Rhein, zieh' nicht an den Rhein . . .

the old song tells a deep truth of the witchery and the peril.
I know. Especially if one must live elsewhere thereafter
. . . in the noise, in the ugliness, in the hatreds of life.

I was on my way, via Nuremberg, to the walled village
of Velberg in the Oberpfalz, where I sojourned two weeks
with the sister of the village-surveyor, the first Yankee that
had ever entered its nine-hundred-year-old ramparts, in the
limestone foot-hills of the Bavarian Alps. It was for me
another village four miles from the railroad, with a dialect
still more alien than Bolton's. The sister of the village-
surveyor, Der Herr Geometer Stark. What did I want
with Fräulein Stark? Who was Fräulein Stark? Fräulein
Stark, thin-lipped, sharp-witted, and sharp-tongued, sallow,

black-eyed, sinewy dame of fifty, had been the housekeeper
of our fraternity in Boston University days. Was she glad
to see one of the boys—who had rescued her from her job
as governess in the Back Bay? She was. It was in the district around Velberg that, with the permission of the burgo-
master, an amateur archæologist, I visited the astonish-
ing cave described in "Two Lives" (Part III, XXVI).

To Göttingen, through little visited Regensburg with
its Roman ruins, all day in a fourth-class car, full of folks,
jostling and joking all, red-cheeked peasant girls, foresters
in green felt hats, dumpy middle-age, and *Burschen,* frank,
irresponsible, and shabby. Though I've never worked with
the workers (beyond a New England hay-field), in my own
poverty I've often knocked about with them. The people on
earth I have always felt most at home with are from the
so-called intellectuals and the so-called proletariat—analytic masters of human reality by isolated thought, instinctive masters by commonalty of toil. So I enjoyed that ride.
The small boy who gave me apples from his basket was
doubtless in 1914 saving civilization for the rest of us,
along with the millions on either side of all the war-fronts.
I spent a year in the quaint old rainy city, where the sun
was at best a diffused splotch of yellow glare in gray skies
from November to March and the winter snows were without shadows; and in wistful mood I wrote the sonnet (in
"The Vaunt of Man") which, as recited sonorously later
in New York, made young Ludwig Lewisohn's eyes pop and
spine tingle, as he recounts in "Up Stream." My poetry
brought me a friend for life. It has not been, you see, a
thing in vain.

On all my wanderings in the villages and hills about
Göttingen, on all the trips from city to city about Germany,
and up and down the Rhine from my residence in Bonn, in
Switzerland and France and Italy, there accompanied my
intense interest in the sights of nature and of strange civili-
zations and memorials, this surging thrill of freedom and
self-reliant morale. I enjoyed nothing more than entering a

city, as Geneva or Rome, where I had to trust to luck for
both language and lodgings. I was so secure in myself, and
mankind was so friendly, though in the linguistic confidence
there was of course the added psychological moment of intellectual assurance. Nature was so friendly too . . . or
rather I felt in the very silence and majesty of even her
bleakest peaks a silence and majesty in my own spirit that
made me at home. I had many perilous adventures. Truly
perilous, not merely so seeming in retrospect to my condition of to-day that takes fright on an orcharded hilltop a
half-mile from my door. The gray mountain wall just back
of Geneva, Mount Salève, is not as famous as the Lake or
the white peaks ranged from Dent de Midi to Mont Blanc
beyond the borders of the Lake; but it should be more
famous than it is. A greater than Lamartine should dedicate
it a stave. It towers precipitously on its Geneva side a mile
in air. You can clamber to the ten-mile-long plateau through
the gorge in the wall. I went up the gorge—but not of that.
Let us take the circuitous roadway of eight miles on the
end toward the lake. I was traversing its familiar ascent on
one of my Sunday afternoon rambles, when I thought to
cut off the last two miles by striking up through the brush
and furze. I was soon in a dense fog, in danger any instant
of stepping through a bush off the precipice into the talus
a mile below. Totally lost also. I wander on, curious, delighted, thrilled . . . for an hour . . . in the cool white
mystery that shrouds me from all I ever knew. Suddenly I
seem to hear singing somewhere in the mist, many voices,
eerie, shrill, and yet happy. To-day I would, with reason,
think them voices of old memories, singing as if from far
away in both time and space . . . such voices I have heard
so many times now, singing voices and far whistling and
bell-ringing, cow-bell and engine-bell . . . in the twilight
sleeps of my clinic . . . sometimes too even when reading at my desk. But then I had not even this explanation.
Curious, delighted, thrilled . . . yet realistic too. I
thought of angels and fairies, but only in sportive fancy.

Yes, singing voices they are, a chorus, and louder. Children's voices—I would have known them for the happy voices of children of earth, if I had heard them in the craters of the moon. And still louder . . . children's voices of France or of Switzerland, for Salève divides the countries. And weirdly I light upon a dancing-ring—little hands clasped in hands and a pink little face and a pink little smock-frock in the middle. Ring-around-a-rosy, or something like it, in the misty mid-region on high. They stop, as surprised as the intruder. "Where is the mountain-house?" I ask in that French I once spoke so nonchalantly. "Why, it's right here," says the child in the ring . . . I was within twenty feet of the rear door. . . .

Let me complete the tale of the surprises of that day. The fog sank toward the valley and left the stone mountain-house foursquare in the crisp and clear October breeze of sundown. Between me and the Alps lay an aërial ocean of cloud forty miles across, billowing in transcendent golds and reds, with Mont Blanc the highest island among a chain of islands, all fiery peaks. A glowing surge without spume or breaker or sound or salt or sail, with vast distances between the larger billows . . . and a cosmic calm ere this billow or that would heave so slowly and silently or roll again, as if by an accumulated energy of its own, in rhythm with no wind or swell. It was a scene from Greek mythology. I would not have been astonished to see Perseus flying toward for his Andromeda, or Poseidon-Charioteer and his white horses bounding up from below. And all the while underneath, in the valley of the Arve, the farmers looked up to a commonplace sky, overcast and threatening rain. So much depends on the point of view.

To-day the imagination, or rather subconscious memory, gives to even the placid familiar places an alien terror; in those days even the strangest and most alien places stirred the imagination unto delight. Even when the self realistically confronted danger, as of death or of sickness, it experienced not panic, but a problem. You recall, from Chamonix, where the Arve debouches, muddy and turbulent, out of ice-caves at the foot of the Mer-de-Glace? I had left Batschinsky, Russian fellow-student in Göttingen, my traveling companion, protected from the drizzle in a pine-grove, for a climb up the steep lateral moraine, banked there in old times when the glacier's course had been farther out into the valley. I wanted to look down on the Mer-de-Glace from above, just where its ice front formed the precipice. I wanted to compare its edge with Niagara Falls as seen from above. There was a lateral path far up along the ridge of the moraine, by which I intended to descend. But some hundreds of feet in air I became too much exhausted to climb to the path, far higher than it had looked, and found the direct descent itself impossible with its loose rocks and gravel. I sat helpless on a partially projecting boulder. The long River of Ice lay before me out of its lofty fiord, amid such summits of snow as made meaningless the measure of its distance in terms of human miles. Mont Blanc beyond to the right . . . Coleridge's "Hymn," "Manfred". . . Space was a different thing, even from space in the White Mountains. Time too on a larger scale . . . that was why the River of Ice seemed not to flow. My speed was not its speed. Torrential rain makes rivulets all about me, and the little Arve is boiling in the boulder-strewn meadow. I think: "Well, you damn fool, you have preached cosmic nature in your damn rimes—and here you are—and here you end. A damn fine end for a damn fool." In those five minutes I was, subjectively speaking, in the presence of death in as awesome a spot as you will find on this earth. And without terror. I think again: "You will tumble down eventually; why not tumble, while you still have your wits and some strength to help make the tumble systematic?" I stick my traveler's checks in my inside vest-pocket, stuff a handkerchief in either hip-pocket, and start sliding down, my back pressed to the declivity. I keep a quick lookout for bits of boulder on which from instant to instant my heels a little check my speed. I dig elbows and hands into the rolling grit.

Little Slider-downhill. On the wet grass by the Arve I lie, I can't say how long, with tongue out like a dog, unable to budge. At last I hobble to the pine-grove, in shreds, palms bleeding. Batschinsky leads me to an inn. I lie in bed all day. The French maid sits beside me with brandy and jokes. Batschinsky goes down to the village and brings back the only extra pair of pants in Chamonix.

Here I faced death—with ironic humor and resourcefulness, and at most with anxiety. I faced disease in the same way—disease now always a ghastly shadow I have to fight back, though I stand in the very fortress of many years of physical health. I had overdone in Rome. The Ancient City of half my dreams was truly as a city to which I was merely returning after long homesickness. But, like one returning, I was the more eager to see all the old familiar places. I was underfed and incessantly on the go for ten days, up and down and over the Tiber, out on the Campagna, on each of the Seven Hills . . . though I was twice unsuccessful in my plans to brood, silent and alone, in the Colosseum—first by moonlight, because of a fiddler and impromptu dancers of the folk in the shadowy arches; second by sunshine, because an elderly German led a party of ladies into the arena, and seating them on the fallen plinths, began reading in a loud voice from Baedecker. It was useless even to quote Byron. . . . I had overdone in Rome, and, weak and feverish, I cut short my stay in Florence, to get over the Alps as soon as possible into Munich, where Fräulein Stark, my nearest friend, could look after me. I am at the station in Venice, awaiting a change of cars. The day has broken raw and drizzly. But to sit till nine o'clock shivering here in this dingy corner, with Venice unvisited perhaps forever. This shall not be my memory of Venice. So I button my frayed overcoat tight; I drink whisky; I walk forth . . . in the rain . . . over bridged canals, through winding alleys, to St. Mark's and the Doge's Palace, and the Bridge of Sighs. I return up the Grand Canal, past the famous stone façades, and under the Rialto, not by gondola, but by a chugging truck-steamer, warming my spine as usual against the stack. I have another twenty-four hours by day and by night, through the Brenner, through Innsbruck, to Fräulein Stark, without sleep . . . but also without disease, after all. Two weeks later the Campanile fell, and I laid down my copy of the "Tageblatt" and quoted from Byron's "Ode to Venice". . . .

A loud lament along the sweeping sea.

The reader must not forget the purpose of these stories of adventure. In themselves they are of little moment; in comparison with the hardihood of brave men in lonely peril on polar ice or Sahara sands they are nothing. They have significance only in contrast to the later mental states of the subject of this study. It was in Munich, after this flight north, that I experienced the first typical recrudescence of the childhood traumas—a then unaccountable dread and shame, a double motif, that kept me from paying a second visit to the family of my two years' fellow-student, Heinz Pringsheim. We were close intimates in the same house at Bonn, I in a hall room at the top, he in a suite on the ground floor with a grand piano and Lenbach's portrait of his sister (now the wife of Thomas Mann). He had sought me out in the pro-seminary of Leo at Göttingen, having become interested in the ragged stranger. He was later to lend me the money for my passage back to America . . . still later, so much later, I was to send him the few dollars I could for his sick wife and child when he had laid down his sword but could not take up his conductor's baton. He is to-day writing the best musical criticism I've ever read, when not slaving at his desk in the government offices over Italian reparations. His people in Munich, his father the famous mathematician, had heard of the American and wanted to show him kindnesses. I was too horribly afraid and ashamed to get to their door that day, though I had been there the day before with a welcome. I couldn't understand myself. I thought it was the contrast of their magnificent home and my poverty; but the contrast was only the stimulus, perhaps related to the contrast in childhood between Mary's home and ours. Later, in Philadelphia and Madison, the earliest manifestations of my manhood phobias were these spells of panicky shame, sometimes suddenly attaching themselves for weeks and months to a single individual. I felt the same dread and shame for a few days with Pringsheim himself after I got back to Bonn; which I falsely explained to myself as embarrassment for my apparent discourtesy to his family. I would have the acutest dread, utterly unmotivated, of facing a given person, always some person with whom I was on the friendliest footing, more often a woman, but often enough a man, so that I found sex-embarrassment an apparently irrelevant explanation . . . not totally, however, as the analytic reader must recall . . . for there had been little Mary. I could ward off these attacks best in company where I didn't have to face directly the troubling glance of my friend or by *hiding* (as behind a *shelter*) behind dark eye-glasses. It was a premonitory symptom. Life's exhaustions, of which I have still to speak, were wearing down my resistance: the panicky shame of the railway-station of 1878 and of the school-house of 1885 were getting their chance at last. Curiously, the shame-phobias decreased, though for years vaguely intermittent, after the now characteristic phobia of flight-to-shelter set in. I have had practically no shame-phobias in the last ten or twelve years—whereas the flight-to-shelter phobias have at the same time enormously vindicated their power.

If the spirit of physical adventure during my European sojourn was in such contrast both with the timidities and terrors of childhood and with the constricting phobias of middle age, the spirit of intellectual adventure, with a new language and civilization and with new subjects and technique, was but the unfolding of the spirit of curiosity and wonder, alive in the two years' child on the railway-platform—and alive within me still. Unlike the over-compensations in the spirit of the free and adventurous physical roamer, this spirit owed nothing of its excess, I believe, to the Locomotive-God—at least until after the actual phobias of maturity. I cannot believe there is any psychological meaning in the suggestion that, just as that shock indubitably fixated certain terror-reactions, it may have fixated an intellectual reaction, and turned a momentary mood of childish inquisitiveness into a life-habit and life-passion. Nor have I the slightest clinical evidence. My intellectual curiosity at the station was an aboriginal set of mind, fostered by training in childhood; as little fixated by the Locomotive-God as annihilated by the Locomotive-God. The Locomotive-God has affected my intellectual quest only through the concrete conditions of distress and frustration established first by the chronic neurosis. The practical result of the phobias, not the psychological complex itself, has been the modifying factor. Psychoanalysts have affirmed that my intellect has been roused to greater independence of action, to greater confidence in itself, by compensation for the actual collapse of self-confidence in other ways. My intellect has certainly sought out new interests in compensation for interests denied; it has, for instance, traveled imaginatively by books and by maps, as well as achieving its escapes by an absorption in scholarship more exclusive than if I lived with a thousand free paths from my door-steps. But this compensatory escape-motif is fundamentally rather a deflection of intellect than a stimulus, the intellect's more exclusive preoccupation with books, often too as substitutes; and, as to the compensatory confidence-motif, it is hard for me to make out any vital difference between the intellectual self-assertion of my practically constricted present and my intellectual self-assertion of earlier years when free to assert the self normally in all other ways. If there is any difference at all, besides an external difference in social tactics, I conjecture sometimes a difference in the direction of less self-assertion and even less self-confidence; as due, however, to the humorous irony that comes with the mellower years of thoughtful men and not to any specific disheartenment of a life defeated by phobias. But the phobias have obviously challenged intelligence to understand them, even as they have thus far defied intelligence and will to master them. They have deflected intelligence to a long study of abnormal psychology: this remains the outstanding achievement of the Locomotive-God in my intellectual affairs. *Elan vital of* phobias on the one hand, *élan vital* of intellect on the other: the reader will have marked how the two *élans* have woven so dominantly the plot of my life-history. And the dénouement seems to be this: my intellect, after roaming through the libraries and the lands, finally deploys all its energies, as awakened in all its curiosity and as commanded by pressing practical need, in turning upon and making the subject of its search the sinister energy that dwells in the same personality with it, until, after tracing that energy through a thousand shapes, it finds the aboriginal form and names that form for the thing it is. The intellect that began by trying to understand all the world ends by understanding something—alas, not all—of a phase of the single self. In one way or another that is where all intelligence ends . . . or it is not intelligence.

An allied question that I had originally intended to defer is this: is my creative energy, whatever of poet there is in me, psychologically involved in this complex, either in its latent or its manifest form? There is much loose talk about artists as being necessarily neurotics. In my case the known aspects of the situation seem capable of very simple formulation. My phobias (latent or manifest) did not make me a poet, though they furnished many an unsuspected line in my poems; and my poesies did not make me a phobiac, though they may have sometimes lowered nervous resistance to phobic attack. Neither is the birth of the other. But likewise neither was *necessarily* involved in the other: genetically, I could have become a phobiac without becoming a poet or half a poet, and vice versa. But there does remain a connection: a sensitive, imaginative, emotional organization is the prerequisite for becoming either half a poet or a good phobiac. The poet is by constitution more exposed than most mortals to initial shock; the poet is more exposed to the subconscious effects of initial shock; but all men are exposed in some degree. And the poet may escape this exposure or the calamities of this exposure, as most poets or other artists have in fact escaped. I was one who did not escape; I was one who, through circumstances, humanly speaking fortuitous, had to pay the price for his temperament which life does not exact from all. Possibly too the poet and the phobiac are similar in having a similar relation between consciousness and subconsciousness. In each the subconscious tubes into the consciousness may be more numerous and more open. . . . Perhaps this holds for the whole class of the more highly endowed of mankind, and most completely for the man we call the genius, who works so largely without apparent effort or conscious design or the dictates of society and convention. Yet something more than numerous open tubes is implied too: the subconsciousness itself must be a rich ferment of good things with energy to make them bubble upward. My crude imagery and incomplete science can get no farther; but at least I know that they can get no further . . . and that at best they haven't got very far.

Such speculations were, however, far enough from my thought when I settled down as a German student and as a student of German. Learning a new language, not as something of new words and combinations that comes into one's mind (with whatever vitality) from the printed page in the study, but as a function of one's *entire* experience both in taking in and giving forth, as organically a phase of both the individual and the social self—the process was indeed not unlike the birth of a new mind within me. I had postponed, for other more immediate advantages and interests, the study of German in college from the time I began to look forward to studying it on the ground. I did wisely. In six months I had learned among the Germans more of their speech than I could have learned in six years in an American class-room. But this comparison falsifies the time-relations: the six years would have been composed of a series of brief moments isolated from one another and from the rest of the six years' living. The six months were German on the street, in the shops, at the café, on a walk, at a lecture, in my reading, German with man, woman, or child, with book or newspaper. All day long, with all the day's thoughts and emotions, all day long—while in the night sleep in its own way reworked, to more organic results still, the linguistic experience of the waking hours. It is truly one thing to study to read a language and another to study to live by a language. But let no one suppose the process repeats the child's learning of its native tongue. The "natural method" is applicable but once in any human life, and then too without the pedagogics of the new education. But once; for we have the child's *mind* but once, and we find ourselves but once in that *situation* where we are learning life *per se* at the same time that we are learning talk *per se*. The process would be different if only for the fact that another set of linguistic habits has to be, in a way, unlearned before we can acquire the new set. The child has no previous language in the way, between experience and the names and locutions. Yet I can trace similarities between my learning English and my learning German. The memory of the latter adventure is of course fresh; but I have perhaps an almost unique memory of the former—I can remember at least the latter stages of "learning to talk." In each was the vital interest in words both as *meaning* and as *sound*, the zest to make them mine by use, the relatively high facility to remember, to imitate, to manipulate, and, above all, to create my own combinations, in accord with the subconsciously perceived laws of the language, as worked out quite as subconsciously by the million talkers of past generations. I had the so-called linguistic talent organically from birth (compare my mother's diary), along with the organic physical "talent" to become six feet tall with a rangy,

rather than a stocky, physique. I have as little right to brag
of one as the other—*natura fecit, non ego*. But linguistic
talent in maturity controls a consciously analytic instrument
besides. It studies grammar. This study, however, need not
be by a grammar-text. It may be, as has been mainly the
case in my own study of all languages—I know something
of twenty-five—an analytic study of usage in books read or
talk heard: I generalized a German grammar from the
living language. This was possible not simply because of
linguistic talent, but in great part because of prior scientific study of linguistics. My linguistic talent is correlated
with the creative artist in me, the study of linguistics with
the intellectual quest. But, in spite of "talent" and linguistic
science, I bungled and floundered into the new knowledge
and power. Even my old friend Prokosch of Bryn Mawr,
gifted in language beyond any man I have met, blunders
and flounders in contrast with what either he or I can
ideally project, from our practical linguistic experience, as
"the perfect linguist." Talents in any field, more or less
above the ordinary, are the best reminders of the limitations of all human intelligence, that is, of the enormous
access as yet unattained.

I discovered too in Germany that above languages is
language—that all men speak essentially with the same
physical and psychic apparatus. I discovered that the little
German I had so laboriously read was already, so far as it
went, not only a language but language and had revealed
its intrinsic messages, even its intrinsic overtones. I had felt
the essential "Lorelei" of Heine as I had repeated it on a
Boston trolley; it did not become a different poem even
after a talkative year in the Rhineland. So I suspect that
Vergil's language is not dead—unless pronounced as English. So I believe I already hear Sappho in Sappho, though
I can never visit the Lesbos of 600 B.C. Beyond languages
is language, and beyond language is the common life of the
race. A language is only dead to dead souls.

The German universities were a new experience, more

222

momentous even than the German language. Here was a
civilization where the life of mind was to the state what in
Aristotle's conception it was in the economy of the individual, in the hierarchy of the goods of the good life—the
culmination, the *summum bonum*. It needed to make no
apologies. It was its own justification; or rather it justified
all else in civilization that was justified at all. The free, the
utterly free spirit of learning, organized, but organized for
freedom, the meaning of learning, both as substance and as
method, how much more profound than I had ever known!
And lesson-getting forever at an end; written reports to
pedagogues forever at an end. My own free choice of book
or lecturer. The scholar dedicated to truth, to its discovery
—to its discovery, no less than to presentation. The driving power of all, the organizing power of all, for the pur-
suit of truth to the very center. Individual minds, both
teachers and students, I had met in America fully the equal
of any I met in Germany; but the total impression was overwhelmingly as of something in its very essence and aim of a
different, a higher order. I discovered in short the reality
that from childhood had been troubling my spirit in its
dreams. In the German universities I was for the first and
last time of my life in my own intellectual home.

I am not bitter toward our American universities. I
have more right to pride in Wisconsin than any German
colleague has to pride in Göttingen, Bonn, or Heidelberg.
Wisconsin is a great school, a great cultural force; and if
not as a whole a university in the German sense, you can
find there among its eight thousand something that is becoming a university, say of twelve hundred, though at present desperately entangled in administration and personnel
with the traditional undergraduate college and the recent
technical schools. And my pride is that this vigorous institution was founded but seventy-five years ago, and founded
in the wilderness, shaped by and helping to shape the very
framework of the commonwealth. It is my pride, but it
can never be my intellectual home. The hierarchy of the

dominating values is aboriginally and eternally alien for me. Alien for me as mind; sympathetic to me as American— a conflict I can never fully resolve. The creative energies it puts forth, in spite of grievous wastage, it puts forth to ends I call humanly desirable . . . but humanly not most desirable. They are not my ends, except in casual and fragmentary moments . . . and except, let me say, in the research laboratories. I came to realize that the German universities had not only been the chief centers of the discovery of truth in the nineteenth century, but that they had given to the world a discovery still greater, the discovery of scientific method, the technic for discovering truth. Yet it has been my lot, off and on, for thirty years to hear American teacher or colleague smile tolerantly at the heavy and useless learning of German books. If there is more pedantry in Germany than in America, it is simply because there is so much more *Wissenschaft*.

I came to Germany when some of the great elder generation were still lecturing. I heard Moritz Heine on Old Germanic life, Leo Meyer on comparative philology, and eighty-year Bücheler on Horace. I came when some great reputations were still being made. I heard Roethe on Goethe, Morsbach on Middle English and Burns, and Bülbring on Anglo-Saxon; Wilmanns, perhaps in both groups, I heard on Germanic grammar. But this paragraph is not the vita of a Ph.D. dissertation. I heard these men. I heard their peers. I was in their seminaries. I was in their homes. And no one of them ever noticed my clothes. I corresponded with one or another . . . till they dropped one by one . . . even during the war. . . . The German universities had doors open for all the world. They charged no higher fees to the Americans. They welcomed the Americans perhaps over all other students. They certainly taught them more. They taught, indeed, some of us the very scientific devices and knowledge which, as worked out in American laboratories, became later timely instruments for saving civilization from the Huns.

I had gone to Germany to prepare myself for a position in Latin at B.U. But the scholarship of the masters over-whelmed me. The scholarship of student-friends over-whelmed me—there was one who quoted Catullus and Vergil and Sappho half the night on many a night, Rudolf Borchardt, the now famous critic and poet. I had high ideals. I wanted to be among the best in my own scholarship. Perhaps in the strange environment I exag-gerated the disparity; perhaps the difference between my own broken preparation and the German schools made only too real a difference. I surrendered Latin. I went into English (and Germanic) philology, where I felt I could compete on an equal footing. Counsels of an American in Göttingen, himself a professor of English on leave, Henry Snyder of Wofford, weighed too. I gave up the practical certainty of a life job at Boston University for an uncertain ideal. It was an ideal that concerned me alone; I would have been equal at least to the job ahead. Was it foresight or folly? I had a chance for my ideal. But I did not—for long—find my chance for a job wherein to work out my ideal. And I never succeeded in frustrating something more aboriginal than ambition's ideal, the love of a thing for the thing's own sake. I did not then know that the love of the classics was the deeper thing; and that it was to avenge itself on my disloyalty by reiterating its lure all my life to prevent me, along with other distractions, from being the top-notcher in reputation in the field itself of my am-bition's ideal. I have a respectable name in two worlds of scholarship; a venerated name in neither.

But there were to be more immediate issues than this from my surrender of Latin and the job at B.U. Some trou-bles of life it would seem have simply come to me, even as the Locomotive-God came; where at worst my defect of wits was in not knowing how to get out of the way or how to give them a turn. But the long maladjustments due to this change of career were due to my own choice in the change. Still, to regret the choice would be to overlook all the realized meaning life has had ever since; and realized meaning is the only success I understand. . . . Perhaps I should cancel my earlier comment on my father's choice in leaving his pastorate. . . . There are three attitudes to the what-might-have-been: regret, which naïvely assumes the issues would have been happier (the world's way); repudiation, which as naïvely assumes, to save one's face, that whatever is is ideally better than what might have been (the New-Thoughter's way); acceptation, in terms of reality, of the values that have come, especially of the values that have come as earned, for there is not a choice or a chance in life whereby life cannot find value or make value. This is the way of the sage. . . . I have tried to make it mine. A part of my story is how I have tried to make it mine.

But meanwhile I was unwittingly reorganizing my life for subtler and more spiritual maladjustment. I was beginning to see in Germany the ideal state, with individual freedom through organization, as the creative unit, in contrast to the amorphous aggregate. Reveille at the Göttingen barracks around the corner, or the goose-step when the crown prince drove by in his tandem on Bonn's Coblenzer-strasse, were for me spectacular or comic externals; the realities were the clean cities, the schools, the concerts, the theaters, the wise laws and the people who obeyed them, not as cowards but as coöperators—the manifestations everywhere of a commonwealth intelligent unto highest ends. And was I not right, after all? Reveille and goose-step are gone . . . the Germany I loved remains. Reveille and goose-step were the comic externals—the same as in France . . . Russia . . . England . . . Italy . . . except for the patriotic nuances of brass and boot . . . till the grotesque fantasy, common to all, became the Devil's holiday. Nonsense of reveille and goose-step are gone . . . but only in Germany. Germany won the war.

I began in Germany to assemble my thoughts on society from reality, not from patriotism. I conceived a new ideal of my American citizenship: I would be the wise American, not the cheering American. And I would help other Americans to think and to create by thought and to give over the cheering for a while. I would be to America the revealer of this great country, this Other Country of my childhood. Yet Republic must vindicate itself against Empire. My estimate of actual America went down; my ideal of America rose. I thought: "It is glorious to *live* for one's country. Emerson found it glorious . . . why not I?" For the more one lives creatively for one's country, the more one lives for the world. Emerson does, Goethe does, Edison, Ehrlich. And neither parliaments nor kaisers ever declared war to prove one or the other has the greater Man or the greater Statue of the Man. Reveille and goose-step *are* comic.

The troubles ahead for me from my unhappy convictions about the German commonweal were a long way ahead. The troubles from my love of the German people, though playing a part in the later troubles, were to begin with my return to America. I discovered unfortunately that in character I was a German. My German friends discovered it too. They said I looked like the young Goethe of the picture, where he lay brooding beside the Roman ruins. German, in my search for reality, in my indifference to form except as organic form, in emotional depth rather than in emotional display. German in an ineradicable naïveté of self-revelation and trust, German in my hierarchy of ethical values—loyalty to truth and friend and self—German in my wit and particularly in my humor. Now, in an equally friendly environment, say, in China, I would probably have discovered that I was a Chinese, a union of Confucius and Li Po; and it need not have been the same sort, it could not have been the same sort, of an environment. There is so much human nature in all the more highly developed and complex individuals in all races and nations that any visitor, if he gets into their real world, through the differences of technic and dialect of life, will discover enough of himself to feel, as if by a revelation, himself already theirs. And those who take him in will take him as theirs. My English friends say I still prove the breed . . . my Spanish friends say I am a typical Andalusian . . . it is only my American friends who insist on rejecting me. But was there nothing at all in this discovery of Teutonic affinity? I have enough complexity and plasticity of temperament and enough joy in humanity to find some affiliations with all races—I have had acquaintances among almost every stock on the planet, including Eskimos, Zulus, and Polynesians; yet (let me confess it, now ten years after the war), when I most crave solid comfort of body and both relaxation and enthusiasm of mind, and a little understanding of the reasons for my existence, I will seek out a German, or an American . . . or an Englishman . . . or Spaniard . . . or Japanese . . . who is as near like a German . . . like me . . . as I can find. . . . I mean as near like the particular variety of German that I like.

The boat will be bringing the young man back to America very soon, with all his bigger troubles ahead. We dare not linger too long, drinking our beer and talking philosophy and politics either in the tavern on the October hills back of Göttingen or in the balustraded garden by the midsummer Rhine. We won't visit now the Kneipe or the Mensur with caps and colors—to smile at their picturesque excesses, along with the German fellow-students that smile too. We won't drink Maibowle around the lamp-lit table on the garden piazza with the hostess of our Bonn lodging-house, *das gnädige Fräulein von Zitzewitz* and the yellow-haired *Backfisch,* her pretty niece, Emmie, really witchingly pretty and demure and soulful. For now it is all a reality; and it will all go back across the Atlantic as a memory. And reality may become, as this did, more potent as memory. And memory may create, as this did, new reality.

The young man was to take back to America another memory, too, the memory of an American comrade in Göttingen. This too was destined to create new reality; and the comrade, becoming himself strangely my comrade again in this Western city, was to coöperate in the flesh with this memory of his old self to make this new reality indeed very new and unforeseen. Jack was the first fellow-countryman I met in Germany. We were for the first weeks in the same pension. Both of the class of '98 in American colleges, both with a year or so of high-school teaching; both of about the same build, both above the rest of the American colony, I think, in intelligence; both well-wishers of our fellow-men, with decent ideals of conduct and strong ethical urges. I liked him with all my heart . . . and better with the months. He liked me . . . though, I am sure, far more casually. Yet he wrote me at Christmas from Copenhagen, where he was stopping with his fiancée and her sister and father, playmates and fellow-townsmen from the Middle West. He wrote that the sister was ill. And he wrote me from his researches in Paris when I was at Columbia. And in the spring he had me meet his lady in Göttingen. She was a lithe tall girl, with large eyes and soft wavy hair, molded chin and high color—the European's very ideal of the American girl, when the European is dreaming at his best. And I remember her too. She was the only American woman of my age I saw for over a year. I liked her . . . and wanted to see her again. And he had me meet the old gentleman—not so old, a Grand Army man and paterfamilias, with white goatee and quick jokes. Yet Jack and I were very different. I would probably not have been so welcome in his cozy rooms opening out upon the little gravel path and the fruit-tree if we had been in America. I must have seemed, too, something of a fool to Jack. He had clothes, a secure past, a secure future. Many years later indeed he was to say in words of an address read all over the United States: "Fortunately or unfortunately, I knew neither the handicap nor the incentive of early hardship." He had a most definite aim, a mind made up and already equipped for one thing. He had come to study under the greatest mathematicians of Europe. My bursts of intellectual excitement, my spurts of intellectual interest in all directions, above all my exterior, clean enough but always shabby and unkempt, must have amused him, perhaps annoyed him. I think right then and there he acquired a life-long impression that was to play its saddening part in the relations that turned out so disastrously for me . . . the impression that Leonard wasn't a fellow to be taken very seriously. He needed no incentive of hardship to develop his extraordinary energy as scientist, man, or leader of men. But hardship might have helped him to understand men . . . and the Göttingen fellow-student. Yet experience, however rough, cannot transcend personality; and his personality instinctively gravitated to its own set, its own social kind; and really respected intellectually only its own intellectual kind. Though he played the violin, it was for escape and diversion; the conception of the artist, especially the poet, as anything more than the ornament and entertainment of civilization was beyond his vision then . . . and, I think, later. My long-haired and restive loquacity in Göttingen was, I fear, not exactly the influence to convert him; but later in Madison, after I had made the welkin ring before five thousand with an ode at the unveiling of the Lincoln statue, he said to me words that revealed I had not converted him yet. By way of ingenuous compliment, he said, "Now, that was really a situation where after all only a poem would do." Poetry, my poetry at least, was still only a social ornament, though on occasion a very acceptable ornament. But then and always for me there have been two supreme greatnesses, from Aristotle and Homer to Einstein and Goethe: the Scientist, the Artist; the Finder, the Fashioner. I understood Jack. He never understood me. He never will understand me. This year he received the doctor of science from one leading university in the East; I have heard that this same year I might have received a doctor of letters from another . . . had my disease not prevented me from going. I know about Jack's degree. He will never know about mine.

XII

I HAD lived two years on a thousand dollars, part of it borrowed. I had wanted both Italy and the German degree. I had chosen Italy. But I had been awarded a fellowship in English at Columbia. I was returning to write my dissertation and to get in touch through Columbia with professional opportunities. The desire to do was crowding the desire to know. Columbia generously exempted me from routine limitations. The English faculty welcomed me. The library facilities were most excellent. But my heart collapsed. The Rhine was between America and me. Those halls of brick and stone seemed a factory. The professors, though genial and cultured men, seemed fussy or idle dilettanti beside the masters I had heard. . . . Except for the professor under whom I was preparing my "Byron and Byronism in America." Trent, largely self-taught though he was, alone seemed to have the instincts and technic and materials of scholarship. I didn't know rare George Woodberry till years thereafter . . . now my best friend among the elder gray-haired poets that I have overtaken in gray. Things have perked up at Columbia since then.

The graduate students thought Columbia the Mecca of all intellectual pilgrimages. Several had known no other institution, even as undergraduates. Even John Erskine, the best of them all. And he is still there, after a year long ago in the provincial Amherst Hills. Yet he could write "The Private Life of Helen of Troy," even as Columbia educated and Columbia educator. A best seller among the best people whose laughter is thoughtful in two countries. What

231

might he not have written with a rangy and variegated academic experience like mine! I began, for the first time since childhood, to be at odds with folks. It is a wonder the chaps and young blue-stockings in the seminary workshop remained on the whole as friendly as they did. I made unseemly jokes. I exalted philology. I piffled at poetry. I told Erskine that Venus would have done better to send Adonis to a medical specialist. (That may have started him on his realistic vision of classic love-affairs.) I was least unhappy in my lodgings with the Vierecks, where I could still talk German. George Sylvester was then sixteen, a cerebral elf. On my first interview he had followed his mother down the corridor and, agitated that the stranger had not noticed him, popped out from behind her skirts with the anxious cry: "Ich bin ein Dichter; ich bin ein Dichter." He was. A German lyrist even then. He became a lyrist in English, with a recognized note, exotic but rich and passional. With poems even in those standard periodicals of morals and taste—"Independent" and "Literary Digest." Then the literary Vigilantes decreed him dead as bad poet because of bad politics. He had founded the Poetry Society. So they expelled him from the Poetry Society to help win the war. They still keep him out of the Anthologies. And Haldeman-Julius reprints him in his Little Blue Books with reprints of Swinburne and Wilde and Villon and other pariahs. To my corner bedroom at the Vierecks came also one other miserable, the future author of "Up Stream" and "Israel." Ludwig Lewisohn has painted my portrait in his American chronicle. Full length, excited, and unshorn. I would choose to sketch him half length, seated and unshaven, but no less excited. Seated at the typewriter in my corner room, ticking off my verses from my lips as I lay on the bed. His stocky frame, supporting an eager, kindly, leonine face, of pronounced Jewish cast and swartness, sat night after night at the table-job, with chubby but delicate fingers and sonorous interjections. He was younger than I, with at that time a more provincial experience, a sensitive and aggrieved South Carolinian, but his reading in English and German and Latin was extraordinary in range and in organic integration with his spirit. Poetry meant the world. And poetry was not of yesterday but for to-day and forever. My verses lay about in scrawls that nobody could read. Mankind should read them, especially our professors. I could not typewrite. He could. I cite his humble and mechanic task as a fine witness to the reality of his passion for the creative life. I have his typewritten manuscript still. I got it back from the professors with tired comments. And now my students get their manuscripts back with comments often quite as tired. Whenever a concrete fact of experience, as a mountain or an event, gave the poem its start, it sometimes said something that I stand by still; but too often a mere mood was the start, mainly the yearning or the restive mood, and the result was at best iridescent gas. Moreover, I had not yet closed the traditional English gap between literary feeling and life, a process which makes my best verse something as different from the Romanticists as are Frost's or Sandburg's. Of the realistic German contemporaries, I knew best Wilhelm Busch, the humorist. Ludwig and I swapped innumerable of his trenchant couplets, when we weren't swapping Catullus.

But in spite of George Sylvester and Ludwig, I was increasingly homesick, in all this brick and noise, for the mellow year of the Rhine. Also a little love-sick for Emmie, to whom I was sending verses—German verses . . .

> Ich hatte 'mal ein Zimmerlein,
> In Bonn, in Bonn am Rheine . . .

I felt a deeper pang still. I was in sober earnest in those months, a man without a country, though the stars and stripes floated by Grant's Tomb and yonder somewhere on the Palisades. I could not live in Germany . . . and I certainly was not living in America. And yonder too in Boston was the family already in want. I recognized, however, that

I was in a depressed and irritable and almost hysterical state, and decided, like a man, to pull myself together. Though heart and soul were still in Germany, I had packed up with me my sense of duty. I knew I owed Columbia courtesy and gratitude and hard work.

"Like a man." I tried to rehabilitate the American in me by seeing something of Maude and Annie in the home town near-by. I yearned, like the sick scholar I was, for the mood of our old summers in the White Mountains. Perhaps, I thought, Europe has tired me out. Maude was more hurt than Annie that I had let our correspondence lapse in the last year. Annie was studying art in New York with Christie; so I saw more of her. Perhaps this hurt Maude too. One can never know the inner story of the girls he has known best. I began to feel more like my old American self. Something of the White Mountains came back . . . as if beside the Rhine. Annie said something a little coyly and cold, when I put my arm too tenderly about her on the deck of the evening ferry-boat. I intended to write an apology. It turned out a proposal. Her reply came on my birthday . . . perplexed, grieved, frightened, negative. Good Mrs. Viereck assured me it was undoubtedly negative. I had never had a serious love-affair. I had never known practically anything about the passion that was now to harass and astound me. That negative turned mere fondness into a turmoil of yearning, sorrow, sinking, agony of wounded pride, and uncontrolled resentment. I pleaded by letter and interview—anything to remove that negative. Marriage apparently was only a formal idea with me. Sex-union itself in the concrete scarcely even a formal idea. But that negative. My reaction was more than intellectual pride or masculine conceit . . . though these too. The negative had roused the whole sex—and then blocked the whole sex. And sex was manifesting itself in desperate sublimations. I suffered an acute form of love-sickness, as real a disorder as thwarted Nature can devise against us. My symptoms were conventional enough. It pleased Ludwig to call them the grand passion. He knows himself more about these matters now. But what was not conventional was the relative superficiality of the cause. I had been no more seriously in love with Annie than she with me, though in a disordered state of nerves and emotions. I was puzzled myself, for I have never known suffering, however acute, that altogether destroyed self-observation and analysis. I know the specific cause now. Psychoanalysis has revealed emotional and ideational relationship between Annie and the little Mary of the Station: I was losing little Mary again. The relationship with 1878, in additional factors, comes out strikingly in the following episode. Obeying the counsels of an acquaintance, I had written in March an ultimatum: I was not to be trifled with; there had been too many evasions; she had acted yes and said no, etc., etc. There was an ominous spunk in the chirography on the envelop that was not long in coming. I rushed to my corner room. I tore into the envelop. The answer began: "Ellery, Ellery, Ellery, Ellery, Ellery"—five shrieking Elleries, each in progressive deviation from that amorous and orderly Spencerian script of the girls of twenty-five years ago. She discarded me for a villain. An instantaneous surge of horror and terror seized me, and I ran like a madman to find the acquaintance of the counsels. He stayed with me till midnight, somewhat skeptical of his wisdom. I was in an acute and unmotivated panic, consciously identical in tone and behavior with the phobic seizures of later years, and subconsciously identical (as clear from associational data of twilight sleep) in the source of its curiously acute over-reaction, yes, identical with the seizure in infancy before the locomotive. Even though I laughed sardonically, the initial attitude of masculine aggression, as in 1878, collapsed before attack as in 1878. The letter was the Locomotive-God. I was losing Mary again, with new complications. The Locomotive-God was not bearing down on me to separate me from her and to destroy her. She herself was now the Locomotive-God. And again, I was now to feel, not humiliation because Mary

235

thought me a fool, but degradation because Mary-Annie thought me something far worse than a fool. And the reaction during the next year—for I was nearly two years in getting over the emotional effects—of blind resentment in more than one letter and verse was resentment against the Locomotive-God. I am not excusing myself. I could have controlled the expression of the resentment even so. And the beautiful psychology, or the sublime irony, or the perfect comedy of the situation was that the confidante and comforter whom I *sought out,* in visit and letter, was none other than the mature woman who had been the little Mary of long ago. . . .

And now indeed the White Mountains came back. No hypnosis nor twilight sleep could have produced a more living total recall. But the subconsciousness is awakened in the clinic for only a few moments; here the emotional tension, acting on the subconscious and reacting from it, produced a state continuing for months. And again a difference: the super-vivid recall of the White Mountain days, that now reduced Columbia to a shadow, and the Rhine now to a forgotten legend, was an exquisite torture of the *no more, no more.* Homesickness is real, but it has its hope of intervening and estranging space to be eventually traversed. What I call *past-sickness*—that is, homesickness in the dimension of time instead of space—is in the nature of the dimension hopeless. And in this case, to the hopelessness of revisiting *as of old* the reality, was the added torture of the destruction of any eventual revisiting in the spirit. Annie haunted every skirt that rustled in the street, every girl's plume that tossed. Maude's big black eyes haunted me, for old affection's sake. The light and silence and majesty of the White Mountains haunted me with each glance at the Palisades, and with every New York Central whistle, echoing from their walls. I wanted to forget, not recall. And upon all this, settled the incubus of remorse—my fault, my fault (as in the remorse-motif of '78):

236

Du hast sie zerstört, die schöne Welt . . . Du, du, *du*.
Guilt. External reality was totally distorted; but internal
grasp of reality no less. In these later years external reality has been subject to far greater distortion; but I never
again lost the intellectual mastery of the distortion. In
other words, I never lost my head again. In a world of
normal senses and sense my silly proposal would have become in a few months a joke for all three of us. To my
tortured condition, though without hallucinations (in spite
of appetite gone and sleep gone), Annie became the
Ophelia, Rosalind, Portia, the Messalina, the Cleopatra,
whereas she was in fact but an innocent, distracted,
wounded girl. The only griefs that had a basis in reality
were two lovely friendships utterly ruined . . . and my
work at least half ruined. In spite of my research trips to
the libraries of Cambridge, Boston, Brown, and about New
York, my studies had become more a search for distraction
than a search for Byronism in America . . . or anywhere.
The preoccupation with Byronism, be it added, seems not
to have augmented my emotional confusion—it was shadowy, intellectual, comic, though there may have been subtle effects of my own Byronism of adolescence. The pain
was the realest thing in my life yet; the ideations the most
unreal before or since, except for the infantile ideation of
the Locomotive-God itself. Hence the poems that I wrote
were true, as sincere expressions of my experience, though
my experience had small objective truth. Many of the
world's poems have come out of such subjective reconstructions. Yet not, I believe, the greatest. And, even with
me, as between my Marguerite sonnets and the "Two
Lives," the difference is in the stark objective basis in the
ideations and emotions of "Two Lives." Subjective reality
and objective reality must be one at last, in art . . . as in
life. . . . I am not referring of course to mere accidents
as date and place. . . . Many years later I wrote the two
girls for forgiveness. But though they must by then have
realized that I had been in some way unbalanced, they

never replied. I do not know whether they are married or single, living or dead. I have not seen the White Mountains again; but I know they are still there.

By the end of April, I had a craving, like thirst in the desert, to escape to the Rhine. Intellectually, too, I decided that was the only resort. There had been no self-help, nor friend-help, on the ground. My poor father said he could "secure me a loan." He spoke as if certain. The loan came—he never told me but I know it was out of his own tragically small capital . . . from "the farm." I took the first boat for Rotterdam as one takes the first train to the suburbs . . . by grim irony the same boat and the same state-room as a few months before when homeward bound. I had tried to play Annie and the White Mountains off against the Rhine and Emmie. Now it was Rhine and Emmie against Annie and the Mountains. "Spielen Sie uns eine Comödie?" asked Viereck senior . . . with a bewildered yet sympathetic grin under his Teutonic mustache, by way of good-by. Of the Columbia professors, Trent was the only one in whom I confided anything of my state: "My mind seems to be going to pieces." His anxious and solicitous look said that he feared I was right. For the sake of that look, among other things, I am glad I did not go to pieces. The Rhine and Bonn and Emmie and all old German friends helped beyond all else; and on my second return to America, that October, I had other troubles than either Annie or Emmie, White Mountains or Rhine—no money, with debts to a thousand dollars, no job, no degree, and no very enthusiastic academic backers. "Brilliant, but dangerous to recommend," was the general formula. And, besides, my clothes. Could I blame them . . . the only puzzle is how they admitted the initial adjective.

In the railway-station at Cologne on the way thither, I had experienced for a night and a day the first of the fiercest solicitations of the then Unknown God. Behind me were many months of emotional tension and physical exhaustion, in no small part already his handiwork. I was

238

changing cars for Bonn, with ticket in hand. Midnight. The engine-bell was ringing. And ringing again. Sudden and nameless horror, of unsheltered isolation and helpless loneliness. Paradoxically, sudden and nameless shame and dread of meeting my friends in Bonn. Sudden and inexplicably intense craving for home, my own parents. Sudden emotional distortion of all spatial concepts, without any intellectual distortion of spatial facts: the distance back up the Rhine to Rotterdam, back from Rotterdam over the salt, unplumbed, estranging sea *felt* inevitable and immediate, as being rich with meanings for my strange and lonely need, whereas the brief miles to Bonn filled me with a surging sense of the impossible and the far. To my feeling, home and parents were nearer than Bonn, however much nearer Bonn remained to my intellect. This phenomenon of a double and contradictory reaction to reality will meet us again in still more amazing forms. It is characteristic of my chronic neurosis: a *feel*, especially as to distance, that converts a half-mile, or even two blocks from home, in terms of subjective need and powerlessness, into an infinite remoteness, at the same time that it remains to eye and estimate exactly the same half-mile or two blocks it is. This is an extreme form of a double reaction to experience that underlies much so-called normal conduct, where we *do* according to the more overwhelming evidence and urge of reality as *felt*, in spite of our intellect that knows better. In my case the conflict is readily analyzed: the *feel* is the reverberation of the feel in childhood trauma; e.g., the *feel* of infinite distance is the infantile subconsciousness with its infantile feel of the distance down the platform of 1878—and, as such, split off entirely from the eye and estimate of the mature intellect. It is really a phenomenon of double personality. I could not get on the car for Bonn. I sat in the dim and dreary station, waiting for the seizure to pass . . . drinking (of all things) strong coffee. At dawn I dashed to a hotel, forced myself to send a telegram to Bonn that I was sick, called a doctor, and went to bed.

The doctor said I was nervous and gave me a pill. I couldn't stay in bed. . . . *Relaxation made me worse.* The reason is now clear: relaxation was giving the subconscious reverberations of the Locomotive-God the better chance. I then did, by instinct, what I've done so many times since. I deflected attention, in desperation trying to shake off the spell by the commonplace business of shave and hair-cut. Coming out of the barber-shop, I bumped into Fräulein von Zitzewitz, who had taken the first train after receiving the telegram. The spell snapped instantaneously, and she took me back without difficulty. I suffered no ill effects, beyond physical tire that passed with a night's sleep. I still had great reserves of endurance. The Locomotive-God would have to wait still . . . for a better chance. I was as fully aware of the abnormality of the experience then as now; and its general outlines were never forgotten. It was associated, however, with no memories of infantile terrors, until the psychoanalysis (of 1922 to date). It was, then, one of the first experiences to grow near and vivid, and I recognized at once that the ringing of the engine-bell somehow (it was still long before I recognized just how) set off the disturbance. Wait . . . wait . . . the engine-bell will ring again . . . in 1911.

I had been delayed in my passage back, because funds had not come, till after the American schools had begun the fall term. A teacher's agency had a job waiting for me in German and history in a famous private school for the rich and swaggering sons of senators, bank directors, actors, divorcées—with a tragic little group of serious and gentle lads, none the less lovable because rich. Up the Hudson, where the private schools are as numerous as castle ruins on the Rhine, though less picturesque and less useful. The article I wrote for the "Boston Transcript" is still in manuscript . . . they said they had too many advertisers in their educational columns who would froth. Other journals said the same. Here I had my first experience with the typical Foxy Man. I had created out of all previous experience, as well as out of my own nature, a spontaneous faith in the ingenuousness of mankind as functioning in my own group. The confidence-men, the smart fellows, they belonged in another group—as a matter of course. For an intelligent man, I have made many blunders, groping my way through the world. Intelligence is now defined by our philosophers as successful adaptation to environment. I will think this over. I wonder what kind of a showing Shakspere's intelligence would have made among the Choctaws. It would seem that when I am at last aware of a Fox, I can watch him, to his discomfiture; that I can be fooled, without being a fool. I found I had accepted a salary less than half that of any of the other masters. I had always assumed that in business relations men of our group paid for services rendered what they seemed to be worth in themselves. This was my first awakening to the bargaining motif in American education. I had had no power to bargain. "He needs a job desperately, he comes back too late to find a good one, and I expect to get him for a third of what he is worth," the Foxy Man had told one of the masters (in confidence), who told me (in confidence), as I now tell the public (in confidence).

The swindle lasted but a few months. One Sunday after supper, I had strayed into the big library to warm my coat-tails at the comfortably blazing hearth. Some ten loungers there, football fellows, as big as I, were soon trying for sport and vengeance to jockey me on to the middle of the great rug, while another was getting ready to shut the door. I jumped to the exit. I threw one cub and felled another. The Foxy Man heard the rumpus from his office. He walked in, cool and masterful in his Prince Albert: "Well, boys, it's rather close in here; better open that window a little wider" (the window through which a millionaire's son had already jumped as I lunged for him in reckless fury). Then to me, under his breath, "Come at once to my office." He had something to say to me. I came at once. I had something to say to him. We both spoke at once;

and it would be a nice question whether I resigned or was fired. I received by note anonymous threats of violence next morning. I announced to him and to the ringleader that I was going to stay over till Tuesday, and would treat any young ruffians who entered my quarters as I would housebreakers. I bought a baseball bat in the village, barricaded my door that night with a bureau, chest, and trunk in a straight line across the room to the outer wall, and nailed up the transom. And slept—undisturbed. Still without fear, though taking no chances. Still without fear, in spite of the Locomotive-God and the nervous strain of many months.

Tuesday morning I called for my December salary. It was the beginning of vacation. He handed me my check. Twenty-five dollars. "That is not the full month's salary," I said. He explained that I was being paid, not by the month, but by the teaching day and hour. I couldn't tear the check up and throw it in his face. I had no bargaining power. It was all the money I possessed in the world. I was paying off the thousand dollars. As I walked through the outer office, I saw a newly opened box of fine Havanas. I stuffed every cigar into my frayed overcoat pockets, and, meeting the mathematics master on the train for New York, divided with him. "Here are some smokes for the fellows—on the Old Fox and me." The masters had given me a farewell dinner in the village . . . of congratulation and God-speed. I was known among them as Sunny Jim . . . *lucus a non lucendo*. The Latin master, an Oxford M.A., after I left, used to write me Horatian Sapphics, celebrating the Old Fox with detached gusto. In after years, I have heard, I became an informal asset to his establishment: "Professor Leonard, now of Wisconsin, a poet of no mean distinction, was formerly on our staff."

Back to Boston. My people give me springless cot and board table in a narrow back room by the alley fire-escape. I am sitting in despair at that table, cursing life. My father,

in the small doorway, chokes as he tries to encourage and
console, and turns away, hurrying his handkerchief from
rear pocket to his face, and steadying himself, confused, at
the jamb. I am startled out of myself into anxious solicitude
for him. "What is it, father?" "I want my son to be happy;
I want my son to be happy." I had never seen him cry. I
had never seen any old man cry. One doesn't . . . very
often. I had never heard a human call from so deep . . .
Curiously, it roused my energies. I scribble a series of articles for the "Transcript." I haunt teachers' agencies. I
write up my Byronism notes in five weeks. I get the dissertation typewritten, sent to Columbia, and accepted with
entire approval. I substitute two weeks in another private
school, long enough to make the head master wince, shame-
faced, for expelling a fourteen-year-old, frightened to death
and ready for death, because discovered in auto-eroticism.
I substitute for the spring term as the German teacher in
the Lynn Classical High School. I teach the grandsons of
Lydia Pinkham.

Lynn is a concentrated memory of sea-winds and friendly folks and long sleeps. I had a top chamber, big as a per-
golaed roof-garden, airy as a lighthouse, on a foreland
hill by the ocean where the Neck runs out four miles to the
headlands of Nahant. I could stand, like a liner's captain,
and see from my triple windows the Atlantic north to Mar-
blehead, south to the Bay and Marsh, and east to Egg-
rock Island and the long open horizon. Standing, sitting,
or lying, awake or adream, in sunlight or thunder, I had
space, winds, brine, and the sounds of the breakers on the
shingle. I strolled up the sands to Swampscott, and sailed
impromptu in a frail dory three miles out to Egg-rock with
a stranger who had been whittling on a piled fish-net. I sat
on the giant cliffs at Nahant where the spring tides came in,
under the spring storms, roaring into the chasms a hundred and more feet below and throwing spray up the clefts,
like a geyser, a hundred feet over my head. There is no
strength in motion so powerful as the sea; there is no

strength unmoving so powerful as the mountains. Two voices are they, each a mighty voice. And there were woods to the landward, great and organic. Here at Lynn was Nature a Meredithian source of spiritual recovery for me. Here I wrote a series of sonnets celebrating "Natura Magna," and sent to Ludwig Lewisohn. "What a breath of fresh air blows through," he wrote. One lavender twilight, when the banded clouds were still red and yellow behind the Lynn derricks and iron stacks to the southward, I heard, in my wanderings on the beach, a strange piping, an eerie melody pitched so high that I fancied on any merely mortal instrument it would have to be harsh and strident. Where and what could it be? What bird-throat or wind in the wires? Or siren-song by Red-rock? I followed after. Down behind a boulder, looking out toward Europe, sat a fifteen-year-old Sicilian boy from the shoe-shops, barelegged and bareheaded, trying out his home-made flute. . . . Theocritus. . . . But I can't capture these things in my verses. Our range of discovery and reflection and feeling is always far wider than our range in art. Art is a specialization of a part of us, and only a part. Yet *which* part is surely the revelation of what we *most* are.

But I told the episode to the friendly boarders and hostess . . . for I was housed once more with my kind, of whom I have known so many . . . Yankee people, like the Germans I like . . . though only a shop-foreman, and his mother, a veterinary surgeon, and young woman high-school teacher, who was keeping up under a broken engagement . . . of her own breaking after a surgical operation. Said this girl once: "Don't be discouraged over your job—when you can write a poem like that; the poem matters more"—returning a manuscript. The large fame folks used to forecast has scarcely come . . . but I testify with Floyd Dell to an American environment of persons as friendly to the young poet as he deserves. The young American poet will always find American company enough to keep him company in this America of realtors and politicians and fundamentalists; and he will find them often at the boarding-house or in the market-place.

There was, however, good reason to be worried about the job. It was plain that I could not stand, even temporarily, the strain of school-teaching in spite of revived spirits. I got through the term only by resting on my bed an hour or two hours every afternoon. The principal said, in all kindness, that I wouldn't do: "The children in the classes, after their class with you, are unmanageable, not undisciplined but mentally over-excited, over-stimulated." The teachers, men and women, advising with me, generously decided that " if I was more unfortunate than they in that kind of work, it was because I was more fortunate than they in being meant for higher work." But where was the higher work? I had gone down one week-end to New York, tired and without preparation, and now had my degree. I realized, however, that Columbia was scarcely more than half convinced. "Dangerous to recommend." And I asked no favors. I would fight my way to something with my scholarship and brains as sole weapons. I did not know what I know now. For many years I have myself taken part in calling likely young academicians as teachers to Wisconsin. My own decision in committee usually depends on the backing of the two or three professors, be they at Harvard, Columbia, Yale, or wherever, with whom the man or woman has worked; and these professors heartily back only those in whom they see disciples and worthy carriers of their own renown. Choose your professors well, my lads and ladies, and stick close and work for them not less than for knowledge and wisdom . . . for therein is knowledge and wisdom and the job whereby you can live, and not for bread alone. I have taken my part, too, in backing my own disciples. If I had been a professor at Columbia in those days, I would not have backed me as a disciple. But I might have taken a longer chance than they dared to take. Left to shift for myself as I was then, I have ever since taken the long chance in backing the Queer

Dicks and Insurgents from A.B.'s to Ph.D.'s. I have made more mistakes than the conservative backer whose motto is "safety first." But the majority of my Queer Dicks and Insurgents have vindicated me. They have become editors, writers, actresses, university teachers—though not without propensities to radical thinking, I admit. On the other hand, I won't absolutely refuse to back a young person, male or female, just because not a Queer Dick or a Queer Dora. . . .

Because Columbia did not take the long chance, I had to accept through a teachers' agency a post as associate editor of the Lippincott's Dictionary in Philadelphia. The enterprise, originally a modest revision of Worcester, had developed into a six-volume project, something between the Century and the Oxford, and the staff was undergoing reorganization. I was the new philological editor. I entered upon my work, in a large suite of finely furnished rooms on the eighth floor of the Bourse Building, carpeted with rugs and walled with a costly library of many thousand books in scholarship and all the sciences, among them a first edition of Dr. Johnson's Dictionary, and frequented by some twenty-five workers of both sexes, older and younger, all eating their hearts out for one reason or another for which no publisher could be held responsible. Ex-college instructors with wives and babies . . . but at last comfortable salaries. Ph.D.'s, like myself, who had failed to become college instructors. Cultured ladies whose masculine relatives, fathers or husbands, had gone bankrupt. Librarians who had been fired. And that floating population of American hacks that drift unknown from publisher to publisher, the unappreciated Grub-Streeters of our encyclopedias and lexicons, a specialized proletariat of intellect. And elderly little Dr. Flinch, the melancholy Dane, who had known Hans Andersen and Georg Brandes and Victor Hugo, with his shrewd repartees. "Don't quote Aristotle at me, Flinch," said a bumptious colleague on our staff, one of those querulous in discussion; "I know more about philosophy than Aristotle." "And I," said the whimsical Flinch, "know more about Amayrica than Coloombus." And there was the gracious and genteel Mr. Savage, another elderly and saddened gentleman, who would read me Vergil aloud in my room when my eyes ached, son of the African Missionary who had first identified and described the Gorilla (as Huxley will tell you). And Mr. Z., the courteous business-manager, who had risen splendidly from office-boy, and Miss X., the marvelous woman of iron, in general charge of dictionary form: two people of brains and bustle, terror of office laggards. The secret feuds underneath our impeccable professional demeanor, as we consulted one another, jealous of our scholarship and resentful over mistakes discovered (usually by our chief enemy) where one task crossed another. The incipient friendliness between this lady and that gentleman, to the disapproval of this other lady or that other gentleman. And all in such a world of external peace and decorum in those sunny chambers, up above the commercial streets of the City of Brotherly Love, where we all watched the hands of the afternoon clock in the Tower of Independence Hall slowly creeping on to five.

And the solemn end to it all on that day in March, 1906. I had noticed, on consulting a book in this room or that, a strange distracted look in this lady's face, in that ex-instructor's face. I had noticed from my own desk Miss X. strangely pallid and mechanic and angular at hers. I had seen a messenger drop a note on Mr. Savage's desk at three o'clock. Then he dropped one on mine. It announced the unwilling but practically necessary closing-up of the enterprise immediately. I ventured to speak to Miss X. She said: "I have given some of the best years of my life to this work . . . my days and my midnights." She had. There were twenty-five of us, and all jobless. The suite had never seemed so much like home before. We had never liked each other so well before. The great enterprise had never seemed so great. Mr. Lippincott's intended spir-

itual monument to his father, the founder of the house,
never so noble. But in spite of the immense financial loss,
Mr. Lippincott gave each of the twenty-five one hundred
dollars, and to the five men who, as university teachers,
would have no regular job till fall, an additional four hundred. My objections to our capitalistic society are impersonal and philosophic: one capitalist gave me an education;
another probably saved my life.

For I was now far nearer collapse than I had ever
been. My eyes had troubled me for the first time, almost
from the beginning of the dictionary-work. There had been
glasses and new glasses. Oculists and new oculists. And
"nothing wrong" with my eyes—in Philadelphia, in New
York, in Boston. Aching and aching, month after month,
for two years of unrelieved pain. There had been sleep
from four to seven, from five to seven. No sleep. And the
next night no sleep. Sometimes five hours' sleep the week.
Then all day at the office. Magnifying-glasses. Evenings in
my room in the dark . . . composing my poems (now in
"The Vaunt of Man"), about the Drudger and the Poet
in the City and others. . . . Walking back and forth between Bourse and West Philadelphia, over the Schuylkill
River—the river . . . the river . . . "I have covered the
loan with life-insurance—will suicide cancel the life-insurance?" Changing my lodgings again and again to escape
the noises that tortured raw nerves. Consulting nerve-spe-
cialists, who so kindly undercharged . . . and could find
nothing wrong but "nervousness" and "overwork." Sunday walks ten miles up the Wissahickon valley in the forested ravines, alone or with a friend. Two years of
unrelieved pain. And I dared not give up my job . . . it
was all the money my father had. The return of the loan
with the interest, in instalments of fifty dollars a month,
kept my parents fed and sheltered. My sister had given
up her job. I had friends, especially on the faculty of the
university: Professor and Mrs. Newbold, with a suite in
the same pension; Tait McKenzie, the sculptor; Hermann

Ranke, now Egyptologist at Heidelberg; Morris Jastrow and Albert Clay, Assyriologists, now dead; Schelling and Child in English—these and many others. And there was Croll, now at Princeton, and Tupper, now at Lafayette, among my co-editors. They were kind to me; but their kindnesses and companionship could not cure the two years' ache. How did I stand it? We stand what we have to. By a free act of will I could not have stood it a week. My thumb and fingers were pressing on my eyeballs for two years in Philadelphia . . . and many months of a third year elsewhere. And I worked seven hours a day. The only oculist who told me anything said, on his second examination three months after the first, that I was becoming strangely myopic, and I would go blind if I did not give up at once all work involving the eyes. He lied, and I knew it: his second test showed exactly the same results as the first, despite his pretense of meticulously consulting his records—for my memory was exact. He lied, and I knew it, but that was not the knowledge which could cure the ache. He lied to be rid of me; I had come complaining too often.

The cause of the aching was certainly neurotic. The office confinement, my unmastered distaste for a work to which I was ill adapted, the really heavy demands on the eyes, perhaps naturally my weakest organ anyway, and the harassing sense of responsibility to the debt and the parents, all combined their forces of strain. There are many different kinds of suffering . . . perhaps I have not known all—I have never been toasted under the armpits or crotch by the Apaches, for instance—but I have known several. The Philadelphia kind I call *misery*. That it was neurotic is clear (given the fact that examinations revealed no optical trouble beyond slight astigmatism) from the way it hung on during long months when I scarcely used my eyes at all, and vanished, while I was actively using my eyes and wearing the same glasses, but under normal living conditions. Clear also (given the above facts), from the association of the aches with miscellaneous bodily aches,

in thigh, arm, or neck, of the same tone, that disappeared
at the same time. Clear from intermittent and unmotivated
moments of mild recrudescence in subsequent years, especially in these last four years with their accentuated phobic
neurosis. Clear again, from the curious fact that, on writing
these very paragraphs, the aches, reverberating in a tenuous
memorial form, are flitting through my eyeballs this very
moment twenty years after. And that the phenomenon is the
work of the Locomotive-God seems more than likely. We
have noted already that the God had begun to move again
with audible and unmistakable reverberations. And, in my
clinical analysis, one night, the thought of those old aches
popped into hypnoidal consciousness, in association with
the fright of '78 and with other items already definitely
established as associated with that fright. There followed
a brief moment of ache relived—i.e., an actual physical ache
in the eyeballs like the old one of 1904-06, and hard
upon this relived ache, another ache relived—the sudden
heavy twinge, half ache, half shooting pain, of the infant's
astonished eyes before the Locomotive-God in 1878. And
each of these associations was accompanied by the simultaneous bodily shudders that I have learned by long observation to interpret as verification of ultimate psychic connections, usually causal connections. Remote as the phenomenon may seem, it tallies with dozens of instances of
mysterious pains in maturity that I have traced beyond all
doubt to these early traumas.

An instance or two right here, for the better recollection of matters in earlier chapters. Three years ago, when
my trail had got to the beginnings of the school fright of
1885, I suffered for two weeks a pain in my left jaw for
which the dentist could find no physical cause. In twilight
sleep one afternoon, it grew of an instant fiercely more
acute, as I felt myself hit by a tin can and heard it, in a
dream-noise, bang along before me in whispering metallic
repercussions. Instantly in the midst of the most violent
bodily shudders the memory of a moment (already de-

scribed) in the school fright and flight returned, and the pain disappeared. Another instance. For several years, even before I had begun this psychoanalytic investigation, I would be awakened every month or so at night by an excruciating pain in the neighborhood of the rectum, lasting from five to fifteen or twenty minutes. I called it neurotic, though the frequency with which my elderly colleagues were being taken to the hospital suggested alarmingly another explanation. I subsequently traced it, through the pain of the boy in the school-room of 1885, to the pain from the escaping steam below the piston-box of the Locomotive-God of 1878. And it has disappeared, except for infrequent slight twinges. Twenty-five years ago I began remarking, "I must be a somatic freak—no doctor seems ever to be able to explain my pains." I can explain nearly all of them now myself as one phenomenon or another of somatic memory; that is, reverberations (in one or another defined spot of the nervous system) of specific pains experienced long ago. Indeed, if I get a new pain nowadays, in the midst of my psychoanalysis, I say to my wife, not, "I wonder what is the matter with me," but, "I wonder what that *means*." And in a few days, or weeks, or months, I know. As already suggested in chronicling the original traumas, many conscious intellectual memories have been restored precisely through these subconscious somatic memories. I could write a book on this phase of the case alone. My whole life is one organized plot. So is the reader's, though he may never know as I know. May he never need to.

I hung around Philadelphia, with my five hundred dollars. I got a reporter's job on the "Philadelphia Ledger"; I had no strength. I tried to tutor; I had no strength. I was suffering, too, annoying returns of the then inexplicable shame-phobia, that robbed me of comfort from friends. Meantime I had published (at my own expense) my dissertation, my father having corrected the difficult technical proofs in Boston as best he could to spare my eyes. Meantime Bliss Perry had published four sonnets of mine in the

"Atlantic." Meantime, too, I had proved to Columbia I could hold down a job. But I was not waiting for Columbia to find me a job. I did my own finding in part. Columbia found me a professorship in Coe College in Iowa; I found (with shrewder tactics than one might suppose) an instructorship at the State University of Wisconsin. I chose the latter. I premised that my religious and political heterodoxy and my scholar's ambition would get me into less trouble in the larger school; I was beginning at last to think of career in terms of job. But, out of work, and seeking, not sought, I had no bargaining power. Coe was for a thousand dollars too. I came to Wisconsin, only too gladly as an instructor at one thousand dollars; but, with my training and my affiliations with the professorate at the University of Pennsylvania, I should have started at Wisconsin as an assistant professor. And the start is much. How colleagues place you at the start is much. Even in later years, since competition has become more strenuous and our standards more exacting, I have seen many a man of thirty start here as assistant professor with much less learning, and no more facility to hand in correct reports on time or to walk across a drawing-room like a gentleman. I had no bargaining power. Nobody was to blame.

I could hang around Philadelphia no longer. I took train for Massachusetts with good-bys only by letter after my flight, phobically ashamed. I went to Bolton, to the cottage of Dr. Stone's widowed daughter and golden Ella, then already a young woman, to rest till fall. I read but a half-hour a day . . . in the centenary edition of Emerson . . . and corresponded with the editor, Emerson's son. Emerson was my companion . . . so nigh is grandeur to our dust . . . not from a vain or shallow thought his awful Jove young Phidias wrought . . . the pine-tree sung "my hours are peaceful centuries." . . . I am the owner of the sphere, of the seven stars and the solar year, of Cæsar's hand, and Plato's brain, of Lord Christ's heart, and Shakspere's strain . . . spirit that lurks each form within beckons to spirit of its kin. . . . With eyes aching as grievously as ever, I feigned myself back in the Greek ages where books didn't count. All summer I played Aristotle. It was an interesting game. What is "playing Aristotle"? It is walking about learning, by direct observation and unaided wits, all that you can about the look and the ways of the clouds, the flowers, the birds, the people. It is sitting before a busy ant-hill all the sunny morning. It is picking up and comparing the different kinds of oak-leaves and acorns. It is looking at a horse's teeth and hoofs and then at a cow's. It is studying the lines of force in a blacksmith's muscles as he drives home the nail. It is watching a rivulet in the gully dig a new course through sand and mud, like the Mississippi or Amazon. "Playing Aristotle" is the same as "playing Lyell," "playing Darwin," or "playing Vesalius." For a supposed man of books, I became quite efficient at playing Aristotle. It implied for me a relatively new attitude to nature, the scientific attitude. Nature became organism, laws. Friends have demurred that as a poet I am always talking scientific facts, the causes of the sunset, not the beauty of the sunset. The ultimate poetry in nature as in life is in the realities. The ultimate, the highest use of the poetic imagination, acting on life or nature, is to enforce for humanity the facts of life and nature; to give the emotional values for mankind of the facts, after science itself has established the facts . . . which does not mean, however, that the sciences, especially the humanistic sciences, may not find that the greater poets have sometimes preceded them in science. There is beauty in the sunset as a celestial show; there is greater beauty in the sunset when we understand the show. Aristotle . . . Emerson. You don't see the connection? Well, lay down your copy of Mrs. Wilkinson's Anthology (revised to 1926) or your Vachel Lindsay (collected works) and examine closely (for the first time) the poems of the one major poet this country has produced. Emerson's science is not always mine; but his poetry is the poetry of the scientific spirit.

253

I had one companion in the miserable flesh: Peter Pence, an ailing electrician of forty, who had been sent up to the Edes farm as a melancholiac apparently now convalescent. We roamed about together. He too loved to pry under logs and poke up the soil and feed squirrels. He was a very gentle spirit, loving all things, and expressed himself, as we all tend to do, in terms of a philosophy that fitted his nature. The poor fellow was just then a follower of Christian Science. So Cowper translated his insane gloom into Calvinistic theology. Pence was apparently rational except on one theme, his will-power. His half-brother, he believed, had stolen his will. Here too Madam Eddy's system was to the purpose. The scientific fact of abulia and helplessness and the legal fact of his half-brother's guardianship he interpreted in the terms of "malicious animal magnetism" of the New Witchcraft of the Lynn Seeress. It is sometimes a nice question just where philosophy merges into insanity. Mrs. Eddy herself is a clinical case. I tried, as an amateur alienist already interested in abnormal psychology, to disentangle his delusions for him. Of course, vainly. One afternoon he turned on me impatiently with the argument that to him was unanswerable: "I have not had a movement of the bowels for four days." That is, his half-brother, a doctor, had not only taken his money and job away from him, but had been unscrupulous enough in his lust for power to deprive him of the inalienable right to the control of his own digestive apparatus. Poor Peter Pence. I missed him for a week. So I strolled up to the Edes farm. Farmer Edes was mending wall by the roadside. "What's become of Peter?" I had already told Farmer Edes about the bowels. So he answered: "He's been sick abed for days: the spell seems to have been removed from down there" (with a meaningful slap on his own, more normally functioning, abdomen). We shall meet Peter Pence once more.

The time drew on to fall, as the old sagas say when they begin to tell of new events in the Icelandic winters.

254

My eyes were no better. I had swellings and aches in arms and thighs. Neurotic too, but unexplained still. The rest had not cured me. Emerson and Aristotle had not cured me. I sat with my father on the slope of the Common by the old church which he had so pathetically left. Under the great oak in its vigorous green yet unturned, with a strength in its trunk older than *Mayflower* rib or the flagship of Columbus. We talked about my future. . . . So nigh is grandeur to our dust. . . . I had decided to become a carpenter. Carpentry would not need eyes. It was out-of-door work. Work with the tools, plane and saw, that I had loved as a child. Work with the stuff I liked—clean timbers and fresh-smelling planks. There was satisfaction, I said, in driving a nail till the head was flush with the wood, by two inerrant blows with the hammer. And with my intelligence I might rise to become master-workman or even a contractor. I was only thirty. I had a right to hope. My father tried to see cheer in the prospect. I would telegraph to-morrow morning to Professor Hubbard at Wisconsin that I was compelled to resign. But to-morrow morning I started West, with all my aches, unable to carry my dress-suit case in my swollen right hand. I risked the expense of the trip on a chance that seemed only too desperate.

I have noted myself making these sudden abysmal reversals of decision, several times in critical moments of my life, in complete defiance of common sense. They seem to indicate a subconscious control of my conscious mind, not unlike in some ways the phobic control, though usually creative of better issues of life. I will record another instance, which, if my main purpose had been chronology or drama rather than psychology, would have been recorded some pages back. I had, as a matter of fact, been dismissed from the dictionary staff Saturday noon after the first two weeks, as inefficient—brilliant but useless. I was sitting, stunned and tearless, on the already moving train, when spontaneously a great light burst within me. I rushed without baggage down the aisle, jumped off, and made my way back to the office. I found Mr. Z. and Miss X. gathering up my relics, amazed at the pallid apparition. "I've come back to say I've given you no chance to know whether I'm efficient or not. I was supposed first to be learning dictionary form and office routine; but I've been giving Miss X. and the rest of you all lectures on Germanic philology. Let me take a set of proofs, and you examine me on dictionary form Monday morning. And if I pass, let me have desk-room for a week, before you decide. It might save you trouble too." They liked my cheek (or my humility) and took a chance. So I stayed till we all left together two years after.

What if I had not jumped off that out-bound train? . . . I would at least not have been so exhausted and ailing from two years' drudgery when I came to Madison . . . with all that resulted in Madison from being so exhausted and ailing. But if I had not jumped off the train, it is likely I would have jumped off the Jersey City ferryboat. I was in no condition to cross a river that day. . . . Then I would never have come to Madison at all. . . .

XIII

I CAME to the City of the Four Lakes in September, 1906, at the age of thirty. Here I have paid my debts, earned keep for myself and others, written most of my books, established myself in my profession, served others as I could, and made or developed most of the friendships now dearest. Here I have first seen death close by . . . and many times . . . here are graves I would visit if I could—here all but two, my father's and Uncle Oliver's. Here I first knew declared enemies . . . and now many of them are here . . . out at Forest Hills . . . in graves too. And here I was stricken, and here I have suffered, and here I have lost . . . and won. Madison is my home as no other spot of earth.

In September, 1906, I needed these quiet inland lakes and bluffs, these wooded shores, these long coulees and sunny oak-openings, and these west winds of Wisconsin as badly as any one who ever came. I needed them even more than I had before needed the Mountains or the Sea. But had I not needed them as a weary man, sick in nerves and spirit, my eye would still have drunk in the beauty of town and country-side with eager delight. And age cannot wither them nor custom stale their infinite variety, through the four seasons, of flowers, leaves, snow, clouds, and starlight. Almost from the first hours, Madison was to me the Peculiar City, a Capitol Dome on one hill, a University Dome on the other, and each Dome, as in no other city, mirrored in water, and her homes and factories and stores, as in no other city, girdled with neighboring fields of corn and neigh-

257

boring woodlands of wild flowers and (twenty years ago) an occasional tepee. Here was my ideal for the dwelling-place of modern man: an organic civilization in close touch with organic nature. A city far over whose roofs, twice a year, the wild geese fly. Why is not this the most famous city in our country, I thought. I will make it that, I thought. Longfellow's poem is but a conventional fancy, made to order in the studio. But let one live here, deeply and long, and he will write the poem that will give this city to America and the world. So I thought. And in the end so I tried to do.

But this book will not be repeating the city or the story of "Two Lives." Whenever it touches on the same scenes and events, the main purpose will be entirely other, to trace the further evolution of hidden psychological forces in one human being, as those forces reacted under new and unforeseen conditions; and whenever it differs in objective facts (especially of time-relations) from "Two Lives," it presents scientifically what "Two Lives" was distilling into art in ways I shall refer to later on. The peace and restoration I achieved here during that first year, with the mastery of at least the worst aches in eyes, with the closing of eyes far oftener in normal sleep, and with the doing of pleasant tasks from day to day, and with the walkings, the boatings, the swimmings, the skatings, was literally the first peace I had known for about four years. I had in that period almost come to expect troubles as my normal lot, with each trouble worse than the preceding. What next? was my habitual attitude, in trying to make my way out of each new difficulty. Unwholesome, embittered, perhaps unmanly—but the fact. And meanwhile the ancestral drive and physical constitution had kept me going . . . and here I was in peace at last. I had a quiet attic room in one of the town's old mansions by the lake. A famous professor and his gifted wife had rented the main portion, as if to assure the young scholar of as good house-companions as he had found in the Newbolds in Philadelphia . . . the wife who passes away, almost as I write these words, friend of twenty years through all. The other occupant was the owner . . . none other than the genial Grand Army veteran whom Jack had introduced me to on the streets of Göttingen. He was no longer in the diplomatic service abroad. He had returned to his old post, as professor at Wisconsin. He was professor too in the same department with me. Famous he was through the Northwest for his debates with Donnelly on Bacon *vs.* Shakspere. Jack had meantime married his daughter, and was established at an Eastern university. His other daughter, who had been ailing in Copenhagen, was away for the year at a sanatorium. She had left the day before I came to Madison. I shall call her Agatha. It is Greek for "Good" and an old name for home-loving girls in the New England I had come from. I shall call the professor Dr. Greylock. Jack's wife I shall call Esther. Dr. Greylock showed me, the very day I came inquiring for a room, a photograph in his study of Jack and Esther and the baby. He never showed me a photograph of Agatha; but that of the young family-group persuaded me anyway, as a symbol of friendliness, to live in that house. The quiet attic room too. I told Professor Greylock how ailing I had been; and he thought the quiet attic just the place for me. In the course of the months, I fear, I acquainted him in many wearisome details with all my nervous troubles then happily in subsidence.

I have had so many significant remeetings and momentous coincidences in my life that what we call chance plays a more important rôle in my thought about human affairs than it does in typically modern thought. But not more important, apparently, than it did in Shakspere's. If the Hamlet problem is, on the one hand, a temperament in conflict with a duty, it is on the other (and still more amazingly) the element of chance and, more specifically, the irony of chance . . . where an event or situation, originally created either by chance or design, recoils by chance and not by design to the destruction of the one who was about to use the original event or situation to his own advantage. Thomas Hardy's novels are likewise studies in the unforeseen accidents and their long results. My life makes me strangely at home with their art: I do not feel it to be fantastic or unreal. They report with supreme insight the way of the human world. But whether the victim be their Hamlet and Tess or myself, both in their fictions and in my life, I find the ultimate *determinants* so profoundly in particular human character, sometimes in its own creative cooperation with "chance," certainly in its own reaction (Hamlet's or Tess's or my character, and not another's) to the chance events or situations created, that my interpretation has never been supernatural. Yet I can well understand how a mind, obscurantist by nature or religious schooling, would trace, with very satisfying proofs, a career like mine to the guiding hand of a Providence . . . divine or diabolic, all-wise or all-cunning. Certainly nothing in my career would support that argument more plausibly than the accident of my coming to Wisconsin, and finding myself a lodger under the same roof with the father-in-law of my old Göttingen acquaintance, Jack Dayton. Jack's own accounts of Wisconsin long ago—the beauty of the place, the new emphasis on research, the loyalty of its students ("A fellow would die for Wisconsin," he had told me in Göttingen)—had doubtless played their subtle subconscious part in deciding me for Wisconsin against Coe, perhaps in directing my inquiries toward Wisconsin in the first place. And here I was, too, only three doors from his own birthplace and homestead on the corner I passed every day to class. The humor of it struck me then. But the accidental was to work out its results, as my own character became more and more a dynamic factor in the initially accidental . . . my own character, and Professor Greylock's character, and Jack's . . . and the buried memories of little Mary and the Locomotive-God . . . my own character and all my past sufferings and struggles and dreams. I am not thinking too precisely on the event. Nor am I seeking rationalizations, *a posteriori* and factitious, of my own motives; I am simply analyzing event and analyzing the subconsciousness in interaction with event. For any one who reads me, interested not alone in a neurotic case, but in the web of man's life and the gathering of the strands into a pattern—mine here, another's to-morrow—the demonstration will be tolerably clear. The time was to come when the humor of it ceased to strike me.

But before that I was to revisit Bolton once again and complete one other experience that was to be an important dynamic factor. And I was to leave behind on the desk of Dr. Greylock the record in verse of some of the experience chronicled above in prose. I had printed that year (1906) in a small private edition a selection of my poems (written between graduation from college and Madison). This came under sympathetic eyes. Arthur Symons had welcomed me as an authentic new poet in our common tongue; so had Edward Dowden; the laureate had sent me an inscribed volume of his own poems; Thomas Bailey Aldrich had written:

I find a large sum of very beautiful poetry in your little book—

and it was, perhaps, the last letter that gracious artist ever wrote. George Woodberry had made himself my friend for that book's sake. John Burroughs had it at Slabsides. But no one, I believe, ever read those humble pages—their honest words for mountain, sea, cloud, and flower, for human toil and ambition, for human love disappointed and craving love, the neo-romantic note not without (I declare it) some homely vigor and realism of thought and speech— no one ever, with keener vision and with heart in closer tempo with its rhythms, than the unknown blue-eyed lady Agatha who found the copy that summer on her father's desk at Madison . . . while I was in the hills of New England. I was gathering a new experience, unknowing, which was to make her history and personality the more intelligible, awesome, and tragic to me; while I had left behind me, unknowing, my own history and personality to work its effects upon her.

The experience I was completing in the Bolton Hills was not the revision of my little book in prose, "The Poet of Galilee," for young Mr. Huebsch's new publishing establishment in New York. Nor the correcting of the last proofs of the translation of the "Greek Fragments of Empedocles," for the Open Court Company (of Paul Carus, philosopher and friend), an interest aroused first by Hermann Diels in Germany and fostered by Newbold in Philadelphia. The experience to be completed was to see life through with Peter Pence. I had heard rumors that he was now a perfectly well man, happy all day. And he had invited me to spend my first two weeks in his cottage two miles from the village on the ridge along the road to Harvard Village. Wise Mrs. Edes had shaken her head. "Peter," she told me, as I started wheeling up the hill my dress-suit case on the handle-bars of a borrowed bicycle, "Peter is in as bad a way as ever; his present gaiety is as ominous as his depression last summer." He welcomed me with pathetic grace and joy at the door of the long abandoned farm-house; and, with step springy as an Indian's and arm eager as a boy's, hurried me in to see all the new things. He was going to be a farmer. That very summer. His half-brother had given him back his will and his money. The barren little parlor was piled with new hoes and rakes and spades and a great shining plow with red frame. On a box was a stack of agricultural bulletins and of Christian Science Journals. In the middle room was a wooden box and a cot. In the kitchen, there were oil-stove and ten or so cardboard boxes of crackers and breakfast-foods. Upstairs was nothing . . . or, rather, more piles of bulletins and Journals . . . for here was to be his study. In the barn nothing. It was past the middle of June . . . and he was still reading agricultural bulletins. He wanted to be a scientific farmer. The country-side, he said, had no conception of the recent advances in agriculture. And he had been getting ready for my visit by thinking for days about where he could get a second cot for me to sleep on. I said, realizing that in kindness I must stay there at least that night, "there's probably one over in Edes' shack." It was on the farther brow of Huckleberry Hill beyond the chestnut-woods, and a good mile and a half in the hot dusk. He told me on the way of the wonderful cure. He had joined the Baptist Chapel—Christ had saved him . . . as Christ had once saved the poet Cowper. There had been much rejoicing among the Bolton Baptists—till they learned that shortly afterward he had also joined the Unitarians. "But," as he explained, "I got so much good from one church that I felt I would get still more from two." Though I had read much theology, in Edwards, in Calvin, in Augustine, in Pfleiderer, this was to me a new slant. We got the bed back. The poor fellow, emaciated and haggard though he was, sat on the edge of his cot singing and whistling and talking agriculture, Christian Science, Baptists and Unitarians, and his love to God and man and his therapeutic regimen till midnight. I couldn't sleep. I said it was the whippoorwill on the roof-tree of the barn. He got up, went out, among the elms and untrimmed syringas, and talked to the whippoorwill: "Whippoorwill, you must stop annoying Mr. Leonard." He believed he had a peculiar influence, like Thoreau, over birds, squirrels, and snakes, and all God's creatures. But evidently the whippoorwill didn't quite recognize him in his night-shirt. The little brown torment answered with a fiercer crescendo to the moon. At four we arose . . . first over to the spring in the meadow to wash . . . he believed in the morning cool and in cold fresh water all over his pale white body and tousled graying head and beard. He paddled naked in the spring . . . interminably . . . then splashed himself some more . . . singing and whistling like Pan. In time we got a pailful for the eggs (I dipped in somewhat above the outflow that had been his matutinal lavoratorium) and bought eggs and milk at a farm-house down the road . . . where he talked with the restive wife a half-hour by the side door. In time we got the oil stove lighted (the wicks and screws were out of gear) and the water on (fifteen minutes in finding a pan), and the eggs boiled (they had to be hard to suit Peter) and the grape-nuts into two saucers (it was I who finally found the two saucers . . . among the Christian Science Journals). Breakfast was ready by eight. I then explained that I rather feared there were too many whippoorwills in the neighborhood . . . "I guess," I said, "I'd better arrange to stay in the village after all." He was distressed about the whippoorwills (for it never occurred to him that any gentleman could lie), but confessed he didn't believe he could stop them. I said I didn't believe he could either. . . . I told the village doctor about Peter . . . Good-by Peter. . . . Three miles or so beyond Peter's cottage Bronson Alcott had once reigned over Fruitlands: there they ate, like Peter Pence, no flesh, but also no vegetables with the edible portions growing downward . . . for spiritual aspiration was Alcott's aim too . . . and they had molasses for butter . . . also on spiritual grounds. And Alcott puttered his whole life away . . . not only the last two years or three. Peter died in an asylum, a manic depressant, not long after. Bronson Alcott still figures in the history of American philosophy. I had never heard the sweet bells of the human spirit jangled out of tune before . . . but I was to hear them . . . again . . .

During the summer I bethought me to write Dr. Greylock that I would not be staying at his house next year: "The little girl who came over did not look after my room very well." I had not complained how tipsy my table and how the bed-slats sometimes dropped out from under and cut short my best dreams. But he replied:

I apologize heartily for your last year's discomfort; however, my daughter is now back and keeping house for me; which puts another complexion on the matter. I'm sure you will be satisfied.

So when I returned, I returned to the same attic room.

But it was not the same. . . . The year above sketched disappears entirely from the poem "Two Lives," as under the commands of the reconstructing imagination, where nearly five years beneath that roof are reduced to two, and only those moments matter that are relative to those Two Lives. Yet here, as with every other alteration of the raw stuff of life, there has been, I believe, an unerring, subconciously guided emphasis on some spiritual truth that the raw stuff in fact blurred or distorted. It is true chronologically, and for the purpose of this study important psychologically, that there was this year before the daughter's return. But the new meanings of life and the new life itself, Madison itself, really began for me not with my coming, but with my coming back. Of course this comment phrases a critical judgment of to-day, not of the days long gone when the poem was making itself under my pencil. But the scenes in and about the white house by the lake and about this city were no reconstructions, nor the spiritual relations of the people to one another and to me, and mine to them. The character of Agatha is no reconstruction. In her wistful majesty, in her playful girlish humor, in her alert and cultivated intelligence, in her unconquerable selflessness, in the very manifestations of the fatal inheritance, the raw stuff of life gave me a completer loveliness than art, as art goes, usually creates from the elusive suggestions in the best of ten good and lovely women. "The perfect portrait of my dear dead classmate," wrote a friend of hers and mine. And nothing touched deeper the man in me and the artist in me. Possibly it is literally true that there is not a word in the poem about her and my thought of her that is not a transcript. The poem is art first because life itself was the terrible, beautiful artist, and second (and only second) because it omits, not adds. I shall return to this.

So I say I am not telling that story again. In a week we were in love, though we did not know it then. In four months we were plighted. In a year and a half we were married. And about two months before our second anni-

versary she had left the house by one door and I by another
. . . she to join her father, dead three weeks before; I to
be joined by mine—summoned desperately from the East.
That first year in Madison was the first year of golden
peace for five years . . . and the last, forever, it would
seem . . . for the peace I now have is an iron crown.

I shall not now open, except for an instant or two, the
doors of that house during my four years there with
Agatha; but I shall open more widely than in the poem the
doors of my subconscious mind. I know far more about
my mind than I did then, though what I then wrote needs
only supplementation, not revision. The history of my
mind, conscious and subconscious, in that house was the culmination of antecedent experience and itself the experience
that, in conjunction with antecedent experience, has modified my mind's entire history ever since.

Few men would have risked their whole life and career
as I did in such a marriage. I myself would have been the
first to warn another both for his sake and the woman's,
even with the little knowledge of the specific conditions
that I had on our first acquaintance. For I had heard
rumors of melancholias of old under that roof in more than
one gentle soul, and Agatha herself, though now in such
bloom and joy, seemed ominous in her very song and spon-
taneity. There needs no psychological analysis to explain
loving her as a human being. To know her was to love
her. All loved her. That all loved her indeed was paradoxically one reason that thereafter so many hated the
widowed husband. No analysis to explain a man's loving
her as a woman, nor the fact that love, man's love or
woman's, was deepened by pity and anxiety, and man's particularly by the protective instinct. Her personality itself,
given everyday human nature to work upon, would inevitably have created the reactions recorded in "Two
Lives." Indeed, had already more than once created them
. . . but in vain, for none had given her wifehood, the
dearest dream of her spirit. But with me past experience

brought to bear initially several specific additional influences. The long after-effects of my disordered emotions over Annie had been such as to make me both crave love more and dread it more than a normal man. I dreaded above all lest the love-emotions, reawakened, should again be rebuffed. And, lo, here was love growing within me and for me, quietly as a flower. I had realized too that with my small earnings and the needs of parents I could not support a wife. And, lo, here was love awaiting wifehood, eager above all to give of its own toward that support. Probably the most degraded of the slanders subsequently in such lively circulation against me was that I had coldbloodedly married Agatha for her money; but even slander is welcome to the above confession. On the other hand I had more than a normal man's horror of sweet bells jangled out of tune. The tragedy of Mr. Pence was still fresh. When I had first known him, he had been normal, except for the presence of one fixed idea and the brooding sadness associated with it; and when I next saw him, in his very gaiety he had exchanged idea and sadness for conditions far more ominous. Mr. Pence was in my imagination now like a *danse macabre* among the Muses. Well and supremely happy as she seemed now, her very goodness and gentleness, combined with the rumors I had heard, brought good gentle Peter Pence to trouble my thoughts. But, above all, I knew my own neurotic make-up; however little I knew of its causes. Though I felt restored sufficiently to do my day's work in the world, I knew, as Dr. Greylock knew, that I was not in a nervous state that could abide unusual strain. I felt I was not the man to cherish Agatha, either in health or in sickness. I have among my papers letters of her father to her that indicate how difficult a task it had been even for him in a previous illness. So, when I saw love in the offing, I left the house for other lodgings—on her account and her family's, no less than on my own. This item too fell out of "Two Lives": it had no bearing on the spiritual values of the poem.

But it has bearing on the history of my mind. I realized in absence how much my feelings were involved. I worried about her feelings and especially the possibly disastrous effects upon her mental health. A note from her, so humorous and sensible, soon relieved me on that score; but at the same time opened the door to the thought that the rumors of her melancholias must have been exaggerated. The thought never occurred to my agitated mood that any girl whosoever, in such a delicate situation, would most naturally and properly take counsel. Agatha had no mother; Dr. Greylock himself was her only helper. Her note to me was far more poised than my farewell note to her in my attic room had been. So I began to wonder if marriage was after all so much out of the question. Her sister, in the most robust health, had married. Her brother, once a famous athlete and then a medical man, had married. The father was the soundest of heads and of nervous organizations. She herself was life abounding. The strain was surely pretty sound, in spite of what I had heard. Mental disorders were, like typhoid or measles, possible in any family. But the family, I was told, would oppose her marrying. So I wrote her brother, frankly and asking for frankness and especially, in case he desired to remain out of it, for the address of some medical man acquainted with all the circumstances. He replied briefly and warmly, referring to a "nervous break" some years before in Paris, due to emotional strain; and urged me to talk with his father. He gave me too the address of an old friend of his, the head physician in a sanatorium. I took train to the sanatorium. The physican had just received a letter from the brother. He said, "Marry her; keep her happy, and it's all right." He gave me few particulars, and I dreaded to ask. But his hearty pleasure and assurance was pleasure and assurance for me. I had previously consulted two other physicians who knew something of the circumstances; but this last interview swept away all traces in me of their dubiety. And I talked with the father, as best I could.

Agatha never knew what we had been so busy at. She had a simple faith that love itself would solve everything. On my birthday she gave a party. "So we're now engaged," she said when the guests were gone; as if mildly relieved that one more rather unimportant external of life had been gotten rid of. I came back to live in the house. Jack and Esther were in the East, and had had no knowledge of my perplexities. But now came their good-will too. Jack wrote:

It has been plain for some time from Agatha's letters to Esther what must have been going on. . . . Well, I'll try to make the best of it with a poet for a brother-in-law.

And he sent me a print of a photograph he had taken in the garden by his room at Göttingen. There I sit in a chair, with an apron tied about my chin, a crowd of merry American students holding me down, and the grinning German barber (hired for the occasion) standing with shears ready. I too am merry in the print. I have it yet. Esther wrote the words that fell so easily into the rimes of "Two Lives."

Father and brother and head physician doubtless believed, as the brother himself had written his father and had subsequently told me, that a happy marriage would be the solution for Agatha. But, though, as the poem says, the imperfect information chafed my pride during our marriage with a feeling that they thought me a simple and a useful man rather than a keen and dignified man, to be dealt with man to man, I still realized how dearly they loved their sister, and how hard in any case for kindred to speak out in such matters. It was only after her suicide, when the Mob was upon me, that this inexactness of their information truly grieved me. For it was true, as the Mob said, that they had told me; but it was not true that they had told me all, and most that mattered most. It was true, however, that I knew All when I married Agatha; but it is not true that I knew it from the family. I had learned it meanwhile (as told in "Two Lives") from her own innocent lips, verified only too completely by a woman now dead. And father and brother and Jack and Esther, who knew all, never knew that I too knew all. And Agatha never knew that it was from her I first knew all. There was, as I see it, no gross chicanery, perhaps no deliberate attempt to mislead me at all; but, aside from the effect upon my psychology, I believe the readiness with which I acquiesced in all the transaction without further query, tended to develop in their minds the fatal mistake that Jack had made, on other grounds, about my character. Mr. Leonard was naïve, impulsive, more or less irresponsible, not to be taken too seriously. All through our married life I had little indications of this that wounded me. From Jack too, who was then on our faculty in Madison. Moreover, Agatha was to the family something childlike; and to the family her husband naturally became something childlike. After the suicide, I was to pay a still more grievous price for their mistake. Outcast, as I was. And perhaps in the end they too pay the price. For but give the laws of life long enough time and they work out. Jack, particularly, I fear knew more about the laws of the atom than the laws of the human spirit. Otherwise he would have known that no man of my character and temperament, provided he lived at all through the abysses and darkness into which I was cast, would come out into day without seeing the issues of truth through to the end, both as art and as science. Indeed . . . and indeed . . . otherwise he would have foreseen that, in eliminating me forever from his life, not only would he help to create for my life the conditions out of which the two books have grown, but would certainly eliminate from my life all question of deference to the wishes of friendship and family-group. I trust he has not known of "Two Lives," and will not know of "The Locomotive-God"; and that none but the local group who already know will ever know what Jack's famous name really is. For I have no wish to embarrass, to hurt, or to anger. But the ethos of the matter is simple: I owe him, under the circumstances, no obligations whatever as against intentions of a bigger scope than family privacies . . . neither him nor his circle that mobbed me. The laws of the atom . . . the laws of life. One should know both, to live wisely. And it must surely be at last my right, in broad daylight alone before the world, to make an ethical and philosophic use of those slanders, once multiplied by so many in darkness . . . even though some good people have now passed on to the place where they can slander me no more.

But there was another motif impelling me to Agatha, only touched on in "Two Lives." The motif of service. At thirty-one I was saying to myself what Schiller put into Don Carlos's mouth when the Spanish prince was eight years my junior:

> Drei und zwanzig Jahre alt
> Und nichts für die Unsterblichkeit gethan.

I was feeling frustrated in ambitions. I was still only a college instructor. I was still hardly known at all as a critic or poet or scholar. I felt, too, a deep discontent with my life, as essentially a struggle for self. The young scholar may well feel it often. Here was escape. The feeling brought a strange exaltation. Paul Carus, in Chicago, whom we called upon on our wedding trip to the East and my people, took me aside: "Your wife's beautiful face looks like the Transfiguration." And I had wrought this. I had saved her. The more terrible then what came after. But I was happy too in serving the family. The good dowager next door said when we were back: "What a cloud you have lifted from this roof." And I served the father and heirs by caring for the house and grounds. Twelve times, for four summers I mowed that great lawn of six hundred feet from pavement to lake-shore. I served the father in his sickness . . . and in the most menial and repellent of services. The more terrible then when the surviving kin cast me out. In my simplicity, I never thought, till long after we were engaged, of any advantages that might accrue to my professional career from her father's distinguished influence, or to my social career from a connection with the very best society of this inland city that takes its society so seriously. Still so seriously . . . though dynasties have come and gone . . . since then. And the thought never loomed very important, at best. I was of quite as good family myself . . . scion of pioneers no less old. The less my disappointment . . . but not the less my surprise when later I realized that precisely this connection with the best families . . . as diner-out and fellow-entertainer . . . was what rendered me so helpless in the end. In this group I had chiefly lived. When they turned upon me, they the most respected and influential homes in the community, what remained for the stranger? But, after all . . . something remained, as we shall see.

But first some significant memoranda of the days before the end. I had experienced one return of acute stage-fright . . . and it was in our own home. It had come Dr. Greylock's turn to be "the host of the Madison Literary Club"; and, though Dr. Greylock was visiting his son far away, there was no by-law in the constitution and no precedent in the sessions of that august and venerable institution providing for a modification of its annual calendar. Thus Agatha and I ordered the ice-cream and the chocolate and the wafers from the caterer and the folding-chairs from the undertaker, and arranged the setting and seating, with lamp-lit table by the portières between living-room and *salle à manger* and our best upholstery either side of it for the president and "the reader of the paper." Agatha was calm and resourceful. But it was the first social responsibility of my life on a grand scale. And with it too an intellectual responsiblility, for I had accepted the invitation to open from the floor "the discussion of the paper," and knew how for two solemn generations it had been the club's custom to give outsiders of extraordinary promise this gracious op-

portunity to win their coveted way to membership. And
I was only a little over thirty-three and only at the beginning of my career as an assistant professor. And I had
heard how such occasions had sometimes spelt disaster:
how, for instance, an embarrassed and untimely jocosity on
the part of a brilliant young scholar many years before had
not only eliminated him for all time from consideration for
the club but had held up his promotion in the university
twelve years. I knew how important the club's favor . . .
and how austere its elections. Its number was inexorably fifty
and, though larger than that of the French Academy by
ten, still the fifty best of the intelligentsia in the glaciated
area of the north Mississippi Valley, including too the
watershed of the Missouri and the Ohio. Twenty-five from
Gown (representing wide interests, economics, history,
natural science, belletristic, and the highest administrative
officers in the Academic Body Politic) ; and twenty-five from
Town (justices of the Wisconsin Supreme Court, family
solicitors, eye-specialists, abdominal surgeons, eminent
bankers, dowagers, retired authors, etc.). No one could
get in unless some one went out . . . and no one went out
except as he died or left the city; and no one, thus honored
with membership, ever left the city if he could help it. One
black ball was decisive. The candidate had to be *persona
omnibus gratissima.*

Our guests began coming . . . all on time, for eight
o'clock was the tradition . . . ladies and gentlemen . . .
the ladies' wraps in Agatha's bedroom, the gentlemen's hats
and canes in Dr. Greylock's. Our guests began sitting . . .
expectantly row behind row, elegantly but informally at-
tired (for another admirable tradition was that of a spiritual and civic intimacy among the Chosen which evening-
dress would have marred). My nervousness had begun
days ahead. I had revived my old habit of the High School
Debating Society, in spite of the not forgotten public fiasco:
I had learned by heart my extempore speech, having had an
advance look at the paper (the traditions of the club always

permitted this) ; and I had prepared for reading aloud a
translation of a poem by the literary man about whom "the
paper of the evening" was to be, in case I forgot my speech.
I had fortified myself too by emergency notes on a card.
But with every new entrant through our household door,
my pulse went faster, my tongue drier. In vain I kept
thinking, as I walked about welcoming, "There's only one
man and one woman besides the reader who knows Norwegian"—(Björnstjerne Björnson was the subject)—"better than I; and the woman is an awfully good friend of mine
and the man won't be here" (because he presumed to know
even more than the evening's reader about B.B.). In vain, so
I made a last minute dash to the bath-room. A fatal misstep.
I met an elder colleague of our department descending. He
saw me eying distractedly the card in my hand: "Leonard,
Leonard," in a frightened, furtive, solicitous whisper, "it's
absolutely against the traditions of the club to speak from
notes" . . . I stumbled and wabbled back into the company,
dizzy. The lights were lowered, all but the table-lamp. Our
familiar rooms, with all these familiar faces sallowed in the
red-litten ambient glow, were transformed into a chamber
of horrors. Exactly at nine . . . no paper ever extended
beyond the hour . . . the sonorous voice stopped. I arose,
shaking and gagging, from the rear, at the summons from
the chair, my card in my vest-pocket . . . help so near, and
yet help fatally withheld. But by beginning with the reading
of my translation of "Faederlandssang." . . .

Ja vi elsker dette Landet . . .

I got myself together "for my few informal remarks."
When I began teaching after my breakdown I feared this
phobic weakness might end my career; but it soon developed that the one place where I was to feel most self-confidence for the rest of my life was the class-room. I ac-
quitted myself, however, without imperiling my future that
evening; and acquired, furthermore, a unique distinction for
life—as the only host of the club in all the traditions of

the club who was never a member of the club. For other matters soon concluded my chances.

Such a comic stage-fright is sufficiently common; but that in this instance it was symptomatic of specific neurotic conditions in integration with attacks of adolescence seems clear from the fact that my subconsciousness, even my co-consciousness, was vibrant all that evening with reverberations of those two earlier stage-frights (during the high school debate and during the Latin play in college), and that but about a year back, three days before my marriage, I had recited from an open-air rostrum, before thousands of people, an ode at the unveiling of the statue of Lincoln on the upper campus, with the most buoyant confidence. Yet how far I had still been from direct phobic bondage to the Locomotive-God may be best illustrated by a *railroad* episode during my second year in Madison. The train had come to an unexplained stop at the further end of the bridge over Lake Monona; and, getting out with many others, I found the conductor extending a cup of water to some one under the rear truck of our car. No doctor being aboard, I soon found myself more or less in charge. We drew him out, a seventeen-year-old lad, only too conscious with pain and horror, his right leg all but severed just below the thigh, his eyes bulging like the eyes of a deep-sea fish. I sent into the train for towels, which I ripped and twisted to a tourniquet, got him on a car-seat litter on to the floor of the baggage-car and instructed a hand to run and telephone to have a hospital-ambulance at the Madison station. While the train was backing into town, I got his name and address, and stilled his worst agonies with brandy; and wrote out a telegram for his father, a farmer at Mount Horeb. And then having delivered the telegram from the door of the baggage-car as they lifted him out, and having wiped the blood from my fingers and wrists, I made my way to my seat, and resumed reading. And read all the way to Chicago. Nor did I feel any after-effects whatever. I had had no course in "first aid" and no experience; but my mind seems to have drawn subconsciously upon chance instructions, framed on the walls of waiting-rooms, and perused long before to kill time at various railroad junctions. And the practical problem itself inhibited both pity and fear. The lad died that night.

Meanwhile the difficulties grew more and more dreadful in the House by the Lake quite as "Two Lives" reports . . . the college girls rooming there (because of aging Dr. Greylock's anxious thrift—and not one year but two, and a far worse strain in the second year) . . . the decline of Dr. Greylock . . . Agatha's divided worries between father and husband . . . her alarming mental symptoms . . . her father's death, with the shock and the neurotic feeling within her of an old prop and control now taken away. My increasing distraction and irritability and terror . . . all three the worse because I cherished her. Above all, the secret, corroding

> Dread lest on some morrow she
> Should witness nature's old fecundity . . .

I was indeed not the man to have cared for her . . . I with my nervous record. I can blame myself roundly for delinquencies. No one else has the like right . . . unless he has suffered the like. That very day, a half-hour before she took poison, Jack's own mother had said to me in all sympathy: "We must get Agatha to a sanatorium at once for your sake as well as hers. You are breaking down too." After the poison, that same day when all thought that I had saved her, by intelligent prompt treatment, from its lethal effects—when Jack and all applauded me as the resourceful brother and hero—Esther had replied to my remark over the phone that I was at the breaking point: "Oh, no, no, you must not say that" . . . with a sister's fear and solicitude that sounds very far away now. That was the last word she ever spoke to me . . . the last greeting. I have never blamed her. She believed what she was told . . . and what she was told to.

In the meantime, had circumstances not been preparing for the Locomotive-God? To live four years in the same house with any human spirit that you know has been desperately insane is a test of one's own sanity. To live those same four years, haunted by the reminding memory of a friend who died in insanity, is another test. A third test is to live those four years, besides, when that spirit is your beloved bride and wife. My condition was not only distraction, irritability, anxiety. Chronic phobias had set in over a year before her death that point directly back to 1878, and directly forward to 1911–26. Once when she was off on a picnic, with another group, a thunder-storm precipitated in me at home a fierce and irrational panic of hopeless loss (as of Mary on the platform). Frequently, I would be startled out of my initial doze at night by what I used to call "seizures or attacks of consciousness." I would be at the very verge of sleep, and instantly, with a surging onrush, preternaturally wide awake as if consciousness had *burst* up and *flared* forth from its hiding-place within. Something very different as phenomenon from those twitchings we have on going to sleep. But identical in general cause, though the psychology books don't tell me. The mind, in sinking into "twilight sleep" conditions, is giving the subconsciousness, particularly its buried memories, a chance to act freely upon consciousness. The so-called nervous twitching of drowse is with me the somatic registration of a buried and troubling memory, even as the somatic pains above referred to are another registration. I am not theorizing. The psychologists shall know I am not theorizing. In my recent experiments, I have had many times these "nervous twitchings" on approaching the dividing line between sleepiness and sleep (the hypnoidal state so often referred to already), and have identified them almost immediately (or sometimes only a year or two years later) with one or another specific buried memory of past experience, even as far back as the platform of 1878. One time, my hand jerked: it was the incipient repetition of my

277

clapping hands to face before the Locomotive-God. Another time, my foot jerked: it was the incipient repetition of my beginning to run from the Locomotive-God. I have many other instances among my notes, particularly concerning the school-fright of 1885. These swirling "attacks of consciousness," accompanied as they were, so mysteriously, by incipient rush of *sound,* have repeated themselves, in my recent experiments, again and again, under circumstances where psychological meaning has been perfectly clear—where, in short, they have been followed by the associated idea of the Locomotive of 1878 and by the bodily shudders, as indeed they were in a vaguer fashion already associated with a locomotive in their earlier manifestation. In the light of my whole neurotic history, the attacks of 1910—11 can have had no other meaning. My exhaustion in manhood had now gone so far that for the first time since early childhood's reverberations (in phobias of bells, railway bridges, etc., etc.) the original Locomotive-God was directly and continuously reverberating again, and in a form of onrush and noise more nearly *literal* than even in childhood's phobias. This indicates, as nothing else, how profoundly the strain of these years under that doomed house had shaken my mind.

But more pervading was the strange new phobia of water. In rowboat, canoe or launch, I had for terror to hug the shore, though I had always previously crossed the lakes from point to point over one mile or four of open wind and wave. I could not swim to a raft anchored a hundred feet out, though a sturdy swimmer from boyhood. I knew they were phobias. I was already intimately acquainted with books on abnormal psychology . . . not alone from scientific curiosity, but in the vain hope to help Agatha. I tried to master these fears, by the elementary device of "try and try again." To no purpose. I tried for the raft fifty times. Terror would drive me back . . . terror of being *so far* from safety. I took my boat and vowed to row the half-mile across University Bay, alive or

dead. Dread when at five hundred feet . . . but I rowed
. . . terror unto death in the middle . . . but I rowed
. . . and in blind terror to the other shore. The result
of this "cure" was thereafter I found my normal rowing-
limit from shore reduced from two hundred feet to fifty.
I would not have—I could not have—repeated the horror
for a kingdom. In every characteristic phenomenon this
experience was like those of to-day. And, on reliving that
rowing-phobia in twilight sleep, I recalled that a train was
passing near-by, which doubtless increased its intensity.
These water-phobias were simply phobias of distance from
safety: the wide waters exaggerated the difficulty of getting back. At this stage all *land* was equivalent to safety
(or to "getting back"), in the same way that my *immediate*
environment, my home, is now. They were not phobias of
drowning or of any neurotic "notions" about water as such,
as if slimy, crawly, or engulfing. Probably the external fact
that water is less the native element of security of the land-
animal man was the chief psychological foundation for this
particular form of the subconscious recrudescence of the
childhood trauma. Possibly the foundation was subconscious memories of two water-frights, one on the ocean at
six, one on a pond at thirteen; but these were in themselves
unimportant; and I have found, in my subconscious, few
ideational or emotional associations. But, like so many other
of my phobic phenomena, the phobia was associated (subconsciously of course) with a specific memory of 1878—the
pond that then so fascinated me and the man rowing. The
very multifariousness for my infant mind of the objects
experienced that afternoon laid the foundations for multi-
farious phobic associations and stimuli of manhood. The
water-phobias were a serious handicap, I thought, to my
freedom and pleasure. The following winter (the winter
before Agatha's suicide) I found myself uneasy and phobic
if far out on the ice. Another handicap, I thought. I have
all these to-day on water and ice, in a far acuter form. I
can canoe, swim, or skate, only if within a few yards of

shore. I used then to think, "Well, at least one can't get such notions with terra firma underfoot . . . one can't get such a feeling of insecurity on dry land." I didn't know much then of the diabolic resourcefulness of phobias . . . nor of what strains were to come that would give them far wider scope . . . on dry land too. Yes, the Locomotive-God was preparing to return . . . had returned. And I was trying to play the game of life against the odds of mental collapse of my wife and nervous collapse of myself. I needed help. I needed friendliness . . . no man ever needed friendliness more, friendliness of neighbors and wife's kindred above all.

My wife took poison . . . to save herself . . . to save me . . . her mind had been breaking for months. She had rushed at me. I never forgot how she rushed at me. But once in my twilight sleep the memory became immediate vision and feeling, and I found it linked, in the very lowest abysses of my subconsciousness, with the onrush of the Locomotive-God. She was indeed Death rushing upon me . . . even as she was little Mary indeed lost forever. She lived two days, dying in a sanatorium the morning after she had been declared out of danger by the family physician . . . now dead too. I did not sleep till after the funeral. When the news came that she was sinking, I was seized with intense (though partially controlled) panic, not merely the normal grief and dread of even an exhausted husband. Friends . . . I had friends, though not among neighbors or kindred . . . came running in. Thomas Dickinson (the now distinguished interpreter of the drama), and Ludwig Lewisohn (that year an instructor in German here) and his wife. Another physican came. He gave me a hypodermic. As I sank away, I underwent exquisite horror, as of the whole world abandoning me. I can never take an anesthetic again. I called every few minutes in a low voice to Mrs. Lewisohn in the next room. "Are you still there, Molly?" "Yes, I am still here." It was from this anguished sleep that I was prematurely awakened to go to her death-bed, and saw Jack standing over me and heard him saying to the bystanders what I chronicled in "Two Lives" . . . verified afterward by friends.

It was Dickinson and Mrs. Lewisohn who had accompanied her to the sanatorium. Jack had his own wife to think of. I had been too broken, and both physician and neighbors had told me to keep out of the way. I never had even a chance to say good-by to Agatha. But she sent good-by to me . . . and "be good to my poor husband," was her message to her kindred. Even with the poison corroding her body and the hereditary taint corroding her mind, she still maintained toward the laws of mercy and love and justice an integrity and a sanity that rebukes, more wisely than ever I can rebuke, the irrational collapse of those laws in the others. Our funeral carriage accompanied the hearse to the railway-station. I saw the casket lifted out of the baggage-car. I had a seizure of horror and despair. I heard the locomotive bell. Another seizure. Do I need to indicate further this new relation between Locomotive-God, Death, and me? They put me in the first carriage behind the hearse. I was still the husband . . . for an hour . . . still . . . and something still was due to good form. I rode in the carriage to the cemetery with Dickinson, the son, Dr. Greylock, Jr., and an elderly lady, a neighbor. I read in the silent and averted attitude of two something besides mourning for Agatha and sympathy with me. I read hostility. I said, in inner panic (again controlled outwardly) : "Dickinson, get out with me; I must walk." But the old lady said, "No." And I sat through Despair, Grief, and an attack of the Locomotive-God.

Returning to the house, after the funeral, I found in the front yard my white-haired father. He had taken the train west within an hour after receiving the telegram that, with Lewisohn's most urgent counsels, I had sent immediately after her death. He was seventy-four years old. "I need you, my son," was his greeting. But that night, not

under the old roof (under which I never slept again), he
wrote in his diary:

I hope my presence is to be of some comfort to our dear Ellery
in his desolation.

It was. Two weeks later he wrote:

To-day dear Ellery and I moved from good Professor Smith's
house to a furnished house on Prospect Avenue which Ellery has
rented for the summer. . . . Ellery has arranged to have his mother
and me live in Madison with him. This is providential . . . for
our need. . . I am enjoying greatly the opportunity given me as
a guest of the University Club to meet the teachers of the university.
They are a fine lot of men. . . .

Good Professor Smith was the professor of Greek. The
furnished house was a young widow's—whose husband, a
professor, had committed suicide three weeks before . . .
but I was in a grim realistic mood, unterrified by whimsies
and superstitions. . . . The need was in truth extreme
indigence. He had but about two hundred dollars; and he
was paying this forth week by week (as I discovered afterward from a pile of canceled checks) to my sister, out of
work in Boston. I was already paying for his life insurance
of $3000 in one of the fraternal orders which, already com-
pelled enormously to increase its rates for the old men,
finally went to pieces, leaving his widow $500 . . . one of
the minor ironies in the financial history of the Leonards.
Their sole support for their three years in Madison was
the phobiac whom some townspeople of wealth and influence were trying to get dismissed from the university—the
phobiac, who, if dismissed, would have been unable to take
the train to seek another job. The teachers of the university, with a few exceptions among the intimates of Jack,
remained my well-wishers, even through all the ugliest
noises. The first evening in the new cottage, Professor
George Sellery came over with cool drinks. We sat on
the porch. He was a good neighbor. A week later:

282

We had the pleasure of welcoming the mother . . . this afternoon. It will seem like living again to have such a notable housekeeper in charge of things. God bless her and bless us all, the absent one in Boston with the rest. These are surely trying days for our little family. May each one prove his faith and trust in Divine Love.

To go on. Nine days later. On the dedication of the new Parish House of the Unitarian Church:

The pastor very kindly had me down for parts in the services, but I was unable to be present because I was needed at home.

He was needed at home. I had been brought by a stranger's automobile back to the house that day in the collapse which will make psychologically the most significant moment in this entire book. He was "needed at home"; the more terrible life became for him, the quieter and briefer his words. Needed at home. These are the last words of the last entry for nearly two years. And there is only one other:

This is the second anniversary of my arrival in Madison. I have not kept a minute [record] of our life in the little home [my phobic condition had meantime compelled our removal to an apartment *near* the university], because the main features are such as one could not [illegible], consisting as they do of the brave struggles of our son . . . the life of the good wife and mine had but this one purpose . . . may his handicap pass away very soon! . . . What a joy that will bring to all our hearts . . .

"Will bring," not "would bring"—there is much of his ever hoping character in that "will." There was seldom a subjunctive in his speech.

My father's diary was silent for two years, and then, after a moment, silent again. I wish I too could be silent. But I have an austerer purpose, other than peace or hope, a purpose to make my life count for other men and women, in its very failure of peace and hope, toward the deeper and wiser understanding of life itself. I must fill in the silences of my father. And that will mean going back to the day after the funeral.

I shall say very little on the psychology of grief. I have such a lecture, on Tennyson's "In Memoriam" in my course, "Philosophy in the English Poets," that those follow closest who have grieved most. We are all much the same down in the deeps. A woman friend grieved for a mate gone, in a grief uncannily like mine, even to minute reactions to daily life. We talked about it together, even while we grieved. But each grief has its specific moments. Mine the moments of release from long anxiety, and of the tragic solace that she could suffer no more. Mine the reverberations from the child-Mary of infancy. Mine its intense moment of remorse, of guilt, beyond that familiar phenomenon of self-accusation that death of loved ones always so accentuates in all unbrutalized, but imperfect, mankind; for my reason—that knew well enough her doom was through nature, not through me, however much I had fallen short of ideal husbandhood—had to fight against both the psychic suggestion of guilt so noisily abroad in the community as well as the unknown solicitations of guilt reverberating within me from the overwhelming horror of guilt (associated with *death*) in infancy at the station. Mine too had the moment of an added grief, the loss of Esther and Jack. Esther in chief. I needed to hear her voice, to see her handwriting; she would have been something of the voice I could not hear under the grass. She passed me on the street the day after the funeral with averted head. I later besought a tress of my dead wife's hair from a drawer I knew, as I tell in "Two Lives." I received no answer. She believed what it was well, perhaps, for her own good that she believed. She too must have been in anguish, and under shadows not mine. She has never spoken since, in street, in hall, in shop.

I said "the moment." But moment has another meaning. As to time, the grief was not a moment but years. Grief in its acuter pang with most people spends itself mercifully in six months, becoming quiet sadness. Mine kept its original intensity almost uninterruptedly for over two years. As to time, the slander too was not a moment but years. Two years after the funeral, a man prominent in local public life, between whom and me there was bad blood in this matter already, raised his cane before me on the street. Don't mistake—it was not to strike. But to point to the just skies of God. "In the name of Agatha Greylock," he called out. "What's that!" and I drew close. "Don't you suppose we all know who drove that poor girl to her death!" I drew closer, with a look about me. "You mean I murdered my wife?" "It amounts to that!" What to do? I had not lost my head. I had had two desperate years' practice in not losing my head. What should I do? What should I have done? I drove my heel into his foot (and I did not wear rubber heels then) that he might not topple over and make a public spectacle for me when on the next instant I drove my fist in and up under his jaw. "You viper—that [as I trod] is symbolic." He hobbled off, holding his face. He is the only man I have struck since a man. This is an honest book. I don't believe at all in this sort of thing. Yet the crack did me good; and it does me good to write it up. Maybe it will do the reader good. He was more fool than rascal. He had been reading old books about how the courageous village minister of Puritan New England used to rebuke sinners on the highways, and he had forgotten that I had read them too.

But it is two years yet to that encounter. What chiefly mattered happened before that. I am not dependent upon mere reminiscence, as I remind the reader again. The confusion and horror of those first days indeed produced for years both amnesias and distortions of facts. I even dated her death wrong by over a week, in the biographic note for "Who's Who." But part of my later attempt at a psychological cure was to retrace, under hypnoidal conditions of recall, the precise events of my life with Agatha and the first years after. I have them clear and in order, integrated with the recalls of all the years before back to the Locomotive-God. I am not reminiscing, not sophisticating: I am recording the findings of clinical science. Many data have been objectively verified, though some cannot be, of course. The psychopathologist who first worked with me, for instance, had conjectured that my phobias might be in part the symbolic inversion of a horror of some cruelty to Agatha that the conscious mind had suppressed. I was scientist as well as patient. "It may be," I said. We went on this trail. My hypnoidal mind recalled many intimate details, some sorrowful enough, but no forgotten cruelty. "It may still be," I said; and I gave him the addresses of two people who might help him objectively, truthfully, scientifically. One was a lady. I scarcely knew her. But Agatha had known her and been with her day after day (unknown to me) in the three weeks between her father's death and her own. Had there been any cruelty of mine, physical or mental, Agatha, always so innocently frank and at that time under the neurotic's peculiar impulse to talk, would have told that confidante. Indeed, she went to her specifically to talk, in her confusion, about herself and about her husband. If there had been any cruelty, physical or mental, Agatha would have told her. I know just how she would have told her. She would have blamed herself; she would have been worried about it as a symptom of my nervous condition; but she would have told her. But what in fact did Agatha tell her? She told her how considerate her husband had been, especially since her father's death. The sister of the lady wrote me this of her own accord long ago; I carried the letter in my pocket for years . . . like a message from the dead. The other to whom my psychopathologist went was an engineer in Boston, a son of a John Hopkins professor of medicine, who had lived at our home when a student—till her death. He was glad, even after twelve years, to testify he knew nothing. Let the reader note: my friend did not consult these two strangers to him in the capacity of a lawyer hoping to cajole witnesses for the prosecution in a suit for defamation of character; he went as a scientist, and explained why, saying: "If you know anything, Mr. Leonard himself wants most of all to know too." I think this is at least a partial objective verification of the failure of psychoanalysis to find any buried memory of cruelty. If there are details forgotten, of cruelty or of kindness, they must be buried even deeper than the spirit-house of the Locomotive-God.

I have, I believe, the events, even to the minutes, under command. I believe the mind forgets nothing . . . that all is there if one knows how to hunt for it. A friend was telling me how, as a four-year-old, he heard a low voice under his pillow (the pulse in his ear, probably) ; but, being so sleepy, he didn't bother to listen. He said to me that for weeks afterward he had regretted he never knew what the voice said. I told him he could yet know. He would only have to relive the original experience. Rivers in one of his books speaks of trying in vain to recall for two years an upper room of childhood; it took me nearly four years to recall suppressions at thirty-five, of which I have soon to speak. Rivers could have recalled that room to its very window-shades with my technic and more patience: that room was there. Everything is there. A psychologist once assured me there were no reliable memories before six. Perhaps not usually, for mere reminiscence. But I have them to two years and three months, April, 1878, two months before the locomotive, through hypnoidal and other induced states. And I have them in plenty for 1911 and after. Memories not only of my states of mind, but of the words and actions of others.

The reader may have, like myself, an interest in social as well as individual psychology. An interest in the psychology of rumor which so often deviates into slander. But in spite of all I remember, I cannot know a whole group of other minds from within as intimately as I have come to know the single mind of myself. Possibly all would be clear if I could know but one of them, say, the inner workings of Jack's consciousness and particularly subconsciousness during those days. What motifs were at work to turn those people of her old circle against me so fiercely? Evans had come to me in the afternoon of the funeral, white and frightened, to tell me I must leave the town at once. And he himself apparently more than half believed. And I had already heard and seen enough. I was dazed before the insoluble and unforeseen. I had in the preceding months looked forward to the poor comfort of an increased sympathy from the circle after the disaster that I felt coming. And now this to bear. I could not understand. The worst possible should have been a passing coolness, with the hysterical suspicion that I might have somehow prevented the suicide that her father and others had several times prevented before. But this. With all that I had borne, to be made to bear the responsibility for her death. I could not understand; but I told Evans I would die before I would run. I was the maimed cat, but I would fight. I had many helpers, however. The good sense of outsiders. The careful reports of friends at my request. I knew in time the precise source of precise stories. I knew how some passed from one kitchen door to the next, with the passing of maid-servant from one employer to the next. I knew, in time, much from individuals who, though at first in the Mob, had later withdrawn, as some in old Salem days had withdrawn from prosecuting the witches. But, for many months, I never knew who was going to speak to me and who not. I was cut dead by fifty. The best people. But the whole phenomenon had its grotesque comedy. Families were evidently divided. A mother would greet me with marked kindness, her daughter with a loathing scowl. Husbands would chat as ever at the University Club, wives would draw up their skirts in the shops, or, with painful obtrusiveness, turn their backs. I was the Devil, apparently, of a new mythology; but not all were converts. The hideous factitiousness, the fantastic artificiality, of the whole ideology was clearest in Jack's own house. Jack's father remained my friend, though we never spoke of Agatha or Jack; and when I remarried three years later none pressed my hand more warmly. Was there some too terrible story believed in the innermost group that I have never yet heard about? I doubt it. The family physician, an old chum of Dr. Greylock, Jr., hinted that if I did not pay the full amount of his exorbitant bill he would be compelled to go into court and divulge dark things. . . . My lawyer told him we had nothing to fear. He settled for half. He did not go into court.

I will explain the motifs and causes as far as I have been able to think them out. . . . They may serve others in other cases.

I. *The Social Attitude: General Motifs.*—(1) The whole subrational atmosphere of horror and pity and confusion, an emotional matrix in which any idea, however absurd, might find lodgment. (2) The craving to wreak the effects of these emotions on a concrete agent, a scapegoat. (3) The need of an objective symbol for one's own subconscious feelings of joint responsibility. (4) Resentment against ghastly disappointment in a too readily assumed solution through marriage of Agatha's mental condition. (5) The stranger in the home town. (6) Normal society's latent suspicions or misconceptions of "the poet," or any somewhat noticeable deviation from type, except as a creature for social exploitation. (7) The familiar revulsion against the atypical person who has been favored with patronage (I had been locally one of the little lesser lions). (8) The familiar preference for the dead against the living, and often for the woman against the man. (9) As to the credulity of the town at large, the fact that the sad truth of the hereditary taint of insanity in that household had naturally been kept from the general public.

II. *The Social Attitude: Special Motifs.*—(1) The

transfer to me of a pent-up dislike among a certain group
toward old Dr. Greylock for alleged harshness in his family
(pent up and unexpressed, because he had been so powerful
a member of the community . . . dead only three weeks
before). (2) The protection to be obtained from the
solemn shadows in the haunted house if the suicide could
be referred to a moral agent, instead of to heredity and
mental constitution. (3) The resentment that an outsider
should inherit anything of the old familiar properties. (4)
My refusal to accept a cash settlement. Dr. Greylock, Jr.,
on the morning after the funeral offered me out of hand
five thousand dollars for my withdrawal. I said I couldn't
think about money matters just yet. But I felt myself in
spirit what I was soon nominated under the laws of Wisconsin, "The Executor of the Estate of Agatha Greylock
Leonard." I felt it was of her right that I was the defender,
even as I had taken charge of her right in the three weeks
after her father's death. This disagreeable motif of the
heirs was originally in "Two Lives." I did wisely in cut-
ting it out; but it hurt me to cut the following lines . . .

> . . . defender of her defenselessness,
> O still the guardian of her right—a fool,
> Whose eyes, though they had seen the coffin hid,
> Whose ears, though they had heard the sod on lid,
> Still saw, still heard her . . . as a child from school,
> Who feels its own dead mother on the stair,
> And sets her place at table and her chair . . .

(5) The grotesque misconception of my business intentions
and actions. I was forced, in my broken condition, to ask
a lawyer to take charge of settling my wife's estate. He
was a university professor, a gentleman, and a friend of
mine, and in nowise hostile to the other heirs; our purpose
and our practice was throughout to accede to all arrange-
ments consistent with dignity. The interest I took, aside
from this feeling of loyalty to her interests, was an effort
to find distraction and substitution. I had said in one mood

to Herbert Quick, the novelist, then living in Madison: "I believe I will refuse to inherit a cent." He replied: "You haven't inherited, you have earned." The unfortunate fact is simply this: it angered some good people—all the people were good, and hence the instruction for us all in this analysis—that I evinced more sagacity and firmness in business affairs than a poet is entitled to evince, even if much the poorest of the heirs in the end. (6) The misinterpretation of my external manner. Outwardly I was matter of fact, commonplace, going on with my lectures, mingling with colleagues. I wore no mourning. I adopted no ritual whatever. Inwardly I was in such torment and so *distrait* at times that my external manner, gesture, speech, gait, was often like that of a mechanical toy, only still working by virtue of a spring well wound up before.

III. *The Specific Legend: Causes.*—The above items possibly motivate the social attitude of the circle; the following, possibly, the origins of the specific legend, and those simulations of reliable detail and source so characteristic of gossip, especially when most malignant. (1) The indubitable fact that I had had spells of irritability and moodiness. (2) The maid, as usual in such cases (solicited for information by Jack, flattered by her new importance, grieving for her mistress, and of course stupidly ignorant of all the essential conditions). (3) The six college girls (likewise flattered, likewise ignorant, but with the additional solicitation of personal spite). The girls there in the second year are those to which "Two Lives" refers. Moreover, old Dr. Greylock was away for months, ill at his son's, and Agatha and I had charge without adequate authority. They did much as they pleased; and disliked us both, but me the more of course. After Agatha's death, I had to close the house. Under their indignant protests. I interfered with their convenience. They were a ghastly revelation of the selfish thoughtlessness of flapperdom. Two or three of them hated me particularly for one final word. As they were romping and shrieking in the upper hall that morning after

291

the funeral, I rushed up with flaming eyes and cried out:
"Stop, stop, you young fools; this is the house of Death."
Of course no gentleman, especially if a university professor,
loses his urbanity like that. They furnished the maid ample
support. (4) Talk of mine imperfectly overheard through
our bedroom window by the neighbor, a woman more or
less *in loco matris* besides. It was indignant talk, and may
well have seemed in its tones convincingly brutal and quar-
relsome talk . . . but it was simply over the home having
been turned, contrary to expectation, into a lodging-house.
I paid a heavy price for a bad habit I have not altogether
mastered yet. I lose myself too readily in an emotionally
repudiated fact or idea and then hold forth to my companion as if he were responsible for the fact or idea. But
Agatha understood. The ill effect on her was worry over
me. (5) A certain appearance of inconsiderate masculine
authority even in public places, as in the local restaurants
(due partly to a temperamental oblivion of appearances,
partly to the attitude to Agatha engendered by her childlike nature and past history, partly to the irritability under
which I was trying to support life and her life). (6)
Agatha's own naïve ways of speaking about me. When
asked why she did this or that, she would sometimes reply,
"Ellery told me to." This became evidence that I nagged
her and browbeat; yet "Ellery told me to" were words of
naïve and happy pride, uttered often in my own presence,
with a look at me. It would seem that some people misunderstood her—or chose to misunderstand her—as much
as me. (7) The indubitable, but misinterpreted, fact that I
did attempt to direct her beyond what a husband normally
does (in my inexpert and anxious efforts to help her to self-
possession and health). (8) My letters of mingled self-
accusation and self-extenuation to her kin—the full import of whose hostility I was too long in realizing—letters
of self-reproach such as Shelley's wife wrote in the first
weeks of agony, except that mine added the cry for help.
(9) Our very moments of romping play became evidence

against me . . . evidence of the worst thing of all. She had escaped me, out of her bedroom. I caught her in the hall. She called in her laughter—"Girls, come help." A couple of the young women stuck their heads out of their doors, hearing racket and call. In retrospect, when the hue and cry had begun, they decided that she had been only pretending it was play . . . in order to shield the husband from being discovered in a brutal assault. She *would* have done just that, to be sure. As late as ten years after, a lady, prominent in club and church, answered a visitor who doubted my imputed villainies: "What can you say when I tell you there are eye-witnesses to testify that he beat his wife?" The visitor reported to me next day. My gentle father, to comfort me with companionship in injustice, recalled how when he too was in his thirties the calumny had spread, even in his home town, that he manhandled my grandfather. Passers-by had heard the ancient man moaning and calling: "Will, let me go, let me go." Sitting with failing faculties in the very room where his son and son's son had been born, he suffered the delusion that he was in Chicago, begging to be allowed to go home.

At the same time that both fashionable drawing-rooms, campus, and barber-shops were circulating the explanation of Agatha's suicide, they were circulating the explanation of the suicide of the young professor in whose cottage I then lived. His wife had given birth to a negro baby . . . or a Japanese . . . the hospital nurse had told the secret, they said. I had talked with the mother, as she held the baby. I can assure you it was very fair. This type of story is almost folklore; I have collected five or six cases in my own studies of slander. Possibly there is some objective foundation in the physiological fact that new-born white infants, besides having negroid or, particularly, mongoloid features, are sometimes yellow for a few days with jaundice. I do not believe that it is alone my own experience that convinces me that the credulity, brutality, and cowardice in human nature achieve their completest ex-

293

pression in mob-slander. These notes of mine may sometime serve the sociologist.

There was nothing for me to do but to live through it
or die under it. Nothing for my friends to do. Some have
since told me how in attempting my defense they were themselves made in effect partners in my crime. Society did not
give the young university professor that day in court which
it gives even to the thief and the thug. I could not demand
that day. I knew the libel laws of Wisconsin; I knew specifically five or six individuals against whom I had legally
secure cases—and one individual would have been enough,
under the law. But my neurotic disabilities aside, the law
was obviously out of the question. Could I involve my
friends in the ugly job of the witness stand? "The family
had opposed the marriage": could I read their letters in
court? "Agatha had never been insane before": could I
read in court the clinical report (still in my possession)
sent me by the Northern State Hospital? The law is often
enough no protection for a decent man.

Acquaintances, new to the community and hearing only
kindly words about me, have questioned if I did not exag-
gerate or imagine the abuse of past years. And some reader,
realizing that it is a neurotic writing on a neurosis, may
question if I did not have a persecution-mania then . . .
and still perhaps. I have received between 1911 and 1925
letters that might precipitate a persecution-mania, but which
need no persecution-mania, as a hypothesis for their interpretation. Within a week after her death they began to come.
The first was from the physician who had given me the
hypodermic: it warned me—while the girl's body was still
warm in the earth—against ever subjecting another woman
to the catastrophe of being my wife. The physician subsequently canceled his thought—but that did not cancel the
pain. Shall I quote a letter as late as December 1, 1925?
It is on fine paper (Brother Jonathan Bond is the water-
mark), with engraved personal letter-head in purple, carefully typed with typist's initials in the left-hand lower cor-

ner, and the author's signature in purple autograph. I
have never seen Mr. ——. As far as I know, he has never
seen me. He is a physician in another city. He had just
finished "Two Lives" . . . No, I will not quote . . . except one sentence. He calls me the liar and the coward,
as himself "one who knows much of the truth"; and the
precise source of his information is plain from his letter.
"One who knows much of the truth" . . . *O sancta sim-
plicitas!* One hostile letter once literally knocked me down,
and my father had to snatch it and destroy. But that was
from an old lady and friend, and that was long ago in 1911.
For an instant Mr. ——'s gave me a touch of the same
horror—the phobic seizure on attack (as on opening the
letter from Annie); but only for an instant. My reaction
was otherwise impersonal, intellectual. That is, though the
attack-motif in Madison precipitated (as I shall show) the
chronic phobic neurosis that still remains uncured, I seem
to have achieved some normal emotional resilience over
against actual attack to-day. I scarcely felt even the natural
man's and the literary craftsman's impulse to reply. Mr.
—— still awaits proof that I ever received his letter.

But when friends have uttered the old commonplaces,
true enough for some occasions and for some natures, about
forgetting the past, I have answered them thus . . . out
of perhaps a deeper experience than theirs:

> You tell me (you in life and books well read):
> 'Let your Past die with all its grief and riot."
> *Let* the Past die!— The Past is never dead!
> Not at high noon! Not in the starry quiet!
> My Past is gesturing in this limp you pity,
> And whitens in this scar against the blast,
> And not a tree, a book, a song, a city,
> But has to-day its meaning from my Past.
> There is, good friends, scant wisdom in this "letting";
> I *am* my Past so long as I am I;
> And in a brave reshaping, not forgetting,

Is my one hope and action not to die:
The Past that might have killed me if it could
I sternly mold to art and hardihood.

The verses might have been inserted in "Two Lives." As inserted here, the last line needs some revision. I am analyzing that past as a scientist, not molding as an artist. But perhaps that too has its hardihood.

So imperfect is any individual that, even in a friendly environment generally tolerant of his imperfections—the only environment that makes normal living possible for any of us—the spy and delator can readily find materials to his sinister purpose. But the individual in an unfriendly and already suspicious environment can neither live normally from within, nor get fair judgment from round about. Right and left, for years thereafter, humanly respectable conduct of mine, in itself nowise related to my marriage, was likewise misinterpreted; and year after year, on the other hand, I stumbled and blundered into one or another minor act in itself blameworthy, but still the clear result of these social forces against me. I was, in short, "in bad"; I have discovered fuller meanings in that brief idiom than any given by the dictionary. The study of these secondary derivative results of the mob-attack, quite aside from the results of the direct perpetuation down the years of its own slanders, would make an ingenious chapter. They played their part in social opportunities cut off, in professional advancement deferred, and in personality distorted. But another force was to play a part far more powerful; call it nervous breakdown or chronic phobias, or—Locomotive-God. Did I not already have what we so nonchalantly call "rather rough sledding"? Why should the neurosis have had to come too? Why?—precisely because the sledding had been so rough—too hard, at last too hard, in fact. Alone in "The Green Cottage by the Brook" of the poem, with parents and the loyalest friends a man ever had . . . none loyaler than big burly Herbert Quick, now dead . . .

alone with Vergil and Goethe and the quiet, undarkened, unhampered memories of the dead girl at rest over yonder down the lane at Forest Hills, and alone with the twilight and evening star, I would have pulled through. At thirty-five I was practically as brown-haired and athletic as at twenty. I was constitutionally robust in lungs, heart, and stomach, in muscle, in nervous and intellectual energy. For Nature, who made me curiously sensitive to suffer, had made me tough to bear. I had also still hope and will, and above all will to live . . . in spite of all. With rest and peace, and a new start, I would have escaped the Locomotive-God, even then—escaped at least all but the submerged and intermittent rumblings. What finally knocked me out was the Mob . . . the Mob of 1911 from Madison's fashionable Langdon Street and Wisconsin Avenue, with reinforcements from Milwaukee and Chicago, rushing to join forces with the hooligans of 1885 from Plainfield's back alleys, in order to stone a defenseless fellow-creature already in pain, like the dog that attacked the maimed cat. Many of both mobs are dead. Death is great Death, but He is not great enough to silence Truth. What brought on the neurosis was the Mob—the Attack, Onset and Uproar. That set loose the Locomotive-God.

XIV

THE attack of the Mob set loose the Locomotive-God. This is not a figure of speech. There are few figures of speech in this book. One service of this book indeed is to discover for many an outworn figure its more significant realistic meaning. Such, for instance, as "frightened almost to death." If you understand my figures, you will find them not rhetorical ornament, but psychological facts. The two Mobs did join forces in my subconsciousness. Review the first Mob, blended, as it dashed at me down the school steps, with the wraith of the Locomotive, before you read of the bigger work of the second Mob . . . in the story which follows . . .

My father and mother and I were living in the cottage, at the other end of the town, beyond the oak-grove and the then scattered houses of University Heights, in a quiet hollow far from Langdon Street and the rallying quarters of the Mob. I had paid the undertaker and completed my university tasks. I had held my head up on the street, walked, canoed, swum, and talked with colleagues and student acquaintances, and attended baseball games and theaters. My mental condition made one single instant of mourning perilous. I must keep alive through this, through all this . . . there will be time enough to mourn, I thought. For me the anxious foreboding, at least, was ended; for her all suffering was ended. I wrote in verses some thoughts of her. I prepared to publish my poems for her sake.

Kind eyes were in many faces, kind words on many lips. But the whispers were spreading, and some eyes and some lips were soon not so kind. The Mob robbed me of the holy right to an uncontaminated sorrow for my dead. It sullied my grief by precipitating in me a defiant, a consuming resentment; it thrust between her memory and me an ugly and sordid problem. Spiritually that was its most tragic work. But that is not the specific work that concerns us here. The Mob was beginning to get me—psychically. I was beginning to feel an abnormal, a neurotic dread of the Mob. I thought I was just nervous and edgy. A long walk will set me up, I thought, as physical exercise had so often set me up when nervous and edgy before. I did not know that I was "all in." I had never yet been *all* in.

I took the walk of a hot June morning, seven miles to West Point on the opposite shore of the lower end of Lake Mendota. Charles E. Brown, curator of the Historical Museum, was with me. We were going to make a survey of some Indian mounds, as we had done so often before together, and as we were never to do again. The *external* facts (recovered by autopsychoanalysis) that I am about to give have all been verified within recent weeks by conferences with Brown, in his office over the way from my apartment. He is amazed at the vividness of his memories of details, after fifteen years. Why has he never forgotten; and why had I forgotten so much? For him the events, as so unusual, emphasized a portentous day, but without any profound psychic upheaval to induce amnesia; for me the events were a traumatic shock down into the depths, and, moreover, affiliated with internal processes which had been in the depths of the subconscious since infancy. For Charlie the day was a profound *im*pression; for me (in all but the superficial phases) a profound *sup*pression.

We had dropped in at a road-house, near the end of that seven-mile walk, for a glass of beer. I had already complained of feeling queer . . . queerer than I had ever felt in my life (as far as I then knew). Seated at the board table, I suddenly seemed in all truth to be dying. I was facing the side wall. On it a huge map of Wisconsin in red and yellow. Through the center of the gaudy map, a passenger train was depicted as dashing head-on down a track, as if bursting out of Wisconsin (i. e., subconsciously the infantile *Past* plus the present Locality—remember, too, the locomotive picture on the Ætna calendar in Uncle Oliver's insurance office, beside my father's sanctum, that had flooded my mind at the first coming of the Locomotive-God). Head-on. Right at me. Hideously hostile . . . huge . . . God . . . Death. . . . To destroy me for my guilt, as myself the destroyer of my wife. The objective fact was still there—the map and the train—I recognized it as a familiar advertisement of the Northwestern Railroad. I suffered no delusion. But here again was the old split in the personality, creating this split in the objective world: the picture, to the *eye* an old map on a tavern wall; to the *feel* a horrible alien monster . . . Death . . . God. G O D . . . the very core of 1878 at last . . . Locomotive-God, visible again to the naked eye . . . with death instantaneous, exactly as it had seemed instantaneous to my infancy at the railway-station. I think (though my recall here is uncertain) that the pictured boiler head became even a wraith of the God-Face with the gaping maw of 1878. My introspective intelligence performed the identical process it had performed at nine years when in the school-room I had had the seizure of panic. It recognized the phenomenon as psychically abnormal and precipitated in my emotions a secondary panic based on the recognition of this abnormality as a desperately critical symptom. So, as in the school-room, I felt the terror of death twice over: first, directly, from the reverberations of the aboriginal Locomotive-God of 1878 (merging with the present Onset and Attack of the Madison Mob); second, indirectly, from the deductions at the moment about the state which the reverberations had induced. In other words, I became panicky over my panic. Only far more fiercely than in the school-room . . . for much had happened since 1885.

I am convinced this is my last hour . . . perhaps my

last minute. The Locomotive-God in the Map on the Wall. Menace. Destruction. I say to Brown, "I'm feeling awfully bad" . . . in a low, controlled voice. I drink more beer . . . to get my eyes off the map. I take out a pencil from my vest . . . bite it, first on one end, then on the other, repeatedly (Charlie's vivid recollection of this was the stimulus to my own recall—he imitated the original act) . . . I take out an envelop from an outside coat-pocket . . . open and show Charlie a paragraph. It is from Henry Holt, apropos of an arrangement (later dropped) for publishing my poems, "The Vaunt of Man" volume. I comment on Mr. Holt's objection to my use of "fore-word" instead of "preface" . . . with that irrelevant interest in trifles . . . anything to hold myself together. I lay the envelop on the table and draw aimlessly two pictures—one large, one small . . . they were two *locomotives*. Charlie remembers that they were locomotives. We get up . . . pay at the counter by the door . . . I buy a *cigar* . . . light it in the doorway . . . just as a train is passing over beyond the meadows. And my eye, above the match, turns by an unconscious fascination once more to the map. The Locomotive-God, with thrust more malignant still, seems as if leaping out at me across the tavern-room from behind the bar. I suffer the intensest seizure of terror yet. The feel of onrush is so fiercely authentic that my very reason spontaneously omits the rational explanation (i.e., absurd hallucination), and repeats to itself that the locomotive can't really be rushing at me because in the map-picture it never passes beyond the gate-beam (with a man behind it) depicted at the left just in front of it on the cross-roads. And I keep looking to *make sure*. I say nothing to Charlie, and my external manner is merely agitation.

Let the reader note well the extraordinary associations with the cigar. The Stocky Man at the station in '78 had been smoking a cigar close to my nose as the engine bore down on me. My first overwhelming *feel* that the Locomotive-fright (already vaguely recalled) was more fundamental to my phobias than the school-fright came in twilight sleep, a little over two years after beginning my experiments, with the pungent odor of a phantom cigar, accompanied by the most violent bodily shudders. This pungent odor—so sharp and fresh that, had I been an expert, I could have identified the brand, a very good one—returned with the exact aroma many times in twilight sleep for the two subsequent years. It assailed me, indeed, several times in broad daylight when I was occupied in commonplace errands on the street during the garish day—so pungently that twice I retraced my steps and looked into doorways to make sure that it was really a phantom odor. So it was indeed . . . and wafted down a generation in my brain (like the acrid stench of the school privy). For two years I traced the associations of the odor. I traced them readily and speedily to the school-fright episode—when the whole Locomotive-God episode was, as I said, still only in the first stages of emergence. But all associations came to a stand at the point where, on leaping down the steps (from the house where I had been cared for), I confronted the Catholic Chapel, just as the locomotive-whistle blew. It will be recalled that, at this whistle, the Chapel Front became entirely to my feeling, and half to my vision, a locomotive rushing head-on at me. I analyzed the association of the cigar with this point as indicating probably the cigar of the janitor who, as will be recalled, came up to the gate of the house. But I cannot yet remember that the janitor was smoking at all. I think now that the association, persisting for many months, of the cigar-odor with the neighborhood of that Chapel Front was occasioned simply by the *dominance* of the Locomotive-God's reverberations precisely at that point of the 1885 trauma. The cigar-odor was so intertwined with the '78 trauma that it linked itself in association with that moment of the 1885 trauma, which most nearly inherited the meaning of the former. The phantom cigar had been preceded several times from the beginning of my search by half-dream images both of some

one *else* lighting a match and of myself lighting a match,
accompanied by shudders and the feeling of association with
old frightful experience. These images now recurred and
associated themselves with the mysterious and illusive cigar.
Somebody somewhere in the long history of my frights
had been lighting and smoking a cigar. That was clear
. . . where? . . . who? In time, by a process of associations so long and intricate that two hundred pages could
not tell the tale, I got to the cigar in the hand of the Stocky
Man of 1878. It took a year more to pass from his cigar
to that cigar I lit in the doorway of the road-house, June
11, 1911. I arrived at many other details of this June day
of 1911, only after having first recalled the associated details of that June day of 1878. This inverts the normal
clinical order of recall. Which cigar had I smelt in my twilight sleep in my bedroom and on Madison's streets—the
Stocky Man's of '78 or my own of 1911? It was apparently
something of both—but the odor was certainly more his
than mine. . . . I recall the identical aroma, when he used
to puff away luxuriating in my father's sanctum. I actually
get an evanescent faint whiff as I write these lines in 1926.
The Rector has been dead for more than a quarter of a century. His cigar lives on. . . .

To return to the narrative of 1911. I light a cigar in
the doorway . . . just as a train is passing over beyond the
meadows . . . my eye sees the horrible phantom in the map
once more. I suffer the intensest seizure of terror sensations. . . . I say nothing . . . try to "walk it off" . . .
within a hundred feet I throw the cigar away, saying it
seems to make me feel worse (a truth uttered by the subconsciousness, with different purport from that intended,
while the throwing away was an attempt to get rid of the
unknown factor of torment). I recover a little. The train,
however, continues to torment. I am obsessed with a *feeling* that fellows are playing ball in the meadow by the track.
I look and look at the meadow. All is empty to the eye.
The *feeling* is inexplicable and ominous. (The reader will

not find it inexplicable if he recalls the ball-players by the track of '78.) The train passes and I feel relief . . . Some. We walk the scant quarter-mile around to the woods by the further side of the lake. After a half-hour among the mounds, I say again, "I'm feeling awfully bad" —I had not dared weaken to the point of speaking much— "it's sultry in here, and the beer and cigar seem to have affected me. I'll go out into the open by the bluff."

Traversing the four or five hundred feet from Charlie, across thickets and pasture bluff, I stand looking out over the silent and vacant water, in the blue midday . . . across the half-mile to Merrill Springs, down the lake to forested Eagle Heights, off to the Capitol Dome shining seven miles away. There is a sail out on Mendota far toward town. That is all. The summer cottages on the bluffs are still closed. And not even a cow has strayed this way, from the farm-house hidden between the cove and the side-edge of the woods. I stand attending to the want of nature that had occasioned all the terror of the school episode. (Note this motif from 1885.) I feel a sinking loneliness, an uneasy, a weird isolation. The locomotive-phase of road-house and cigar of less than an hour before has already entirely lapsed from consciousness. I take off my hat; I mop my head; I fan my face. Sinking . . . isolation . . . diffused premonitions of horror. "Charlie" . . . no answer. The minutes pass. "Charlie, Charlie" . . . louder . . . and no answer. I am alone, alone, in the universe. Oh, to be home . . . home. "Charlie." Then on the tracks from behind Eagle Heights and the woods across the lake comes a freight-train, blowing its whistle. Down the same track. Less than an hour after the passenger-train. Instantaneously diffused premonitions become acute panic. The cabin of that locomotive *feels* right over my head, as if about to engulf me. I am obsessed with a *feeling* as of a big circle, hogshead, cistern-hole, or what not, in air just in front of me. The train *feels* as if it were about to rush over me. In reality it chugs on. I race back and

forth on the embankment. I say to myself (and aloud):
"It is half a mile across the lake—it can't touch you, it
can't; it can't run you down—half a mile across the lake."—
And I keep looking to *make sure,* so intensely in contradiction to what the eye sees is the testimony of the *feeling* of
that cabin over my head, of that strange huge circle hovering
at me. I have not recalled the exact time-relations to the
minutes; but somewhere in this stage I was obsessed too
with the *feel* of the presence of Agatha, and with a peculiar
crescendo of horror at Agatha's death—and at my guilt
for her death . . . even as the Mob was shouting at that
very moment over yonder seven miles away at the other
end of the lake. Agatha was hovering there with the phantom Cabin and the phantom Circle. The circle was of
course the reverberation of the head of the cylindrical body
of the Locomotive that became the Hideous Face of a
Devil-God in '78. Attempting to summon strength for self-
possession from the depths of my being—those very depths
from which came my distress—I chanced to sweep the
Heavens from above Eagle Heights and Black Hawk's
Cave, past the glare of the sun, riding high over the ancient
Winnebago camping grounds. Was the impact from outer
space of that great light on my eyeballs the fatal stimulus?
I don't know. But the summer's cloud to the left of the
sun, with all its arcs of white and gold, kaleidoscoped in one
onrush, into a vision of two tremendous shining horses
head-on, before a canopied chariot, in which was a bearded
man and a fair young woman, that *felt* to me like the Last
Judgment. And over the woods, farther to the left, on my
side of the lake, pictured in the unclouded blue regions,
stood a gigantic negress in a red-and-black plaid bodice.
An Apocalypse. . . . I think Patmos Isle and Ezekiel
flashed across my horrified brain even then . . . the biblical
data are obvious . . . but John and the Prophet had
Heaven on their side. To me it was not alone a vision but
a destroying menace. The horses and chariot were dashing at me. *This* at last was no mere *feel,* nor no wraith;

305

this was complete hallucination in all three dimensions of space. The Locomotive-God had emerged again from the sky with all his aboriginal power. But in a new distortion, integrally compounded in part of elements that merely surrounded Him in 1878: little Mary, the negro nurse, Mary's father, his carriage and his horses . . . and the horses have turned white. Simple, but preposterous, psychopathic reverberations—and no abstruse psychopathic allegory in so-called typical symbols of the Freudians. Locomotive-cab, Mary's phaëton, biblical memories of celestial wagoneers, project from within me, as from within a cinema, these monstrous canopied wheels out, far out, upon the skyey screen, with a subtle fade-in from the steam fire-engines of my childhood (then always a terror and a fascination). And lost Mary, riding away from the station with her father, fuses with my lost Agatha, rushing toward me, about to die. Guilt . . . punishment. Reverberations, not allegories. Deep called unto deep on high. June summoned June, across the continent and across thirty-three years of my life. Literally, the Vision knocked me down. I collapsed to my knees. It lasted at most but a few seconds—possibly but four or five. I cannot say. The negress lasted longest . . . over the woods. I leapt up. I rushed about, chattering aloud: "Miracles are impossible; miracles are imposible." I come to a stand. I fumble out my note-book, even as the hysterical Hamlet took out his, after a vision too. I write in wild jottings brief arguments against miracles, repeating consciously the arguments in my "Poet of Galilee." I am thrashing about me with the broken sword of reason against Monsters more puissant that all reason. Reason could not destroy the Fear of this Apocalypse; autosuggestion could not destroy it. For this Apocalypse was not the cause of the Fear at all; the Fear was the cause of the Apocalypse. Reason could not destroy either the Hallucination or the Fear. But, note, neither Hallucination nor Fear could destroy Reason and Reality. I knew both the Hallucination and the Fear *for what* they were, however little I then knew *from what* they came. Once upon a time it was different: Saul of Tarsus on the Damascus road saw a vision too, and far less monstrous than mine. And thereby he founded a World Religion.

Meantime the freight chugs on toward Middleton. The torture of its chugging supplants even the horror of the vision. My subconsciousness knows what the torture is; and makes my voice shriek, as I rush back and forth on the bluffs: "My God, won't that train go; my God, won't that train go away!" I smash a wooden box to pieces, board by board, against my knee to occupy myself against panic: I watch the train . . . it seems so slow . . . so slow . . . if it will only get across the flats . . . out of hearing. I am obsessed with a half-feel, half-wraith of a red-brick railway-station down the track, as when I ran in the school yard of 1885 . . . and my mind is flooded, not with Agatha but with Mary. (I cannot remember whether distinctly as in her childhood or in her maturity—in twilight sleep and crystal she has always appeared as a child, in my dreams, however, as a woman.) I am intermittently still shrieking, "Charlie, Charlie." I am all the while mad with the terror and despair of being so far from home and parents; and when I look back toward the distant city my mind is flooded not with the image of either the Langdon Street Mansion or the Cottage in the Hollow, but with the feel and wraith of the old Homestead of my childhood; as if verily beyond those hills and bays, beyond Eagle Heights. I am running round and round in a circle shrieking, when Charlie emerges from the woods. His presence is psychic support. The panic subsides into mere diffused dread, a relative relief. I say: "I seem to be in an awful nervous state. We must get back to town." We begin to walk hurriedly along the dirt road. I talk about girls . . . trying to fight back another seizure . . . not about Agatha, nor about Mary, but both these are the real girls on the fringes of my consciousness. I have another seizure. I try

307

to run it off, Charlie with me. In vain, though not of the intensity of the former. I think it is sunstroke. At the pump by a picket-fence (recall the picket-fence of the Washington School . . . picket-fences were long in my phobic dreams) in the hamlet of Pheasant Branch where the dirt road enters the highway, I bathe my head and wrists and feel my skin and pulse. I know from the symptoms it cannot be sunstroke. But I do know I am in a critical condition. I approach a standing automobile. "Boys and girls, I'll pay you anything you say, if you'll get me back to town at once." I insist on Charlie's accompanying us. I need psychic support. They drive fast. I breathe deep, holding myself together. Counting the landmarks, mile by mile. The distance into town. We get out at the Cottage. I pay the boys. Two dollars. Charlie goes inside with me. My parents are there. I lie on the davenport. I shake with terror. I say in a low voice: "Father and mother, this looks like the end. I guess I am dying." Charlie tiptoes about, lowering the shades. The spell passes. But my father does not go down town to take part in the dedication of the Parish House . . . being "needed at home." I sleep long that night. In the morning, though feeling strangely weak in body, I start out on a little walk down the street. Within a hundred feet of the house I am compelled to rush back, in horror of being so far away . . . a hundred feet away . . . from home and security. I have never walked or ridden, alone or with others, as a normal man since that day.

The relations of the trauma with that of 1878 (and incidentally with that of 1885, itself the derivative of 1878) even to the hot day and the sheet of water, must be clear to any reader; as well as the same split in personality (rational self-directive intelligence on the one hand, subconsciously conditioned torture and confusion on the other) which we have noted before, where intelligence was shut off to the task of controlling and managing the self in its terror, but powerless to control and manage the terror, as such.

Unique, however, is the swiftness and completeness of the suppression. Mr. Brown and I estimate he remained at most twelve minutes in the woods after I came out. The slow freight had but little more than disappeared behind the groves of Middleton. Upon the sudden relief—almost itself with the force of a shock—of seeing him emerge, perhaps a hundred feet away, I forgot—and forgot for fourteen years—all the factors that were associated with the Locomotive-God; the Cabin, the Circle, Mary, the torture from the chugging train, the brick station, the homestead, and the entire vision in the sky. I talked feverishly with him at once, but not of these. I recall perfectly the states of my consciousness as we traversed the short dirt road to Pheasant Branch: the Locomotive-God complex had already sunk below consciousness. Mr. Brown's clear recollection of our conversation supplies verification. I retained for a couple of weeks, or a month, a vague memory that the whistle of the train had started the panic; then that too disappeared for fourteen years. I retained a vivid memory only of the landscape, itself already long familiar from many tramps, and of the general quality of the panic as such (my feelings of terrified isolation and my calls for Charlie). And the experience recalled to consciousness nothing whatever from the traumas of 1878 and 1885. In 1917, during a brief period of lessened phobic intensity, I revisited West Point with friends (I could not have gone so far even then without the psychic support of friends). I tried to recall the entire experience of six years before, here again on the very spot. Nothing came back. I still had only the general, the superficial memories—landscape, Charlie, panic at being so far from home—and still supposed these were all. The preliminary seizure in the roadhouse had disappeared from memory as completely and as speedily as all that followed, and even more deeply, for my psychoanalysis recovered the Locomotive-God in the Roadhouse only after it had recovered the Locomotive-God in the Sky.

XV

THE story becomes now, with more and more concentration, the story of that God. The seasons and the years become less defined, as the issues of life become more and more dominant over the revolving sun and calendar dates. The world with its million ships and giant chimneys and suburban door-yards shrinks to the scope and intensities of one mind; the people will be more and more shadowy; the trees and the waters and sunsets farther and farther away. And if from time to time images of faces and bulks of nature or a bird and a flower flash into light, they will be more and more but the scenery through which passes the Locomotive-God. And some of these faces will be of people devastated too by the same God; for the story becomes now not alone what He did to me but what, in distorting and torturing my life, He did indirectly to distort and torture the lives most closely associated with mine. But above all it becomes more and more intimately the story of one man's concentrated fight for rehabilitation of Health, Hope, Freedom, Career, who for long years was still fighting in the dark, not knowing the God, and discovering him late . . . possibly too late.

We must live through this first summer, the reader and I, together there in the cottage with my father and mother . . . but we must take it, like much else that will follow after that first summer, with self-possession. The problem becomes more and more how to tell of suffering, without suffering anew and harrowing others, yet with words that report vitally the psychological facts. Suffering under the microscope must remain suffering if we are to see and understand it; yet we will be in no condition to adjust eyepiece or make drawings if we suffer too readily ourselves. Any study of the neuroses calls for a peculiarly nice balance between sympathetic insight and analytic detachment.

That first summer, I had found myself the morning after my collapse at West Point driven back to the house after the first steps of my first walk. The second morning, abnormally timid, I started out over the adjacent University Heights with my father. Among the flowery homes on the sunny hilltop came up, from the near marshes by the bay of Lake Mendota, the whistle of a passing train. "Get me back, father; get me back to the house. I am dying." And the old man with arm and voice gets me back. And no one of us leaves the immediate sidewalks, meadows, and groves till autumn. The goldenrod bloomed and withered . . . the hickories became a glowing bronze.

I called in a doctor. He told me that when I felt queer on a walk I should just sit down in the shade and think how silly it was. And he gave me a pill. A week later, in a spell when I could barely control a mad impulse to scream, and could not control at all a mad impulse to pound my thighs with my fists, another doctor gave me another pill. He said I was nervous. A third doctor, later in the summer, said that my phobias would disappear with restored physical energy . . . which seemed reasonable, for they were indeed beginning to diminish their intensity. Off and on for years afterward, other doctors, in casual conversation, used to tell me that all I needed was to get a good grip on myself —or to take a trip to Europe. I wrote, too, that summer to good Professor Münsterberg. He took the trouble to write out in his own hand a letter full of astute "suggestions," assuring me my phobias would pass in a few months. I carried it in my pocket for years, till I destroyed it along with all our later correspondence . . . which had been not about my neurosis but the neurosis of a war-mad world. It was the enlightened and honorable correspondence of two thinking men, grieved for their respective countries, at a time when most thinking men were no longer thinking; but I feared for him, should a member of the Defense Society visit my files. We had dinner together two weeks before he died at his cathedra, facing his students.

My condition that summer was what used to be called nervous prostration. I became forthwith too weak physically for a cold bath or for five minutes with the lawn-mower. I guided the nozzle of the hose at sundown about the parched grass, or held the wooden posts for George Sellery across the way as he tamped them down for his new wire fence. And I walked a hundred . . . two hundred . . . two hundred and ten . . . feet down the lane . . . in a weakness more than physical. Sounds tortured me, not in the old phobic manner of childhood, but simply as nerve-racking, like a chalk-crayon's strident squeak grating on a blackboard. We plugged all bells, and my father and mother walked about very quietly. That summer all reading or thinking or talking with emotional content of any sort, except filial affection or sardonic humor, was torture. For three weeks I worked on the sixty-two pieces of a picture puzzle. All I had left of zest and intellectual ambition was to concentrate, morning after morning, night after night, on an effort to reduce my speed-record in setting the pieces together on the dining-room table. My father sat beside me, with open watch in hand. Fifty minutes . . . forty . . . twenty . . . two . . . clever fellow. I read Wilhelm Busch, as I had read him up and down the elevated in the pain of New York days . . . "Der Heilige Antonius," "Die Fromme Helene," "Der Verhinderte Dichter" . . . laughter. I turned Æsop into rime, with Busch-like modifications of situation and moral . . . the swindle and the smug pretenses of mankind . . . with veiled symbols (not unrecognized in my consciousness) of my own state . . . I was the sick lion . . . and the cackling geese and the braying asses were over the hill in town. Most of the fables were written with frantic speed to ward off overwhelming seizures of grief, of indignation, or of terror. . . . The Laughter-God fought the Locomotive-God in

a strange new mythology . . . but, after all, the wars of
the gods still go on over the earth . . . and they are not
mythology. When friends visited me, I did not talk about
Agatha or my phobias; but I would recite my new Æsop.
And we would laugh together. My father copied some of
them, and I typed others. They were published quietly in
1913 under the title of "Æsop and Hyssop," by the Open
Court Publishing Company of Paul Carus, philosopher-
friend. Properly exploited in the book-market, they might
have got me into the list of contemporary American humor-
ists . . . except perhaps that their real purport was too
subtle. It is this book to which I refer in "Two Lives,"
as multiplying for man the medicine of mirth from the
springs of pain . . . for, after all, some people have
chuckled over it.

And I felt strangely drawn to Robert Burns, unread for
years, in fact since Morsbach's lectures on Scotch dialect in
Göttingen. Indeed, I wrote one of my fables in Scotch, in
the Burns stanza. My mind was turning for self-rescue
to Germany so far away. But my "Burns revival" was
something more than that . . . farther away than that. I
spoke at the beginning of this book of the part played by
the Locomotive-God in my serious interests of maturity.
The following, though the most incredible, is the most complete example. From early in my auto-psychoanalysis, I
remarked recurrent dreams about Burns, especially about
the Burns cottage. It was a little white frame-house, not
simulating any auld clay biggin at all, not simulating Allo-
way, Lochlea, Mossgiel, Ellisland at all. Much less Dum-
fries. And it was situated in a country not the Burns country, with Jersey hills over yonder. But I was always trying
to get to it, with phobic anxiety, for safety . . . and comfortable in it, with Jean and Robert . . . Jean once sang
me one of Robert's songs in that dream-cottage. My first
analysis explained it as dream-interest in my university
work; I was actually giving a seminary in Burns and the
Scotch dialect. But why did I never dream about other

313

courses? And why, too, had I chosen the unacademic Burns for a seminary . . . against some mild demurs of colleagues? I eventually traced the dream-cottage to the white frame-house toward which I was running down the platform. But, again, why had I identified the cottage along the track just beyond the railway-station of Plainfield in 1878 with the dwelling of Robert Burns in Scotland of a century before? I have the answer to this likewise. The platform-cottage was vividly associated in 1878 with *Scotland* : as I stood crestfallen by my mother after my run and yells, I kept noticing that laughing Highlander, with plaid and kilts and bare knees, who stood near-by, with bagpipe just silenced . . . such an itinerant and picturesque seeker of livelihood as I remember to have seen again later in childhood. Of course at two years and five months I knew nothing about Scotland; but the subconscious which preserved the image did in time relate it to the Scotland I came to know about . . . and to the chief Scotchman that all the world knows about. The trail occupied several months, with several false scents: as when, hearing myself say in twilight sleep, "Mr. Scott," I conjectured associations between Sir Walter and an untitled gentleman of the same name who had painted my father's portrait. I then imagined this Mr. Scott must have been the swart Stocky Man that I already vaguely recalled as with me on the platform . . . whom I ultimately discovered to have been the Episcopal Rector. But behold how well my subconscious served me in thus leading me to Robert Burns. Burns, in his very own right, was my man . . . he too had fought poverty and detraction with laughter and with song. I would win as he had won: "Do not worry; people will respect me more after a hundred years." He had precisely the humanity I needed to have near me. Of all the poets in all the languages I know, Burns is the fellow, quite aside from his rank and his fame, whom I would have foregathered with most heartily . . . whom I have foregathered with most heartily. Byron has gone.

314

I want to reinforce the lesson of this : an interest, because stimulated by such a mechanism of subconscious associations, is not necessarily invalidated as ultimately associated still more with the higher values of one's character and intelligence. My "Lynching Bee" reflected (unbeknown at the time of composition) my horror of the two mobs that assaulted me (of 1885, of 1911), also my horror of the World War (though it says nothing of the war) ; but it reflects no less a man's judgment on the Monstrous American Crime . . . and the judgment can stand, as sound, in its own right. It is not invalidated by psychoanalysis. So too my minority opinion on the World War that cost me and some friends such pain. I was a revisionist before the revisionists . . . from 1914 on. Subconscious or half-conscious contributory factors were indubitably my reactions to the mob (i. e., *I was Germany,* resenting misunderstanding and resenting irrational attack) ; and they were reinforced by dear memories. But there were the factors of a mature man's study of economics, history, diplomacy—and human psychology . . . and there was that mature man's vow in August, 1914, to keep his head through what he so clearly foresaw was to be the most tragic upheaval of society on the planet. Of course, I over-reacted at moments . . . in confusion, in wrath . . . and it is a tribute to some ineradicable persistence of the loyalties of life that my friends (all but one), themselves so dedicated to other and fiercer opinion in fiercer action, yet remained my friends even in 1917–18. But did the subconscious factors urge me nearer the truth or farther from the truth than Wilson . . . than Versailles? Ask a hundred years from now.

We return to 1911. The wraith of Agatha hovered over my head . . . literally . . . even to three years thereafter, as I might be serving the ball in tennis. A sinking despair of failure in the high cause of Agatha's salvation repeated the sinking despair of the infant failing in masculine courage in 1878 and the school-boy failing in his work in 1885. And it drew reinforcement from these earlier failures. Again and again in my remorseless clinic I have noted this phenomenon as typical: an emotion, an idea, itself born out of present circumstances, gets added intensity of tone or sharpness of outline from forgotten analogies of the past; even, as above remarked, a past stimulus may generate a present interest which has its own integral value. The defection of Agatha's kin and connections also reinforced the failure. I had hoped to help them too. One afternoon on a walk, when I was struggling in phobic terror to get fifty feet farther than the three hundred feet of the week before, Jack and his wife spun by in their automobile . . . evidently on the way to the cemetery. They saw, and they did not speak. I could not but review . . . though madness lay that way . . . the relations between the two houses. I could not but feel, with bitterness past all speech, that Agatha's kindred had considered me not as a man but as an instrument . . . and I knew what the wise Kant had said . . . but I remembered too how Jack had always spoken so contemptuously of the wise Kant. They had used me, I thought, and now having no further use, they discarded me like an old rag. No further use? I was still useful, after all: the more I could be made responsible before the community for her death, the less the responsibility of the ancestral family-taint of insanity. So I thought . . . I am only recording what I thought. I never could have been bitter merely over the kindred leaving me to suffer and struggle far from them that summer. I was not alone. And they had their tortures, anxieties, griefs— and she who had been my sister bore a child that summer . . . I never could have been bitter for long even if in the horror of the suicide they had felt a little coolness toward me in the first weeks. They might well have realized in time how hard the task I had undertaken, whatever my shortcomings. And in fact they did realize it . . . the fiercer the shame. So I thought . . . I am recording only what I thought . . . that summer. In my dreams I was always trying to drag Agatha from the water or to hold her hand in the yard as an ominous insane heat-lightning seemed to tremble and flash over her sweet girl-face. Sleep was not always nature's kind restorer that summer . . . nor the summer or winter thereafter.

The phobic phenomena were not simply infantile clinging to parents and house. The central terror—craving for safety, reducible ultimately to the fear of death—spread over my entire consciousness, over my whole environment. Every fear known to timid childhood was mine—fear of darkness, of thunder-storms, of dogs, of bodily pains, of blood. And many fears that only maturity has the knowledge to fabricate—as of symptoms of imagined diseases. The hideous components of this three months nightmare . . . thereafter mitigated but never entirely eliminated from the abiding core of the distance-phobia . . . were of diverse origins. Some were direct reverberations of my childhood, awakened with the awakening of the Locomotive-God, as, for instance, the fear of dogs (still present, mildly), and of stepping on a trestle-bridge (near the cottage), though curiously I did not repeat the phobias of bells. Some were accretions from the immediate past experience, as, for instance, a most acute fear of razors. The rattle of a box inside Agatha's room on the fatal morning of the poison had flooded my mind, as I shook the door, with the vision of my razor at her throat. I had to shave with a safety-razor; and for a year and a half my father stropped it . . . out of my hearing. Since then I have sharpened my own blades, but, even at this writing, I feel a constriction as the shadow of the old blade seems rasping my neck. But even this accretion from the immediate past has some general association with 1878, when the terrified child felt a violent convulsion in his *throat,* and perhaps with a *knife* on the table in the house to which the boy was taken in 1885. Some were new buddings, like new tentacles or processes of the aboriginal phobic Octopus, generated by the frightened mind's hyper-anxiety as well as by memories of

Agatha's end. I was afraid of constipation, afraid of poison in food and in sleeping-powders, afraid of swallowing at all, afraid of committing suicide (an aspect of the razor-phobia). And the little boy who fingered so objectively the skeleton had become the man morbidly haunted in hyper-imagination by the white and red coil of all his insides under the skin and under or around the bones. The external order of marvelous nature, after a few quiet weeks with the grove and the evening star, became for two years merely an intellectual affair, recognized as beautiful and sublime with as little emotional appeal as when we recognize that one pencil makes a green mark and another a red and that one is longer than the other; but the Marvel was ultimately restored to me with power . . . before I wrote "Two Lives."

Several times, shaking with the organic feeling of imminent death, I lay on the bed with my father and mother sitting on either side, a hand in mine, talking to me in low tones. Several times my father had to sleep with me . . . or to sleep while I lay in unresting terror. My door was always open . . . and theirs . . . and I could not go downstairs alone at night that summer. That summer my father had his seventy-fourth birthday. We three had arranged a little celebration . . . a cake and household jokes. That was the morning the postman brought me a letter from the old lady who had been my neighbor. I read the first page . . . there were four pages . . . that denounced me for cruelty to my wife and for a "grasping disposition" toward my wife's kin. I fell in a heap on the floor, as I had fallen before the attack-motif of the vision in the sky. My father seized the letter and tore it instantly into bits, while my mother's black eyes filled with pain, not tears. He was not angry at the old lady . . . he was trying merely to save my life—from the other three pages. I cite the episode, no less to illustrate how tragically two worlds of honorable life may be asunder. She had accepted in her distress the local myth about me: she had never seen the inside of our cottage, never the inside of my mind, probably never half seen the outside of my face, even when I used to look up laughing as I shoveled the snow from her door-steps; but she was the dowager of Langdon Street, the wise and affectionate friend of all Dr. Greylock's children and of so many young faculty wives, the widow of a famous professor. She acted as an outraged neighbor might well act . . . if she had acted from knowledge. But in her nature was Revelation, Authority, Judgment; not for nothing was she the lineal descendant of Puritan Michael Wigglesworth, author of "The Day of Doom." She is dead. And she was old. Death and Age are two Sanctities. How do I dare violate them with this tale? I do not violate them. My father is dead; and when her letter came, he was older than she.

My brown hair turned to its present gray that summer. Not overnight, as folklore would have it, or many a story in tragic fiction. The laws of pigmentation are suspended as little as other laws of organic nature even under grief and terror. The subtle changes of life take place only where life is; and the life of the human hair, as of the camel's or sheep's, is at the roots. The gray steals up from the roots, as the new hair grows, lacking the pigments of old days. So the brown of my head lasted on into August. . . .

But I did not take to my bed. Too often when I lay down, especially after the noon meal, I suffered from a wildly rapid pulse and accentuation of the frequent attacks of diffused terror. I now know why. The Locomotive-God was in the subconsciousness just under the surface all that summer; and such hypnoidal relaxation brought him still nearer. In my recent clinical probings there came a time . . . two years in extent . . . to date . . . when, in milder form, hypnoidal relaxation produced intermittently a similar access of phobic feelings and rapid pulse, even after I knew they were the doings of the Locomotive-God. So the terror, on lying down, during that summer was essentially a terror without content (an emotional analogue

319

of feeling ugly or erotic without an object), but a terror
for which the intellect feigned heart-disease as the object—
or (by a still more subtle rationalizing process) invented
the idea that by feeling terror over a rapid pulse, in itself
merely neurotic, I would infallibly cause the pulse to continue
in rapidity so long that the heart would wear out. Much of
the ingenuity and alertness of my mind was turned against
me that summer: my mind found diabolically cunning ways
of rationalizing all my terrors into secondary forms, pseudo-
explanations, as plausible as horrific. For, not having the
true explanation, the reason still insisted by its own instinctive urge upon some explanation. So it was with the innumerable phobias that beset me. Such is the mechanism in
phobias generally, I believe. The real causes are unknown
to the sufferer; and he makes up his causes. If he is of low
intelligence, he makes up palpably foolish causes; if he is
of high, then more plausible causes. Let us say both have
a phobia of darkness; in both the real cause is a forgotten
childhood trauma, from a fright in a wood; the former
will explain it as fear lest some goblin thrust out a white
hand from the blackness; the latter as a fear that some disease may attack him, appendicitis or spasm, with no one
near to help in the night. But in each, even the pseudo-
explanations will take their start in unknown past experience
or associations in the subconscious. Six years ago I wrote a
manuscript, nearly half as long as this book, in large part
analyzing the infinitely varying devices my mind had developed for giving content, pseudo-content, and pseudo-ob-
jectivity, to its phobias. I knew then nothing at all as to
the real causes, but I recognized that the only rational available causes were factitious. I knew I was not really afraid
in the ways my mind devised.

The mechanism in its technique can be made clear to the
reader. We start with a state of terror generated by past
experience. The past experience itself remains in the subconsciousness. Its emotional effect, terror, bursts into consciousness. At times this emotional effect remains merely

a diffused state of terror, in intensity running the whole scale
from vague anxiety to intensest feel of impending death;
and the agonized mind stands balked of any explanation
whatever; except perhaps (as formerly with me) that the
state is a premonition of the organic break-up of death.
The bottom is knocked out of all security, as when, in an
earthquake, chasms suddenly open all about one . . . except that in an earthquake the mind knows the fact *earthquake*, and in my case, it once knew no fact at all. But
oftenest the subconscious experience in addition to terror
generates in consciousness some specific *form* under which the
terror manifests itself, a form of course symbolically, even
literally, simulating the original experience. My central,
dominating phobia of distance is as good an illustration as
one will find. But the *form* of itself will lack adequate
motivation for consciousness. So the mind feigns motivation. And so friendly counselors ask, "What is there to
be afraid of?"—and add to the grievous burden by laughter or by experiments upon the patient . . . of which a
vigorous word later. With the knowledge I now have of
the real causes, the spells of diffused terror have apparently
become negligible, so long as I am in good physical tone;
but "what was I . . . am I . . . afraid of" in going a few
blocks from the house, in 1911 . . . and after? . . . I always knew the terror was without adequate motivation.
I could only say: as soon as I get a certain distance from
home—a distance varying back and forth from yards to
miles in the past fifteen years—I am overwhelmed with a
feeling of insecurity, of terror that I can't get back. The
truest statement of the conscious content is this: I am in
terror of the seizure of terror; and I fear the seizure at a
given distance. There are then perfectly rational sub-terrors
—lest in my panic I make a public spectacle of myself, or
run in front of an automobile, or actually collapse from
nervous exhaustion.

For the emotion in the distance-phobia, as for the emotion in all others, there have been clearly defined degrees of

intensity. Let me assume that I am walking down University Drive by the Lake. I am a normal man for the first quarter of a mile; for the next hundred yards I am in a mild state of dread, controllable and controlled; for the next twenty yards in an acute state of dread, yet controlled; for the next ten, in an anguish of terror that hasn't reached the crisis of explosion; and in a half-dozen steps more I am in as fierce a panic of isolation from help and home and of immediate death as a man overboard in mid-Atlantic or on a window-ledge far up in a sky-scraper with flames lapping his shoulders. The reader who can't understand why I have not merely whistled or laughed or ordered the phobias off my psychic premises, or who thinks that I must be grossly exaggerating a mere normal discomfort, like the initial dread in the dentist's chair, is not the reader for whom I am writing one line of this book. He belongs among the fools, of whom in my phobic career I have met a goodly number already. I would leave him alone. Let him leave me alone : let him, in the future, not meddle again unto worst disaster . . . of which later. It is as scientific a fact as any I know that my phobic seizures at their worst approach any limits of terror that the human mind is capable of in the actual presence of death in its most horrible forms. That I have never fainted away or died under them is due to two factors: first, my physical vitality; and, second, my skill in devising escapes—psychic surrogates, deflections of attention, or actual retreat to safety—before the exhausting surge had torn me to pieces. But more than once the escape has been at all but the last moment. The fools say nothing ever happened from one of these seizures—so why worry. Nothing ever happened? Well, here is what happens always. First, the seizure happens—as well say, nothing happens, if a red-hot iron is run down the throat, even though it should miraculously leave no after-effects. The seizure happens; the acutest agony of the conscious brain happens. Second, the seizure leaves me always far more exposed to phobic seizures for weeks or months; increases my fear of the Fear; and, as in the distance-phobia, robs me of a goodly part of what little freedom of movement on street and hillside I have. "Nothing ever happened." This means simply that to date I've lived through the seizures and continued for fifteen years to teach school, write books, and make jokes at the University Club across the street.

That summer, however, I did not look forward to fifteen years: I hoped at most for five. I would stay on earth at least five years. And I would get well enough to make that stay count. At that time, and for two years after, my parents had not a crust that I did not buy . . . and to the end it was mine to buy half the crust, even after the American Unitarian Association had done its best with the annuity. At that time, my good name was spattered with mud; and then I cared for a good name before the world as indeed I no longer care. At that time, more than from all else, the will-to-live and the supporting reason which it summoned drew their power and patience from two purposes: to avenge by art the dishonor I could not avenge by the law or the pistol, and to save by art the love I could not save with the crude hands of my body. Long before I published "Two Lives," I eliminated the vengeance. I eliminated it, as artist; but art is itself an aspect of the ethical law. Yet vengeance, with the fighting spirit it kept ablaze in my spirit, served me well; in those months, all gentler emotions, except affection to parents and friends, would have precipitated total collapse. My will-to-live knew its business. The service done, I discarded vengeance. The will-to-art knew its business too in its own time. And the will-to-live in the end had other aims, more creative, more abiding.

I was my own physician, careful of physical regimen, in the rooms with the only physicans who could help. I knew I was a "case." I knew my terrors were phobic. I refused by iron thinking to consider the diagnostic of insanity. I even knew they were somehow infantile in ultimate causes. A matter of "infantile regression," I said even that summer.

The source of that conviction is psychologically noteworthy. I was, as noted before, already familiar with abnormal psychology—even as I have since read, first and last (without harm, though without essential help) the chief men in the field, their books and technical journals of half a dozen languages . . . even to eight German volumes of Freud. But the conviction came, not externally from scientific knowledge, but internally directly from my own subconsciousness. All that summer, as I since learned by my probings, the 1878 and the 1885 episodes were almost on the periphery of consciousness; and vaguely reminding my consciousness of its childhood terrors. Indeed, the phobias were possibly as much the registration in consciousness of the suddenly suppressed shock at West Point in June, 1911, as of the childhood shocks that had given stimulus, content, and form to that shock in June, 1911. When I shook with the diffused terror of death on the davenport on the afternoon of the breakdown I was shaking with the reverberations of the already suppressed visions of only an hour or two before. I surmise that hypnosis or even psychoanalysis, under a man like Morton Prince in a few days after my breakdown, would have released, albeit in a terrific psychic explosion, the whole bag of horrors down below, with a completeness and finality that would have enabled my mind to readjust itself forthwith. There was no Morton Prince then . . . or thereafter, though, first and last, I have been in consultation with six or seven generally competent psychiatrists, living or visiting in Madison.

Such betterment as came, came as mere palliatives, as reduction of symptoms, not as elimination of causes. With restored physique—from rest, sunlight, food, regular exercise within my strength—came renewed buoyancy to cope with terrors. The need of good physical tone has been imperative ever since. The one other physical condition that continues to make a difference is external to any control of mine; it is the electrical condition of the physical atmosphere. I am always more phobic in the hours preceding

324

a thunder-storm; and I know from a hundred careful observations that the psychic state is here physically, neurally, and not psychically conditioned. It is electricity, not autosuggestion (conscious or subconscious). On the other hand, a snow-storm makes me worse, i. e., makes me more timid to venture beyond a few blocks, for reasons purely psychic—reverberations from a fright in the snow in 1912 (after my original breakdown). Aside from betterment by bettered physique, all betterment has been "psychic reëducation" . . . getting over the worst terrors by infinitely slow and cautious trying, and patient training in self-confidence. As I gradually felt I could control the terrors if they came, they came less fiercely and soon. But any violent frontal attack always spelt disaster. If I said, "I *will* get to such and such a mark" (a tree or a house, a half-mile down the street), "by God, I will" . . . why, forthwith the Phobia leaped up like a tiger to my throat, and back to the house I flew. This holds still . . . but of my present state an instructive word at the end. The Phobia will stand no back talk from me. So much for the wisdom of those who have so cheerily counseled that I kill it with an ax. Let them find me the ax. This slow process of so-called psychic reëducation was not at all a resetting of the original experiences, not at all fundamental reëducation. It was gradual resuppression and gradual, tragically gradual, autosuggestion; and its results have always proved very unstable. I have "reëducated" myself not to fear crowds, not to fear the distance down Willow Walk, not to fear a little blood as from a scratch, not to fear the shut-off of escape by a closed door . . . over and over . . . and over. I experimented for years persistently with autosuggestion, as a *radical* or *instantaneous* force; i. e., as according to Coué, et al. I have experimented for months with suggestions given me in hypnoidal states by competent associates. Both have been as without effect as the pills of the doctors. I was once preparing to write a book on this; I must dismiss it here in

325

a sentence. I used to say that I was, however, *negatively* hyper-suggestible; for in many a neurotic spell I have had bodily pains that seemed to be due to autosuggestion. But I now know they were reverberating somatic memories related genetically to those very spells—merely another expression of the same forgotten experience. Let the clinicians note this in their diagnoses of their patients. I am a less suggestible type than one would assume on a superficial acquaintance with the "case." Possibly my entire resistance to hypnosis, after at least ten experiments, is correlated with this fact; though it may be a phobic reverberation of my horror in going under the anesthetic the morning before Agatha's death, or in part an assertion of a peculiarly self-assertive personality, or the Phobia's own self-protecting blockage . . . lest I get at Him. Yet by October of that year 1911 I seemed to be progressing famously. I had still a semester's leave with pay . . . earned leave (everything must be earned at Wisconsin) through two previous summer-sessions of teaching. I could walk down town for over a mile. And fifty who saw me returning from the grave . . . Agatha's . . . mine . . . cut me with averted heads . . . (several of them fellow-diners of yore, where covers were laid for eight). I met Jack accidentally on the steps of the University Club. We nodded . . . for appearance's sake. Others shook my hand. I could walk a mile out into the golden year. I had written a little Indian play, "Glory of the Morning," for Tom Dickinson's Wisconsin Dramatic Society . . . in a week of the nearest approach to imaginative escape from grief and terror I had yet known.

I overtook a fifteen years' girl walking down the path of the grove. She cocked her young head archly at me, as I ventured, "Hello." We got acquainted. I was then always hunting for people to speak to. "You're just the girl I've been looking for to play *Oakleaf*" . . . and I told her about the Indian child. And that spring she played *Oakleaf* in the City's Theater. Her name was Helen. She had two sisters; a younger Gertrude, an elder Margaret.

Their home was sunshine, and soon sunshine for me . . . the three little sisters from across the hill of "Two Lives." They all live, no longer children; but Helen, who used to laugh as I read "Helen's Babies" aloud, now knows that babies are no laughing matter—and Gertrude too. Gertrude and I played chess . . . I used to take her queen. The last time she revisited Madison she took mine. Times change. Margaret, ailing for years, often in chair or bed, lives cheerfully and bravely with mother and grandfather. She writes me:

Grandfather was ninety-seven last week. Yesterday he went to a funeral and has been particularly chipper ever since.

I haven't seen grandfather since he was a lad of eighty-eight, interested in street parades and agnostic philosophy.

I returned to my class-room in February. Except for the distance-phobia, which by now gave me a beat of over two miles, I seemed to be practically well. I felt like one raised from the dead. . . even in my unmitigated grief. And many were glad with me. What more was there to fear from the Mob? But one Saturday afternoon I ventured too far beyond my beat . . . over near Second Point in the snowdrifts. I was with *Oakleaf*. I lost the road on a cross-country short-cut. The Phobia seized me. I got home over the half-mile of ice on University Bay, *Oakleaf* holding me by the hand. However, Monday I was still able to reach my classes . . . the shock and the disappointment had not undone too much of the good results of my six months efforts. Then friends were compelled to consult me on a matter . . . friends where I have always found them, inside my own department. Our head of those bygone days, who had been most considerate when the blow had fallen in the preceding spring, was now planning my dismissal. He was soon to tell me my work the preceding year had been unsatisfactory. A belated discovery; he was simply one more convert to slander. The news precipitated a seizure of

327

panic. The attack-motif again; but likewise the normal
anxiety for parents and for job. I had not yet, even in my
best moments, achieved a cure sufficient to take the train
. . . to look elsewhere for work . . . and, if dismissed,
where to look elsewhere? To lose Wisconsin was to lose
all. And in all the years following . . . down to date
. . . to lose Wisconsin would have been to lose all. Much
of my social tactics, in the midst of recurrent efforts from
outside to get me disposed of, has been to conceal my phobic
condition as far as possible . . . with the invention of all
sorts of ingenious excuses for not attending learned conventions out of town or not accepting invitations in town . . .
to conceal, lest the administration find my Phobia the one
decisive argument for my dismissal. To-day, and for some
years past, my services themselves have vindicated me
against the Phobia. I have served adequately in spite of it.
And the Phobia has become too chronically and uninterruptedly acute for concealment. I now tell Wisconsin the
dread she has had for fifteen years within her walls. I
thank the administration of all the years . . . presidents,
deans, regents . . . for letting me keep my job.

But when my former chief in 1912 planned my dismissal,
I could not know that the higher authorities, in spite of influences very close to their ears, were my friends and pro-
tectors. My chief's intention set up such recrudescence of
the past summer's phobias that I couldn't reach my classes:
a new argument for my dismissal. I hired, out of my own
pocket, a substitute. My father visited the dean . . .
though still "needed at home." A day or two later I was
walking desperately about near our cottage, staving off a
seizure of diffused terror, when a lively visitor approached,
cane and all. It was "my pastor" (in the days when, as a
social symbol, I had occasionally attended church). I had
not seen him for many months. It was now up to him, he
felt, to take a hand. He was magisterial and peremptory.
"This moping won't do . . . get on to yourself . . . go
back to your work at once . . . all your friends are thor-

oughly disgusted with you, Leonard." And he said I needed a moral tonic. "For God's sake . . . stop . . . stop it . . . I can't hold up under this" . . . (I still had a list of my friends on my wall . . . pinned there that summer for psychic support.) He followed after, laughing, chiding. A jolly brother. I rushed into the house . . . as wild as when the vision hit me from the sky. I rushed out . . . lest my parents should see me . . . I spent two hours with a neighbor-friend . . . begging him not to let me commit suicide . . . Socially a pastoral visit . . . psychologically the old attack-motif.

My parents and I moved to a furnished apartment across the street from the university . . . in a friend's automobile . . . in dread all three. I was not dismissed . . . but all the summer's work was undone. I could barely get as far as the top of the hill across the way . . . for months. Subsidiary phobias returned . . . to remain in background or foreground. I have never recovered in several particulars what I had gained before my chief and my pastor thus entered into my situation. My story from now on credits much of my suffering in my phobias to others, even "friends." Let the student realize the purport: the phobiac has his being in such isolation from normal feeling and acting that normal people, unless both sympathetic people and wise people, become indeed a desperate additional—vexation, shall I say? One purpose of this book is to make normal people—neighbors, friends, pastors, doctors—safer for the thousands of other phobiacs, in the world to-day or to-morrow. I say I had the fierce work to do all over . . . "psychic reëducation," once more. But I now had the advantages of physical health, of work, and of more companions, with the club so handy. If I name but one of those companions, let it be that more distinguished disciple of James than I—Horace M. Kallen, remembered less gratefully for his sesquipedalian terminology than for his unpretending kindness in always being humanly near when I needed him. I had it to do over . . . for many years

. . . over and over. I was . . . I am . . . like a swimmer, whom wave and tide and alien tribes keep forever from an island shore . . . now nearer, now farther, but somehow never engulfed by the sea. If there be any such swimmer. My parents lived always in or about our dwelling . . . except for brief stolen walks or shopping trips when I was at my teaching on the hill. The old demons reclaimed their dominion. And they brought seven others. For a year now I experienced attacks of acute melancholia . . . usually two or three times a week . . . from about eleven to two in the day. The normal tone of a merely saddened and hampered man would suddenly shift to a sinking such as is described only once in all literature—in Jonathan Edwards's analysis of the lost soul in Hell ("The Future Punishment of the Wicked," especially Section V). All, absolutely all values, dropped out of my being: friends, work, parents, sky. The blaze of noonday was scarcely a candle in the spiritual bleak and black . . . "Cheer up, Leonard.". . . All values dropped out . . . the earth of man, the

congregation of the hopes of man

in the illimitable and invisible air . . . all dropped out. One power only remained—the *will*-to-live . . . the primitive urge itself, though without more content and aim than in a primordial creature bogged in the Jurassic swamps. *One* power? No, *two*. *Reason* remained: I knew the state . . . I knew it would pass. I learned how to help make it pass . . . by running, running . . . by stripping for a cold plunge in the commonplace bath-tub . . . to serve the will-to-live. But I can say no more. Without the will-to-live and without reason it would have been suicide. I can say no more. Only three years ago, I saw a friend go into this state . . . and on to insanity. It was likewise the final phase of Agatha. I survived it. It has never returned. I cannot explain it either in relation

330

to my body (which was well), or in relation to my subconsciousness (which has failed to reveal any connections between it and my past traumas and depressions or my present phobias). As little can I explain the state of diffused unreality, similar to the melancholy but without the melancholic tone, which was intermittent for the first two years; describable as simulating the queer feel of the daylight world to one who has been without sleep for two or three nights. "Nervous exhaustion" is a meaningless phrase, particularly in this case where the victim (after the first few months, when, moreover, the phenomena had not yet appeared) was supplied with plentiful nervous energy for creative activity both bodily and mentally.

This second summer I took up tennis . . . in the adjacent university courts. I wanted a new exercise, something with youth in it too, and something that would keep my mind on the other fellow. But there was a deeper cause urging this particular game now on the man of thirty-six who had never before held a racket. The same cause that created the phobic ideas created the tennis-idea. The game of tennis I had gaped at on the platform in 1878. And the tennis I learned to play in 1912 eventually assisted the recall of the tennis I had seen played in 1878. In my probings in twilight sleep I caught repeated flashes of white tennis-balls in golden air, associated first with recent games of my own, then with a weird feeling of some game long ago in Plainfield; then came a flashed bit of phantom court that I noted was not like any court in Madison. The identification took six months . . . along with many other phantom bits that I was pursuing at the same time. Three years ago I took to playing catch, after I had thrown almost my last baseball nearly a quarter of a century before. The baseball idea was in part from the same platform-show of 1878, in part a recrudescence of active boyhood interests into college days, revived with the whole subconscious stir of boyhood frights. The reader will remember here the baseball motif in the phobic complex of the 1885 episode,

331

and the misplaced baseball field in the psychological associations of my recall of the 1885 episode, and the phantom baseball field by the road-house in 1911. I have noted many other childhood revivals of other happy things, along with the revival of the unhappy. The child is alive within me in devious ways, not all phobic. Young instructors of twenty-five can tell you that I out-throw them on the Lower Campus, right hand or left, with a throw that would still be a feature of the game, and that I am boyishly cocky about it. It would seem that the very persistence of this skill, and even of my muscular tone, and perhaps even of the abiding *feel* of youth, at fifty . . . so anomalous after such long years of trouble . . . owe something to the up-welling of the same subconscious child and boy, as upwells in the phobias. If so, here is a compensation unrecorded even by Emerson. The revivals have been significantly more marked in the last four years . . . coincident with the stirring unto revival (by recall) of the traumas of the old days; and have usually preceded (as in tennis) actual recall of their analogues in my past, as if the first manifestation in consciousness of the particular subconscious memory then beginning to stir—just as a vagrant recent pain has often preceded the recall of a pain from the far past. Reverberations . . . reverberations.

This second summer, after completing the university year, I completed my verse-translation of Lucretius, begun for Agatha. It was my only intellectual work . . . two hours every morning. The rest of the day was outdoor exercise and persistent attempts at "psychic reëducation"—to reaccustom myself, for instance, to water . . . wading two feet in . . . three feet . . . four . . . till by the end of the summer I could swim a few yards off the pier. My mother completed the typing Agatha had begun. Translation now became for me what it had been for Cowper, Bryant, Longfellow—a distraction. So too I translated "Beowulf" into verse . . . later . . . to help me through a war in which I did not believe. Moreover, translation employs the artist, when his artistic impulses and mood, though awakened, are still not awakened with enough energy to grapple initial chaos and shape the stuff of life itself. Critics have both applauded and regretted my self-sacrifice in subordinating original creative work to these long tasks of re-creating original works of others. There was no self-sacrifice. I was good for no original work, and used my time and skill to the best purpose then practicable. I believe no artist has given the world a translation at the expense of greater original work; but some have sacrificed masterful translation to versifyings of the second-rate states of their own minds—a Vergil by Tennyson would have towered far over "Maud" and all the "Idylls" but the "Morte d'Arthur." That I should have chosen precisely "Lucretius" and "Beowulf" is easy of psychoanalysis: in each, in the Roman philosopher, in the primitive epic, was the grim fighter against Monsters against which I too had to fight. The "Lucretius" sought a publisher in America for four years . . . six publishers. It finally landed in Britain, in Everyman's Library . . . a good landing. I had met Mr. Dent in Madison, and I corresponded with him in London many years . . . a courtly gentleman, a Renaissance printer. The "Beowulf" found its publisher at once—the Century. Mr. Ferrin, a younger man, was, like Mr. Dent, willing to publish what he felt was good . . . taking a long chance with the curiosity and sagacity of the public . . . like friend Ben Huebsch, faithful publisher of my "poetical works," and Paul Carus.

Meantime my fight went on. It was good to throw out the chest in the winter air, good to laugh at the club. I wrote two farce-comedies for the club. Here is the title and cast of one:

THE FALL OF THE HOUSE OF OMLET

KING GALLY-CUSS (he's nutty)....Sir Beer-bum Spree
QUEEN DIRTRUDE (enough said).........Evil Tango
OMLET (beaten up at last).........Richard Verbiage

333

DR. FELONIUS (a quack)..........Sir Henry Raving
OATMELIA (she's mushy)...........Yellin' Terryble
RATIO (he's reasonable) ....Edwin Booze
THE GHOST (of an idea)...............Golly Jibber

I never hope to see again as comically lugubrious a face on the boards as that of *Richard Verbiage* (Professor Ernst Feise), when, with controlled realization of the fell clutch of circumstance, he rammed his sword inch by horrible inch down . . . down . . . his gullet, and fell, feet to foot-lights, still a man, though a dead man. It was a five-act play, but the fifth, being a complicated funeral procession, took place off-stage . . . The Laughter-God against the Locomotive-God . . . still.

I taught . . . class after class . . . the wraith of Agatha still back of my shoulder, the Mob and the Phobias still muttering . . . with the loss in the first three years by death of more close friends than I had lost in all the years before. Teaching was obviously a valuable preoccupation . . . a double deflection, though at first after my break-down requiring fierce effort for the deflection . . . and friendly coöperation of my students. Outward to other people, outward to other ideas. Let it be emphasized for our clinical study that, on the other hand, teaching has never sapped my vitality. With a friendly class (and my classes have practically always been friendly, however roundly abused), an hour's teaching has always been at Wisconsin as little a strain as an hour's talk over dinner at the club . . . whether in lecture-hall on Hamlet before a hundred, or in the seminary-room on Beowulf or Chaucer with only six or twice six. Not even the strain of boredom. I know my themes. I like to talk about them. I like to talk them over with competent talkers. I have no pedagogy, beyond knowing my themes, my talk, and my audience, with a profound drift toward forgetting I am in a class-room and a profound reliance on the subconscious resources of my in-telligence. This is analysis, not brag. Teaching is an en-tirely unharried process, with me, though the teacher him-

self be severely harried for other reasons. And I am unharried by much sense of moral responsibility to my students, partly because I forget them readily in other interests out of class, partly because I know that they know I
won't forget them for other interests if they truly need me
. . . as they sometimes do . . . for confusions of mind
due more generally to trying to live than not trying to
study. They know I know a few useful items not in the
curriculum . . . Mamie . . . John . . . Adele . . . Arthur . . . et al . . . for fifteen years. In these last
years, chiefly with graduate students, I have often found
fundamental companionship. But I used to get along, by a
union of ironic detachment and ineradicable liking for
blundering youth, even with freshmen engineers . . . one
class gave me a pipe. Teaching has never been a strain or
an annoyance. Though some of it a huge waste of my
higher powers. My administrative duties have been light
. . . and only such as interested me to constructive ends.
The authorities, very wisely on several grounds, never put
me on the Discipline Committee.

Be it emphasized, also for our clinical study, that my
whole intellectual life, investigation or writing, has never
harried me. Mental effort has not precipitated or perpetuated my phobias; for it has never been effort, except in
the feverish Bolton days (and even there the strain was less
study than ambition to study), and except for the Harvard
stunt. Never effort . . . I hardly know what work is.
I work with absorbed zest . . . and when to the zest suc-
ceeds nervous restlessness (and I have this), I stop because
I must. I have little "morale" in work—the drive is more
organic than morale and looks after itself. Except in preparing a technical monograph, I take few notes in my
readings, and I sort out, memorize, organize very seldom
by conscious effort. Such effort gets me nowhere, unless
the subconscious has been already sometime at the job. If
I don't understand something, I am, like Herbert Spencer
(if I may say so—vide "Autobiography"), unpuzzled, and

335

I don't worry . . . I understand enough already to keep me interested . . . and I always *feel* that some understanding will *come* . . . and some usually does. And long ago I prepared for my Ph.D. in English and Germanic philology by—learning Spanish . . . and this too has achieved its justification. If I can't find the word for the poem, I don't worry . . . I feel it will come if it should come. There seems also no abnormal strain in the double game of teacher and writer, except at times irritation that I have to go to class in the midst of a poem . . . but the poem-vein returns with my return to my sanctum. I wrote "The Lynching Bee" between classes. I can make any half-hour count. I require no fantastic setting, nothing beyond quiet in hall and under my window. My wife does not have to sharpen my lead-pencils. And though long ago I determined to vindicate the Professor as Poet, even in modern America, as my life-work, I have not exactly trained myself into these intellectual habits: I have grown into them . . . Intellectual activity has not only fostered no phobias; it has, more than all else, made it possible to live with them. And any wiseacre who thinks, on the other hand, I have fostered the phobias by "dwelling on them" would do well to make an inventory of the books and articles, technical and non-technical, in prose or verse, I have composed in the past fifteen years, with a supplementary list of the books and articles read and the thousands of letters written. I have been too busy to "dwell on" the phobias . . . except in the clinic (of which more soon). The popular panacea for nervous ills, unselfish dedication to social causes and to individual unfortunates, has proved quite ineffective . . . except to create vicarious suffering and to deplete my purse. The aftermath of the war, in American Red Raids and in European Starvation, gave me a chance to prove that. In short, the easy commonplaces have no bearing on my case. I get out of myself, I get into myself . . . and the phobias, even if a little bothered, survive both operations with unabated vitality.

The strain in teaching has not been in teaching but in fighting for my right to teach. The university teacher works in the open before all eyes . . . before both gown and town. Colleagues and students on the hill see him when he stumbles, or seems to walk crooked. Best citizens, often social and business associates with professors that sit on boards of directors, see him, zealous for the good name of the institution. And a bad reputation spreads faster than a good. I had against me for many years the handicap not only of the Mob's original mythology, but in some quarters the reputation as half-lunatic, half-libertine. Those who knew me least of course knew most. My attempt to live normally in the open, at my tasks and in the street, hampered both by phobias and by misinterpretation of character, precipitated, as already remarked, blunders that helped to give reality to the opinion that I was both queer and vicious. Call a man a dog long enough and he will begin to act like a dog. Then came the notorious University Survey, under a certain efficiency expert imported from New York by the State Board of Control. I never saw him; but, evidently, he was soon sniffing about. However, I had so much company, from the then dean of the graduate school (pronounced a liar) on down to a hundred assistant professors (pronounced ignoramuses), that Allen's critique gave me some honest prestige locally. The Survey was national news and discussion for several weeks. Allen then became the private employee of the new stalwart governor, for reducing the State Capitol to efficiency. I gave him the following God-speed in an ode:

To Dr. Allen on the Job

Though corn be mildewed on the cob,
Though editors corrupt the mob,
Though educators lie and rob,
I am not blue—
For thou, O Allen-on-the-job,
Wilt see us through!

O Expert in Efficiency!
Twixt Tweedle-dum and Tweedle-dee
Thou canst distinguish to a T;
By quart and gallon
Thou gagest cow or Ph.D.,
O Sapient Allen!

Progressives try at playing mystics,
Our senators try pugilistics,
And I, poor ass, try writing distichs—
But Thou, God's Greatest,
Thou Aristotle of Statistics,
Thou tabulatest!

Guard well our Philip, whom from home
Our pride transferred to yonder dome
To make our State another Rome:—
Should aught be lacking,
Be unto him both hair and comb
And boots and blacking!

It appeared in a local paper. Clerks at the Capitol, I have been told, would read it aloud outside Allen's office; it was printed and distributed by some enemy of Allen's as a broadside at a teachers' convention. The editor had at first demurred—"Isn't 'sapient' pretty strong?" "How so?" "Doesn't it mean a sort of damn fool?" But the etymology I gave him was satisfactory . . . The Laughter-God against the Locomotive-God . . . once more.

In the third summer I began "Two Lives." The concluding lyric had been written in the preceding Indian summer; "The Phobiac" (Part III, XXI), much extended beyond its present form, mainly in the preceding winter. But neither was the essential story I had to tell. Prokosch had said, as I sat with him over the steins in a Wirtshaus a week after her death: "Hold your head up; a great poem will come out of this." Whether it would be great with the truly great or not, I knew it would be my own nearest to great. The psychological gestation evidently set in very

338

soon, and the spiritual congestion accumulated into many periods of acute discomfort. The mood, the craving, to create something out of the whole experience manifested itself, with increasing intensity, long before the creative imagination could master the welter of experience to order and to speech. I had scribbled and torn up many sheets. Still on the whole I waited . . . was resigned to waiting. Then on an August evening, sitting without apparent aim at my desk, I began in lead-pencil, hardly aware of what I was doing,

The shining city of my manhood's grief . . .

and so through the first two stanzas very nearly as they now are. And I wrote on . . . until about Christmas . . . sometimes five . . . ten . . . stanzas a day . . . between classes . . . or late into night. The distress of writing was an escape from the worse distress of not writing; yet the distress was labor not as toil . . . but as birth. The poem as a whole had already shaped itself in subconsciousness; only intermittently and in secondary matters, did the critical intelligence devise or direct . . . and even that seems to have taken orders from Below. The austere form itself, the sonnet (if in any organic creation, whether oak-tree or poem, one can separate "form itself" from essence, meaning, end) grew inevitably out of the need, an absolute need, of an especially austere control, masterful and unrelenting, over especially intense and fierce emotional experience, while a certain freedom resulted from variations within the norm (rime-arrangement, management of the "turn," etc.), and from linking the sonnets as stanzas (both in narrative progress and in end-enjambments). "Two Lives" is *not* a "sonnet-sequence." I seemed to be speaking directly to a few friends. The reworking of the raw stuff of life was in part the impersonal urge of art—as in the simplifications of time and action, and in the college atmosphere conceived as a little more intimate than that of a latter-day State university. In part it was the imaginative realization of personal desire, as where Greek, and not English, became the career of the young professor. The Rhine replaced Göttingen. Bolton in Massachusetts fused with Bath in New Hampshire; my parents, with the New England farmer stock among whom they lived and from whom they were descended. My early years in Jersey fell out. The cottage by the brook became the home of three years, not one, and the brook was moved up from the Mendota marshes; the vow not to budge from town against slander was left unembarrassed by the fact that ultimately the phobias made that vow superfluous . . . albeit there would have been tragic irony in that for the poem, even as there was for my life. But the scenery, the psychology, the incidents, it would seem, were less modified; and it required a naïvely uncalculating forthrightness to deliver some matters . . . for calculation would have feared them as inartistic, because "not true to life." The poem is full, as I discover in my clinic, of reverberations of the subconscious from earliest childhood down through the years of marriage and collapse. The writing affected the phobias neither to my health nor to my harm.

Meditation and brooding and talk with readers of the manuscript had to follow. George Woodberry, in Madison all that spring, helped me to realize a deeper reordering of the sequence of sections in Part III. Five years later another reader, a great character and an authority on "Faust," felt I had nowhere made the protagonist face himself. On that hint I wrote Section IX of Part III. Five years later, still, a sensitive young woman felt I had nowhere adequately enforced the girl's beauty . . . "and Mrs. V—— was telling me only yesterday that her beauty is still so vividly remembered." On that hint I wrote what is now the first stanza of Section VII in Part I. Such is "constructive criticism" from without. In my own rereadings for thirteen years, I gradually came to feel the fundamental tone and meaning which subconscious creation had been striving for, and could eliminate motifs extraneous to the central aims of that creation (where the subconscious had blundered, as it will), however pleasing to me some of the stanzas by themselves. I came to feel two hundred and odd stanza-sonnets in their implicit unity of rhythm, quite as I normally feel the unity of a single sonnet. And I added here and there a stanza to bring out motivation and rhythm. Such is "constructive criticism" from within. But I revised verbally relatively little. Chiefly for clarity. I subjected "Two Lives," first and last, to fifty readers for clarity. Just before final publication separately to two instructor-friends, in rivalry to spot a word, construction, motivation, to be demonstrated as unclear. They reported: "None." I then subjected each instructor to a searching test, as if the poem were Dante or Vergil, and each of them a Ph.D. candidate in text-criticism and interpretation. I could catch them nowhere. Yet one reviewer was wiser than us all: "marred by many obscurities," he wrote. The speech I used I had learned from my father's house, from schoolmates, from New England farmers, from Agatha herself, and from some older acquaintances, like Shakspere, Byron, Wordsworth, and Emerson. For me one organic complex of speech. This was in 1913, remember, before the Poetic Renascence. Hence, some reviewers in 1925, otherwise friendly, regretted an unemancipated diction and "helpless inversions." But English diction in higher art is still for me more than the usage of the twentieth century . . . *o'er* beside *over* on occasion—if you have the instinct for the occasion. And English syntax and word order, in the higher art, loses, not gains, by reduction of its old plasticity to the rigidity of modern French. It is all a question of means to ends— of sincerity too of ends. "O'er" may be a reality—or a jejune and palpable subterfuge for the poetic (as in "Curfew Shall Not Ring")." Hoosegow" may be a reality—or an equally flashy substitute for the poetic. Strain or affectation may be in either direction . . . just at present it is in the latter. My "archaisms" (very sporadic at that) troubled only those who were looking for trouble. It is a professor, of course, who speaks here, in that quiet remoteness from "reality" . . . where a professor like myself dreams his sheltered life away . . . The caption of a review of the "Tutankhamen" volume was "Professor's Poetry."

The mature love-emotion of 1914, though partially and temporarily replacing the original emotion about Mary (as both little lover and protector), could not reorganize the profounder habit of the subconsciousness. It could relieve but not break the tension of the tangled mythology in which the subconsciousness in its deepest deeps still believed . . . and still believes. The Locomotive-God won even against Aphrodite, goddess of manhood. My young wife found herself in two strange worlds amid ghosts of a past not hers: a social world where she suffered very soon the snubs of those unfriendly to me; a home-world with a phantom-Monster between us. My own friends welcomed her as theirs; and some faculty-wives, influential in the community and in no wise obligated to me, called upon her with the gracious tact of gentlewomen. But she was soon hampered in returning calls or in accepting invitations to parties, even as my parents had been; and not only did the phobia limit her in the work she would so gladly have undertaken of socially rehabilitating the husband; it gave her no fair chance for herself, it even exposed her to being misunderstood as indifferent to the community into which she had come. The year went by. We tended to withdraw into the small circle of my old friends, most of them living within the small circle of my again restricted beat. She inherited in a few months the direct effects upon me of the death of Agatha: the phobia now borrowed a new form for the new home from the old; and I have always suffered an abnormal anxiety, which in the times even of her slight illness becomes sometimes acutely phobic, that she will suddenly leave me forever. And she became thereby more and more the specific object . . . and the other victim . . . of the infantile Mary-complex. The love-emotion that had at first subdued the complex subsequently surrendered the more abjectly to it. The Locomotive-God, after shrieking over the grave of my first home, had invaded the new hearth.

The year went by . . . and the years went by . . . at

351

times the phobia somewhat receded and our hopes would rise. We could picnic in the quarries, on good days. We could get as far as theaters and stores around the Square. For several years she could visit her mother or sister for a few days . . . hurriedly, anxiously . . . in cities nearer or farther away, if I stayed with Madison friends or they with me . . . every minute . . . if possible with friends in *skirts* (the aboriginal Mary-mother-shelter complex). She could attend alumnæ banquets of her sorority sisters, if I went with her, and spent the evening near-by in a hotel lobby . . . waiting. Meantime, her deprivations became distorted gossip in the very group that had snubbed her; and my cruelty toward her, like my cruelty toward my parents, became further proof of my cruelty toward the woman I had driven to suicide. The very mob that shared so profoundly with the Locomotive-God in creating this sit-uation for my wife was damning me in my struggle to brave and better the situation. I am intelligent enough to per-ceive this bit of irony: it is not always a joy to be intelligent.

We had built a simple cottage overlooking Lake Wingra and its woods, in the second year. We feared it was rather far out from town and my work; but the scene out there was so lovely, so quiet, and our best friends had their flowery homes out there. And we felt too that it might be an incentive . . . that I might "reëducate" myself once for all by accustoming myself to a home . . . out there. While it was a-building, we could ride over on our bicycles . . . every day . . . or twice a day . . . in July, stakes along the green earth cleared of brush . . . a brown square hole . . . cellar beams . . . frame up and attic beams checkering the blue sky . . . the shape of a house already . . . we could see where the kitchen and the study were to be . . . talks with the kindly contractor on the precise brick for chimney and for fireplace . . . by October, twilights on the sun-parlor seat, as yet without paint, amid the saw-dust and shavings with the same pine-smell I had loved in boyhood's carpenter-shop. We were really living there

long before we moved in. Early the next spring I graded
the lawn with my own arms and back; and planted . . .
a year after . . . new trees and shrubs. A poplar . . . a
tamarack . . . a pine . . . a cedar . . . a mountain ash
. . . elms on the tree-lawn . . . the glad gifts from the
private nursery of next-door neighbor, a suburban Thoreau.
Wild honeysuckle bushes from my foragings in near-by
thickets . . . flower-garden of larkspur and hollyhock and
all the other names of blue and gold and scarlet . . .
with the thriving pillage from thickets and meadow, such as
a border of sumac along the rear of the lot by the lane
and a bed of goldenrod. An oil-painting of the garden
by the artist Mrs. Chase, then next-door neighbor, hangs
in our apartment now . . . in the next room. I never lost
but one growing thing in all my hundred and more trans-
plantings—a little hickory, though I had grubbed it up to
the very tip of the tap-root. And even the hickory-tree
took two years to die.

We had, too, a vegetable garden in a vacant lot beside
the cottage . . . for me an entirely new interest. And
several neighborhood friends had theirs. So there developed jealousies, acrimonies . . . as, for instance, over the
size of our tomatoes and their dates for ripening. I had
wagered on the biggest tomatoes—and these, too, to be ripe
and red by the first of June. A horticultural miracle. But
on the evening of the first of June, I telephoned to house
after house: "Come and see the tomatoes." They came,
bringing their wives . . . "You're a liar," said O'Neill,
professor of rhetoric and oratory, as I escorted him thither
at the head of the procession. Then a circle of gaping
mouths and some masculine "I'll-be-damneds." They
fingered the huge scarlet fruit to see if I had not tied it
on. No; everything was according to nature. Eventually
they refused, however, to pay the bet . . . learning too
soon that I had got the plants (after dark) ready-grown
from the laboratory of an unscrupulous plant-pathologist,
experimenting in nutrition.

Meantime, my wife created all the indoors . . . year after year . . . of the cottage. But I cannot look in now. . . . The curtains in the dining-room were pale yellow . . . in her bedroom, blue . . . in my study, brown to match the built-in bookcases . . . we sat behind the wood-bine vines of the sun-parlor in hot-moonlights . . . and we had when the time came a wood-fire in the living-room grate, or the study's. Neither of us ever cared for property: but a home, owned and paid for, and a curtained window from which two can watch . . . spring after spring . . . the bark of the willows on the lake-side turn yellow and the bark of their own osiers turn red . . . and count fifty varieties of birds in the thickening foliage of their own trees . . . is something more than property . . . especially for two who have been sore beset, before . . . and after . . . they had come together . . . and still the more, not the less, if there can be no child in the house. "Why don't you have children, Leonard? They might cure the phobia." The stock is sound, to be sure . . . on both sides.

Some two years after we had been compelled to abandon the cottage, I wrote a poem suggested by her anomalous situation. The "Nation" printed it after another magazine had rejected it on the ground that the theme was too peculiar for their readers' literary interests. It appeared afterward in the same "Tutankhamen" volume which some reviewers found so coldly academic and dull.

THE WIFE

Ten years you've sat (within the room you wrought)
To guard me from the Fear,
Except for hurried trip (when I was out)
Down town . . . and near, quite near.

Ten years you've sat, except for stolen walk
(With scribbled note on shelf),
By lake-side lane or neighbor's hollyhock,
Anxiously, by yourself.

Ten years together we have hugged our home
Because of this fierce Fear,
And made our prison-close a world to roam,
Counting so dear, so dear

Our swims, our skatings, picnics, we together,
Our phases of the moon,
Getting our changes from the changing weather
From June around to June;

Viewing our lake (from hills behind our door)
With its blue miles of light,
While those far woodlands on the other shore
Turned green . . . then red . . . then white;

Calling a luncheon at a near café
A journey on the train,
Calling a neighboring concert, lecture, play
A voyage to Greece or Spain;

Reading by lamp of Rome and Gipsy Trail,
Where friends go, two and two
(Whither I'd hoped with bride of mine to sail
While yet this curse was new) . . .

Ten years . . . and you have still such youth and grace,
One born to see and do . . .
While even in Town-and-Gown your woman's place
My Fear withholds from you.

You dream no more (though long the dream was dear)
Of any child at breast,
Playing the mother to a cureless Fear
(Cureless, for all my quest).

Ten years . . . and though I try to think my wife
In spirit still is free,
And in so cherishing my wretched life,
Works her good works through me,

355

Yet gnaws me utterly one grief and shame:
You've paid, because you could,
For a foul wrong to me, before you came,
That broke my hardihood.

The "foul wrong" meant of course the Madison Experience, particularly the Madison Mob, for I did not yet really know of the Locomotive-God. But let it stand. Without the Madison Mob, as we have seen, the Locomotive-God would not have come back . . . at least not so near. The case is "civilian shell-shock" as more exactly of a pattern than I then knew with the innumerable cases, from all fronts on both sides in the World War . . . except that in the World War the shell-shocked victim was not compelled to go on fighting. At least till cured. But I need to keep my wife out of these pages, as far as possible. During the past four years she has scarcely been five blocks from our down-town apartment . . . and many things that we'd both like to see or hear are in the sixth block or the . . . seventh. Theater . . . music . . . store-windows about the square. We look with curiosity down State Street to the inaccessible steps of the Capitol. Our cottage is as far away as the Rhine. And I have become a landlord. With tenants who find it as lovely as we did . . . and that is something.

My father died in 1920, aged eighty-three. I need no clinical experiments to recall the last time I saw him. The morning their bondage was broken, I said good-by and fled out of the apartment before the taxi came. But something led my distracted steps, timing them with fatal precision, to a street-corner as my parents were hurried past; and I glimpsed unseen his white profile framed in the window. He was leaning forward on his cane, looking out beyond the wind-shield into eternity. I found a note from him when I came in. The Locomotive-God had undone him too . . . more than his old age. His own God had not been able to protect his gentle participating nature from the wear and tear of the son's distress. They had one large chamber in an old-fashioned rooming-house of Roxbury . . . their last home . . . bedroom, parlor, kitchen in one . . . for six years. He broke down almost at once, haunted by an insidious feeling of unreality and of insecurity, and clinging to my mother, who for six years scarcely left his side . . . an uncanny repetition. When she came back from her half-hour shopping, he would be standing there, at the head of the stairs, his face happy again.

I could not go to my father. I could not let my wife go. I wrote a physician, a stranger to me in Roxbury, inquiring, urging good services upon him, and trying to explain my own disability. His reply was:

You are simply passing the buck—an old game. One more son deserting his old parents. I know their hearts are breaking over your desertion of them—and yet they are trying to shield you with excuses.

Probably the phobiac, in his deceptive and paradoxical condition of physical health, intellectual energy, and normality of conduct when not under strain, yet striving to play his part hampered by the most hampering of the typical neuroses, is the most grievously exposed to misunderstanding of all unfortunate men. And this drives one more nail into the cross. I could give other instances . . . many.

I could not go to him, even when I had gone, during an interval of betterment, to New York in 1916 . . . on that uneasy trip with wife and friends, a trip ventured upon in part to give my wife a chance, in part for what seemed alarmingly urgent professional reasons, and in part in the very expectation of going to my father. In New York itself, where I had wandered so freely about since earliest boyhood, I could go off nowhere—but once—without my wife; and often enough only when others were with us both . . . and often enough not at all. And I had an overwhelming horror of taking the train to my birthplace—a horror now more explicable than then. I could not go to Plainfield even to see my Uncle Oliver: so he ran up to the Bronx to see us, puzzled but reticent about my inaction. The phobic relation to Boston seemed different. New York seemed to mark my utmost limit, precisely as in acuter conditions a house a mile away, or a tree five blocks away, marks the limit. The phobic scale had undergone the enormous magnification to a thousand miles from the few feet about the door of the cottage in 1911; but the phobia itself remained the same in tone and in technic and in inhibiting power. Probably there was some, even yet undiscovered, reason relating to my parents for the subconsciousness thus marking New York off from Boston, or all directions toward Boston. But with all the mind I was conscious of, with all the mind that grieves and longs, I desired above all else to see my father. Yet the best I could do was to arrange by letter a long-distance telephone-call. On the appointed day and hour I rang up. My mother answered. Immediately. I could actually hear his hurrying steps—could almost see him reach in his trepidation for the receiver in my mother's hand. We talked three minutes. The telephone was invented the year I was born.

In the last months, his spirit seems to have shrunk from all reminders of the world. He was not physically bedridden. He was not mentally confused, but he had utterly withdrawn. The aged journalist would not, could not, look at the daily paper, nor read any mail more . . . all news had become the possibility of dreadful news. The war had helped here. His letters to me, though to the last in a firm hand, ceased. My mother finally wrote me that he now had her lay every letter from me aside. . . . "Read it to me later, Mattie" . . . and Mattie was the girlhood name he had seldom called her by since she had become "mother." And in a few days thereafter still, "No, read it to me later." "But, Will, don't you want to think about the boy any more?" "I hardly think about anything else," he replied absently. In this true book, is such a report an impiety? It is not. But to the impiety of America, with its blatant organized emotion for Father's day, it may well seem impiety. His last illness was brief and painless, with hand in his Mattie's. He had never spent a day in bed before. I have two snap-shots of him at eighty-two, in a full beard, in which I had never seen him . . . which he had not worn since he was a theological student riding horseback with a young girl along the Genesee. In the profile, he looks like Bryant; in the front-view, like Whittier. This is not a fancy. Nor an accident.

After his death my mother sent me such papers as he had preserved. One was of very recent date, a birthday letter from Uncle Oliver, who had died only the year before my father. It was from a man of nearly eighty to a man of eighty-one.

Dear Will:

All my days I have wanted to tell you how much your character has meant to me, but I never have found the words. From earliest boyhood you have always been my guiding-star, the profoundest influence upon my whole life. . . .

Your brother,
OLIVER.

Uncle Oliver . . . for sixty years the clerk of the First Baptist Church . . . Uncle Oliver, the Santa Claus . . . the Funny Man . . . the old corner brick-block in Plainfield . . . second floor . . . glass doors side by side . . . "Central Times" . . . "Ætna Fire Insurance." Father and Uncle Oliver . . . two Americans.

My mother expects to join him. I do not. Whatever the anthropological explanation of the far-off beginnings of the belief in immortality—whether in dream-visions of the returning dead (horrendous or consoling) or in the animism that stocked all nature, every tree and river and rock, with spirits—the belief has been perpetuated and conserved, during thousands of years, chiefly as an asset to the affections and as a projection of the will-to-live. And in both these aspects it has depended upon the fact not of death, but of untimely death. Indeed, if every human life had come full circle and had simply faded away like an autumn sunset in extreme old age, the idea would presumably never have occurred to the race at all. In those deaths I have known in which old age was a reckonable factor, the will-to-live weakened peacefully, as a phase of the peaceful weakening of the physical functions; and the mind looked back over its youth, if it looked anywhere, as it sank into its last sleep. There would be no projection of the will-to-live beyond the bourne, if all men lived out their hundred earthly years. And, as little as they would crave immortality for themselves, even so little would their kindred crave it for them: the elder kindred, the sons and daughters, would be themselves aging, yet still involved in their remaining will-to-live and human relationships in a world of their own, with their own sons and daughters, their own terrestrial responsibilities; and the buoyant and blooming third and fourth and fifth generation, without hardness of heart, would yet mark the passing of the patriarch as the far end of a long journey . . . far indeed from them. Tears there would still be at such partings . . . but how much more amenable to the sanative forces of time than those we must shed. And there would be no orphans, and the desolated widowhoods, however tragic, would be isolated anomalies for human compassion . . . at best over a few years . . . too isolated to create for the race on their behalf the surrogate of reunion after death. But the world of life is not so. Untimely death makes us desperate to deny death. This is for me proof only that mankind is still in intellect and in morale too weak to confront reality . . . too weak to acknowledge how hard and heroic life is. Furthermore, though metaphysics can make it plausible, and though science does not prove it impossible, the idea of immortality seems to me psychologically disassociated in mankind from his other beliefs, as such only half a belief, even a subconsciously feigned belief. Observe, with subtle union of sym-

360

pathy and analysis, the demeanor of the living over new-made graves. Do they *really* believe in immortality? . . . But neither for himself nor for me has my father's life needed to borrow from that belief any intrinsic value of grandeur or beauty. . . . Do I desire immortality for my father?—Yes, that his life might still work in the universe. Have I the desire to see him again?—Yes. But I have found my desires seldom warranties of the laws of life, except as I could create for myself, according to those laws, the fulfilment of desires. . . . Do I desire immortality for myself?—not on the terms I have had consciousness thus far. Do I want to die? Not yet.

Meantime the roar of the cannon that had begun in Europe the very day of our betrothal had grown wider and nearer. It had helped to undo my father; it beat upon my neurosis to my own further undoing. For the first two years,

> I'm visited each night in sleep
> By much to make a strong man weep,
> As Europe's hosts on hill and plain
> Resmite each other *in my brain*.

I am dreaming, over and over, of being in desperate con-ferences with the crown prince, my classmate in the Faust Lectures at Bonn, to get the boys out of the trenches by Christmas. Long before Henry Ford, I commandeer and man my own Peace Ship . . . in my dreams. Literally. In waking hours I write and print prose and verse (signed and unsigned) against the partizan ideology of our intel-lectuals, against our tightening financial entanglements with the Allies, against the sinister and perilous growth of a new mythology of Ahura Mazda battling Ahriman. I trans-late and publish a book from the Dutch. I collect my own verses, satiric and epigrammatic, into the book (with a long political prose preface), "Poems, 1914–16," from which I have just quoted. America declares war; and the entire edition, just off the press, goes into a dark corner of my cottage-cellar. I sprinkle dust on the bales and bid the spiders get busy. I burn letters. I shut my mouth. I make notes (late at night) for two years for a book to be called "Intellectual Reconstruction" . . . and keep the notes hidden. Yet nothing is in my thoughts or in my papers that need shame, before a judicious world, my character as an American whose ancestors had helped build New England. I grieve that I share so incompletely the vast patriotic emotion of the hour. Indeed, in this grief I first fully learn the deep foundations of my own patriotism. I grieve like a man without a country. The flag in which I had been swathed by my mother in the old-fashioned sentimentality of America's centennial year, the flag I had saluted on the passing ships in mid-ocean and before the embassies of Europe, in Berlin too whither I had gone with a letter in my pocket to Andrew White, becomes an alien symbol—not precisely as hoisted over the transports, but as draped over Bank-grilles and as wrapped around the Political Shysters, the Profiteers, the Sadists, and the Nincompoops and Ninnies now all-potent in every village. There seems an inversion of all values. Things are in the saddle. More and more. The German issue disappears in the American issue. What will become of my country? I learn what patriotism means to me; but I learn that, for me at least, in the end nothing is sacred but the integrity of my own mind; and I comfort my failing Americanism with the thought that Emerson, one of the greatest Americans, had first given me this thought, and that perhaps this thought is the leit-motif after all of the deeper, the abiding American spirit . . . or if not yet, that I will help to make it so, when my time comes.

I have here sketched briefly in a paragraph what I had once expected to develop into a book. The glory or the disgrace of my "war record" does not concern us here; I chronicle only my state of mind. It was obviously no state for a phobiac. There was also private grief. It hurt me to hurt my friends who had been besides such friends, and I did hurt them. "Leonard," they would say, "what pains us all is that, now when the great vision has come to the skies of America, *you* cannot see it.". . . Il gran rifiuto . . . But I had already seen one great vision in the American skies . . . in 1911 . . . over the woods at the lower end of Lake Mendota.

And, again, the anxiety lest I lose my university post. Others elsewhere were losing theirs. The Old Madison Mob, which had hated me too for my politics as a supporter and friend of La Follette, our discredited fellow-townsman, might get its deferred opportunity at last. Besides, one New York newspaper had smoked out the traitorous activities of my pen in 1914–16; another had discovered that I had once taught German in the public schools of Lynn; another that I had long ago written a sonnet—a very poor one—on the Kaiser in Bonn (having been momentarily buncoed by his imperial splendor as he passed down the Coblenzerstrasse at the head of the parade). Fortunately no one discovered that I had been a classmate of young Wilhelm Kronprinz. But the University of Wisconsin did not surrender its independence. Nor quite all of its patience and sense of humor. It did not ask me for a contribution to its War-Book; but on the other hand it did not ask me for my resignation. I forgive her for the first oversight; I applaud her forever for the second.

But it needed something more sudden than the strain of the war to precipitate the acuter phobic conditions that finally robbed us of our cottage. After the return from New York, where, though haunted and shaky, I was a well man as compared with now, for three summers we were able to make three and four all-day trips for forty miles up the State by train to Devil's Lake . . . our precious vacation substitute for the trips of our friends to the Adirondacks and Glacier Park. Those gigantic bluffs and crags of quartzite, the relics of the Archæan, later washed by the Paleozoic seas, and only yesterday thrusting their impregnable ramparts against the glaciers, tower all about the beach and the little outwash-plain and gave me the needed feeling of sheltered security. And we were never in our climbs and rambles more than a mile from the station and adjacent cottages, which formed my transferred center of safety for the day. It was always necessary for us to go with a party of two or three, however, as if by their protective encirclement to decrease the sense of strangeness and farness. . . . It was the only trip I could seem to manage at all.

But an acquaintance of many years, who shall be named in these paragraphs simply as the impersonal force that made the fatal difference, had coaxed me into the thought of a trip to Parfrey's Glen. The station, Merrimac, was on the same road as Devil's Lake, and some miles this side. The difficulty was with the "two and half" miles' walk from the station. But it was a straight road, he said, with many friendly-looking farm-houses, and not much farther, he told me, than from our own cottage to the Madison Station. And we'd have a large party, with him as the Guide. I knew he liked to guide parties. Let the student of the history of this phobia not forget that I had always taken the affirmative attitude . . . to do, to risk, what I possibly could. The years had been all try-and-try-again. But interested persons were reiterating more and more their worry and pain over the outrageous bondage to which I was subjecting my wife. And they worried me . . . and my wife. And they pleaded with me and they chided me . . . and few then, and few either then or later, had any scientific or much human realization of my case. He whom I name the Impersonal Force had often shaken his wise head dubiously. The remorseless objectivity for which I am striving in this story compels me to register this fact . . . though I well realize how it exposes me to the commonplace charge of blaming one's troubles on others. To some friends indeed I owe most that makes the phobia more tolerable; to some Interested Parties I certainly owe much that has most made it more intolerable.

The day came. A party of ten or twelve. At the start in Madison my wife whispered to the Guide: "He's feeling a little shaky; don't try any experiments" . . . and we had had that sort of experience before. I make the railway trip . . . anxiously. For the first mile and a half out of Merrimac I was almost normal and buoyed up by the glory of being almost normal that mile and a half. Only a mile more—yes, I could make it finely. Then a sudden suspicion —"this isn't the straight road—down here on this sandy curve by the Wisconsin River." I inquire of the Guide. He admits he is taking the six-mile roundabout way by Owl Head—the great hill over in front. It is so much more interesting, he says.

I am done with details of psychological description. I say it briefly: the bottom dropped out of all. I was suddenly in a world as alien as the moon. And my chief psychic support, my Guide, had suddenly become the trickster I could lean on least of all. The region was in reality utterly barren of life all the way, with four or five empty farmhouses and a bleak, overcast sky, and not one automobile, wagon, or stray cat. Such folks as lived on that sparsely settled rolling prairie were in Merrimac at church. I got to the Glen—thinking of my wife—and keeping always in the *midst* of the party, my moving shelter. I got to the Glen, with my tongue like chipped beef and my throat constricted as if by a hangman's rope. In the Glen some relief . . . shelter . . . cozy fire. There was a Fool in the party . . . the one person, outside my wife, who saw how excruciating my suffering . . . and in his incessant whimsical talk there was some relief, but more in the psychic support of his unexpressed sympathy. The shorter walk back by the *straight road* was under far less strain: my mind had prepared itself before the trip for that road, and I was supported by the idea that every step was nearer home and safety, and that the worst anguish was over. As a Man, my Guide had simply tried a casual experiment; as an Impersonal Force, he had given me the

last blow. He who by a kindly interest—though charac-
teristically officious, yet kindly—had devised to procure me
. . . and my wife . . . release from bondage and the
gift of freedom, had in a single hour riveted the chains
shorter and tighter and despoiled us both of what freedom
we had so laboriously earned during all the many years
of our hoping and trying. He thought, doubtless, how
happy I would be if the experiment succeeded. He forgot
to reckon how unhappy I would be if it didn't. Never afterward did he mention that day either to my wife or to me,
but he explained to others that Leonard himself had told
him how much he'd like *sometime* to get over to Owl Head.
Quite true . . . My Guide, in his purpose to do me good
by a trick, along with the Clerical Gentleman referred to
before with his purpose to do me good by a lecture, are
the two outstanding illustrations of what may happen
when Interested Persons, practically emboldened by confidence in their own judgment on matters totally beyond
their experience and ken, have taken quite unasked a
hand in this phobia. I do not blame them for not understanding the disorder itself. I blame them for the implicit distrust in my character and my intelligence; that is,
for not realizing that I was doing my best with all the
morale and brains I had. And I blame them for frivo-
lous meddling. And, even as the clerical lecture precipitated
the crisis that had driven me from the rented cottage in
1912, this trick precipitated, though with slower development, the crisis that drove me from the cottage of my own.
And, as another of the ironies of my life-story, I recall how
this cottage of ours had been during his bachelor-years the
chief refuge of the Guide, and how, when he was about to
bring home a wife to a belated cottage of his own, it had
been my pen that had scribbled and my fingers that had
pinned the verses of welcome which they found on their
door.

After the trip to Parfrey's Glen my mind reacted with
damnable consistency, according to its inveterate technic.

A fight, long protracted, went on between the subconsciousness that insisted on keeping what freedom it had gained for me and the subconsciousness, the phobia, which insisted on taking more and more freedom from me. The trip left me phobically unstable—extraordinarily so. For the first few days I could not get a half-mile, a quarter-mile, from the house, and for a year and more I would have these extreme relapses intermittently, especially in bad weather or if in the least agitated by the normal difficulties of life that we all meet. . . . And . . . I guess . . . some acuter difficulties that we don't *all* meet . . . (among the many unchronicled things of this life-story). Yet I made, albeit with increased agitation, two more of the precious excursions to Devil's Lake, before the fight between the freedom-loving subconscious and the phobia was won by the latter. . . . Others, with other Phobias, have told me how, in the same way, the worst effects of a shock or strain are deferred: they can do a dreaded thing once or twice afterward, only to meet the overwhelming inhibition on the third attempt.

The practical situation became gradually but surely worse; attempts to meet it involved me in a still worse situation, still less understood, in which my own misjudgment and desperation now played a distinguished rôle. Interested persons were again busy . . . busier than ever . . . I am brief and indefinite here. Not to spare myself, but to spare others—among them these well-meaning but horribly blundering Interested Persons who found in the new situation new opportunities for Service, Moral Sentiments, and Excitement. My wife was now in New York, released for a freedom she was in no condition to enjoy. My widowed mother, summoned by telegram, had come West to keep house and to keep me in her absence. Another Winnebago play of mine, "Red Bird," was given on the local stage, by the Curtain Club, our Faculty Dramatic Society. I had not been able to get to the rehearsals, and I got to the matinée performance only, and then on my bicycle, by slow stages beginning at ten in the morning. I

367

was missing my classes more and more, making my official
excuses as plausible as possible, till the distress evolved into
complete inhibition and I could not get to classes at all.
Nineteen-eleven was repeating itself. It was even the end
of April—the very season of the Catastrophe of 1911.
Reason had to combat new obsessions concerning Doom and
Fate. The Gods were to *get* me at last, I felt. I did not
then know the Locomotive-God.

Much that we call Superstition is really Phobic Fear,
not understood as such by the victim or those who gird at
the victim; even as Phobic phenomenon have surely been a
prime source, feeding the speculations and prepossessions of
theologies pagan and Christian, of the belief in witchcraft.
Grettir the Strong, in the Old Norse saga of like name,
in his tragic fear of the dark, was clearly a phobiac, though
the saga refers his affliction to the spell cast by a dead
man's eyes . . . "And this is the curse I lay upon you,
Grettir," says the ghost of Glam: "You will be outlawed;
and your lot shall be to live forever alone; and these eyes
will be ever before your sight. You will find it hard to live
alone." (Chapter XXXV.) Up to three hundred years ago
(or less), I myself would have been notorious in the prov-
ince as a case of demoniacal possession, with no one more
convinced of the fact that I myself . . . haunted and seized
and ridden, as I have been, thus long and thus desperately,
by an invisible power so malignant, so *alien,* and withal so
cunningly, so devilishly, *personal* in temper and conduct
. . . and some toothless old hag would have shrieked and
shriveled in the flames for my sake. There were probably
phobiacs wandering about the Sea of Galilee.

I was forced to telephone the chairman of our Department to come out to the cottage for an interview.
We had been excellent friends. I had long admired his
honesty, fairness, scholarship, and an undeviating sense
of duty veiled under a casual, dryly ironic, exterior. But
I had concealed from him, more even than from most
other closer associates, the long abnormality. He was

my professional head; and, moreover, he was, I thought, in temperament and experience the last man to understand; and some counselors had thought so with me. But he did understand—both the disorder and the struggle —in five minutes. He arranged for a substitute for my large undergraduate lecture-course. He arranged to have my small classes of graduate students meet at the Cottage; and the walk in the spring air and the sessions out in the sun-parlor overlooking Lake Wingra made a pleasant academic diversion that some of them, men and women, will perhaps always remember. He enabled me to finish out the year, pending the return of my wife and a moving of our household down town for the fall. The chairman understood me. And now I understood him. We only really know people when the real issues come up: the phobia has brought me many revaluations of people —and of books. I can speak thus freely, for he is no longer at Wisconsin.

My mother was seated quietly in the living-room with neighbors, awaiting me, when I first saw her again. Eight years had gone by. Two in widowhood. She had become an old lady. Seventy-two. I would not have recognized her on the street. We had a month together . . . oatmeal and cup-custards . . . feeding the cat together . . . talking about the six years in the room with my father. She talked too with my young students and with my famous friends on their travels, as Upton Sinclair, who has so much in his head besides socialism. Age had laid after all only a thin veil over her face. I watched the familiar lines about the firm mouth take shape again. I got back the same troubled but unconquered gleam in her black eyes. She returned to Boston, feeling that was best—her errand fulfilled, her service done.

For my self, I feared that, if she made her home with us, the phobia would again fasten itself upon her. The wife had first become the phobia's surrogate for the mother; the mother now the surrogate for the wife: and there were alarming symptoms, while they were for a few days under the roof together, that they would both become its victims, even as both father and mother had been before.

XVII

THE phobia, as said, now made changing our home a necessity. But this necessity involved us in a new problem. The cottage had now become so acutely a center of safety, with all its familiar interior, that to strip it for the moving-van was to leave me frightened and lost. The tension was relieved only by a careful selection of articles to go the first day, such as might be set up in the apartment at once by friends working there—to make it seem a duplicate center awaiting me; while enough articles remained with us that night in the cottage to keep it still somewhat like home. I had had to stay in a neighbor's house, and leave it for my wife to look after the men. Then on the morning of the second day, before the van came to get the rest under the superintendence of a neighbor, friends hurried me with my wife in an automobile down to the new "center," where other friends were ready to welcome us. Friends at each house, friends on the mile-and-a-quarter highway between. Not until all things were in, and in place (and eagerly I helped now), did my mind begin to readjust. Such was my abnormal incompetence to perform a commonplace action. The phobias of the human mind may take infinite forms and intensities, from irrelevant whimsies dormant in one's ordinary activities (like the phobia of high places) to domineering terrors that radiate their effects into half the daily affairs of life. But the phobic suffering and the grotesque bustle took our minds off the grief of leaving. We brought with us everything except my boat, my garden-tools, my boxing-gloves, and . . . the cat. Our apartment is now famous

371

for the sun through the Murray Street elm-tops, for its airy rooms windowed on four outer walls, and for the color and coziness of its interior. I raise a few marigolds, zinnias, calendulas, poppies, and nasturtiums in the back yard for the bowls and vases. I can look down upon the flower-bed from the rear window of my study. So can my wife from the kitchen-porch with her duster, or when she throws peanuts to the squirrels.

And we have our half-mile beat, within which the abnormality leaves me normal, aside from intermittent minor phobias. The reader will by now have grasped the psychological anomaly: when not under the obsession of being blocked from home or wife by distance or some barrier (as a crowd or locked door), these fifteen years have not modified perceptibly my external conduct among men. I may wince inwardly when some acquaintance rhapsodizes to me about a glorious tramp in the White Mountains, or when another, back from a summer in Europe, asks me where I went on my vacation; but he never sees me wince. And though on my walks that alien whisper just back of my ear, warning me not to walk too far, may trouble for me the song of the redwing in the willows or subdue the zest in the blue of the distant hills, my acquaintances never know that either. I am in my goings and comings about the Campus, the University Halls, at the Club, along the street, at the bank—anywhere under aphobic conditions within my beat—a normal man. If I have any oddities (i.e., ways of my own)— aside from an acquired flowing tie (purple)—they are the same as in student days or in the free, first years in Madison. They come out of me, not out of the phobia. That is, not out of the phobia as such, though some, it would seem, come out of the same childhood experiences that engendered the phobias. Even if at times the phobia makes me irritable, it is presumably less often because of subconscious phobic irritability than because monotony and disappointment get on one's nerves . . . a normal enough reaction, surely, however regrettable. So I continue to live, as I always have lived, except that I seize and hoard the little diversions with more avidity.

Unable, for instance, to get to my friends for return dinners, I am the happier when they basket their cuisine and lay it out, as hosts, on our table. Compelled, for instance again, to do my skating on a short stretch offshore instead of striking out in the blow to Picnic Point with my tattered skate-sail, I entertain myself, between grape-vine twists and figure-eights, with the son of the sometime governor of Shantung who knows more about Chinese philosophy than American winter sports. I stand, coaching: "Remember, Tsai, the initial motion is just a shuffle-along. It's not a walk or a stumble. Like this . . . not like *this*." Or between swims, I stand looking down from the pier into the translucent green water as a girl's shimmering scarlet trunk, with rhythmical legs white to the thighs, glides up to the ladder, though not sinuously enough to suit me. "Let's see you do that Columbia River stroke again, Miss Sanders" . . . and she does it again . . . "Why, you have the right-side kick for the left-side arm— try it the other way." And she does and she glides faster, and I am pleased. Or I ask for a lesson myself . . . in skating or swimming . . . when some master is at his stunts. I may see at a fall smoker in the club some young instructor in Spanish just up from Chile or Argentine, who looks homesick and interesting, and invite him to call on my wife and me, across the way. I was particularly perspicacious in one case: a tall, dark chap, strangely reserved but not timid, who had noted me too because in the corner-causerie my ignorance of South American literature was a little less dense than some others'. And he seemed most anxious to call. When he did, I asked him the conventional question: "Why had he come to the States?" But his answer was not conventional. Son of a fine Chilean home of affluence and culture, he had seen father and mother and brothers and sisters wiped out week after week by the epidemic. When he arose from his own bed, the old family mansion was a tomb. He had to get away . . . far away. So we became great friends, all three. Exchanging gifts across the Equator . . . "Two Lives" and Araucanian rugs and the *poesias* of Pedro Antonio González.

My wife's sister and husband pass this way in the family automobile, bringing the two children and the children's widowed grandmother, on their trips to the North Woods. The years lengthen out since my wife could make even a hurried visit to her kindred, and it is many more since I could accompany her. They love her dearly and miss her sorely; and they have forgone too the happiness any sojourn of mine might have given their hospitable home. My ailment is something very strange, very unreal, to them. But all these twelve years they have never complained or chided, though I myself feel as if I had robbed them . . . which touches their visits to us with sadness for me. But I can forget, when their Barbara with her sea-blue eyes and blue bathing suit slides splashing from the Mendota raft like a mermaid, or Sonny on our couch, with my ball and mitt in hand, listens gaping to my personal reminiscences of Ray Shalk, White Sox catcher, up here to train our baseball squad last spring (what would it have meant to me at ten to have had an uncle who knew Buck Ewing!) . . . and my vivacious sister-in-law's teacher of philosophy in college was the loquacious chap that had been in James's metaphysics class with me . . . though she seems to have listened to him more reverently than I . . . My brother-in-law of to-day, compelled to work early and hard, with no formal schooling after thirteen, is a trusted commercial expert for a great house. I like the frank, open friendliness in the face of the silk-buyer . . . it announces the square deal, come hell or high water.

And Madison is not only the City of Famous Folk (in "Who's Who" its native roll-call is far longer than any

city's of the same population) ; it is the Stop-over of their
Main Traveled Roads . . . European statesmen, men of
science and letters from America and all other lands, and
Minstrels of the Modern Show ("Hear Chesterton, England's Supreme Genius," read the placards on every other
telephone pole . . . and we hear him, though he costs
$750 an hour—an expensive joke). And some of them
spend moments of their stop-over with me. After a surprise telephone-call from a local hotel, I run out down
the street. I've never seen my visitor—but I know him
. . . there he comes; lank and loping along with cigarette
and freckles: "Hello, Lewis." "Hello, Leonard." I
bring him home. He is still in the door, when I see Gertrude out in the sun-parlor with my wife. "Gertrude, have
you read 'Main Street'?" "Half of it . . . I couldn't
stand it." "Well, meet the author, and tell him about
it." Was Gertrude fussed? She was not. Was S.L.?
Scarcely. At dinner he gave us advance-information on
"Babbitt"; describing, for instance, what he called the
clergyman's "short, snappy prayer." He half expected
then to settle in this klein Paris . . . but it is perhaps as
well for him (and some Madisonians) that he didn't.
Hergesheimer has been here too . . . grubbing in old
American Manuscripts of the Historical Library, with his
preternatural zest for antique details. Sitting betweenwhiles on the porch of the University Club, he overheard
(I owe this to a bystander, leaning against a pillar) a respected colleague of mine repeating the familiar academic
whine over the intellectual shabbiness and indifference of
undergraduates. "Excuse me, sir," said the stranger,
turning his head, "do you talk like that to the boys and
girls . . . and in that voice?" "Why, I suppose that's
my talk and my voice." "Well, if *I* was one of your students, damned if I wouldn't go *swimming.*" But later
he sat in my sun-parlor . . . again counseling an academi-
cian: "Leonard, don't be so noble." Carl Sandburg
drank a whole pitcher of home-made grape-juice between

ten (after his lecture) and 2 A.M. . . . though I am not sure of the legal aspect of our hospitality. Vachel once recited "The Congo" and "General Booth" . . . booming away only three yards off. But I could never get over to the La Follette Farm to hear the senator read Irish stories . . . and he had other things to do besides visiting around town.

The last time I saw him was in the rotunda of the Capitol at the inaugural reception of the post-war Progressive governor . . . truly Fighting Bob's victory, but ours too. For me also a good joke. I, whose politics had kept me so long under a spiritual cloud, had been in the official receiving-line, shaking hands magnanimously with many a quizzical university official, astutely present on that dramatic and historic occasion. I could get as far as the Capitol then . . . to the great funeral I could not go. My wife and I went down to the corner of our block, to stand quietly . . . an hour . . . as the Hearse went by . . . and the long, long train behind it . . . out University Avenue to Forest Hills . . . "There are still a lot of things I could do." . . . Well, perhaps young Bob will do them for you.

'Gene Debs (I confess it) came up from Chicago,

The bald, lone tall man of the Plebs.

He recalled Atlanta and the strike of '94 . . . and I recited a poem, "The Old Agitator," which I had copied out in longhand and sent him, in the one-sided correspondence for two years between Wisconsin and Georgia. My letters had been so much longer than his . . . his, in pencil on the inside of the cut-out backs of my envelops (all prison-marked 9653 on the address-side and forwarded from Theodore, his brother). He told me how he had read the verses in his cell . . . and for that they seemed worth while to me. I liked him, Alsatian though he was, for the New England tradition of Garrison and Phillips . . . one

more incorrigible old man that wouldn't shut up. I only
wish I had a faith as firm as his in some solution of the
economic order. I know with his kind that it is really disorder . . . that something will happen . . . that freedom of toil and of art and science are constricted under
capitalism . . . but no man's doctrine has solved the
thing for me . . . there is always some other doctrine in
the way. But the Radicals are at least aware of a problem; and there is more chance to think in their company.
They also have been in jail. Their ideas are their realities.

Yet a brilliant Oxford don, distrait two whole semesters
from wife and six children, in spite of many (I understand)
dinner-parties, came to our sun-parlor, and told us with
mellow voice of wistful affection about the intimate life of
Corpus Christi: our Oxonian, as a good Tory, will offset
Debs, I trust. One of the two or three most distinguished
authorities in ancient civilization, Rostovtzeff, the Russian,
has talked here with Sommerfeld, the German, one of
the most distinguished of modern physicists, about the
issues of the war, as have a young Junker-lieutenant here
with an English musician, each having his scars . . . old
battles without hate. Our sun-parlor is greater than
Geneva or the Hague.

And, across the street, in and about the Club, is all
civilization, not only every branch of learning. I smile at
the outsider's superstition about the narrow, unworldly
experience of all these professors who are so canny in real
estate and sit with upturned forefingers in an acute angle
on so many boards of directors. And yonder, reading the
"London Times," is a professor that escaped from the
pogrom-belt, when less stoutish than now. That laughing
Spaniard, with a copy of the "Mercury" on his knee, was
a sailor before the mast from the North Cape to the
Horn; the Norwegian, with thumb in vest, to whom he's
talking was formerly a fisherman on the Lofoten Islands
. . . now an authority on the diplomatic history of Eng-

377

land. That sandy Scotchman in the doorway, big and bony as Lincoln, once stopped off on his travels for a note-taking chat with the hapless black villagers of African Angola, and now, if he turned up on the streets of Lisbon, he'd be mobbed in an hour.

Hamlin Garland was this way again last spring, and told his hosts of the English Department the enthralling story of the Custer Massacre, as he had it years ago from some grizzled Sioux of Sitting Bull's day who had reason to know all about it . . . they reminisced, said Garland, like a group of old Grand Army men about Gettysburg. Their version of the coming of the government troopers was not that of the histories . . . and none but Indian eyes saw them fall. Few of the Indians were killed, said the old fellows, but many were wounded in the ankle . . . where the foot projected from under their ponies' bellies as they circled round . . . and round . . . and nearer . . . and nearer. Pop . . . pop . . . pop. And so the rest of the regiment, riding up, found its three hundred dead . . . out near the Black Hills. I was back in my childhood . . . so were we all, even though Garland had just laid off his new robes, insignia of his honorary degree.

Professor David M. Robinson, archæologist of Johns Hopkins, was this way, after his digging in Asia Minor, and told a dinner party of classicists at the Club how, on forcing the stone door of a buried Syrian tomb, he suddenly saw (he vowed he saw), lying on the marble slab in the torch-lit dusk, a lovely Greek lady who collapsed and crumpled in a few seconds to a golden comb, a bit of pearl necklace, and strewn powdery ashes. Not even the beauty of the story, nor the courtesies of the evening, could keep me from injecting an explanation out of my own thrifty experience . . . I too had seen visions, though not often one, I said, so "clearly the creative projection of psychical tension of anticipation." And the golden comb in the powder helped, said I. But other archæologists energetically backed Robinson's tale with others as leery

. . . giving a physical explanation of the preservation in motionless air of a body-shell, which raised for me new difficulties . . . how could a shell so tenuous support the weight of the comb and the rondure of the necklace, etc. I was getting disagreeable; so we turned to Sappho, whose precious fragments (including the new-found) Robinson was now editing: I forgot my brooding over the dead lady in the Syrian tomb for the deathless lady of Lesbos . . . and began soon to turn all the six hundred lines of her fragments into English verse. Those done are in Showerman's "Century Readings in Ancient Classical Literature." If I ever do the rest, they will make a little volume in white vellum under the title "An Ægyptian Papyrus" . . . to lay beside the twenty or so dainty volumes a year of those radiant poetesses to-day on that other isle of song, sea-breezy and sail-girt Manhattan . . .

> Love, like a mountain-wind upon an oak,
> Falling upon me, shakes me leaf and bough.

Or say this:

> Round about me hum the winds of autumn,
> Cool between the apple-boughs; and slumber,
> Flowing from the quivering leaves to earthward,
> Spreads as a river.

Say it again . . . with your eyes shut . . .

Hans Driesch of the University of Leipsic was this way, our "Carl Schurz professor" for a semester. Twelve years before it had been my difficult but pleasant task to present to our Philosophical Colloquium (a faculty group of biologists, philosophers, and humanists) an outline of his theory of the autonomy of life, "Driesch's Vitalism," as expounded in his Gifford Lectures at Aberdeen, then just published. And I had so many questions to ask him . . . as I have still sundry to ask Plato and others.

But my chance finally came . . . face to face. We talked too on the foundations of ethics. He had begun at one end long ago, with the dividing cell of the sea-urchin and moved in thought on to man, the Finder and Fashioner; I had begun at the other end, rather long ago too, and followed the line backward, as best I could, from man to the sea-urchin. And I found that my thought met his thought. I can never forget Driesch, neither can Wisconsin. The wise, kindly twinkle in his eye when his countenance puckered into wrinkles, the unruffled detachment in his speech, the childlike simplicity of mind and manner, and his instinct to pry around in friendly curiosity into all our affairs, even to football games and Rotarian banquets, made him veritably for us Socrates come again . . . as wholesome, whimsical, brooding, human as ever, with the old facial lineaments still recognizable, only considerably improved in the modeling.

A professor from Göttingen was this way, and a colleague gave a luncheon . . . all former Göttingen students on Wisconsin's faculty around one table . . . Jack and I chatting across one table after a dozen years . . . chatting for the first time at all after a dozen years . . . reminiscences about unforgotten streets, taverns, castle-ruins. . . picture-post-card greetings to old Göttingen professors . . . Jack's autograph and mine on the same card for the first time in almost twice a dozen years . . . since we were fellow-students over there, sending greetings back home. Jack played the game. I played the game. For the sake of our host and our visitor. Jack is not at Wisconsin now. I am. In the half-mile beat.

Our half-mile circuit is the navel of the earth . . . but it is not our theme. Sometime perhaps . . . when I am an emeritus. With chapters too on such things among many others as: The University Woods, The Boathouse, Muir Knoll (and the Moon), The Ski-jump, The English Seminary, The Biological Laboratories, The Patched Mammoth in Science Hall, The Library Stacks, The Art-

Exhibit (Madison Artists), The Art-Exhibit (Traveling Frames), Maison Française, Deutsches Haus, Casa Cervantes, Arden House, International Club, The Lower Campus, The Lesser Shops This Side the Square, My Letter-File (e. g., Woodrow Wilson and Henry Mencken), My Terrestrial Globe (twelve-inch, with meridian ring and analemma). It would be a long book, with so much ready to hand; and besides, the shorter the walk from one's door the more one learns to see and sees to learn. Imprisonment stimulates the spirit of prowling and sharpens one's observation and wits. And inner needs and resources create richer values for the outer resources. It would be many times a longer book than Thoreau's "Walden," for it includes his waters and his woods, and so much else. When I am an emeritus perhaps . . . but I must leave these interests now for some account of the Cat.

Jimmie's career, both as associated with our lives and as a phenomenon in my phobic neurosis, is of specific importance to this book. Jimmie himself too, as an extraordinary personality with eventually a neurosis of his own. But we must first go back to the cottage. We had found him, a four-weeks-old kitten, in a litter of four one November afternoon on our front door-step. We had barely got them in out of the cold, when they began scurrying into corners and under chairs, and scratching so furiously that they had to be handled, not with gloves, but literally with leather mitts. We returned them, as infested with chicken-lice, at once to our neighbor's Jemima, a well known, and fecund, but shiftless, Maltese of the Back Lane. But the most desperate little scratcher clawed his way out of our hands, and hid somewhere in the withered jungle of iris alongside the basement-wall of our cottage. We set a saucer of milk and a blanket on our front steps that night. He was there in the morning. And, as my wife opened the door, I shooed him inside. He was a little subdued by cold and bewilderment. So we could look him over. Tiger-stripes of rich gray from nape to tip of tail, tinged with yellow where they softly merged and whitened under the belly. Symmetrical white markings on the face. Knowing eyes and winsome muzzle. I cite his appearance not for its beauty, but for its singularity. His identification marks were indisputable; no other kitten ever looked like Jimmie. It will be important to remember this later. We soaked out the chicken-lice; and he took to us at once as soon as he recognized us as his kind of folks; and he set about justifying our choice. In a week or two, my wife discovered the black string of the tail-end of a mouse just disappearing between his closing teeth in the kitchen; in another week, he had jumped out of a second-story window on to the frozen lawn, unblanketed with snow. All to show us what he could do. After racing and springing all winter over the house, upstairs and down, behind a bit of twine trailed from my hand, or tearing his way out of the involutions of a streamer of black silk for my wife on the living-room floor, or blindly backing away and pawing gropingly at his neck when I tied a paper bag on his head, he found by the middle of May life's most zestful hours in a sort of jungle-tiger hide-and-seek in the striped grass about the cistern-top or under our border of raspberry-bushes. He never left the yard, beyond a few rods down the Lane or into our corn-rows. When tired out, he lay under the raspberry-bushes. He would come at call . . . but only when he felt like it.

The next summer I began to note that I was getting phobically uneasy when I couldn't find him. I was pestered, not with any worry about him (he could take care of himself), but with the obsession that I needed to have him around for psychic support. I was dumfounded. My previous phobic obsessions had seemed to me, after all, abnormal only as abnormal exaggerations, chiefly in infantile patterns, of fears in themselves normal: the abnormal fear of being far from home, for instance, had seemed, however irrational, merely an extension and a recrudescence of the state of mind of a child that has got too far away from its mother and its doors. Even my intermittent need to know just where my personal copy of the original Æsop was on my shelves, I could explain as the shadowy reminiscence of the help I had got by turning its pages into rime during the awful seizures of the breakdown. But this need of a cat! Was I insane after all? To no purpose did I refuse to yield to it, lying on my study-couch when I couldn't find him and repeating in phobic terror the hocus-pocus of autosuggestion slogans; to no purpose I'd flee to friend Bruns's house to deflect attention by talks on Hebbel's Dramas or Kant's "Critique," or what you will. I tried to conceal the obsession even from my wife; but my explanations of my harassed interest in Jimmie were almost as bizarre as the obsession itself. Finally, I could let him out of the house only when set in a little harness, with twenty-five feet of clothes-line tied to the apple-tree, or to a weighted flower-pot that I could move for him from place to place. He romped around and round and would get tangled up chasing a wild rabbit or robin. Some people wondered at my cruelty. When we were about to move, we arranged a home for Jimmie. He was entitled to his little life; and, once gone, he could hound me no more.

However, two days before, he took matters into his own hands. Startled by a workman dropping planks, he dashed the length of his cord, overturned the pot, thus releasing the stone weight, and smashed the pot itself to bits as he trailed it wildly out of sight around a shed on the alley. I followed. He had disappeared. All normal interest in the welfare of a domestic pet was swallowed up in the hope that he was gone forever, releasing me. The subconsciousness, when compelled to action, sometimes surrenders its obsessions . . . but not always. The cat's sudden departure was one thing; that of one or another human being would be another. There was a cloud-burst that night, and my wife, after sleepless visions of Jimmie

strangled and drowned in the thickets, called all a morning hour up and down the borders of Vilas Park and then
advertised for him in the suburban drug-store. Three
weeks later, on a bicycle-ride at sunrise, I saw him, far off,
emerge from the grove by the Zoo, strolling about with
eight or nine other cats. Some one had removed the rope.
The Zoo always smelt meaty; and Nero, the lion, and
Cleopatra, the tigress, his primordial kinsfolk, were over
there. He recognized my call . . . but he wouldn't come
. . . yet a while, at least. He wanted his fling first.

Late in October a former neighbor telephoned he was
back in the cottage yard, meowing to get in. They
brought him down to us, after dark, on the trolley, sleek
and fat. He knew us. It was a curious joy to remark
his bewildered curiosity and joy. He scooted under the
davenport, he poked his whole body into the opened
dresser-drawer, and did all of twelve old tricks; yet where
were the stairs, where was the hearth-mantel, and where
the cellar-door? But the lease read "no cats"; so, after
forty-eight hours during which he was not outside the apartment, the original consignees took him off, covered over
and in an automobile—a second journey of a mile and
more, and in another direction. His new owners had
been well instructed in his habits and tastes—olives and
tuna-fish and raw eggs and green peas (not too hot). But
he moped in a corner for two weeks and disappeared.

All winter my wife would look out the window every
time she heard a cat. One morning in bleak March, she
said: "Jimmie has come back; I know his cry." Was
this an obsession too? I thought. All day she listened
. . . and heard it again after dark: I acceded to her
whim, and went down with her into the street. "Jimmie,
Jimmie, come, Jimmie." A wailing creature bounded into her feet out of the blackness. She picked him up, as he
struggled frantically to get into her cloak. "Look out, that
stray beast will claw your face to pieces," I said. She
said, "It's Jimmie"—and Jimmie it clearly was, even to

me, as we got into the lighted entry. Down to four pounds and a half from ten; a dirty, feeble little skeleton which could scarcely stand up . . . which would infallibly have perished in the blizzard that came that very night. We laid him on the sun-parlor couch and sat down beside and fed him, where he purred awake or asleep for forty-eight hours, nearly shaking the skin from his ribs. The landlord said we might keep him. I have been careful to state the exact conditions of his return. That he found his way back to the familiar cottage even after four months, was of course characteristic cat-psychology, but by what mysterious psychic power, farther still beyond our own human power, had he found his way back to the apartment, an alien spot, with meaning to him only as far as people (to whom cats are supposed to be indifferent) gave it meaning. And what of the memory and affection in that stupid small cranium which kept those weakening legs on the hunt all winter? The more I know of animals *close to,* the more I respect and wonder at life.

He picked up. His spine wasn't injured as we had thought. But we soon discovered that Jimmie too had a shelter-phobia. If we took him to the open window or out of the house-door, he wailed in horror like a human baby (a cat has many cries). He had evidently been taken in, fed, and thrust out from house to house for many cold months. That is, his phobia underwent no transformations as in the somewhat higher psychic processes, which I think (with all regard to Jimmie's intelligence) I can claim as mine. It was direct reflex-action; even as the dreams of children and savages are direct wish-fulfilments, untransformed into symbolism. For two years he raced up and down the skidding runner of the hall, or leaped like a playful dog at my legs from his lurking place behind the davenport and then skedaddled to "goal," as madly as if I were the dog. "Goal," or "safety," was a certain chair in the corner of the dining-room. We never mauled him there; never took him off. His most notable humorous stunt was to squat, paws out, up there with complacent satisfaction, when we tried to catch him nights to put him in his basket, with kitchen-door closed off. Life was such fun. Or he curled himself up with a greeting in my wife's bosom when she lay reading. He remained in abounding health, more full of frolics, if possible, than ever before, though nearing five. Except for a certain late-developing weakness in personal habits. We had to dispose of him. The veterinarian came. Jimmie should not be put into the street again—perhaps to be sold by some small boy to the medical laboratories. When I returned from my classes, my wife was busy in the kitchen with lunch . . . and unusually matter of fact. I found his cat-nip-mouse and his rubber-ball in the middle of his sand-box, which she had set out of sight on the back-stairs landing. . . . Though the limitations of our childless diversions and the appeal of his struggle to find us may have added a special tone to our grieving, several grown-ups of both sexes, far from sentimental, have confessed to me on inquiry similar emotional entanglements with animals. What does this mean? It means something momentous.

Our grief over Jimmie's death was normal. But what of my amazing phobia over Jimmie? It is, in fact, more readily explained than the grief. It was for the subconscious in part an extension to another *member of the household* of the father-mother-wife-need, an extension that has several times started to develop toward transient visitors at our home, particularly women. But it went back in its own right directly to my childhood and to my infancy. In my clinical probing I have often *felt* that there had been a cat at the station in 1878, even as I remember distinctly there had actually been a dog. The feeling has never emerged as definite recall; nor can I by any deductions of reasoning about the data of all the recalls concerning the station convince myself of the likelihood that any cat was down there. But even if a cat was there (eventually, perhaps, in the yard of the adjacent house), the resurgent and vigorous cat-idea in my 1878 associations must have been transferred thither from the experience in 1884 at Atlantic Highlands, where the eight-year-old boy saw with such pity the cat maimed by the *Locomotive,* and with such admiration saw it fighting for its life. My subconsciousness was clinging to Jimmie as a sustaining reverberation of the heroic, as the example of fighting morale . . . against the Locomotive-God and the Mob that had maimed me too. My cat-phobia strangely inverts the familiar form, where the sufferer is in terror not of the cat's absence, but of his presence.

XVIII

THE general procedure whereby I arrived at such discoveries of the subconscious drama of my life has been already sufficiently indicated to make a brief résumé sufficient here. I had from the beginning of the chronic phobia been speculating on the psychological cause, according to one or another of the theories of the specialists. That it was precipitated by the 1911 catastrophe, especially by the mob-motif, was clear. That it simulated infantile attitudes was clear. Clear too that the fear-objects were not what they seemed. But what was behind? Had 1911 simply shattered manhood back into the world and reactions of infantility? Had earlier experiences contributed anything? There was the vague memory of bell-fears and of a fright and flight in early school days, and of the strange fear-seizure in Cologne—were these causes or merely analogies, premonitory symptoms of a generic neurotic tendency to phobias? Was the anxiety and the gloom in adolescence over sex a factor? Or the strain of the dictionary years? Innumerable dream-records, many of which I have preserved, yielded under analysis of the manifest dream (i. e., the raw stuff as distinct from design, the latent dream) innumerable relics of childhood, but no analysis of the latent dream led me into the ultimate dream-motifs (that were still there, as I now know). One dream (among the later) borrowed its stuff, its scenery, and its people, recognizable even then, all the way down my life from early childhood to the night before the dream, including the school-fright of 1885, my college days, my Guide to Parfrey's Glen, and Mary (as grown woman); it was also a phobia-dream, i. e., a dream

(like so many) in which I was laboring to get somewhere in phobic distress. I made by associational exercises and ratiocination a complete and correct analysis of its raw stuff (the façade of the dream); but my analysis of the latent dream, its symbolism especially as wish-fulfilment, was a grotesque blunder, in the light of what I now know. I know by experience the wish-fulfilment type of dream (as, for instance, a dream of kicking the head of a clergyman I detested down the aisle out of the door, like a football); but I know that the very *core* of the symbolism in many dreams is simply a direct reverberation of the past. My probings of the last four years have restored not only immense stretches of my waking life but, as said before, vast terrains of the shadow-lands of sleep: I have recalled perhaps twenty dreams even from before puberty, and several were indeed reverberations of precisely this latent phobia (as one of a head on wheels—i. e., the face that formed on the front of the locomotive-boiler; and one, a fierce nightmare, of a locomotive bearing down upon me). Wishfulfilment and reverberations, especially of shocks, may combine, of course, in one dream (as in my dreams of being free of the phobia). In these studies of my dreams— anterior, be it remembered, to the investigation of the past four years—I noticed many sex-factors, associated particularly with my mother and Mary; and so I speculated on some gruesome suppression of incestuous desires and infantile erotic fixation, with the phobia as the conscious manifestation of the horror and revulsion of my moral nature; but I could never correlate these putative factors with the obvious factors of 1911 (even as then remembered). I speculated too on remorse: the phobia might be the fear-expression of my sense of guilt; perhaps for Agatha, perhaps for Annie too, perhaps for the life-series of misdeeds of an erring spirit with a Puritan conscience—for often I felt a *diffused guilt*, especially in the years just after the suicide. And I would think, in the words of Fernanda in Valdez's "El Maestrante": "Dios mío, ha sido grande el pecado,

pero qué castigo tan terrible!" Of course I conceived the
punishment as the vengeance exacted, not by God, but by
my own moral nature. The close reader will remark, I
think with interest, how all of these dreams (and there are
a hundred others) and indeed all of these speculations
(which were suggested, in fact, less by independent reasoning processes than by direct influence of the troubled subconscious stimulating reason) were reiterating for me,
in forms not understood, the actual causal series, as discovered later and as recorded in our preceding chapters.
More and more was I challenged by the increasing frequency of Mary in my dreams, as a grown woman (though
she had passed so long out of my life), and in situations
where I was always about to lose her (though I never, to
my recollection then, had worried at all about wanting or
losing her). This for a time convinced me that the phobia
was somehow rooted in sex; while, on the other hand, the
phobic seizures in their analyzable emotion were so damnably obvious as expressions of the self-preservation instinct.
I vacillated for years between sex and self-preservation as
the leitmotif. The reader will note the reason for this:
both were in fact leitmotifs intertangled all the way down
from 1878 to 1911 (and the secondary complications thereafter). But all my observations for eleven years had got
me nowhere. And all the explanations of amateur or professional psychologists and neurologists in the vicinity had
got me nowhere, being inconsistent or superficial, or frankly
tentative. And all my varying technic of cure had got me
nowhere. I had tried *every conceivable attitude* toward
the phobia, even to that of living well *inside its bounds and
forgetting it and all its works for months at a time.* I
knew at last that autosuggestion was buncombe (for me),
suggestion by an operator buncombe (for me). I knew
only that I had palliatives: in the unconscious suggestion (if
you will call it that) of an alluring sunny day and scene or
other buoying influences, and in the self-confidence, as safety
and refuge, furnished by my own physique and by my own

acquired skill in deflecting attention under attacks. And these I knew only too sadly were very inadequate. I realized finally too that mere habit explained neither phobia nor "reëducation." The phobia had suddenly started and dropped, without apparent cause, various secondary "habits"; the "reëducation" had often lost its "habits" almost overnight. And I was unable to "try Christian Science"—having lived in Lynn, Massachusetts. Just before quitting the cottage, in the extra strain of the last weeks, I had noticed how rapid was my heart-action (unexplained by indigestion, etc.), on after-lunch siestas or on retiring, and how my mind was always dozing off to the half-remembered fragments of the school-fright, with the incongruous recurrence of an inexplicable gaping Face, subhuman and ferocious as a pagan idol. This gave me, I think, an unconscious set toward suggesting that fall a thoroughgoing analysis with a new member of our Department of Psychology, a young scientist whose articles dealing with neurotic cases of his own I had read in a technical journal. Moreover, some memories recovered in 1920 by systematic reminiscence with closed eyes, though later proven by the deeper explorations of twilight sleep, etc., to have been imperfect, superficial, and merely peripheral, were yet so numerous and unsuspected as to make startlingly plain how little after all I had guessed as a mature man about what had gone on in my conscious life years ago—and about what was still going on in my subconscious life. I knew indeed there was something *down below*. What was it? I estimate by (careful computation) that my efforts to answer this question have been to date equivalent to *four semesters of laboratory research of a seven-hour day*. I have been sustained in the long quest both by scientific curiosity and by the hope of cure.

My colleague, whom I will call Professor A., and his associate Professor B. (now both at other universities), met with me every Saturday evening for from two to three hours, for two semesters and two summer-sessions, with the school year between when I worked alone in their absence. On the other six days I relaxed by myself into conditions of twilight sleep or lay crystal-gazing; in periods (consecutive or interrupted) of from one half-hour to six hours, exercises continued (in briefer periods) to the present date. They took organized notes for their year and a half. I kept mine up for over two years (to the central discovery, the Locomotive-God of 1878), till the task became too tiresomely repellent even for my scientific interests, in spite of many extraordinary details continually popping up. Professors A. and B. have all the notes. The cards fill two boxes, each a foot long. An analytic study of the processes of specific recalls, dates of recalls, channels of recall (crystal, twilight sleep, dreams, etc., etc.), specific associations among the hallucinations (i. e., the images, sounds, words, odors, actions, tactual and temperature sensations), and especially the *time elapsing* between the appearance of hallucinations and of a complete recall of what they stood for (ranging from a second to four years), might reveal important data on memory and temperament and many other psychological problems. But I leave this work for them. Their union of scientific spirit and friendly services, freely given and so patiently continued, was itself a rare experience for me. If their efforts have not brought the results we all hoped for, they bear no blame for either bungling or neglect. Nothing was undertaken without my full consent, and Professor A. was several times in consultation with specialists on his trips East. An analytic study of the whole intertangle of hallucinations and associations, with a refollowing of all the trails crossing and recrossing one another in devious ramifications, with an account of all the detective activities of the observing reason, would be possible only for me, as necessarily including phenomena of the past year and a half preserved only in my memory. If possible at all. And even then it would be impossible for the reader to grasp without many rereadings of the text and repeated examination of a hundred accompanying diagrams. It would involve at least fifteen thousand items, probably twenty thousand. But enough examples have been given in the course of the narrative to render the process intelligible. The investigation itself has been perhaps as complex, ingenious, and adventurous as the last expedition to buried Egypt or to the covering sand-dunes of the Gobi Desert, and as the experiments now going on in the chemical and biological laboratories of the University of Wisconsin. But the great difference is clear. My results, except for some possible by-products on method and general psychological laws and human personality, can be of primary concern only to me: the discovery of the Locomotive-God is in the end only my discovery. The Locomotive-God cannot be exhibited beside the Mummy of Tutankhamen or the Eggs of the Dinosaur; it cannot be ground up and distributed about the earth, to the good of mankind, like a new arsenical compound.

When we undertook the investigation, none of us knew most that the reader himself already knows. "What is causing these phobias?" was a totally unanswered question. We were to compel the dank caverns of the subconscious to give up their brood of vipers. Hypnosis and automatic-writing did not work at all. Experiments with word-associations were barren: the mind of the patient, philologist and verse-man, simply played with the words as words, by associations of rimes, puns, cadences, and familiar quotations, from entirely other regions of the subconscious, its Elysian Fields, its Islands of the Blest; or drew with grotesque whimsicality of subconscious *humor* on its stores of scientific and miscellaneous information. It always took my friends a half-hour or an hour to get me into even a drowsy condition, though I have seen Professor A. put a colleague under deep hypnosis in three minutes. The technic was sometimes by B.'s revolving his finger in front of my eyes, or by A.'s repeated suggestions of "sleep" (through the monotone rather than the idea, probably), or by their having me stare at the crystal while one (usually A.) talked, sometimes to fix my conscious mind on it, sometimes to deflect conscious attention. The room was darkened; the voice always low. When they had the patient "under," as far as he would go, they directed his mind by asking pertinent questions, sometimes to stimulate associations, sometimes to force an immediate recall; or by reiterated affirmations in order to jog and jolt the buried matrix. They showed much ingenuity in the verbal devices, especially in following up some clue given by a crystal-image or a chance idea in my brain. I was, of course, continually telling them during the clinic what I saw in the crystal and what notions occurred to my wandering consciousness. They made occasional, and less successful, use of free-association; that is, getting me to mumble off serially the spontaneous drift of my ideas. Gazing into the crystal brought images the first night—including an image of the Latin-play (a fright-motif), as already reported. And more and more the images, either as erratic shapes of the spot of light itself or sometimes as little pictures (more or less distinct, like those in the finder of a camera), and more and more the recalls or the associations were *leading* us into the territory of the school-fright of 1885. The initial lead—I emphasize this—was from the subconscious itself. In a few weeks we were devoting ourselves to a planful following up of that lead, by fixating attention on a given hallucination, by collating it in fixation with another, by stimulating associations, etc. That lead itself made the subconscious reveal other leads, to other buried frights, and these too we followed up. We were far from knowing then the one ultimate whither of all the leads. For instance, we misinterpreted the crystal-image, so early and so often repeated, of two grown-ups, apparently women, with one small child beside them: the small child we thought meant *me* in 1885—but the picture, of course, was of little Mary, and of her mother and mine, to all of whom I was running down the platform in 1878.

I keep even now discovering the ulterior meanings of some of those earliest hallucinations (whether of crystal, twilight sleep, or dream), which we interpreted then often so imperfectly. There came to me in one of my own private twilight sleeps, but a few weeks after the start, an image, strangely clear and intimate, of a small girl's face, cocked in friendly wise at me—as if thrust out at me and withdrawn *instantly* (whereas many hallucinations, whether of sight, smell, taste, sound, or diffused light and warmth, etc., remain several seconds). It generated instantly a feeling of acquaintanceship, peacefulness and affection, that only faded back into time after several days. But it would not yield its identity. It roused too a curiosity more than merely scientific, as when one is troubled by the familiarity of a sudden face in a strange city. I traced its associations with the following recalls, which were suggested by it and subsequently intelligible to me (though not of course to the reader) in their varied and subtle connections with it: a girl in a swing as I ran by in 1885, a swing on the picnic-grounds by childhood's Washington Rock, a swing in our homestead yard, my sister as a small child, a child in the rear door of the last car that passed over the bridge on my 1885 run. Above all, it suggested the feeling of Mary as if present during the 1885 run. For a year or more I have been convinced by a series of deductions that it must have been Mary's face near mine at the depot; but it is less than a month since it became a memory.

Again, for the first three years I kept seeing in the crystal every week or oftener the blurred tiny image of a man, like an unfinished *homunculus*. It brought into consciousness, well before the end of the first year, the gentleman who stopped to watch me from across the street by the school in 1885, when I leapt the fence. But it continued to reappear, a clear indication that there was some other man in the case. My cue was still: *cherchez l'homme.* He seemed now to be blurred across the middle, especially as if behind some sort of cross-bar. But he meant nothing; and the associations seemed to mean nothing, except that the bar suggested "locomotive." And he flitted up from so far below that his popping into the spot of light never produced any emotional reactions whatever. He simply stood there, motionless, indifferent, homuncular. Then he ceased to show himself altogether . . . many months ago. I had entirely forgotten his phantom existence. But now I know him. For a fact he never existed anywhere in the flesh. He was but the simulacrum of a simulacrum. He was, in a word, the man depicted in the tavern-picture of 1911, as standing at the cross-roads behind the lowered gate-beam to the left of the locomotive that seemed to be dashing at me out of the map. It will be remembered how I stood at the tavern door in a seizure of horror as a real train had just whistled, arguing to myself against the reality of this pictured onrushing engine, on the ground that it never actually passed the beam: I had been for a few awful seconds fixating my mind on that cross-beam (with the man behind it) as the one concentrated phenomenon in the universe that could make me feel safe. The depth of the subsidence of this buried memory is a notable indication of how abysmal was the shock of 1911. And there is an image-flash of great vividness from a twilight sleep of about two years and a half ago for which I have no recall whatever—an arm, with bandage loosened from a suppurating sore. The associations were almost immediately with vaccination and with the Family Doctor; and I now know he was actually at the station. It is vaguely as if he and my mother had been talking on the platform about my exposed arm. If that ugly sore was mine, and mine at that time (and the image came within a few seconds of another that I since identified as of the 1878 complex), my physical condition (as a newly vaccinated infant) must have contributed seriously to my fright.

A few miscellaneous notes in a paragraph or two. The sessions with my colleagues resulted in fewer finds than those by myself. My mind seemed discouragingly recalcitrant to others. But their probings stirred up the earth, or bored down part way, and made my own borings easier.

My gains were distinctly slowed up after they left—but owing also, doubtless, to the strata being now so much deeper. The recalcitrancy can be explained perhaps as egotistic independence—the preference to do things for myself —but probably not as egotistic vanity of taking the credit of the cure away from them. If it was that, they are well avenged—for there has been no cure . . . to date. The diffused light above referred to adumbrated three sunny days now all long ago . . . 1878 . . . 1885 . . . 1911. Sometimes I have conjured up in twilight sleep, or with merely closed eyes, shapes of light, even pictures as of a bit of doorway, or boiler-head of locomotive, as golden and bright as the crystal-vision. I can't get down town as far as the moviehouses; but I have my own movie in my head, portable like the old-fashioned diorama . . . and sometimes with eerier music . . . bells . . . whistles . . . bits of piano-tinklings . . . rumblings over rails transferred to a higher pitch, as being far away. In both twilight sleep and crystal-gazing we all used the method of leaving unhampered the free play of the subconscious along with that of directing it by fixation on a given idea, by association-stimuli, etc. For a crystal, we used an inverted tumbler, suspended eight inches from half-raised eyes and held steady by taut guy-strings, with light-spot cast by a dimmed electric bulb a little back of my reclining head. Commonplace enough; but our psychological tactics too, as will have been observed, involved no recourse to anything but commonplace states of mind—we merely induced them artificially and turned them merely to uses not commonplace. Every one has looked into a fire glowing or flaming in the grate, and "imagined" pictures—which were really unrecognized projections of his own buried memories or fancies, stimulated by the chance shapes and colors without. Crystal gazing is the same thing, merely under conditions more favorable to the subconscious, but still only commonplace conditions of abstraction, quiet, concentration of light, etc. Every one has experienced what I call twilight sleep, the dozing state between waking and sleeping, and noted the chance fragments of faces and landscapes seen or of sentences and music heard. The state may be lighter or deeper, or shorter or longer, and one can learn to "hold" it. And every one has his dreams. I have found I can achieve the deepest state (differing from that sluggish drowsiness of physical exhaustion that passes into full sleep a few seconds or minutes after we touch the pillow) by rising early (say five), dressing, eating a bite, reading an hour, and then lying on my side (either side) on the bed. In that deep doze I have seen things farthest back with most vividness and (I think) with most success in recalling them as old experiences (i. e., either immediately, or later with less assistance from associations and refixation on the thing seen). In that doze I saw, as vividly as in a deep dream, the hilly landscape I saw in reality from the platform of 1878; but I was aware, like a waking man, that I saw the landscape (and in time aware of what landscape). I have called it dreaming with one eye open. The next deepest state comes by lying down after an interval of a half-hour's reading, after the noon-meal. I get less in the doze preceding the night's sleep, and still less from the doze preceding rising. Somewhat differentiated from the doze has been the more actively induced semi-trance (extreme relaxation of body and abstraction of mind); but it tends to merge into the former, and I have used the term "twilight sleep" for both states. Scientifically speaking, the hallucinations of the doze are "hypnagogic," of the trance "hypnoidal." Alcohol dopes me; and I have been phobically unwilling to try the effects of drugs. I have got, both by crystal and dreams, hallucinations from events and scenes equally far back, but I think those in the crystal have oftener been the slowest to take on emotional tone or meaning: an analytic study of the cards would be necessary here. I have certainly got the most data, earlier and later, all told, from twilight sleep—having gradually discarded the crystal and dream-analysis. The shudders, of which I have spoken as surely indicating meanings, come sometimes at once with the ultimate meaning of the hallucination, and sometimes long before (as in the odor of the cigar), even sometimes where the hallucination has no meaning at all even in itself as image, etc., till months or years later (accompanied then by a repetition of shudders), though hallucinations may rise from such deeps that it is years before the telltale shudder comes (as the mind remembers its earlier appearance or repeats the hallucination itself). Analogously, though less frequently, in twilight sleep and crystal-gazing, I have had terrific smarting of the eyes, bodily twitches and itchings, sneezings, gaggings, tears streaming down my cheeks (even while in conscious emotion I may be mildly amused or acutely curious). The smarting, if in front of the crystal, has several times been so painful that I have had to cease looking into it, as if the phobic subconsciousness, in telling me *something* was stirring, were putting forth especial protective resistance against my finding out *what*. In a few days something important turns up. These other bodily phenomena seem, however, to differ from the shudders in one other particular: they are often identifiable as a somatic integer of the original experience (as gagging at the station before the Engine)—while the shudders seem emotional reactions of the mature subconsciousness, mainly of its terror, but sometimes largely of its surprise and triumph in discovery. I think the order of both frequency and significance of the hallucinations in the three chief states (twilight sleep, crystal-gazing, and dreams) has been visual, auditory, tactual (pains, etc.), olfactory, gustatory (chiefly the brandy in the house of refuge, 1885); but here again analytic study of our cards would be necessary. In a class by themselves are the many hallucinations in twilight sleep of myself as doing something—running, shaking my fist, or writing (where the writing stops just as it is about to mean something . . . something at times revealed later). The bodily pains, in my waking hours, those somatic reverberations, are to be reckoned too among the hallucinations. Sometimes a slight diffused phobic spell or accentuated irritability has preceded for an hour or so some recall. Except in the first few months, I have experienced few recalls when about my ordinary affairs; that is, only a few memories have "popped into my head" irrelevantly when wide-awake; and those of only peripheral significance. I have spoken already of recalls stimulated by photographs, manuscript accounts, and maps. And of the many verifications by those instrumentalities, involving me in much correspondence with many people, some strangers (like the rector of Holy Cross in Plainfield, successor of the Swart Stocky Man, who looked up my baptismal record).

Aside from my dreams, I have experienced but one hallucination (it was in twilight sleep), among many thousands, that I could identify as basically wish-fulfilment, i. e., as a fancy and not as a reverberation of experience. And even that one contained a moment of reverberation. And this fact suggests that the few identifiable wish-fulfilments in the dreams are approximately all there have been, and that the rest of the phenomena there too are basically reverberations of experience. At least, I do not believe the plastic power, the creative energy of the dream, is exclusively the wish, or in my own case dominantly the wish.

It will be remembered that my laboratory investigation of my own dreams antedates the clinic of the past quadrennium by eleven years, and that the clinic includes scattered dreams recollected from twenty-five years back of those eleven. I doubt if any other investigator has dream-data extending over forty years of his life. Not excepting Freud himself, who is as much the discoverer of Dreams, as Columbus was the discoverer of America. But just as Columbus made mistakes in charting his New World, it seems to me the great Freud has made mistakes in charting his. At least I owe it to science to notate where I have not found my data verifications of his. (1) Though I could give apposite examples illustrating many phenomena discovered by Freud, my dreams have not only not been dominantly wish-fulfilments, but, more specifically, not dominantly wish-fulfilments of a sex-nature, realistic or symbolic. (2) The symbolism of my dreams is looser and more plastic than according to Freud, or especially according to Freudians. Flying, for instance, usually in an airplane, has recurred several times, when it was clearly an expression simply of the wish to be free to wander (i. e., free of the phobia)—as distinct from an analogous dream of a certain buxom, vibrating young woman of my acquaintance, where it was as clearly an expression of the wish to be free to woo (i. e., free for the satisfaction of sex-desire)—and I have myself had flying-dreams of this sort too. In each is the common craving for expansive freedom of personality in a vital particular: but the particulars differ. So too I have read of a man in a prison-cell dreaming forever of flying. That symbol in proverb and poem has always had this wider application; why should the dream, which is but human nature after all, limit that symbol's meaning to sex? But that there can be close relations between sex and flying I know also from the localized sex-sensations of adolescence when coasting down a long hill on my bicycle. So of the other symbols. Freud's disciples become sometimes as arbitrary in their allegorical interpretations of dreams as the Second Adventist allegorical interpreters of Scripture . . . and for the same reasons that make allegorizing always more or less capricious guesswork. (3) I have not found the symbolism of my dreams, except in a relatively few instances, due to the "Censor." Though of New England spirit and home-training, my conscience has apparently waged few very fierce battles with my dreams. The symbolism seems to have illustrated more commonly two quite different mechanisms than conflict between a bad wish and a horrified or even disapproving moral nature. (a) The mechanism of self-preservation, where the mind didn't dare face the unsymbolic, literal reality, and where, too, the sudden wakening (as in nightmare) was not moral revulsion but scare at the instant where the symbol almost merged into the fact it stood for. (b) The mechanism of parturition, when the subconscious was laboring to give birth to something, especially in the remote deeps of buried memories, and could not disentangle it from the associational matrix. And these three notes are applicable also to my crystal-gazing and hypnoidal states (twilight sleep). But to return to our narrative.

A little before my friends finally left Madison, I had got back the complex of the school-fright and apparently had assimilated it to normal consciousness, reset it into its proper circumstances and subordinated it as an episode long done with in my life. But though I had been a little extending my beat, I had not at all recovered the relative freedom I had achieved in many periods before. I believed with them that the school-fright was the cause, believed with excited hope, that, with mastery of the cause, would be coming speedily mastery of the disorder. And, lo, I was not cured. Faith in the cure had produced no "faith-cure." "Holding over one's self the thought" had created no reality. But I had begun vaguely to recall an earlier scare from a train at the depot (as recorded in my mother's diary) during the first year I had worked alone. Then one midsummer afternoon on Willow Walk, attempting to continue when peculiarly phobic, I had a violent seizure and had to hail, as if dizzy and faint, a coming automobile—the automobile itself which must have precipitated the seizure. For the Locomotive-God, though yet an unknown God, had been *stirred* to new, and more virulent hostility against me. The seizure itself and the automobile spin simulated the episode of 1911 more closely than anything between. Strictly speaking, the consistently unalterable half-mile beat dates from that walk. All the old palliatives, as the try-try-again, have become utterly powerless. The phobia has become stable at last.

I have before indicated how the Locomotive-God and his works of 1878 emerged into my consciousness by way of the 1885 trauma. From the beginning of our clinical search in 1922, there had been continuously recalls and reverbera-

tions of locomotive-experiences—as a ride in the cabin of a
switch-engine at four, a rusty locomotive-boiler by a saw-mill
whose hollows I used to make ring with my brass-edged ruler
on the way to the Franklin School at ten, and a strange
shape in the crystal reminding me strongly of both a plow-
share and a cow-catcher, accompanied by a shuddery diffused
feel of iron and brass. These, with sundry others, drawn
from both childhood and youth, and some of them involving
bridges, I supposed were resolved, when I got back to the
memory of the train passing over the Liberty Street bridge
in 1885. But more kept following. I had a dream of sitting
by a negro woman, as a child, at the end of a railway bridge,
eating a grape-fruit and choking on the seed. In the dream I
could not understand why I choked; I found experimentally
that I could both breathe and swallow, and yet I choked, and
was much agitated lest I choke to *death*. I woke with a distressing and unsubsiding constriction in the throat (which
was my heart in my mouth before the engine of 1878), then
as unexplained as the grape-fruit which I knew was not a domestic edible of my childhood (it was the orange I sucked
after the scare—I have relived that orange, even to the
aroma and the hole into which I stuck my finger). Meantime
I had begun to feel that the actual train of 1885 was not the
only train of that morning of 1885, nor the more important
train. And I kept thinking of the gas-tank as by the Liberty
Street bridge of 1885, though I knew it was not there.
And a casual twilight-sleep image, supposedly of the red-
brick parochial school, which I had insisted for the first
year—it came a few days before we began our clinic—on
misplacing across the street from Liberty, turned out to be
the wraith in air of the red-brick railway-station seen, or
half seen, in that phantom position on my run across the
school-yard, and I began recalling the locomotive-wraiths
around the boys rushing down the school steps and around
the Chapel Front. So I moved all my researches a mile or
so up the tracks to the station. The first suggestion of the
god-idea behind the locomotive was an image in twilight

sleep of a circle. I had had in twilight sleep innumerable hallucinations of circles before—finger-rings, hoops, barrel-ends, etc., as likewise, in the crystal's light, round black hollows in the middle and crescents gouged out of the side of the light. But across this new Circle were three distinct capital letters. Those three letters were: G O D. Of course as a two-and-a-half-year-old I couldn't spell; but my mature subconsciousness, taking the inarticulate message from the subconsciousness of the illiterate infant within me still, translated it into printed speech for my conscious mind of maturity. This God-circle associated itself soon (my notes would indicate just how soon) with a crystal-image of at least a year earlier;—the spot of light that had shaped itself into a clearly defined disk, which, though objectively as motionless as a dead firefly and not more than one fourth of an inch in diameter, had seemed to my shuddering feeling the Dominator of all Horizons and onrushing, annihilating Menace. Thereupon the association (God-circle plus disk-menace) was followed by those renewed and more violent shudders that always seem to say, "Now you're 'warm'—keep after it," and by a secure feeling of conviction that Disk and Circle were One and the Same Thing.

The toil, the ingenuity, the suffering of the quest was from now on infinitely greater than all hitherto. And I made it alone, except for a half-dozen clinical sessions with a friend, himself an amateur. The resistance of the God was tremendous. I had the Locomotive as Locomotive long before I had it as Locomotive-God, and the Locomotive-God long before the Locomotive-God *with the gaping maw*. It is only in the past few months that in my twilight sleep I have not started in sudden wakefulness with horror as I had drawn him forward to just before the moment of emergence. It is only in the past few weeks that there have become relatively quiescent the perpetual all-day constrictions in chest and throat, the occasional eye-aches and head-aches like those in Philadelphia, and the boiling in the brain that has postponed sleep during two years for two or three hours a night unless I subdue the subconscious turmoil by a glass of whisky (legally obtained). It is no longer a question of a directed *searching* for Him. It is He that stirs, when I doze, whether I look for him or not. It is now as if, infuriated that I have found him out, he were writhing in the Twilight of the Gods, but refusing to die. Or, at times, as if a supreme fear of facing him, a fear more powerful than all his fire and steam, blocked his onrush by a charm . . . just below consciousness. Yet, curiously, he appears only rarely in my dreams, and then without occasioning emotional stress. And if I go to the Roundhouse of the Illinois Central a few blocks down my street, and, squatting on my knees to the diminished height of a child, watch the switch-engine puff and clang toward me, I experience but the shadowiest tremors; yet concentration upon the same switch-engine in twilight sleep brings profound agitations, as if there it merges with the Locomotive-God in a union anything but divine.

In these phenomena I find the only plausible explanation of the failure of the cure. I have certainly found the cause, and its chief effects through forty-eight years. For these earlier frights did not associate themselves in my recalls or my shocks as mere analogues of the later. I have tried to make plain how they contributed to the ideations and emotions of succeeding frights; and how at times they created the very stuff of the frights. I need hardly review the evidence, but let the reader recall especially the wraiths of the locomotive in different moments of 1885, the panic before the locomotive in the map in 1911, and the vision in the sky as the train passed by across the lake; and let him remark again the similarity in essential pattern between the phobia and the infantile traumas . . . specifically the flight to home and skirts. And let him note that, with the accentuated suffering from the Locomotive-God in consciousness, has come in the conduct of my life the more consistently severe phobic domination, concentrated now more exclusively in the distance-phobia and need of wife.

Twilight sleep itself has created for me one picturesque
phenomenon strikingly symbolic of the dynamic continuity
of the attack-motif: it has shown me again and again the
vague Locomotive-Face in annihilating menace *merging*
vaguely into the menacing and annihilating Face of one or
another of those who were hostile to me in 1911 or after
. . . even though my conscious mind laugh at both Faces.
And twilight sleep has revealed many specific items of the
traumas of 1878 and 1885, besides the Locomotive,
that have been subconsciously dynamic in the long series of
specific phobic seizures since 1911; as the milk-wagon of
1885 that precipitated a seizure when another milk-wagon
passed me in 1912—though it was not till my clinical sessions
of 1923 that I either remembered the milk-wagon of 1885
or recognized in the milk-wagon of 1912 any connection
with my seizure: a recall and a linkage that came by a
curiously insistent association between a certain picket-fence
on Liberty Street in Plainfield and a certain unfenced lawn
of Prospect Avenue in Madison . . . each with its passing
milk-wagon . . . 1885 . . . 1912 . . . I have, I repeat,
certainly found the cause. If my story is not scientifically
correct, in the main, we had better surrender psychology altogether—to the Behaviorists, say. Professor Köhler, the
Berlin psychologist, too much identified in America merely
with his book on his monkeys in Teneriffe, was remarking
to me in a conversation on the porch of the University Club
a year or so ago, "We are just beginning to know the human mind"; but that beginning includes surely such psychoanalysis as this book records. I have *found* the cause.
But why not, then, the cure? It must be for this: I have
not *mastered* the cause. I have seen but not overthrown
the God.

The evidence is partly in the phenomena above mentioned. And I can compare, likewise, the 1878 recall with
the 1885 and the 1911. The 1885 is absolutely integrated
with my waking life, as real as its old self, including its reverberations of 1878. The 1878 is, in its core, still at a

stage of relative remoteness identical with a specific transition stage of the 1885 recall, and so too of the core of
1911. Possibly no reader could detect this difference by any
comparison of my accounts of 1878 and 1885 and 1911 in
the former chapters; yet in the 1878 and 1911 traumas my
subconscious energies in the writing supplied the vividness
of some central details, whereas in the 1885 I wrote entirely under the stimulus of vivid memory itself. And, moreover, words are inadequate to reveal the more delicate, but
all important nuances of experience: the real differences remain forever our own secrets. I have not completely relived the instant of facing the locomotive and of rushing
into Mary's arms, or of the vision in the sky of 1911:
either in objective vividness or in emotional tone. I am
still like one who sees vaguely, beyond a near landscape
itself sharp of outline and warm of color, a central vista vastly farther away, blurred, ominous, and vol-
canic. For instance, the memory of looking at the standing boiler-head beside my mother in 1878 (and examining
it for the Face I had seen upon it but a few moments before) is as of yesterday, while the direct memory of the
actual onrush of the Face is indeed as of many yesteryears
ago; the memory, too, of hysterically writing in 1911 in my
note-book about the "miracle" just seen in the sky is as of
yesterday, while the memory of seeing the "miracle" itself
is likewise of many yesteryears ago. And, though my waking consciousness and the upper strata of my subconsciousness fully realize that the God with the gaping maw was
nothing but a commonplace locomotive, coming along toward a commonplace platform, secure on its rails and physically harmless to me (as the issue proved), the aboriginal
infant mind within me (of the instant of shock) still refuses
to realize it, more unconvinced even than it was when my
mother led me round in front of the standing Thing. How
little the infant mind has realized it, I know too from ex-
tremely rare and brief but grand moments of accentuated
realization, that, however, I cannot capture and aggrandize

and that are not potent enough to affect my phobia-pestered waking life. It may be that only deep hypnosis could accomplish this reliving and this resetting; and, if there be any master, east or west, eager for a supreme demonstration of his powers, let him come to Madison. I won't be able to meet him at the train; but I can send a taxi.

This explanation is accepted by all (but one) of my necessarily few acquaintances who have had professional experience in abnormal psychology. If wrong, then it will challenge the theories of men like Rivers and Prince, even as the etiology of the case clearly challenges the theories of several other schools (as the Freudians, the Jungians, the Adlerians), or at least embarrasses them with an anomalous exception. But, again, if wrong, the alternative, according to all available evidence, cannot be an explanation in terms of a subconscious purposive mechanism, using the phobia for its own designs. I have unearthed many subconscious purposes in my mortal conduct, some of them contemptible enough. But negatively considered, neither my co-investigators nor I have unearthed anything, even by long and direct probing, that remotely suggests subconscious purpose in my phobias. And positively considered, my mature mind is clearly getting nothing out of them but handicaps (even aside from all phobic suffering) : they have kept me from all professional associations with colleagues at national conventions, kept me from accepting a hundred lecture-invitations around the country, kept me even from mingling with the estimable anthologists and prospective reviewers of my poems in New York, kept me from considering any one of some three calls (and telegrams pointing to three other calls) from major universities or of using them (in the established and approved manner) for boosting my rank and salary at home—in short stripped me of all bargaining power in my professional career, equally with all come-back in my personal relations. I am a full professor at fifty, after hardships for which no university was responsible, only because the University of Wisconsin has given me a chance. They have deprived me of normal sonship and husbandhood, and of fatherhood altogether. They have deprived me of a thousand simple pleasures that belong by birthright to every man under the skies; and rendered tenfold more difficult the performance of a thousand simple duties that every decent man feels privileged to face. They have kept me from burying my dead. Grant that the urge to find out knowledge and wisdom and the urge to create art are profoundly rooted in my personality: wherein has the phobia achieved anything there? By compelling me to write this book, you say cannily (for even every sorority-house porch now has its psychoanalysts of subconscious motives). Well, the phobia had a long look ahead, say I. And, for a fact, I wrote this book partly as a last experiment in cure. The phobia satisfies a desire to appear "different," as a genius and an afflicted genius? Whence then the *profound urge* (aside from practical policy) to be ashamed of it . . . to conceal it even when concealment was futile . . . for many years, till it finally became an objective problem? No. My mature mind has got nothing to the good out of the phobia. The phobia has not served even to avenge me on my enemies, who doubtless see in it (with satisfaction) the immutable workings of divine justice, nor to mortify with chagrin the blundering friends . . . for I had it (with analogous symptoms) long before they blundered. The phobia has not been necessary to excuse me from disagreeable tasks otherwise beyond my ingenuity to escape (such as reciting my poems at Rotarian banquets about the country).

But is my infantile mind getting anything out of it? This is a far subtler problem. That this infant-subconsciousness is getting an infant's satisfaction out of being over-mothered seems a vague generalization, with no data directly from the subconscious states as actually revealed back to 1878, except possibly satisfaction from Mary's coddling—and the infantile eroticism. Am I still running down the platform, frightened nigh unto death, and still standing in such infantile shame, merely for the repeated pleasure of little Mary's arms? I know the pleasure was once there. If I realize its absurdity will I be well?—not, I believe, unless I recognize too the absurdity of what sent me flying there: in other words, it is dynamic only as part of the unrelived part of 1878. The only proof available for the theorist who believes in some subconscious purposive mechanism is the fact that I—still have the phobias. But I cannot see its appositeness. I am here giving, of course, the same theorist his best opening for a rejoinder about my "defensory-mechanism" and about the impossibility (even after nearly five hundred pages) of any man "psychoanalyzing himself." Let him say so. But let him then psychoanalyze the amused indifference of my mental state when he says it.

I hope I am not speaking fractiously to the experts or contemptuously of them. I hope some will find value in this case. The books and technical journals report too exclusively the cured cases. Not every expert, it would seem, has the candor of Freud and Rivers. The reason is simple: the psychoanalyst is not only an investigator; he is also often a practitioner. The biologist tells what has happened in his laboratory for the sake of truth alone, be the results positive or negative; the psychoanalyst is under the (very natural) temptation to tell what has happened in his clinic partly for the sake of his practical career, and so his scientific interest in reporting his negative cases lapses. The library shelves distort the true situation: the too numerous uncured cases are too seldom available for study. I once read of an interesting complex successfully destroyed; I happened afterward to become accidentally acquainted with the patient (anonymous in the report), and found him still suffering from other complexes uncured and unreported. The clinical picture was inaccurate. I myself might have reported how I cured the year-long pain in my rectum, omitting the sundry more painful ills I have failed to cure.

There is no evidence, either, that my condition has been perpetuated by any psychological strain of the four years' investigation. In the first year and a half I was improving, if not because of analysis, then in spite of it. During the whole period I have done much other intellectual work with no more effort than before; and made indeed one other discovery beside that of the Locomotive-God—the discovery of the meter (and the origin of the meter) of the Old Spanish Epic, "The Cid," in which one scholar's varied interests—as in versification, phonetics, psychology, literary criticism, Middle English, Spanish Civilization, Germanic and Romance philology, and classical and medieval Latin—are, I hope, at last vindicated against academic critics of his defects in specialization (to be published by the Centro de Estudios Históricos, Madrid, as a monograph in a Spanish translation by Jesusa Alfau de Solalinde, one of our sun-parlor group). The investigation of the neurosis, like that of the Old Spanish, has had many moments of absorbing interest. The relaxations have been certainly helpful to my physical organism, including the nervous system. The intellectual stir was stir only of a mind always stirring. The emotional stresses during recalls have registered old strains *below,* not created new strains *above.* Nor has the writing of this book made any difference, except to bring into clearer consciousness a few minor memories: writing of emotionally painful moments has harmed as little as writing of expansive moments has helped.

There seems equally little evidence of perpetuation or accentuation by "practising the fear," as some experts might say. I have put myself into an attitude of terror only a few times . . . to stimulate recall . . . as when I would imagine myself in flight down Liberty Street or paralyzed before the engine. Most of the fear-practising technic was in connection with the 1885 complex, and thus at a time of temporary improvement. I have not used it practically for a year and a half. In this connection, I might note for what it is worth a twilight sleep habit extending

over two years, during my engagement and first months
of marriage to Agatha (i. e., before the chronic phobias).
I would amuse myself on going to sleep with the construction of a blockhouse in the Indian lands on a bluff over a
river, protected landward with ingenious devices (as suddenly lowered doors spiked at the bottom, electrically
charged stockade-wires, unsuspected loopholes, tank against
flames, etc.) and provided with a secret trap-door
into the gorge over which it stood, in case hostile Indians
should be successful in breaking through. And there with
two or three companions, carefully chosen for intelligence
and courage, I would spend my imaginary summers, though
not without trepidation. Several fearful raids there were,
as the hatchets were brandished and the fire-arrows flew
and the war-whoop rang. In this fantasy, I was certainly
practising a fear . . . but without the slightest effects of
fear in my waking life. And a fear, interesting too as
strangely symbolic of my subconscious attitudes and the
craving for safety in my early traumas, as well as prophetic of my phobia and of certain minor symbolic forms
of Indians in the early images seen in the crystal. Of course
it differed from all factual fears in that I was always *safe
at last:* the Indians were uniformly in the end even more
stupid than Cooper's. Incidentally, these imagined scenes,
so long repeated in imagination, never increased in vividness, like my recalls of actual experience; and later furnished me by comparison with a clear definition of those
differences in the *feel* of reality between experience
imagined and actual experience relived on which I have insisted so often.

No. "Practising the fear" has not held up cure—
any more than the *much more persistent* "practising freedom and safety" has achieved cure. For fifteen years,
originally indeed more as a spontaneous wish-fulfilment
than as a principle derived from psychotherapists (Nancy
School or Emmanuel Movement or Coué or Psychoanalysts)
I have projected myself, awake, or in twilight sleep—with

analogous projections in dreams—as gloriously wandering, alone and confident, over hill and dale, through cities and across seas and mountains . . . and for fifteen years all these wanderings have remained in the regions of fantasy, except for such limited range as I have recorded.

Again, the perpetuation of my phobias can scarcely be due to failure in intellectual analysis. It must be that I understand them. The reason is bungling no longer with pseudo-reasons, factitious rationalizations. Moreover, auto-suggestion could now operate with a tool in which I have complete confidence: it could say to my fear-states, without rousing in me an *arrière pensée* of hocus-pocus: "There is nothing to be afraid of," etc., "The Locomotive-God is a myth," etc. And I cannot name or guess any important complex or other factor still buried: for two years all materials that have come up from the subconscious have been related, and intimately related, to the 1878 complex. Physical weakness or disease is excluded: physicians say I have the constitution of a well man of thirty-five. I seem confined to the one explanation that the infantile attitude remains unbroken, because the infantile experience has not been completely relived and assimilated and reset. And I can report no change here for many months. I seem stalled . . . totally. Its inveteracy seems too deep . . . too old and long. I have succeeded both in bringing the complex nearer consciousness and in widening the highways from the subconscious, with the result that the God-Face on the boiler-head harries me more than ever; but, whether from infantile fear to confront it again òr from some associational tangle, I cannot seem to conjure it out into sunlight . . . and off down a phantom-track into air.

I write this statement, with the quiet objectivity of a physician who, observing in himself the later course of a long disease, has *at last* begun to doubt the prospect of cure, *in spite of long expectation and long belief in his own science.* I write it, knowing the rejoinder of some psychoanalysts. I open my morning mail and read:

You need very much to realize that so long as you are convinced your cure is blocked, blocked it truly is . . . etc. . . . . etc. . . . .

And I answer:

And you, my dear fellow, need very much to realize that, so long as convinced that the failure of cure is due to my conviction of failure, you are simply shutting your eyes, with the prepossessions of theory, to the psychological *facts* of the case. The facts, indubitably, are as follows. In all the earlier years, before the psychoanalytic probings, I lived daily in the profoundest conviction and atmosphere of conviction among my associates that *cure* was *coming* . . . in spite of innumerable set-backs themselves sometimes occasioning disheartenment but not occasioned by it. There was long a great crescendo of faith (amounting to certainty) during the probing both in cure coming *soon* and in the method, in *spite* of further set-backs—that seemed results of the method itself, conceived as transitional results. This faith outlasted a thousand circumstances that would have robbed many men of faith . . . and it was faith *with works,* that is, with daily effort to extend my distance, etc., in spite of the fact that the effort was now so futile, as against some relative successes in earlier years. This faith, created both by *desire* and by my supposed scientific *knowledge,* now begins to wane . . . yet even now there is the general attitude of effort with moments of hope. I am the only one who can furnish these data as to my attitude through these fifteen years; but you must admit that during the years we were together you observed some of them yourself. I have even now not lost all faith in the method, nor all faith that it may yet work out in this case. But the *fact* is that it has not. Doubts have not suspended cure; but suspended cure has latterly raised some very natural doubts. In mental (as too in bodily disorders) few believe more heartily than I in the therapeutic assistance of faith and cheer; but neither their presence nor their absence may be in all conditions the fundamental factor. The psychoanalyst has a nifty advantage over the family doctor: when his diagnosis and prescriptions don't work he can comfortably lay the blame always on his patients . . . for their obstinacy in not letting them work . . . he can achieve no miracles because of their unbelief. Whereas the family doctor can blame only the apothecary.

But I am not sending the letter. And in case my friend comes across it here, let me add for him that neither have I *blocked* cure by *wishing to stay uncured in order to write this lugubrious book:* the profoundest scientific ambition of my life has been for fifteen years to be able sometime to write my life-story with a culminating chapter of complete victory over the phobia . . . a profound artistic ambition too, for art craves the grand finale or at least a last note of quiet victory. . . . But my good friend, with such a good head in so many ways, has never understood the artist. Few psychoanalysts, with the exception of Freud, have . . . and even Freud tripped on Leonardo da Vinci.

And the rest of my friend's well-meaning but ill-considered letter is a reminder that I have omitted to stress above sufficiently the insistent attempt (both in twilight sleep and awake) to *associate powerful counter-ideas* (of safety, friendliness, intellectual curiosity, comedy, admiration, etc.) *with the fundamental ideas of horror* (locomotive, etc., school, etc.). Apparently, in spite of all I have written him, he thinks I have not done so—merely because the doing-so has not . . . as yet . . . brought the cure that according to him it should.

The psychoanalysts, so skilled in readjusting the psychological twists in their patients' thoughts, should perhaps be a little more on their guard against *logical* twists of their own. In three successive years one explained to me the cure of a phobic complex consistently as indeed dependent upon recall of the original trauma, but inconsistently: (1) as a dissipation (i. e., simply a *release* of a buried *emotion*), following *automatically* upon recall; (2) as a *readjustment* of *thought* (i. e., an intelligent realization of the original factors), to be achieved by slow self-help of analytic meditation; (3) as a shift in *emotional attitude* toward the fear-engendering object of the original trauma, to be achieved by the slow self-help of building up a new set of friendly associations in counteraction. It is possible to make some correlations among these three explanations, but perhaps only an experimenter who has tried out each in his own case can fully appreciate the difference in principle and technic. But the disparities in the head of one psychoanalyst are as nothing to those between the sundry brethren themselves.

Yet that there still lurks below an unresolved Something is clear, as said a moment ago—if only from the unresolved Phobias still so flourishing above. But, moreover, the *subconsciousness* has told me so itself, directly, authentically. It whispered into my ear only the other day during twilight sleep the solemn words, "algo más." Algo más, Spanish for "something more." And I realized instantaneously the meaning as *something more unresolved*. This hypnagogic voice was not an *echo* of my present conscious speculations, but an *immediate testimony* from original knowledge possessed from of old by my subconscious intelligence: for the startling and audible hint was followed by fierce and protracted shudders, as if I were about to experience the luminous ascending majesty of some great truth . . . about to . . . but not yet . . . Algo más . . . The subconsciousness has vouchsafed me many such general statements, sometimes even in the form of instructions phrased as imperatives, "do this," "try that". . . which I have forthwith noted and obeyed and found most helpful. Indeed, one of the most astounding of my discoveries has been this tricksy interest of the subconsciousness *as a whole* in assisting my search . . . side by side with the malignant secretiveness of the subconscious phobia-making complex. These general pointers are of course not to be confused with the information furnished by specific items of buried memories. Algo más—a hundred clues, specific items or generalizations, have come to me in such phrases from foreign tongues—Spanish, Latin, Greek, German, Italian, French, Anglo-Saxon, Old Icelandic, etc. It was the phrase "de rodillas" (on the knees), for instance, that ultimately defined the memory of my falling down before the 1911 vision in the sky. And now and then they have come in

416

rimes. Thus even in the intermittent moments of the clinic
there interplay, albeit in fragmentary and rudimentary
manifestations, the three motifs of my life-story—the phobiac, the linguist, the poet. . . . Algo más . . . something
more . . . what? The still veiled Jaws of the Locomotive-
God . . . or algo *más?*

It had been the hope of friends, psychiatrists and lay-
men, that the successful publication of "Two Lives," after
a suppression of thirteen years that was in very truth a
suppression of myself, might shake the neurosis. I had
been twice warned in years widely apart that the Mob
would drive me from the city if I published it. My elder
Madison advisers, with three exceptions, to the last had
consistently advised against publication, even, some of
them, against the private printing of 1922. I had expected
to leave it a manuscript for my executors, if indeed I
should have such. Meantime for twenty years I had been
(for reasons I won't discuss) the obscurest man of letters
in the United States: to be sure, with a page or so of my
verses copied into one anthology from another, but an
academic dilettante not furnishing occasion even for a foot-
note in any popular article, or in any but two books (to
my knowledge), on Contemporary American Poetry—and
the articles and the books have been many. I tried to be
content with my modest reputation in technical scholarship.
But I knew that "Two Lives," though in stuff and style
not essentially different from the best of my so long unre-
garded published verses, had still elements of narrative and
drama that would compel listeners, even in the Radio Age
and the Poetic Renaissance. I could not publish, while in
Madison, apparently; and the phobia confined me to Madison. I had at first waited out of piety . . . out of a feeling too that Agatha's kin and connections might return to
me in friendship . . . for then I would have been willing
never to publish it. But the time came when I felt it my
duty to face whatsoever disaster and my right to receive
whatsoever praise. I prepared the way carefully . . .

with the dedicated coöperation of both the American and the London publisher . . . I had learned with the years to apply what intelligence I had to practical issues, when necessary. But I had written, shrinking from something more than was expressed:

> If ever this book (as Art from Thought and Sorrow)
> Shall lie for sale (with Dante) in the shops,
> Public (like chimes in spires) to fools and fops,
> Then I must front new martyrdoms to-morrow. . . .

And the publication, to my amazement, brought me such a wealth of human fellowship in my city as to make those verses sound ungrateful, cynical, and mock-heroic; even as its reception in other cities, whither I could not voyage in the flesh, put wings on my spirit. Art had won against the Mob. A few new stories, as absurd as ugly, circulated in its depleted ranks feebly a month or two; and one prim lady, who revenged herself by refusing to read it, still scowls on me as I walk my beat, like the specter of my Aunt Cornelia . . . she who had scowled at me when a child, because the child of an alien bride she had not been consulted about. And Art had finally made the White House by the Lake mine . . . forever . . . for it exists, since last July, only in the poem: a sorority is now building its home on the spot, only farther forward where the two oaks were. And Art owns all the rear lawn and flower-beds, all the vistas, and the old pier . . . for the whole quiet neighborhood is now become the fashionable Latin Quarter . . . with many an alley cut and paved from Langdon Street to the lake-shore, and stone fronts or brick, bearing golden Greek letters over lintels that face either alley or street. Art too had set my rejected name on the tomb at Forest Hills . . . and no one can ever chisel it out. The writing of "Two Lives" was an act of faith . . . so too was its publication —in a different sense. And I had now, in sober truth, been justified in my faith. I was not ungrateful, not indifferent.

Yet I experienced no such thrill of triumph, as would have made me a veritable chanticleer years ago. And the publication had no effect at all upon my neurosis. Possibly no thrill, however, could have had any effect, where even the lover's thrill had had effects so transitory. But the evanescent tenure and the flimsy texture of the thrill from the publication seems to have been because the rehabilitating experience came too late. I could not but be reminded, too, in much of the magnanimous surprise, especially in the reviews, how little was still known or understood of my literary work in the past twenty years. I had schooled myself so long in the acceptance of personal frustration. Without losing faith in my own mind's integrity and without the peevish cynicism that would deny, by and large, the urge in society toward justice and intelligence, I had accepted myself as one of the isolated victims of misunderstanding, both in my public career and private, spiritually reinforced by work itself and by a little circle of workers. The habit was too fixed to make a complete readjustment possible . . . and, by implication, to permit any particular craving for readjustment. The chief result for me of the success of the poem was a thought, not an emotion. I said to myself: "This, then, is at last the fulfilment of your boyhood dream among the Bolton Hills . . . to write a poem that mankind would not willingly let die; but the laws of art . . . which are the laws of life . . . would allow that fulfilment only on their own awesome and terrible terms. Would I have dared to foster the dream, had I known? . . . Yes, I believe I would."

These intimate allusions suggest a word (possibly sometime to be expanded into a book) on another relation of my verse to the neurosis . . . and my inner life. I have already noted the Mob in "The Lynching Bee" and the wish-fulfilment elements, so obvious and near the surface, in the animal-projections of the "Fables" and in my autometamorphosis into a teacher of Greek in "Two Lives." Another, only a little less easy to perceive, is the

grim and arrogant projection in the last act of "Red Bird"
—the young Indian chief, caged in the guard-house and
condemned to death for a crime in itself an ideal action
according to his code, and heckled and browbeaten by a
swaggering white sergeant. But more interesting to myself
as a student of psychology has been the discovery of reverberations from my very early life, especially of the Locomotive-God. I note a few. A sonnet (written at twenty-
five), "The Express," in the moment the Engine swoops
into the station, beginning "she comes" and ending

> would mine her hour
> Of large experience and splendid power.

"The Train" (at about forty-three), imagined in its passage
across the continent, containing the line, spaced off in the
printing from the rest:

> A train so often touches me with wonder.

A fragment on "The Depot" (unpublished, at about nineteen), describing the crowd's mysterious faces. The first
two reveal the same glorified interest in the locomotives of
reality as resulted immediately after the shock of 1878,
when the fictitious Locomotive-God detached himself from
locomotives as such for his own phantom career. "The
Quaker Meeting-House" (at about forty-four) adum-
brates the meeting-house seen from the platform. A discarded stanza in the "Phobic Section" of "Two Lives" in
describing various minor phobias that plague mankind (and
they are far more numerous than the public, or even the
victims, know . . . which would make another chapter)
speaks of some people being afraid of the sound of a
drum. The other phobias cited were consciously from my
own experience or those of other victims known to me;
but this was, I supposed, a mere fancy of my own: it turns
out to have been a reverberation of a childhood terror specifically noted in my mother's diary. All these reverbera-

tions, and sundry others, found their way into my rimes long before I had begun the investigation that led to the Locomotive-God. But at a time when I already had recalled the school-fright I wrote a poem, by conscious design, on a trauma supposed to be similar to mine of 1885, beginning:

> She fell, a timid child, beside a gate,
> With crumpled spelling-book and shivered slate,
> *Fleeing a fuzzy pup that bounced at people.*
> But when *he nosed her cheek and pressed his paw,*
> She swooned, *devoured by a lion's jaw,*
> While the last thing in her dear world she saw,
> *As blackness gulfed her,* was the white church-steeple.

The side gate of the house where I was picked up in 1885 merges with the grille gate beside which I had fallen in 1878. The experience in the underlined verses belongs only to 1878, and when I wrote them I supposed it was purely imaginary. The jaw is more the maw of the Locomotive-God than the muzzle of the dog that sniffed over me a half-minute later—or the dog of 1885. Note how I became a *she (apparently a reverberation of Mary)*. I need not point out the intentional similarities with 1885.

I have noted, in the four years' investigation and in the observations of the preceding eleven years, many subsidiary phenomena for which there is no space here. In my seizures I sometimes feel faint but never faint away. I never have shrieked but once—as I stood on the bluff before the vision—and then I was shrieking for specific help; I become white in the face and speak (if another is with me) with a very agitated plaintive quiet, like a dying man who is trying not to make a fuss about it. I never have nausea or any other disturbance of the digestive tract; and headaches or other nervous disturbances follow only rarely. But my interest in these externals of the phobia (recorded so copiously in my manuscript of six years ago) has receded with the progress of the discovery of its inner dynamics and meaning. Some external phenomena, however, have first then manifested themselves, being directly occasioned by the probing—all of them since I got to the levels of the 1878 complex. Some have been already noted. One other was a nervous dread that I was about to fall down. One other still was the sensation of *retching* (though divorced from the sensation of nausea) that I had to make the best of during many hours a day and many days a month, intermittently, for over a year, before the most virulent stuff of the complex *came up:* one more illustration that the metaphors in this book are scarcely metaphorical. These two phenomena seem now to have passed. External phenomena aside, I have already noted that my mind seems to have preserved all experience: I have made experimental excursions with the same psychoanalytic technic into many by-paths of long ago, far from the traumas, and recalled whatever I set out to recall—forgotten playmates, forgotten games, forgotten brook-sides, forgotten tears. I have a vague memory of an April morning with the negress Tina, two months before the visit to the station: I am being coaxed by the little girls in white on the grass and by the rector in black at the door to come into the Sunday-school . . . and, wiser than later, I refuse to come. . . .

The discovery of the subconscious past and of its dynamics and organization down to the shifting present which it forever overtakes has had for my intellect the objective interest in personality as unitary and in life as a self-creative plot; and something of this I have perhaps been able to share with the reader. But the new and awesome subjective feeling thereby engendered I cannot share. In the most literal sense I feel the integrations of 1878, 1885, 1911, as one experience, and all between and thereafter as one. In that one experience there are indeed moments in 1878 (as where I am toddling home beside my mother and Tina and the baby carriage of my infant sister) that seem nearer, as richer in the feel of reality about me and in the feel of my own state of mind, than some moments in 1911 (as

when I stand lighting the cigar in the road-house door, however pungent in recall the cigar-odor itself) . . . how then
is 1878 really thirty-three years earlier for the self of me
than 1911? The dates I have so often repeated for objective clarity lose all their meaning in the immediacy of the
self. And there comes a strange reconstruction in the sense
of time: in spite of all lands and peoples seen and books
read and written and hardships encountered, my life seems
to-day a far briefer span than it seemed to me even as a
seventeen-year-old lad in the New England hill-country. And
so another ancient metaphor flowers into fact: if a thousand years are but a single day in His sight, in my sight
my own fifty years seem but the corresponding fraction of
a day. But the Fraction is not belittled as such. It is for
me still Value, still Power . . . and Time has no meaning
there. If I had only had these things to tell when William
James used to sit so patiently before the fire in his study
. . . listening to my callow collegian lucubrations on the
relations between psychology and metaphysics.

XIX

IF the crowning irony of my lifelong adventures with the Locomotive-God is the fact that I have gained my knowledge of Him, as it would seem, only at the tragic expense of a still greater surrender to his power as Lord of Fears, I still cannot honestly conclude this book in defeat before him. He has been Lord of my Fears; but he has not been Lord of my Life. I have defied him for forty-eight years. My nature is the same as when He first bore down. He has disturbed my temper and my emotions, but they were and are mine, not his; he has distorted my activities, but I evaluated and used the distortions. He has not unmade my essential temperament and character . . . not even in the past fifteen years since he reasserted his claim upon me higher up the heavens . . . over Lake Mendota. He has not undone the aboriginal instinct to know—and I use "instinct" here in an exact biological sense—so strong in the child and in the man; he has not undone the instinct to create. Rather, has he unwittingly furnished those instincts of the scientist in me and the poet in me material of grave and vital import whereon to try their powers. Nor is it he that has taken from me the Divine Love, the God of my father and mother, of Jesus and Dr. Channing. I can find no evidence that my revolt from a personal God to whom I prayed as a child has been subconsciously influenced by this hideous Apparition . . . that revolt, too, is my deed, not his. But in this lifelong struggle against the Locomotive-God, and in the search of the last four years that ultimately led me to his face, I find in meditative retrospect my best clue to the great mystery. We know the stars and the microbes and the electrons themselves only

424

as already immersed in mind: we intuit the world beyond
our minds with our minds, and it is all in itself, in the essential process of our knowing it at all, for us secondary
experience . . . only faith, though I believe to a degree a
just faith, makes us take it even as phenomenon for objectively what it seems. The only primary experience is experience with energizing consciousness, one's own consciousness.
And through such an experience with what for me must be
ultimate reality—I mean boldly with my own mind even in
its strange disturbance—as I have had particularly in these
four years, I feel that it is there that the pulse and breath
of the universe may be best surmised; there the suggestions
to the energy out of which the stars and the electrons, no
less than earth and the cells and the flowers and birds, have
come . . . out of which too all the religions. I have long
since given over, as for me insolvable, the problem of the
Intelligence and the Goodness of this Energy through the
universe; but it certainly achieves intelligence and goodness
under the form man: and the will-to-live in man implies
the will-to-live thoughtfully and well—to live "like a man,"
in short. The end of the rose is a perfect rose, according
to the law of its being a rose at all. The end of the human
being is a being that most fulfils the implications of human
nature: energy unfolding into ethical forms and organized
thought. By the implications of human nature I mean
something very simple and positivistic: the actual complex
of urges, hopes, griefs, ideals, failures, loves, hates, of that
primate called *Homo sapiens,* who painted the caves of
Altamira, founded the Athenian commonwealth, and discovered the habits of electricity and adapted them to his
convenience, but who has actually realized the implications
of his nature . . . in thought, in conduct . . . only in rare
racial moments . . . as yet. From any but this point of
view my own life remains frustration. But, in the end,
this is for me the only definition of success. In so far as
I have realized . . . something in thought . . . something in conduct . . . of the implications of human nature

as a phase of the universal energy, I can claim some measure of the successful life as mine.

The Locomotive-God is a Machine-God. I sometimes conceive him in relation to the individual life sketched in these pages, as a symbol of the age of the machine . . . of Steel and Fire and Smoke . . . constricting and unmanning man. A symbol to me of Material Dominion. A symbol to me of the delusions of a raucous America. And my life has been a fight against this Locomotive-God no less. I have not acknowledged him as so many have—but as many with me have not. Yet he too has hurt me sorely, as he has hurt others. I have not acknowledged him because I would keep the integrity of my personality and those values of life it clings to. I am fifty years old. There may be some years ahead: if so, they will go to the same cause . . . whatever the limits of my beat.

But what would I do, if again, after fifteen years, I found myself free to take ship or train to-morrow? I know. A long time I yearned for Iceland . . . to visit the sagasteads, Herdholt in Salmon-River-Dale of Olaf, the Peacock, and the little offshore islet where Grettir, the Strong, died of his wounds . . . and where to this day is a hospitable and sturdy folk which conserves a language that is as archaic a survival in the life of the Germanic dialects, as the monotremes and marsupials of that other outlying island Australia are archaic survivals in mammalian life. And I would still touch there in my voyage. But I would hurry south . . . to sunny Spain . . . and, arraying myself in the long robe of a twelfth-century *juglar* (such as we see miniatured in old manuscripts or carved in shadowy corners of cathedral portals), I would travel through the university centers . . . Salamanca, Madrid, Barcelona, Sevilla . . . intoning the verses of "The Cid" before learned and laity . . . demonstrating the plangent reality of the old cadences so long lost in the confusion of academic theory, and with an analytic but not too technical lecture proving the metrical pattern of Old Spanish epic verse to be fundamentally but a rougher, more oral, form of the Germanic folk-verse of the "Nibelungen" and derived like the "Nibelungenlied" from old Germanic sources . . . the restored music of "The Cid," like its heroical and ethical substance, being a heritage of Visigothic Castile. That's what I would do. But I can still send over my monograph and my phonographic disks. I will not be outwitted altogether . . . nor altogether constrained . . . by the Locomotive-God.

ADDENDA

ADDENDA

THIS year intervening between the completion of the manuscript and the correction of the final proofs has revealed, in the clinical continuation of the investigation, nothing *essentially* different, and the phobia itself remains the same. Yet there are some additional details of fact or comment significant enough for a foot-note.

1. Proof-reading has rendered some of the recalls in the text more vivid, and stimulated new details of recall (for example, that the terrorizing God-face appeared an instant on the *platform* of a school-house, during an entertainment, when I was sitting in the audience with *Mary,* the winter after the trauma; and that the cow's head in the downstairs bedroom window precipitated the feel of a horrible Face, as well as of horrible Uproar).

2. With regard to my own methods in the investigation, I have perhaps left it too much for the reader to surmise from descriptive moments the specific nature of my own *directive manipulations* of the subconscious and of its data. Though my mind has sometimes lain in my bedroom clinic merely passive to what might pop up, it has oftener initially regulated and limited the field of recall, by dwelling on some specific item or items in the field already remembered, or on some unexplained hallucination in a field as yet undefined; it has still oftener watched the associations and, by bringing varied hallucinations together, watched the new associations and watched for emergent memories (even of trivial details—though *to the subconscious nothing is trivial*). Thus even in the doze or trance of twilight sleep and crystal-gazing, the reader will note the paradoxical activities of this human mind of ours: the *inter*play of consciousness and subconsciousness, and the normal guiding, observing, reasoning activity of *waking* life present even on the border-land of dreams.

3. I have not sufficiently stressed the hints that have come as symbols of searching all along during the (now) five-year search;

431

for instance, in twilight sleep or in actual dreams, I will seem to be turning the leaves of a book slowly, when suddenly I skip leaves and can't find what I skipped; or I try to turn the key in a big iron door and can't get the wards to fit—

Zwar euer Bart ist kraus, doch hebt ihr nicht die Riegel. Yet such symbols have *usually* resulted in discoveries . . . or partial discoveries.

4. I have found by direct clinical experiment that the Locomotive-God, the Face itself, was vibrant in the subconscious in several specific phobic attacks of recent years. For example, the name "Barton," that of a store near the Square, came "irrelevantly" to mind in twilight sleep, and brought back, bathed in the horrible light of the Face, the image of the store on a frightful morning when, unexpectedly returning to the house, I found a note from my wife stating she had "gone to Barton's" . . . on one of those few and hurried errands of hers just a little beyond our beat.

5. I discover that my phobic dreams, i. e., dreams of being too far from home in phobic anxiety, are less the mere troubled imitation of phobic anxiety in waking experience, and more (perhaps entirely) *directly* the result of the same force that causes the waking experience—the solicitations of the God-Face itself.

6. In the continuation of my objective verifications during the past year, I have discovered only two errors in memory, and those only partially errors. The first has to do with ordinary reminiscence. My text (p. 205) refers to the Ellesmere MS. as seen by me in the British Museum. I had a vivid memory of the colored miniatures of the Canterbury Pilgrims, for which that MS. is famous; but I began a few weeks ago to recollect that in 1900 the MS. was in certain private hands notoriously ungenerous in lending it for public gaze. So I wrote to the British Museum. The answer confirms my doubt, but, in a way, also my memory. The superintendent, Mr. F. D. Sladen, writes me: "The Ellesmere MS. was not one of these [MSS.], but the Tellers of the Canterbury Tales copied from this MS. were among the exhibits."

7. The second error has to do with reminiscence mistaken for clinical recall, and is of particular significance to the theme that gives the title to this book. On page 239 I speak of the *bell* of the German engine. Professor Kurt Koffka, the psychologist of Giessen, this last year visiting professor at Wisconsin, queried this point on returning the proofs to me: German engines don't have bells, he said. Instantly and spontaneously my mind became excitedly suspi-

cious. I realized that for the Cologne trauma, so vivid in all the other details (and correct), I had made only a cursory *clinical* search, and so I set to work on further psychological recall. Thirty hours with crystal and in twilight sleep made plain that, while the bell was only a symbol, the Locomotive-God complex had been even more violent in its manifestations than even vivid reminiscence had revealed. The terror was in fact set off by the sight and noise of locomotive and cars in the station; a horrible wraith of a locomotive appeared shortly after, high up in air, at the further end of the waiting-room; and, the next morning, after the physician had left, I jumped up from the bed to make for the barber-shop because of a *specific* locomotive-obsession during my attempted relaxation. I saw while fully awake, though with closed eyes, a picture (as vivid as in a deep dream) of a long wooden railway platform, shining yellow in the sun, and down the tracks the small black bulk of a distant on-coming engine. I was lying on my left side, and turned madly over in order to leave the picture *behind* me; but it moved around and lay there before me again. My emotions were blind, diffused terror (i. e., not specifically of being run down), and a poignant feel of infinitely personal acquaintanceship and of desperate agitation at not being able to identify it in either place or time, except that it felt as from long, long ago and from far, far away. The memory of the picture disappeared from consciousness by the moment I was sitting in the barber's chair; and that night in Bonn among friends my account of the Cologne seizure contained none of these items above. Yet my very manuscript bears witness to an emphatic subconscious memory in the unpremeditated italics of the phrase *"relaxation made me worse"* (p. 240).

8. This now completed recall compels a reinterpretation of my dreams of being again a traveler in Germany, awaiting *with trepidation* the train over and over in *railway stations* . . . at Heidelberg, Munich, Göttingen, Cologne . . . during all these last sixteen years. I had always supposed that they were simply the wish-fulfilments of the hampered confinement of my manhood, pining for that great Other Country of my youth, and that motif of trepidation was an intrusion into the dream of my manhood's phobias. It is now clear that they were reverberations, basically at least, of the Cologne seizure.

9. This dream-like picture of the mysterious platform gives increased significance to the hundred or more visual hallucinations in twilight sleep and crystal during the first two years of my clinic that,

in varying definiteness, simulated or reminded me of a platform . . .
platform . . . platform . . . interspersed with several auditory hallucinations where I would hear myself saying platform . . . platform
. . . platform. I regret, as an artist, that this Cologne material was
unavailable in time for incorporation in the text.

10. On the so-called impossibility of any man's psychoanalyzing
himself (p. 410). Two realms of analysis must be distinguished: (a)
that of subconscious motives and ends; (b) that of subconscious memories and associations. Self-analysis can doubtless go much farther in
the second than in the first; but even in the first, I believe it can go
with some minds much farther than the professional theorists so dog-
matically assert.